A People's History of Soccer

'Correia takes us around the world to examine how soccer has produced the kind of political energy that can change minds and even topple governments. But despite his global jaunt into many corners of the soccer world, there is nothing superficial here. This book is about the politics of passion and they sing from every page.'

—Dave Zirin, Sports Editor, *The Nation* and author of *The Kaepernick Test*

'A fascinating journey through the game's history. While so much of today's attention is on the highest end of the sport- the money and the glory associated with today's biggest stars -[soccer] has always been about so much more: a vehicle of expression, of example and of change. *A People's History of Soccer* tells the stories of how, why and when.'

—Shaka Hislop, former soccer player, anti-racist educator and broadcaster

'Often we lose sight of the real history of soccer ... There are fans, players and teams that built the game and truly harnessed it as not just a sport but a force for good and a way to build long lasting communities. That history needs to be told, archived and remembered. This is an essential history of the people's game.'

—Flo Lloyd-Hughes, sportswriter and broadcaster

'A rich and superbly-researched materialist account of how soccer emerged from feudal origins to become the most popular, and most political modern sport. Soccer fans and players everywhere, in the stands or the pitch, recognize in their chests' pounding the collective heart of a heartless world.'

—A.M. Gittlitz, author of *I Want to Believe: Posadism, UFOs and Apocalypse Communism*

'A wide-ranging and well-researched look at how the masses have attempted to protect and reclaim their sport from the classes, all over the world. An essential read for soccer fans everywhere.'

—Juliet Jacques, writer, filmmaker and Clapton CFC player

A People's History of Soccer

Mickaël Correia

Translated by Fionn Petch

PLUTO PRESS

First published 2018 as *Une histoire populaire du football* by Éditions La Découverte

English language edition first published 2023 by Pluto Press, Inc.
1930 Village Center Circle, 3-834, Las Vegas, NV 89134

www.plutobooks.com

Cet ouvrage a bénéficié du soutien du Programme d'aide à la publication de l'Institut français.

This book is supported by the Institut français (Royaume-Uni) as part of the Burgess programme.

This book has been selected to receive financial assistance from English PEN's 'PEN Translates!' programme, supported by Arts Council England. English PEN exists to promote literature and our understanding of it, to uphold writers' freedoms around the world, to campaign against the persecution and imprisonment of writers for stating their views, and to promote the friendly co-operation of writers and the free exchange of ideas. www.englishpen.org

British Library Cataloguing in Publication Data
A catalogue record for this book is available from the British Library

ISBN 978 0 7453 4876 6 Paperback
ISBN 978 0 7453 4933 6 PDF
ISBN 978 0 7453 4932 9 EPUB

This book is printed on paper suitable for recycling and made from fully managed and sustained forest sources. Logging, pulping and manufacturing processes are expected to conform to the environmental standards of the country of origin.

Typeset by Stanford DTP Services, Northampton, England

Printed in the United Kingdom

Publisher's Note

Although the title of this book in North America is *A People's History of Soccer*, the game is referred to as "football" throughout, reflecting the predominant international usage.

Contents

List of plates xiii

Introduction 1
Football grounds, grounds of struggle
The other face of football 3
Social football club 5

Part I *Defend*: Working class resistance to the bourgeois order

1. **Kicking off** 9
Riotous balls and social control
Political violence and popular justice 12
The soule of France 15
Football under enclosure 17

2. **Normalising bodies, shaping minds** 22
The birth of an industrial sport
Shaping gentlemen 24
'Well-oiled machines' 26

3. **The people's game** 30
Football as a cultural trait of the working class
Taking 'first place in the people's hearts' 31
Decisive pass 34
'The Outcasts FC' 38
Football Railway Company 41

4. **The munitionnettes** 45
The saga of the first women football players in Britain
Under the yoke of male domination 45
From the assembly lines to the green pitches 49

'Much better hitters' 52
A return to the patriarchal order 54

5. Class against class 59
Working-class football in France, an extension of the field of struggle
Social phobia, martial values 60
Play more to work more 63
A new pitch for the struggle? 66
Ball at the feet, fist raised 70
Towards an anti-fascist football 73

Part II *Attack*: Assault on dictatorships

6. 'A small way of saying "no"' 81
Italy, the USSR, Spain: stadiums under totalitarian regimes
Black shirts and blue jerseys 82
Between sporting spectacle and fascist spectacle 84
An indomitable Soviet football 88
'Down with the cops!' 92
Realpolitik 95
The Camp Nou, a bastion of anti-Franco resistance 100

7. Ball at the feet against the iron fist 104
Football's resistance to Nazi domination
A new football for a New Germany 105
A grain of sand in the propaganda machine 108
A paper man facing the iron regime 110
The 'Match of Death' 113
Resistance in troubled waters 115
Clandestine football, weapons in hand 119

8. 'Corinthian democracy' 123
Football and self-organisation against the Brazilian dictatorship
Breaking with the established order 124

Anti-authoritarian jersey 129
Outflanking the military junta 131

9. On the front line, Tahrir Square 134
Ultras Ahlawy fans at the heart of the 2011 revolution in Egypt
From anti-colonialism to guardianship 135
An autonomous youth 138
Everyone to Tahrir! 142
'Oh, Council of Bastards' 146
Lost causes 148

Part III *Dribble*: Outmanoeuvring colonialism

10. The Algerian Independence Eleven 153
A liberation struggle in football boots
Football and national liberation 154
The great escape 157
Football Fellaghas 161

11. When Palestine occupies the pitch 164
Football as a political weapon in the hands of the Palestinians
Restrictions on movement 165
The obstacle course 168
A contested pitch 171
Anti-apartheid red card 173
Gazan football from the sidelines 177

12. Dribbling the ball, a decolonial art 181
Afro-Brazilian identities and indigenous resistance in football
'Something like dancing' 182
Dribbler Social Club 188
The Amerindian gap 194
Zapatista footballs and indigenous rebellion 197

13. Sending colonialism off 204
Football and emancipation struggles in sub-Saharan Africa
The club, a hotbed of protest 205
Anti-colonial pressure 209
Township football against Afrikaner soccer 214

Part IV *Support*: Collective passions and popular cultures

14. 'You'll Never Walk Alone' 223
Hooliganism and subcultures in British stands
A respectable public 225
A crowd to overthrow the world 228
The English disease 233
The Heysel turning point 238
Gentrify to pacify 242

15. The twelfth man 247
The Italian ultras movement: from political militancy to supporter autonomy
From spectator to supporter 248
Left turn 250
Calcio dell'arte 258
Police everywhere, freedom nowhere 264

16. 'God and the devil' 271
Maradona, between popular passion and fan cult
The criollo *agitator* 272
Footballing divinity 275
Saint Maradona 279

17. 'We are lovers, not fighters' 284
Istanbul's ultras and Turkish power
From the stadiums to Taksim Square 285
Football under Erdoğan's thumb 289
Social cohesion vs. martial divide 292

Part V *Outflank*: Facing the football industry: fight and reinvent

18. Football for footballers! From May '68 to the fans' revolt 299
'The players are slaves' 300
Occupy Iéna 303
Beneath the turf, the beach? 310
Playing without barriers 315

19. Tackling sexism Women's football against the French sporting patriarchy 318
A breath of emancipation 318
Women's football turns male 322
Our desires cause disorder 325
Institutional abuse 331
A crumbling bastion 333

20. 'Here it's about punk football' Fan-owned clubs in England 338
In fans we trust 339
Taking stock of a different football 342
'Our club, our rules' 345

21. Playing on the left wing Hamburg's FC Sankt Pauli or the pirates of the football business 353
Red-light district and Autonomen *activists* 354
The pirates of the league 360
Countering the commercial world 363

22. Wild balls, balls on the margins Street football wrong-foots the institutional game 367
Senegal: football at the heart of the neighbourhood 367
Futebol without pitches or boundaries 373

Inner-city football: playing to survive 378
The dummies of the football business 384

Postscript to the English edition 387
Endnotes 393
Acknowledgments 438
Index 439

List of Plates

1. *The Foot-Ball Play*, Alexander Carse, circa 1830. A popular game of football in rural England in the early 19th century.

2. Fevered part of Soule in Lower Normandy. *L'Illustration*, 28 February 1852.

3. The English working team of Blackburn Olympic (Lancashire) in 1882.

4. The working-class footballers of the Dick, Kerr Ladies of Preston in 1921 © Gail Newsham.

5. The stands of the Dynamo stadium in Moscow in the early 1930s. The stands were then one of the few public spaces where it was possible to escape the surveillance of the Soviet political police. © DR.

6. Viennese striker Matthias Sindelar, nicknamed Der Papierene (the Paper Man), opposed the annexation of the Austrian team by the Nazi regime © FIFA Museum.

7. During the occupation of the Netherlands by the German army, Dutch footballer Jan Wijnbergen, from the first team of Ajax in Amsterdam, joined the Resistance in 1941 before participating in a rescue network of Jewish children © Jan Wijnbergen – © Jan Wijnbergen – Collection Dutch Resistance Museum

8. The South African Wanderers team in 1956. From the township of Chatsworth, near Durban, the Wanderers are considered the first Black club in South Africa © Archive Faouzi Mahjoub / FIFA Museum.

9. The Algerian National Liberation Front (FLN) football team in 1961. Rachid Mekhloufi is the fourth crouching player from the right © Archive Faouzi Mahjoub / FIFA Museum.

10. The national team of Ghana celebrates its second African Cup of Nations after beating Tunisia 3-2 in the final, November 1965.

Baptized the *Black Stars*, the team is both the standard-bearer of Nkrumah's pan-Africanism and the best African formation of the moment © Archive Faouzi Mahjoub / FIFA Museum.

11. Nicknamed 'the joy of the people', Brazilian footballer Garrincha alongside an English policeman during a tournament in Liverpool, July 1966.© Sport Archive / FIFA Museum

12. Zapatista team from Caracol de La Garrucha (Chiapas, Mexico) in a match with the Easton Cowboys of Bristol, 1999 © R. S. Grove.

13. Diego Maradona escorted by the police on June 29, 1986, just after Argentina's victory against West Germany in the 1986 World Cup final in Mexico City © Sport Archive / FIFA Museum.

14. Occupation of the headquarters of the French Football Federation on Avenue d'Iéna in Paris by the Footballers' Action Committee in May 1968 © DR.

15. Banner of a fan of FC United of Manchester, a club founded in 2005 by a cooperative of supporters who contested the acquisition of Manchester United by American billionaire Malcolm Glazer © Mark Lee.

16. 'St. Pauli supporters against the right', legendary sticker produced by supporters of FC Sankt Pauli in Hamburg since the 1990s © DR.

17. The Beşiktaş Çarşı ultras in the streets of Istanbul during the demonstrations of May 1, 2014. © Guillaume Cortade.

Introduction

Football grounds, grounds of struggle

Created by the poor, stolen by the rich.

Banner raised by Club Africain supporters at a match against Paris Saint-Germain, 4 January 2017

Whatever team we support, there's no arguing about these results: globalised football has become the epitome of commercialised sport and mass culture; the very embodiment of unbridled capitalism's worst excesses.

The World Cup held in Qatar in late 2022 is a striking example. Human rights violations, corruption, migrant worker deaths on construction sites, the climatic absurdity of it all when the planet is burning, the grotesque 200 billion dollar budget ... The world's most popular sporting event has become a bloated monster with an untenable economic, human and ecological cost.

It did serve, though, to shed a harsh light on what the football industry is today. The big clubs have become vulgar brands, relieved of their social history. Take mythical Barcelona, for example, which one of its own executives recently compared, in jest, to the Walt Disney Company: 'They have Mickey Mouse, we had Lionel Messi. They've got Disneyland, we have the Camp Nou [Barça's stadium]. They make films, we produce content. We no longer look at what other clubs are doing, because our reference points belong to a different universe ...'[1]*

As cynical as it sounds, that executive wasn't entirely wrong. Matches are now treated as commercial entertainment. The supporters become mere consumers. The clubs do their best to attract the best-paying clientele. At the heart of the elite clubs' commercial

---

* All references appear at the end of the book, organised by chapter.

strategy, stadiums are more like theme parks, both family-friendly and cocooned in security measures. In the 2022–2023 season, the lowest-priced season tickets for English Premier League teams cost around £600 on average.[2] An exorbitant figure that testifies to the dizzying commodification of football: between 1990 and 2011, the price of the cheapest tickets for Anfield Road stadium in Liverpool, historically a working-class city, increased by 1,108 per cent.[3] Just like in Liverpool, in Barcelona, Paris and Milan the social make-up of the terraces is changing. 'I no longer know the people around me in the stands', a long-time Barça supporter marvels. 'Half of them are strangers and they change every weekend'.[4] This ruthless gentrification of stadiums goes hand in hand with a disenchantment on the part of the working classes who, driven away from football grounds, are reduced to following matches via the intermediary of screens.

The financialisation of clubs causes transfer costs and player salaries to soar to such extraordinary heights that they no longer reflect economic reality. The practice of naming a tournament or stadium after a sponsor has become widespread, converting the most prestigious stadiums in Europe into advertising hoardings for multinationals: Bayern Munich's Allianz Arena, Arsenal's Emirates Stadium.

The values conveyed by professional football are little to be proud of either. Too often, tournaments celebrate a vindictive machismo around star players, who themselves have become advertising banners and bearers of speculative value. Racist, sexist and homophobic diatribes are common, not only from the stands but in the hushed corridors of the national associations.* At the institutional level, the corruption that plagues football's governing bodies spilt into the open with the 'FIFAgate' revelations. In May 2015, seven top officials of the International Federation of Association Football (FIFA) were arrested on a US warrant and charged with racketeering, fraud and money laundering. The accusations of corruption involved the World Cup bidding process.

* In 2011, the French Football Federation had considered the introduction of discriminatory ethnic quotas in its training centres, in order to limit the number of binational players of North African or sub-Saharan origin.

Ethical considerations are far down the world football authority's list of priorities. Forty years after having entrusted the 1978 World Cup to Argentina, then led by the military junta of General Videla, the awarding of the 2018 and 2022 World Cups to Russia and Qatar, respectively, showed that FIFA is still happy to deal with authoritarian regimes as long as they put enough money on (or under) the table.

The other face of football

Nevertheless, football continues to attract a vast popular following. Every day millions of players enjoy the sport, and whether it is in an organised manner as part of a local club, or improvising on city asphalt or rural pitches, kicking a ball around is an almost universal experience. It transcends nations and generations – and gender too: in 2019, official bodies estimated that over 30 million women play football around the world. As for the fervour of supporters, it is there every weekend behind the railings of the municipal pitches, just as in the stands of the top professional clubs. On the screen, the fans are counted in their billions, whether it's a life-long passion or passing enthusiasm for the big matches.

Football's simplicity is what makes it so attractive. Its basic rules are brief, and since they were written down for the first time in 1863, the '17 laws' that govern the sport have barely changed. Playing requires very little: a ball, which can be quite rudimentary, and a pitch, which can easily be improvised on a street corner or patch of wasteland. This basic grammar of the game offers amazing freedom, allowing it to be played in many different ways, and means football can be taken up by anyone. Kicking a ball is a pure and simple pleasure, one that draws on multiple wellsprings: team spirit, moving the ball around as collective work, the physical confrontation in making a tackle, and the aesthetic joy found in the 'beautiful move'. As the Brazilian player known for his political engagement, Sócrates, liked to say: 'Beauty comes first. Victory is secondary. What matters is joy'.

As a spectacle, football's popularity stems from its power as drama. Every game respects the principles of classical theatre: unity of location (the pitch), time (the duration of the match) and action (the whole game takes place before the audience).[5] Each match has its own intensely dramatic storyline, with an outcome that is played out before the spectators' eyes. Over the course of a game, emotions can shift in a matter of seconds from joy to disappointment, from fear to hope, from anger to feeling cheated. 'Football is the thrill of uncertainty and the possibility of ecstasy', as the former Argentine international Jorge Valdano admirably summed it up.[6] The international football calendar sometimes even shapes the contours of shared memory. The unexpected defeat of Brazil by Uruguay in the 1950 World Cup final remains a collective trauma in Brazilian society. In France, everyone over a certain age has their own memory of the national team winning the same contest on 12 July 1998.

The tension between these 'two footballs' – the football that bends itself to the logic of the market and the football that shakes itself free of it – goes back to the sport's very roots. Emerging in the mid-19th century in Great Britain during the Industrial Revolution, football was born out of a number of popular ball sports played since the Middle Ages. When the rules of the game were codified by British public schools, football became a part of the Victorian teaching model, whose objective was to instil discipline in the offspring of the bourgeoisie and imbue them with the spirit of initiative and competition required by industrial capitalism and colonial enterprise.

Nevertheless, football rapidly became popular among the working classes. Encouraged by a strongly paternalistic British employer class, which saw the sport as a way of teaching respect for authority and division of labour, football spread like wildfire. In doing so, however, it freed itself from the patronage of the bosses: conceived by the captains of industry as a means of controlling their workers and turning them away from social struggle, the sport in fact helped to consolidate class consciousness. Weekly games on factory pitches established the game as a source of enjoyment and forged new social ties. While the first tournaments and professional clubs emerged under the aegis of the industrialists, the local football team reinforced a sense of pride and belonging to the same neighbourhood, and by extension to the same working-class community. Saturday afternoons spent on the stands, wins joyfully celebrated in the pub, factory-floor conversations around the team's performance or recruitment by workers' football clubs embedded a passion for the game in working-class culture. For historian Eric Hobsbawm, from the 1880s onwards football embodied a 'lay religion of the British proletariat', with its church (the club), its place of worship (the stadium) and its followers (the supporters).[7]

As football became a key trait of urban working-class identity, the vast reach of the British Empire and the industrial boom of European economies helped to spread it around the world at the dawn of the 20th century. By 1918 the Marxist intellectual Antonio Gramsci was already using his column in *Avanti!* to analyse football as an indicator of how the capitalist bourgeoisie wins cultural hegemony.[8] Yet, in parallel to the ever-expanding role of this globalised football in consumer culture, another face of football emerged from below, thanks to its popularity among the working classes.

Social football club

It is to this 'other football' that this book is dedicated. Contrary to some critics of the sport who bluntly describe football as a new 'opium of the people' and haughtily regard the millions of people who are passionate about the sport as an indistinct, alienated mass, this book argues that there is a subversive aspect to football and examines those who have made it a weapon of emancipation. Throughout its history and in every corner of the globe, football has been a crucible of resistance to the established order, whether it be that of the bosses, the colonial, dictatorial, or patriarchal order – or all of these at the same time. It has also allowed the emergence of new modes of struggling, of having fun, of communicating – in short, of existing.

In exploring this little-known history, this book avoids a strictly chronological approach. Its 22 chapters pass the story, like a ball, over the vast pitch of struggle that is 'planet football': from Manchester to Buenos Aires, from Dakar to Istanbul, from São Paulo to Cairo, from Turin to Gaza. Meandering and fragmentary by necessity, this people's history of football also seeks to give voice to the lead players in this epic tale, from the stands of Barça under the yoke of Franco to the pitches of South Africa during the dark days of apartheid, from the working-class French clubs of the interwar period to the Zapatista communities of Chiapas at the start of the new millennium.

This book examines football both as an anti-establishment, marginalised phenomenon, as well as an institutional, professional one. Tracing a people's history of this sport entails going beyond the dichotomy between 'wild' football and 'conventional' football. From its very first origins, the rich and the poor, the elites and the people, the dominant and the dominated, have been competing for the ball. There is no watertight border between these two footballs. On the contrary, it is porous and shifting. The history of football is one of continuous recovery and reinvention. Yesterday, the British working class won possession of the ball from the Victorian bourgeoisie. Today, wealthy clubs spend millions on players from the poorest neighbourhoods, while authoritarian regimes seek to channel the passion of football for their own gain, and multinationals exploit the codes of street football to sell their trainers. And the struggle goes on: fans kick greedy speculators out of their clubs or rise up against dictators, women players are calling the patriarchy offside, and amateur players regularly thumb their noses at the professional bodies.

By delineating a new political vision far removed from that imposed by the dominant football culture, this book ventures that the sport remains a powerful tool for reasserting power over our bodies and our lives. At a time when economic liberalism atomises individuals and converts our social habits into a source of profit, football is still synonymous with shared generosity and is a place where the 'beautiful move' cannot be monetised, and where for each player to flourish the team must move as one. As the words of 'You'll Never Walk Alone', the legendary hymn of Liverpool supporters, say: *Though your dreams be tossed and blown / Walk on, walk on, with hope in your heart / And you'll never walk alone.*

PART I

Defend

Working-class resistance to the bourgeois order

1
Kicking off
Riotous balls and social control

To kick up the sand light-footed,
To see the swelling ball leap through the meadows.

Pierre de Ronsard, *Le Bocage Royal*, 1584.

You base football player!

Kent to King Lear, in William Shakespeare, *King Lear*, 1606.

> Now that our lord the King is bound for Scotland in his war against his enemies and has commanded us to strictly maintain the peace [...] And whereas there is a great uproar in the City through certain tumults arising from the striking of great footballs in the field of the public – from which many evils perchance may arise – which may God forbid – we do command and do forbid, on the King's behalf, upon pain of imprisonment, that such games shall not be practised henceforth within this city.

So decreed Nicholas de Farndone, Lord Mayor of London, in April 1314.[1] Promulgated in the name of King Edward II of England, this ordinance spread to other cities in the kingdom during the reign of his heir, Edward III, who thrice repeated this edict limiting the ball game. In a nation soon to fall under the shadow of the Hundred Years' War and devasted by the Black Plague, the first historical references to football are closely bound up with efforts to maintain public order. Thus we see the bellicose Edward III encouraging his subjects to turn to archery and other exercises more military in character than a turbulent 'game of foeth ball'. From the 14th to the 19th centuries, a common thread runs through descriptions of the ball game played throughout Great Britain and north-western France, known as folk football (or mob football), and in French as *soule* or *choule*. Though collective ball games are mentioned in Ancient Greece – *sphairomachia* and *episkyros* – and in the Roman Empire – the *harpastum* played by legionnaires* – the origins of this proto-football so often condemned by royal authorities remain tangled.** The ethnographer Émile Souvestre, who described games of *soule* in Lower Brittany in the 19th century, claims that 'this exercise is a last vestige of Celtic sun worship. The spherical ball represents the day star, and it was thrown in the air as if to touch the sun, and then when it fell to earth again it was fought over like a sacred object'.[2] The term *soule* may come from the Celtic *heaul*, the sun, altered by the Romans to *seaul* or *soul*; a more humble origin, however, would be the Latin *solea*, a sandal.

While the earliest records of the game of football concern its prohibition, it was only in the second half of the 15th century, during the reign of Henry VI, that it was first described as a game – one still marked by a dubious reputation:

> Now the game they were all going to play is what some people call 'football'. It is one in which high-spirited youths of the peasant class propel a large ball, not throwing it in the air but rolling it along the ground, and not even striking and turning it with their hands, but using their feet. A game, that is, altogether detestable and certainly, to my own way of thinking, of all games the most barbaric, low and vile, and one that seldom ends without some injury, mishap or other mischief to the players.[3]

In Chester, north-west England, a municipal archive dating from 1540 describes the custom among the shoemakers of challenging, each Shrove Tuesday, the drapers of the town to a game played with a

* *Harpastum* may be the origin of the *calcio fiorentino*, a ball game played in Florence since the Middle Ages.

** Ball games were also played in pre-Columbian America (*tlatchi*), in feudal Japan (*kemari*) and in Han-dynasty China (*cuju*).

leather ball called 'foutbale'. Yet far from celebrating the practice, the document denounces these 'villainous people' and the 'difficulties' they cause in the city.[4] In Dorsetshire, meanwhile, at Corfe Castle, the Company of Free Marble Workers played a game of football every Shrovetide. The game calendar, generally organised around Shrove Tuesday until the end of the Middle Ages, seems to be closely connected to the Christian festivals.[5]

In 1698, the French writer François Maximilien Misson, in his *Mémoires et observations faites par un voyageur en Angleterre*, describes the game in more appealing terms: 'In winter, football is a useful and charming exercise. It is a leather ball the size of a man's head and filled with air. This is kicked around the streets with the foot by whoever can take possession of it; there are no other rules'.[6] Indeed, the rules of this proto-football were minimal at best, and varied from one place to another. They nevertheless shared a similar set of practices. Two rival teams – or sometimes more – had to get the ball into the opponent's side using any means available.* The head-sized ball could be a leather sphere stuffed with hay, moss or bran, or made of wood or wicker. The place the ball had to touch to win the game was defined by a wall, a field boundary, a church door, an arbitrary line on the ground, or even a pond into which it had to be plunged. The size of the pitch was similarly varied: it could be a single meadow or the whole territory of the opposing parishes. As for the number of participants on each team, this was unlimited: the players could number in the hundreds. A game of folk football or *soule* could last for several hours or even days.

These occasions were almost always male in character, and mostly involved young men. Sometimes, they set married men against bachelors. Yet women didn't hesitate to throw themselves into the game to help their team to victory.[7] On other occasions, notably those organised in urban centres on an annual basis, guilds made up the opposing teams. The ethnologist Émile Souvestre reports:

---

* Some later accounts refer to the rule of the *bann*, which protected the person carrying the ball.

> The most robust and most agile of each parish, with no regard to the total numbers on each side, form two rival camps. In rarer cases, the two opposing sides each comprised contingents from multiple parishes. These made for formidable matches in which the champions were counted in the hundreds, and were pursued for days with indescribable tenacity [...] The exact conditions under which one party would be considered the winner were agreed in advance. Sometimes to be declared victor it was enough to take the ball into the territory of their own parish; sometimes it had to be taken to a designated village; often it required bringing it into a particular house, which was called 'lodging' the ball.[8]

Political violence and popular justice

Despite its rough-and-ready character, this popular form of football was played in a ritualised space that enabled the community – the village or the guild – to affirm its existence. In the case of matches played between married men and bachelors, the game may be understood as a masculine rite of initiation,[9] while also serving to integrate the rural community. The folk football or *soule* matches strengthened the community way of life, uniting individuals in the game just as in agricultural labour: harvests, sowing plans and fallowing were managed collectively at the village scale. During these matches, the game was transformed into 'a veritable combat [...] across the moors and the pathways, the hills and the valleys, the streams and the rivers'.[10] Delimited at the start of the match, the space of play could easily expand during the game: knowledge of the terrain became essential to winning.[11] The embodiment of vitality and social cohesion for a whole community, football games offered victory to those who best exploited the potential of their territory, a powerful symbol to the peasant mind. Finally, these rude ball games offered a space for the transgression of social hierarchies at the time of Carnival and Shrovetide, with priests, nobles, the bourgeois and other local notables engaged in this game of the people – even if this meant that gentlemen were infected by a love of the ball: in the 16th century, the poet Pierre de Ronsard and King Henry II of France regularly played *soule* near the abbey of Saint-Germain-des-Prés in Paris.

Yet proto-football was almost invariably condemned by observers who saw it as little more than physical violence. In 1583, English pamphleteer and traveller Philipp Stubbes described folk football in *The Anatomie of Abuses* as:

> one of these wicked pastimes practised even on the Sabbath [...] more a bloody and murdering practice than a fellowly sport; For doth not everyone lie in wait for his adversary, seeking to overthrow him and to pick him on his nose, though it be upon hard stones? [...] sometimes their legs are broken [...] sometimes their noses gush out with blood, sometimes their eyes start out [...] And he that can serve the most of this fashion, he is counted the only fellow, and who but he?

As for *soule*, it 'hardly went without wounds or bumps, and those who indulged in it must have felt happy if they had neither a broken eye, a broken arm, nor a broken leg'.[12] Drownings were also reported when games took place by stretches of water or the sea. 'What broken jaws, crushed ribs, gouged-out eyes, broken arms and legs in these terrible struggles', Hippolyte Violeau reported three centuries later, describing Breton games of *soule*.[13]

This condemnation of the physical violence hides the fact that these wild ball games acted as a release valve for rivalries or hatred between individuals or districts. A punch to avenge an affront or jealousy, a general melee to put an end to a quarrel among families or neighbours: football games were an original way of regulating personal or inter-community conflicts, a public space for autonomous and popular justice.[14] Sometimes, the vengeance pursued in the tumult of the game took on a more political dimension. The sport historian Jean-Michel Mehl describes a game of *soule* during Shrovetide in 1369:

> In the violent attacks he made on a squire in the game, Martin the Tanner sought revenge on the nobility. A 'class' reflex dictated his mode of play. When we learn that this *soule* took place in the county of Clermont-en-Beauvais, the lesson of this case is clear:

> these are the grudges born of the Jacquerie popular revolt and its subsequent repression, transferred to a sporting occasion.[15]

In 1836, the Breton *soule* became a symbolic and political confrontation between the industrial, liberal city and the agricultural, conservative countryside: 'Often a town enters the fray with a rural population, and the fight escalates with all the hatred of the countryman against the bourgeois [...] It is a duel of beliefs, a battle of Chouans and Blues waged with fists and nails', writes Émile Souvestre, referring to the French revolutionary and anti-revolutionary forces.[16]

The crowds that gathered on the occasion of football games could also be turned towards insurrection, especially in 17th- and 18th-century England during the period of enclosures and the end of common grazing rights. In the county of Ely, in East Anglia, a football game was organised in 1638 with the aim of deliberately wrecking the dykes built to dry out the fens and convert them into arable land – drainage works that were the target of popular protest throughout the 17th century.[17] In Kettering, Northamptonshire, a football game was played in 1740 with 500 men on each side that destroyed a mill taken into private ownership by Lady Betey Jesmaine. A similar thing occurred in 1765 in West Haddon, where the locals, opposed to the enclosure of 2,000 acres of common land, organised a football match on the land in question that was merely a pretext to tear up and burn the new fences. Five players were imprisoned, but the organisers of this anti-establishment protest were never identified. In Holland Fen, Lincolnshire, meanwhile, the month of July 1768 alone saw three football-based disturbances in the fens, involving 200 men and numerous 'rebellious women'.[18]

Denigrated as a simple 'violent amusement',[19] these popular practices also put the body into play in such a way that it became a tool for regulating social and political tensions.[20] As noted by the sociologist Patrick Vassort, '*soule* reflects conflict between generations, classes, orders, villages, cantons, parishes. The durability of this practice demonstrates how effective it was in the role it is assigned: as a popular form of justice with a power of its own'.[21] Yet the uncontrollable disorder caused by football games and their function as a form of 'self-managed local justice' – escaping the state powers and divine right alike – meant they quickly attracted authoritarian wrath.

The soule of France

After that first ordinance against football dating from 1314, at least 30 prohibitions on the sport were recorded in towns and counties across England by 1615. The popularity of folk football was spreading, especially among young apprentices who enjoyed getting on the wrong side of the local authorities and were often the cause of incidents.[22] In Middlesex in 1576, 14 individuals were tried for 'unlawful assembly' and for having 'played a forbidden game called *football*, which caused a great tumult that could have led to murder and serious accidents'. According to the trial records, the accused were playing this match 'with unknown miscreants numbering one hundred'.[23] In 1608 and 1609, there were two rulings in Manchester condemning the wrongs caused by 'a company of villainous and disorderly persons engaged in illegal amusement with a *ffotebale* in the streets', emphasising the large number of windows broken in the course of games.[24] But it did no good, as the sociologists Norbert Elias and Eric Dunning note: 'While the authorities saw this activity as anti-social behaviour, having fun with a ball – even if it involved broken bones and bloody noses – remained for centuries the favourite pastime of people across most of the country'.[25]

In France, after 1319, Philip V, known as Philip the Tall, ordered the prohibition of all *soule*-type games (*ludos soularum*).[26] Charles V, known as Charles the Wise, imposed a similar measure in 1369,[27] arguing that it was a feckless practice. The Catholic Church also mobilised. In 1440, the bishop of Tréguier, in Brittany, banished the *soule* players from his diocese:

> We have learned in reports from trustworthy men that in some parishes and other places subject to our jurisdiction, on holidays and non-holidays alike, for a very long time already, a certain very pernicious and dangerous game is played, with a large, round and heavy ball [...] This is why we prohibit this dangerous and

> reprehensible game, and declare liable to the penalty of excommunication and a fine of one hundred sous those of our diocesans, regardless of rank or condition, who have the audacity or the ambition to play the aforesaid game.[28]

For the Church, it was a matter of condemning the free play of bodies in *soule* and the diabolical matches that rampaged through the places of worship and the cemeteries, and often ended in drinking and revelry.[29] And though priests and canons sometimes indulged furiously in this ball game on church forecourts and abbey cloisters, they were quickly reprimanded by the clerical authorities, in particular by the Archbishop of Paris in 1512.[30] The secular authorities, tired of these untimely agitations and the popular ferment the game caused, also tried to outlaw *soule*, following the example of the parliament of Brittany which in 1686 prohibited this 'cursed game' throughout its jurisdiction.

From the 14th to the 18th century, the widespread censure of football joined a more general regulation of violence in games, closely bound up with the control of other practices – food, sanitation, sex and war. For Norbert Elias, this repression of popular games, and the wider 'control of the emotions' in the different social spheres, is closely related to the emergence from the Renaissance onwards of centralised state structures that progressively tried to secure a monopoly over physical violence.[31] Yet games of football were so deeply rooted in popular culture that these prohibitions from above – whether by a monarch or ecclesiastical power – barely affected their practice.

Rather than simple banishment, some lords and nobles sought instead to control the game of football in order to convert it into an instrument of local power while seeking to contain its inherent excesses. For these noblemen, annexing popular games was a way of developing or consolidating their powers at a time when European nation-states were seeking greater centralisation.[32] In France, the *soule bretonne* was even transformed, from the 15th century onwards, into a feudal right, an obligation that the peasants had to render to their lords. In Caden, Morbihan, the last groom of the year had to pay the Lord of Bléheden a 'new leather *soule* ball with a jar of wine and a couple of loaves'. The *soule* was thrown in the air the day after Michaelmas (29 September), and the bride was 'required to sing a dancing song when the *soule* is thrown in the air to begin the game'.[33] Fifty kilometres away, in Josselin, the *soule* was offered to the last man married on the day of Mardi Gras, with two loaves, two jars of wine and two glasses; if the ceremony was not carried out then the offender was fined.[34] Following the prohibition of the game by the Brittany Parliament, a number of lords replaced the obligation to provide the *soule* with a religious offering. In 1775, the lord of Cherville-en-Moigné, in Ille-et-Vilaine, demanded a half-pound candle on the occasion of the Fête des Rois (Epiphany, 9 January), in place 'of the *soule* that since time immemorial was customarily presented to his predecessors'.[35]

If the game of *soule* survived through thick and thin in the north-west of France, in the 19th and even the early 20th centuries the repression hardened. In 1811, after the death of a man during a *soule* match in Corlay, in the Côtes-d'Amour, the subprefect complained to the prefect about this 'barbaric amusement that a good police force would have forbidden a long time ago [...] This disorder and tumult are frequently an excuse for acts of vengeance and always give way to reprehensible excesses'.[36] The Second Empire repressed these popular activities even more harshly. In 1857, a decree by the prefect of Morbihan forbade the game in the department, and mounted police frequently broke up improvised *soule* matches.[37] However, it was the privatisation of agricultural lands and the rural exodus that were the final nail in the game's coffin. The social activities of peasant farmers, linked to community agricultural production, eroded as the common fields and pastures where the game could be played were fenced off.[38] The end of *soule* in France signalled the entry of farming communities into the industrial age.

Football under enclosure

On the other side of the Channel, the years 1642 to 1646 saw the English Civil War setting the Royalists faithful to Charles I against the Parliamentarians who were leading a revolution under the standard of Puritanism. The decapitation of the king in 1649 and the establishment by Oliver Cromwell of a 'republican' experiment, which lasted until 1660, undermined both the cultural and spiritual hegemony of the Church and the Puritan movement. The loss of control of the people by the religious authorities caused a certain 'loosening of morals' and led to a revival of popular rural and urban cultures. As the British historian Edward P. Thompson describes it:

> Social relations, leisure relations, even rites of passage, were no longer under the control and domination of the clergy [...] In the 18th century, there was a break with the Church: public holidays increased, reaching two or three days a week. We indulged in brutal athletic exercises, in sexual intercourse, heavy drinking, all of which escaped the control of both clergy and Puritans, and were left to the sole control of the innkeepers.[39]

Just as popular festivities expanded across the British countryside in the 17th and 18th centuries, another tidal wave came to overturn these rural territories: enclosure. With the exception of tenant farming and sharecropping established by the lords on their own lands, agricultural production was traditionally based, at the village level, on community farming as well as on the collective management of cereal-growing land and public land, known as the commons – mainly forests, moors, pastures and marshes. But at the end of the Middle Ages, in Surrey and Kent, the first enclosures appeared: the fencing-off of farmland. This system made it possible to rationalise the agrarian system: large collective cereal fields were transformed into private areas, then converted into much more profitable sheep pastures and fodder crops. Enclosure rapidly expanded from the 17th century on, affecting a quarter of the country's cultivable land.[40] The seizing of communal land for the benefit of the rural bourgeoisie went hand in hand with their increasing political power. The British Puritan revolution that overthrew the Stuarts in 1689 brought about a constitutional monarchy that consolidated the role of the House of Commons. The parliamentary regime sought to satisfy the interests of the upper class by affirming the right of acquisition and private property. Between 1727 and 1815, landowners persuaded parliament to vote through over 5,000 Enclosure Acts, accelerating the process of parcelling up land for private exploitation.[41]

The collapse of feudal and ecclesiastical powers as well as the legal seizure of land led to the emergence in the countryside of a real agrarian bourgeoisie: the 'landed gentry'. From the 17th century onward, these landowners, merchants, millers and big capitalist farmers did not see themselves as passive rent collectors, in line with the old morality steeped in duty and abnegation, but as entrepreneurs keen on progress, promoting agricultural innovation and unconcerned to flaunt their assiduous pursuit of profit. This bourgeoisie exercised its hegemony over British rural society – in 1688 the gentry was estimated at around 16,000 families[42] – thanks to a mode of domination quite distinct from the vertical power of divine right: it was expressed in close control of the population, notably reflected in the paternalistic attention paid to popular festivities.

The landed gentry encouraged the festive ferment by promoting games and village festivals and offering prizes or a bullock to roast at each event. They granted their patronage to folk football games, some gentlemen even taking part in the game, in a simulacrum of a bourgeoisie that tries to be near to the people and to 'slum it' at their side. But, in a society that was better regulated and pacified thanks to parliamentarism and the establishment of *habeas corpus* – putting an end to arbitrary arrests as early as 1679 – the gentry no longer wanted games to be synonymous with rebellious outbursts and physical violence.

The privatisation of land gradually stamped out the games of folk football, whose flexible playing fields destroyed agricultural capital and directly threatened the economic interests of the landed gentry. At the same time, in its constant quest for yield and profits, the agrarian bourgeoisie carried out sweeping enclosures of the uncultivated lands, forests and communal pastures. Between 1760 and 1820, almost half of Huntingdonshire, Leicestershire and Northamptonshire underwent this brutal consolidation.[43] Many small farmers, a significant proportion of whose livelihoods still depended on the usage rights afforded by the commons – pasture, timber, gathering wild foods and fishing – rapidly fell into poverty, contributing to the rural exodus.[44] Farming communities progressively collapsed and found themselves dispossessed not only of their lands but their ball game too, emptied of its original social function. Just as rural space was rationalised into more productive agricultural parcels, football would also have to have its allocated space. Due to the enclosure of land, it became impossible to embark on a game of folk football that converted the whole village into a pitch. The gentry could now permit games of football with constraints: smaller teams (up to 30 players), marked goals, a limited and equally divided playing field. Wild and riotous football games were fiercely repressed by the Royal Dragoons, the mounted troops of the British Army created in 1674, and sometimes called in as reinforcements by the local gentry.[45]

As a result, the monopoly on violence maintained by central institutions, together with parliamentarism as a mode of managing power, prefigure modern football. Just as in the House of Commons the Whigs (liberals) and Tories (conservatives) faced each other across a hall divided equally in two, football would henceforth be played on an enclosed pitch, with symmetrical sides and under the control of a higher authority.[46]

In the early 19th century, with the emergence of the first police forces in English towns – notably the Watch Committees, a local police created in 1835 – the spatial restriction linked to the rapid industrialisation and the shortage of free time available to the first factory workers put an end to the urban games of folk football. 'The poor have been deprived of all their games, all their amusements, all their joys', lamented the special correspondent for the *Times* in London in 1842. In parallel, the 1835 Highway Act stipulated that football games were prohibited in the streets, and could only be played in the fields in marked spaces. The ball game struggled to adapt to these new spatial constraints, and there are sporadic accounts of games in rural areas where two teams of equal numbers of players faced each other on a field not exceeding 100 metres in length, with goals marked by two stakes three feet apart.[47] In 1844, a Suffolk clergyman wrote of the peasants dispossessed of both their lands and of their game:

They have no meadows or commons to practice their sports. I have been told that thirty years ago they had the right to a playing field in a particular field in certain seasons, and that they were renowned for their football; but in one way or another this right was lost and the field is now worked [...][48]

2

Normalising bodies, shaping minds

The birth of an industrial sport

> And then it's no joke playing-up in a match, I can tell you – quite another thing from your private school games. Why, there's been two collar-bones broken this half, and a dozen fellows lamed. And last year a fellow had his leg broken.
>
> Thomas Hughes, *Tom Brown's School Days*, 1857[1]

At the end of the 18th century, British public schools were rocked by frequent student uprisings.

> Eton's famous rebellion in 1768 was followed by five serious rebellions at Winchester between 1770 and 1818. In 1770 some of the boys had pistols, and in 1793 they unpaved a court, and carried the stone to the top of a tower to defend their bastion, during a dispute over the discipline imposed by a prefect and other 'small miseries'.[2]

These acts of rebellion spread to other public schools:

> At Harrow, in 1771, when Dr Parr was unsuccessful in his application for the vacant headmastership, the boys, who had supported him, attacked the house where the governors were meeting, and destroyed the carriage of one of them. Order was not restored for three weeks. Eton and Harrow had other rebellions, as did Charterhouse, Merchant Taylors' and Shrewsbury. Rugby had its revolts from the 1780s.[3]

Within these aristocratic institutions, the values inculcated in the future elite of the kingdom were feudal in character: courage, loyalty and tolerance of pain were the main moralising obsessions of the educators.[4] But while the school authorities indulged in floggings and other corporal punishment, they had the greatest difficulty in maintaining order. Power relations were structured more by the age and seniority of the students – the oldest, the seniors, subjecting the youngest, known as 'fags', to the worst outrages – than by the authority of the faculty over the pupils. Each year, the students would engage in a ritual called 'barring out' that would see them occupy the buildings, sometimes for several days, fiercely resisting the teachers who tried to enter the establishment. Regularly, the vain attempts to restore order and discipline in the public schools with strong whippings ended in uprisings by the young boarders until their demands were accepted.

In parallel to their riotous schooltime activities, pupils spent a lot of their free time playing different forms of folk football. Each public school practised its own version, notably since at least 1747 at Eton and 1749 at Westminster.[5] Some games involved passing the ball between teammates to reach the goal, such as at Rugby after 1823 and also at Marlborough and Cheltenham. Other versions, known as the 'dribbling game' and played at Eton, Westminster, Charterhouse and Shrewsbury, were focused on kicking the ball as hard as possible into the opponent's field.

At Eton, pupils regularly played the 'field game', setting two teams against each other who weren't allowed to pick up the ball with their hands. Charterhouse, meanwhile, played its football games within the limits of the school's Carthusian cloister. The limited space forced players to engage in the 'dribbling game', though it still involved furious mêlées of up to 60 students.[6] At Winchester, football was renowned for its violence, with young gentlemen regularly suffering serious injury. The pupils were also prepared to challenge other youths of more modest means. Those from Harrow liked to clash with the navvies who built the railway lines, and Eton's footballers frequently clashed with the butcher boys of Windsor.

Vexed at the violence of these football games, a mirror to the harsh social hierarchy between 'seniors' and 'fags' and a way for all this *jeunesse dorée* to let off steam, the school authorities endeavoured, often without success, to prohibit the games organised by the pupils. The 'wall game', a ritual type of football which pitted Eton's day pupils and boarders against each other, was banned from 1827 to 1836 because of its brutality and the spirit of division it spread.

Samuel Butler, the head of the Shrewsbury public school from 1798 to 1836, likewise condemned football for being, in his view 'better suited to farm boys and manual labourers than young gentlemen'.[7]

Shaping gentlemen

The arrival of the industrial revolution obliged public schools to adopt a new teaching regime, with the aim of shaping gentlemen ready to take in hand the burgeoning British colonial and industrial capitalism. The lack of discipline dominant in schools, the violence inherent in the daily lives of students and their frequent revolts became incompatible with the social and economic needs of the emergent Victorian society.

After 1830, a profound movement of moral reform emerged, driven by Reverend Thomas Arnold, head of Rugby School from 1828 to 1842. In common with a whole generation of new heads and teachers, he was a fervent disciple of the Muscular Christians, an association founded by an Anglican canon after the Battle of Waterloo in 1815.[8] Inspired by the renown earned by German gymnastics following Prussian military successes in the Napoleonic wars, the Muscular Christians posited the educational and moral benefits of physical exercise. Supported by a whole network of reformers, such as Benjamin Hall Kennedy, headmaster of Shrewsbury from 1836 to 1865, Thomas Arnold's ambition was to purge schools of their more anachronistic traditions.[9] He put in place a rigorous teaching system that was more focused on Christian morality and wisdom – 'godliness and good learning'. Arnold also opened the doors of his institution to the children of the merchant bourgeoisie who, together with the young aristocrats, were destined to lead the industrial revolution.

The Muscular Christians conceived of physical activity as a source of discipline and temperance, and so the pedagogical trend led by Thomas Arnold favoured practical games and student initiative. Concerned by the violence of these sports, the public-school reformers and educators trained by Arnold, rather than striving in vain to ban football games, decided to integrate them fully into the lessons. Initially, they allowed the seniors to run the games, thereby legitimising football in schools. However, the disciplinary educational tenets of Muscular Christianity quickly instrumentalised this source of disorder and violence in schools, turning it into a tool for control of pupils. Opportunistically, the reformers discovered in these sports new physical practices that could be codified to improve the students' discipline and inscribe the principle of the law in their bodies.[10] 'I prefer my students to vigorously play football rather than spending their leisure time drinking or fighting in the town's taverns', declared Thomas Arnold. 'Sport is an antidote to immorality and a cure for lack of discipline'.[11]

The first rules of football, intended to reduce the brutality of the sport, were formalised around 1840. The ground surfaces on which it was played had an influence on these new codes. At Rugby, where the terrain was soft, a game with 37 rules was standardised in 1846 that allowed the ball to be picked up – known as 'handling'. The hard ground at Eton favoured the development of the 'dribbling game', and the use of the hands to carry the ball or to block the opponent was forbidden in 1849. At Westminster School, meanwhile, the first match sheets were introduced in 1854.[12] Football swiftly acquired a central place in the daily lives of public school pupils and became the principal physical activity in winter, cricket being played only in summer. Thomas Hughes' autobiographical novel published in 1857, *Tom Brown's School Days*, describes a school life spent on the playing fields of Rugby where he dedicated himself assiduously to his school's version of football to counter the bullying of an older and stronger pupil.

Public school football was steadily invested with educational virtues. The game, played on a space made available by the school and with respect for the rules approved by educational authorities, could occupy a good part of the free time of the students and distract them from rebellious temptations. It also forged the character of the men essential to the development of the British Empire and its all-powerful industries, by articulating on the playing field the spirit of initiative as much as discipline and self-government: 'Cricket and football fields are not merely places of exercise and amusement; they help to form some of the most valuable social qualities and the manly virtues, and they hold, like the classroom and the boarding schools, a distinct and important place in public-school education', reported the Clarendon Royal Commission in 1864, tasked with investigating the general condition of private schools.[13]

Playing sports with rules became almost obligatory in public schools – with Marlborough College making it a part of its curriculum in 1853[14] – and staff were allocated to teach them. At Eton, it was stipulated that: 'Any lower boy in this house who does not play football once a day and twice on a half holiday will be fined half a crown and kicked'.[15] In some schools, anyone who sought to become headmaster was expected to have taught physical education at some point.[16] The Muscular Christian Hely Hutchinson Almond, head of the Loretto School from 1862 to 1903, claimed to have identified in football and cricket a set of essential practices for training the future ruling classes in economic competition: 'Games in which the combined efforts of all lead to victory and which cultivate courage and endurance, constitute the cornerstone of the educational system of public schools'.[17]

'Well-oiled machines'

From the late 1840s, football games escaped the bounds of public schools thanks to the creation of the first university clubs, on the initiative of their former pupils. The expansion of the British railway network facilitated matches between both university and school teams, and allowed the organisation of the first regional tournaments. At each match, however, the inextricable diversity of the rules followed by each institution proved an obstacle. In 1848, at Cambridge University, 14 former pupils of Harrow, Eton, Rugby,

Winchester and Shrewsbury came together one afternoon in a student room, determined to unify the rules of football:

> But the result was dire confusion, as every man played the rules he had been accustomed to at his public school. I remember how the Eton man howled at the Rugby man for handling the ball [...] Every man brought a copy of his school rules, or knew them by heart, and our progress in framing new rules was slow [...] We broke up five minutes before midnight.[18]

This first attempt to standardise football, known as the 'Cambridge Rules', oriented it towards the 'dribbling game', removing the practice of 'handling' dear to Rugby students, and went some way to democratising football across the country's university campuses. The very first football club, the Sheffield Football Club, was founded in 1857 by former students of Sheffield Collegiate School. There followed the Blackheath Club, created in 1858, and the Forest Club and the Old Harrovians in 1859. The game nevertheless continued to become standardised, with a professor from Uppingham proposing in 1862 a regulation in ten articles entitled 'The Simplest Game'.

The birth of modern football, however, can be pinpointed to 26 October 1863, at the Freemason's Tavern in London. Delegates from eleven clubs in the capital and surrounding region took on the task of creating an official organisation for the game, and established the definitive rules, drawing on the Cambridge Rules. That day, the Football Association was officially constituted, though debates continued to rage at subsequent meetings on the use of hands, or the continuance of practices judged too violent by some. Two months later, 14 articles set out the maximum size of the pitch as well as the rules for kick-off, scoring a goal, and for throw-ins. While the prohibition of hacking (kicking the shin) and tripping reduced physical brutality on the pitch, the game remained a rough and individualistic football played by gentlemen fond of the saying 'if you miss the ball, don't miss the man'. The offside rule was introduced in 1866 in order to encourage passes between teammates and, in 1881, the all-powerful figure of the referee appeared in the codification of the game: the man in black – the colour of clergymen – in charge of enforcing the rules of the Football Association on the pitch. The separation from former Rugby students became definitive, and they created the Rugby Football Union in 1871 as a first step towards modern rugby. The rigorous codification of the rules, the appearance of the first clubs, the creation of a federation and the organisation of the first tournaments transformed the 'dribbling game' into a true modern sport, called association football to distinguish it from its close cousin, rugby football.

In line with other sports that became standardised in this period, such as cricket and tennis, association football adopted the leading traits of the industrial revolution. Its standardised rules enabled as many people as possible to reproduce a single corpus of bodily practices in a rationalised time and space. The specialisation of players and positions within the team is a reflection of the division of labour required by industrial society. The organisation of the game under the eye of the referee, a tutelary figure who imposes his law, embodies the discipline and spirit of initiative channelled towards a single production target: to score goals.[19] The first match reports in the press similarly borrowed an industrial vocabulary: the teams were 'well-oiled machines', the players have legs like 'pistons' or transform into 'dynamos' that 'hit like a sledgehammer'.[20]

If the games of folk football aimed at victory at all costs and by any means, the bourgeois morals introduced to football and to modern sports more broadly the ethics of 'fair play'. A direct descendant of the chivalric code of honour that combined the art of war with that of courtliness,[21] fair play is intrinsic to aristocratic societies for which, as historian Johan Huizinga puts it, 'there can only be a question of victory when [...] the honour of the leader emerges stronger from the combat' or when 'the victor knows how to display moderation'.[22] The beauty of the gesture, personal honour, self-control and restraint in the game must take precedence over victory. With the emergence of modern sports, fair play – advocating respect for the rules, the opponent and the final result of the match – became a 'training in moral behaviour on the playing field transferable to the whole world'.[23] Having dispossessed the village communities of their games, the English dominant classes, by rationalising football into a modern sport, transformed it not only into an educational tool but also a new form of sociability for gentlemen.

From 1867, thanks to the unification of the rules by the Football Association, the first inter-county championships emerged between the clubs of former public school pupils. The sports federation organised the Football Association Cup for the first time in 1871, with 15 gentlemen's clubs taking part. The rules established the match duration at 90 minutes, with eleven players on each side. Meanwhile, the network of clubs was quickly growing denser: if in 1871 there were 50 clubs affiliated to the Football Association, by 1888 the figure had reached 1,000.[24] Tournaments with scheduled matches became a regular affair, and hierarchies between both players and clubs emerged with the recording of results and rankings. The exuberant aristocrat Lord Arthur Fitzgerald Kinnaird was as much the first footballing star of the time as the worthy representative of the spirit of the game that inspired the Football Association. Sporting a huge auburn beard and immaculate white trousers, carrying his coach around on horseback during tournaments, this Eton and Cambridge graduate turned bank director was the archetype of the gentleman footballer promoted by the federation. Playing in all positions on the pitch, a charismatic leader of his team and adept at a hard and virile game, he participated in nine finals of the FA Cup and won it five times with Wanderers FC from 1873, and then with the Old Etonians.

Since its creation in 1871 the Cup had been won by gentlemen's clubs. The Cup final of 1883 opposed the Old Etonians, captained by the legendary Lord Kinnaird, and Blackburn Olympic, and would mark a turning point in the history of football. For the first time, a team from the working class won the Cup, signalling the end of public school hegemony over the sport.

3

The people's game

Football as a cultural trait of the working class

A sport is more likely to be adopted by a social class if it does not contradict that class's relation to the body at its deepest and most unconscious level, i.e. the body schema, which is the depository of a whole world view and whole philosophy of the person and the body.

Pierre Bourdieu, *Distinction: A Social Critique of the Judgement of Taste*, 1979

My most beautiful goal? It was a pass!

Eric Cantona in *Looking for Eric* by Ken Loach, 2009

By the mid-19th century, the industrial revolution had already urbanised much of Great Britain and profoundly reshaped Victorian society. More than half of the population lived in towns and cities and, in 1867, almost 70 per cent of them were working class.[1] Benefiting from the right to form trade unions granted in 1824 and by the workers' movement – the International Workers' Association was founded in 1864 in London and the Trades Union Congress four years later – the emergence and expansion of trade union activities progressively led to improvements in factory working conditions that were often still close to slavery. The first regulations focused on reductions in working hours: in 1850, the Factory Act limited the working week to 60 hours, and the British parliament established the first national holidays with the Bank Holiday Act in 1871. But bitter union struggles shook the textile mills of Manchester and Lancashire, with workers demanding the right to have Saturday afternoons off. Increasingly popular among workers, the 'English week' – as it became known in France – progressively appeared in other industrial sectors. With the creation of obligatory weekly rest days in 1854 and a legal limit of six and a half hours' work on Saturdays in all branches of industry in 1874, most English workers now left factories and workplaces at 2 pm.[2]

Initially decried by the British industrialists, this 'English week' swiftly won over factory managers who realised that the weekly rest enabled workers to recover their strength and be more productive in the long run. The establishment nevertheless considered it necessary to take workers in hand to avoid them being left to their own devices on Saturday afternoons and fall prey to the vices that lay in wait for them, namely alcoholism, gambling and idleness. Like the public schools, which inculcated in their boarders a sense of charity towards the poorest subjects of the Crown, Victorian society was imbued with a certain social conscience, steeped in Christianity, hygienism and paternalism.[3] Financed by the industrial bourgeoisie, numerous charitable and philanthropic institutions emerged – on the model of the Salvation Army, founded in 1865 in the impoverished East End of London by the Methodist minister William Booth – to promote the physical benefits and moral virtues of football for the most deprived social classes. The sport was well adapted to the urban living conditions of the workers: the game could be played at any time on any scrap of land, requiring only a simple ball, and the rules were quick to learn.

Taking 'first place in the people's hearts'

The church, together with the pub, being one of the favoured spaces for socialising on Sundays, meant the clergy saw football as the perfect instrument to combat the decadence of a young, depraved generation of workers. Once the 'English week' was introduced, churches set up local football teams that on Saturday afternoons drew growing numbers of workers to presbytery-run sports fields. In Liverpool and Birmingham in the 1880s, one in four football clubs were founded by parish churches.[4] Many of them are still stars of the English leagues: Aston Villa was set up in 1874 by the young Methodists of the Birmingham Bible Class; the team established by the Anglican vicars and professors of Christ Church Sunday School became the Bolton

Wanderers in 1877; and Everton Football Club was founded in 1878 by the Methodist Church of St. Domingo's.

With employer paternalism at its height, the captains of industry sought to take charge of workers' leisure time. They saw football as a tool that at once improved the physical constitution of workers, sharpened their spirit of competition and distracted them from any latent dissent. This was the course taken by Arnold F. Hills, former pupil of Harrow – where he was a star footballer – and owner thanks to his father of the Thames Ironworks and Shipbuilding Company, one of the largest in London. Confronted with large strikes in the 1890s and the consolidation of the trade union movement within his company, he founded the Thames Ironworks Football Club in 1895 with the express objective of bringing workers closer to company executives. 'Our club must bring together workers of all conditions within the same community', he explained.[5] While the team was quickly nicknamed 'the Hammers', in reference to the metalworkers' hammers, the board of the club comprised gentlemen only, and in 1900 adopted the name West Ham United, becoming one of the leading clubs of the English leagues. Many other workers' football clubs emerged under the patronage of industry leaders. The Lancashire and Yorkshire Railway launched its workers' team in 1878 and was later taken on by wealthy brewer John Henry Davies to save it from bankruptcy: he renamed it Manchester United in 1902. The football team of the Royal Arsenal factory in Woolwich, south-east London, was created on the initiative of the munitions workers in 1886. Initially known as the Dial Square FC – after the workshop – the club adopted the name Arsenal in 1891.

Textile workers in Manchester, metalworkers in Birmingham, dockers in Liverpool or miners in Yorkshire: all played football in their spare time on Saturday afternoons and in the bosom of their parish or employer. The club boards were in the hands of clergymen and business owners who had no hesitation in sanctioning players if their private lives were judged too dissolute or oriented towards unionist agitation. At the heart of football's popularisation lay a terrible contradiction. Just as the ball game was becoming a key trait of working-class culture, it was also synonymous with pacification and paternalism, and risked becoming a 'tool of bourgeois control over the working world'.[6]

Other factors rooted in the industrialisation of England contributed to football's popularity among the working class. Pubs multiplied in the low-income districts of industrial towns and became crucibles for countless teams, strengthening neighbourhood ties and worker solidarity. They served equally as locker rooms, places to prepare for matches, celebrate victories and mourn defeats, and for refreshment before and after the match. The backrooms were used for meetings, for organising betting or for storing equipment. The pub owners might even provide the pitch, or sponsor the teams in modest ways.[7]

Local newspapers, major national papers such as *The Daily Telegraph* (founded in 1855), and the first sports magazines, such as *Bell's Life in London* (founded in 1822), began to cover football more scrupulously from the 1880s onwards. The results of regional and national championships could be quickly transmitted to newsrooms thanks to the growing efficiency of telegraph services. The development of urban public transport systems such as trams enabled amateur players to escape their neighbourhood to play in municipal parks and at the first public sports facilities. Train companies offered special tickets allowing workers to cross the country to support their club. At each final of the FA Cup in London, thousands of workers descended on the capital.

> All the long night overcrowded trains have been hurrying southward along the great trunk lines, and discharging cargoes of Lancashire and Yorkshire artisans in the grey hours of early morning. They sweep through the streets of the Metropolis, boisterous, triumphant [...] They all wear grey cloth caps, they are all decorated with coloured favours; they are all small men, with good-natured undistinguished faces.[8]

The stadiums filled up more and more. While 45,000 spectators attended the final of the FA Cup in 1893, the figure had risen to 120,000 by 1913. During the first season of the Football League in

1888–1889, there were a total of 602,000 spectators. Seven years later, it was nearly 2 million.[9]

Just 30 years after it was codified as a modern sport in 1863, football had become a popular passion, a 'secular religion of the British proletariat' in the words of Eric Hobsbawm, with the club as its church, the stadium as its place of worship, and the fans as its faithful.[10] 'The interest in football has become so widespread that today cricket can no longer be considered our national sport in the proper sense of the term', wrote the cricketer and footballer Charles Burgess Fry in 1895. 'Football has won first place in the people's hearts'.[11] An astonishing historical turnaround: while preindustrial farming communities were dispossessed of their games of folk football by the agrarian bourgeoisie, the urban working class became infatuated with the game initially reserved for the industrial elite.

Decisive pass

The 'dribbling game' that prevailed on football pitches was highly individualistic and paid no heed to subtlety: the sole objective over the 90 minutes was to kick the ball far up the pitch so that a forward could try to score a goal alone. This strategy was known as 'kick and rush'. As a contemporary sports newspaper reported: 'The tactics were rudimentary and consisted of punting the ball up the pitch followed by mad dashes by the forwards who, sweeping everything in their path, tried haphazardly to get the ball into the coveted goal'.[12] Steeped in the spirit of fair play, the aristocratic public school clubs like the Wanderers or the Old Etonians sought the beauty of the move or the individual flourish, and passing the ball to a teammate was an admission of weakness.

Another playing style began to emerge among a number of Scottish teams, notably Glasgow's Queen's Park FC. Since its foundation in 1867, Queen's Park FC had always paid particular attention to tactics. The club had internally adopted a more restrictive offside rule to encourage the passing of the ball between the team and reducing the number of attacks on goal by forwards. They also incited their players to train three evenings per week to refine their team game. Furthermore, during the qualifying matches of the first FA Cup in the 1871–1872 season,* the Queen's Park players were highly impressed by the 'irreproachable organisation' and the beauty of the 'smart game' of the Royal Engineers AFC, a British military team that, according to *Bell's Life in London*, had 'learned the secret of winning at football: possession of the ball'.[13] The strategic players from Glasgow quickly adopted this style of play that relies on cooperation between attack and defence.

In March 1872, during an FA Cup qualification match between the Wanderers and Queen's Park, the sports magazine *The Field* reported its astonishment at the technique used by the latter: 'They dribble little and usually convey the ball by a series of long kicks, combined with a judicious plan of passing on'.[14] At the first international football match between Scotland and England on 30 November of the same year, *The Glasgow Herald* described the differences between the two teams as follows: 'The Englishmen had all the advantage of weight, their average being about two stones heavier than the Scotchmen and they had also the advantage in pace. The strong point of the home club was that they played excellently well together'. Charles W. Alcock, administrator of the Football Association and himself a player, extolled the Scottish style in these terms in 1874: 'Nothing succeeds better than what I may call a "combination game" [...] the process of following closely on a fellow player, to assist him if required, and to take on the ball if he be attacked or prevented from continuing his onward course'.[15]

Thanks to the Scottish footballers, who some would call 'the Scotch Professors', the combination game spread through the 1880s to clubs in the north of England. In any case, drawn by the industrial revolution that demanded ever more labour, many young Scots migrated en masse in this period, finding work in the factories of Lancashire and the Midlands, and were also recruited to play in the factory owners' clubs. A number of Lancashire clubs even put adverts in Scottish newspapers seeking local players, who were reputed to be 'courageous', 'robust', 'tough with opponents' and 'technically skilled'.[16] These working-class footballers swiftly developed a com-

* Though a Scottish Cup was launched in the 1873–1874 season, a number of Scottish clubs were invited to compete in the FA Cup.

pletely different style of play, the 'passing game', which merged the style of the Scottish clubs with the spirit of cooperation and solidarity that ruled within the factories. As a reflection of worker culture, marked as much by mutual assistance as by division of labour, the passing game established football as a collective sport, where the fundamental move was no longer to selfishly dribble the ball and try to score but to pass the ball to a teammate and to construct the game together.[17] In contrast to the dribble, which values individual prowess, the pass embodies altruistic action at the service of the whole team.

Thanks to the cooperative game developed by the working-class footballers, the Lancashire clubs appeared more and more frequently in the qualifying matches for the FA Cup. In 1883, its twelfth year, the final saw the aristocratic Old Etonians face off against Blackburn Olympic, a club from the industrial North. The social contrast between the two teams is edifying. The former pupils of prestigious Eton College, already twice winners of the Cup and the current defenders, were playing in the final for the sixth time. Captained by the eccentric bank director Lord Kinnaird, the Old Etonians were partisans of the rough dribbling game and individual feats of prowess, in the purest tradition of public school ball games. Blackburn Olympic, meanwhile, came from an industrial town in Lancashire with more than a dozen active clubs – including the Blackburn Rovers who had lost to the Old Etonians in the previous final. The players trained on a sloping, muddy pitch rented from a local pub, The Hole-i'th'-Wall, and their captain, Albert Warburton, was a humble plumber. The team included several weavers, a spinner, a butcher, a metalworker and a dental assistant. Sydney Yates, a wealthy industrialist who owned the town's foundry, had invested £100 in the club so that the blue-collar players could spend an entire week training in the seaside resort of Blackpool – something both wholly unprecedented and prohibited at the time.[18]

Some 8,000 spectators including 'a horde from the North, roughly dressed and swearing loudly'[19] gathered in a London cricket ground, the Kennington Oval, on Saturday 31 March 1883. The Old Etonians opened the scoring in the 30th minute, but Blackburn equalised in the second half. Faced with the dribbling and individualism of the Old Etonians in a 2–2–6 formation, Blackburn Olympic, before the astonished eyes of the supporters and sports commentators, deployed a collective passing game that was a display of workers' mutual support. The winning goal only came in the 15th minute of extra time. The Blackburn forward Jimmy Costley, a 21-year-old spinner, collected a cross from Thomas Dewhurst, a weaver, and struck the ball home past goalkeeper John Rawlinson, a prominent London lawyer and future Conservative MP.[20]

For the first time in history the FA Cup was lifted by a team of workers, putting an end to the hegemony of bourgeois football and of the dribbling game. The popular symbolism of this victory nourished a certain regional pride, with the residents of Blackburn giving a triumphant welcome to their players. After a parade through the town and an official ceremony in the town hall, the plumber captain Albert Warburton declared: 'We are thrilled to bring the Cup to Lancashire. It will be at home here and will never leave for London again'. With this apparently benign phrase, the player asserted his sense of belonging to the industrial and working North, vis-à-vis the gentlemen's clubs of the South, which had dominated tournaments up to that point.

Another rivalry reared its head in Warburton's words: while the posh clubs of the former public school pupils promoted the nobility of the amateur in the Football Association, those whose players came from the working world – and from the North in particular – were suspected of paying their players.[21] Given the number of working days lost to training and the match itself, a fee for the working-class players known as the 'broken time payment' had been discreetly put in place by factory owners.

Following the victory of Blackburn Olympic in March 1883, the clubs of the bourgeois elite and certain sports journalists, suspecting that the players were paid during their week of intensive training in Blackpool, asked the Football Association to look at this 'sham amateurism' of the Northern clubs. For the governing bodies of the FA, the 'amateur ethic' and the ambition to play 'for pleasure' was a question of principle that should not be overturned, with the gentlemen arguing that it is 'degrading for respectable men to play with professionals'.[22] Yet the Cup was attracting more and more spectators, and the tournament became, to the chagrin of those wanting it to remain an amateur sport, a very lucrative affair (thanks to sales of tickets, drinks and advertising). From April 1883, the FA authorised clubs to cover the costs of players' train tickets for the semi-finals and finals of the tournament. The following season, the textile industrialist William Suddel, owner of a Lancashire club called Preston North End, acknowledged he had paid to recruit Scottish players and was excluded from the tournament. But in 1885, after the suspension of two further teams, the industrial clubs of the North threatened to set up a dissident federation, forcing the FA to officially recognise the status of the professional player.

From this point on, football became a milieu as competitive as other industrial sectors, and club directors applied the same economic and managerial strategies as they did to business. Clubs acquired the status of public companies, such as the Hammers of the Thames Ironworks which went professional in 1898 and two years later adopted the name West Ham United Football Club Limited. The club directors also began to invest massively in the recruitment of promising players and in building grounds. In 1897, for example, the owner of West Ham United built a vast stadium close to his shipyards, the Memorial Ground.[23] Meanwhile, the rational organisation and specialisation of labour continued to make its mark on the pitch with the appearance of the positions of winger and centre-half, as well as the first linesmen. In 1891, there were already almost 450 part-time or full-professional players in England. By 1914, there were ten times as many.[24]

'The Outcasts FC'

Making a short-term profit on club investments demanded more than one annual Cup and a few friendlies. On the initiative of William McGregor, director of Aston Villa, twelve clubs set up the Football League in 1888 with the intention of arranging matches only between professional teams, seen as more lucrative for the organisations and more attractive for spectators. The same year, the

League established a tradition of one or two matches played on 26 December, Boxing Day. A traditional day of rest, Boxing Day – referring to the boxes of gifts for servants and employees – became the day off when working-class men head to the stadium to watch a good football match.

However, despite the growing revenues from the different tournaments, the professional footballers remained tied to their precarious condition as workers. With the appearance of the first transfer fees between clubs – the cost of which had already climbed as high as £1,000 by 1905[25] – club owners established the 'retain and transfer' system in 1893: each footballer became the exclusive property of the organisation and could only leave their club with the approval of the manager and coach. As this little advert published in 1891 reveals, some players were bought, sold and bartered over like livestock:

> No. 163. Right or left fullback. This is one of the most likely youngsters I have ever booked. He gives reference to a well-known pressman, who has repeatedly seen him play and knows what he can do, and has a high opinion of his abilities and future prospects. Just note – height 5 feet 11 inches; weight 12 stone; age 20. There's a young giant for you. This is a colt worth training.[26]

Finally, in 1901 the Football Association imposed a ceiling on weekly wages of £4 – the average salary of a skilled worker – and prohibited any bonus. If footballers had seen their pay to date only as a small supplement to their worker's wages, more and more players began to feel cheated in view of the physical efforts involved, the injuries that forced them to take leave of absence from their factories, and the profits made by the clubs.

In Manchester, where the cotton industry was the seedbed for a robust workers' movement (the city saw the birth of the greatest union of all, the Trades Union Congress, in 1868), football became a new professional sector for unionism to address. Following an initial attempt with the Association Footballers' Union, from 1893 to 1901, the Association of Football Players' and Trainers' Union (AFPTU) was officially founded at the Imperial Hotel in Manchester on 2 December 1907, on the initiative of Charlie Roberts and Billy Meredith, respectively centre half and striker for Manchester United. Trade unionist footballers invoked the 'right of all workers to associate with their comrades in order to be able to help a colleague in difficulty'[27] and demanded the end of wages capped at £4, the abolition of the 'retain and transfer' system, compensation for injured players, and the right for players to obtain a percentage of transfer fees between clubs.[28]

The authoritarian bent of club owners was a particular target for the popular Billy Meredith, who was often fined by Manchester United's managers for 'bad behaviour'.[29] Availing of his media notoriety to promote the union, he vigorously argued against the wage cap, accusing the football authorities of conservatism:

> I have devoted myself to football and I have become a better player than most men because I have denied myself much that men prize [...] They congratulate me and give me caps but they will not give me a penny more than men are earning in the reserve team, some of them perhaps do not trouble themselves to improve themselves and don't worry about taking care of condition. If football is a man's livelihood and he does more than others for his employer, why is he not entitled to better pay than others?[30]

The Football Association and the Football League saw red when in 1909 the AFPTU proposed joining the General Federation of Trade Unions, a powerful trade union federation. Football's two governing bodies wanted to retain their paternalistic control over the players and urged unionised footballers to abandon their protest movement, under penalty of individual sanctions and breach of contract. When the union threatened to go on strike in August, the football authorities suspended all AFPTU-affiliated players for the 1909–1910 season and urgently formed makeshift teams to safeguard the championship. While most of these players fell into line, those from Manchester United collectively refused to give up on their militancy. Even though their club was no longer paying them, the Mancunians continued to train every day and redoubled their union activities.

One morning, the seditious team went so far as to steal trinkets and ornaments from the club offices, selling them on a street corner for cash.[31] The team's centre half, Charlie Roberts, appealed to the press to publish the players' demands and had a photograph taken immortalising the rebels with a sign at their feet reading 'The Outcasts FC' The shocking image did the rounds of the papers and reinvigorated the movement, winning public support from another star player, the Everton forward Tim Coleman.

The Football Association offered to lift the suspension of the unionised players if the AFPTU abandoned its plan to join the General Federation of Trade Unions. In October 1909, the players voted against joining the trade union federation, putting an end to the strike. The AFPTU therefore remained a strictly professional union, and footballers continued to be a distinctive category of worker: the convergence of the struggles of football and industrial workers had reached a dead end. Disappointed, Billy Meredith returned to the pitch in November 1909, complaining that: 'The unfortunate thing is that so many players refuse to take things seriously but are content to live a kind of schoolboy life and to do just what they are told […] instead of thinking and acting for himself and his class'.[32] Although the union wrested permission from the football authorities to obtain match bonuses and succeeded in shining the spotlight on the working conditions of footballers, the salary cap and the 'retain and transfer' system would be maintained in England until 1963.

Football Railway Company

Just as industrial development and productivism were exported across the planet thanks to the geographic and economic domination of the British Empire, so industrial football and sports ideology became international. 'Wherever there is an island, an islet, a haven […] there the Englishman arrives, he erects his telegraph poles, he lays his railway on impassable routes. And he plays football', reported Stefano Jacomuzzi.[33] At the end of the 19th century, the Football Association was already sending teams on world tours to promote the virtues of the game. In 1897 the Corinthians took part in 33 matches in South Africa, and the following year Queen's Park Rangers played in Scandinavia. The Surrey Wanderers and Southampton FC travelled to Germany and Austria after the turn of the century for a series of friendly matches. Above all, though, it was foreign students fresh out of public schools and the main engines of British colonialism – military, missionary and industrial – that carried the Good News of football to the four corners of the world. The Anglophile elites of the countries of both North and South appropriated football, establishing it as a symbol of the 'English way of life', and made it a mark of social distinction and affirmation of industrial modernity.[34]

This meant that the pioneers of South American football were either members of the local upper classes, or the employees of British companies established in the coastal cities.[35] Buenos Aires FC was the first club on the continent, founded in May 1867 by two brothers from Yorkshire, Thomas and James Hogg, employees of a railway construction company. On the other side of the River Plate, the ancestor of the Club Atlético Peñarol, the Central Uruguay Railway Cricket Club (CURCC), was founded in 1891 by four English employees of the British company Central Uruguay Railway Co. of Montevideo. The CURCC regularly met with Albion FC, where the young English bourgeoisie played, then established the Uruguayan football championship with three other clubs in 1900. Charles William Miller, son of a British railway engineer working in Brazil, went to study in a public school in Southampton and played for Corinthians in London before returning to São Paulo in 1894. Hired by the local English railway company, he strived to create a football section within the São Paulo Athletic Club and in 1895 organised a first meeting between a team from his company and players from the Gás Company, another British enterprise. In the United States, meanwhile, association football had difficulty taking root because other ball games – notably American football – were already firmly established within the American educational system. With a few exceptions such as St. Louis in Missouri, where football became popular thanks to British immigrants, in the eyes of the American elites the round ball represented a sporting chimaera redolent of the former metropole.

In Africa, there is evidence of the first football matches – initially restricted to white colonists – in Cape Town and Port Elizabeth in

South Africa, as early as 1862.[36] The ball was quickly perceived as a 'civilising instrument' in East Africa, and football was introduced to Uganda in 1897 by British officer William Pulteney – an Eton boy – and missionaries of the Namirembe Church Missionary Society.[37]

English sailors and the British army imported the game to East Asia from 1873, thanks to one Lieutenant Commander Douglas, an instructor at the Royal Navy academy in Tokyo. The Bengalis, meanwhile, began to play football in colleges established by the colonists; in 1892 a team from Calcutta, the Sovabazar Club, defeated an English military team, the East Surrey Regiment.

In tsarist Russia, football was first imported to Orekhovo-Zuyevo, near Moscow, by two industrialists from Lancashire: in 1887 they set up a team for the workers at their textile factory that was the ancestor of FC Dynamo Moscow. In Turkey, the British introduced football to the Greek and Armenian communities of Istanbul and Izmir in the late 19th century, to the disapproval of the Ottoman authorities; the country had to wait for the Young Turks revolution of 1908 for the sport's popularity to spread.[38]

Back on the Old Continent, football disembarked in Copenhagen in 1876 thanks to British residents, and spread from there across Scandinavia.[39] One of the oldest German clubs, meanwhile, was founded in Hamburg in 1887, while in the heart of the Austro-Hungarian Empire the first clubs emerged in Prague and Vienna in the 1890s.[40]

Football developed in Italy through the major industrial centres in the north of the peninsula. In Turin, the Internazionale Foot-Ball Club Torino was founded in 1891 by Edoardo Bosio, an Italian merchant who had worked for a time in the textile industry in Britain. In Milan, football was played between English gentlemen who came together in 1899 to create the ancestor of Milan AC, the opulent Milan Cricket and Football Club. In Spain, a handful of English engineers from the Sunderland region working for the industrial port of Bilbao founded the Bilbao Football Club in 1894 – forerunner of the Athletic Club de Bilbao (1898); and it was in a Barcelona experiencing an industrial boom that Hans Gamper, a Swiss working in import–export, brought together English, Swiss and German expatriates in 1899 to found FC Barcelona. As for Portugal, it was the aristocrat Guilherme Pinto Basto who, after studying at the Downside School in England, organised a first match in 1888 for young people from Lisbon's high society on the posh beaches of Cascais.

Football established a toehold in Paris in the wake of a school trip by pupils of the École Monge to Eton College, and thanks to English people who came to work for the Universal Exposition of 1889. But the first French club, the Havre Athletic Club, was founded in 1872 by British workers at the Normandy port, under the patronage of Francis-Frederic Langstaff, director of the South Western Railway.[41]

In light of the growing success of football in Europe, Édouard Pontié, editor of the French sports weekly *Armes et Sports*, wrote in the early years of the 20th century:

> All across the Old Continent there are association football clubs [...] Germany and Austria, Bohemia and Hungary have adopted the game, as has Switzerland; Italy has good teams in Turin, Milan, Rome and Naples; Spain has finally shown an interest with Madrid and Barcelona. The suns of winter will soon shine everywhere only on football players.[42]

4

The munitionettes

The saga of the first women football players in Britain

> Football is all very well as a game for rough girls,
> but is hardly suitable for delicate boys.
>
> Oscar Wilde[1]

'The game, from a player's point of view, was a failure, but some of the individual members of the teams showed that they had a fair idea of the game'. This was the cutting remark of the *Glasgow Herald* following the first women's international football match, played between Scotland and England at Easter Road Stadium in Edinburgh on 9 May 1881. The Scottish daily paper preferred to dwell on the footballers' attire: 'The young ladies wore blue jerseys, white knickerbockers, red stockings, a red belt, high-heeled boots and blue and white cowl; while their English sisters were dressed in blue and white jerseys, blue stockings and belt, high-heeled boots, and red and white cowl'.

Although ball games between married and single women are recorded in 1628 in Carstairs, Lanarkshire, and near Inverness in the Highlands in the 18th century,[2] modern football, codified less than 20 years earlier, was in the 1880s an exclusively male affair. While golf, tennis and hockey began to be played by young women from the bourgeois elite as an emblem of social distinction, football remained a masculine bastion, deeply marked by Victorian society's rigid division between the sexes.[3]

Under the yoke of male domination

The female condition at the end of the 19th century was determined by the institution of marriage: a wife, whose legal rights were similar to those of a child, owed blind obedience to her husband, and her social role was to be guardian of the household. Within the working class, women were reduced to a state of quasi-slavery from a young age, while those from well-off families were expected to learn skills in boarding school such as embroidery, singing or watercolour, in order to become respectable wives and good mothers. As for the female body, it was treated as the absolute property of the husband, and as a sanctuary of purity wholly dedicated to procreation. This loss of ownership of the body to the yardstick of Victorian Puritanism was reflected in a strict dress code, especially among the upper classes where women were obliged to wear heavy and uncomfortable crinolines – broad skirts supported by metal hoops.

The *Glasgow Herald*'s disparaging remarks and sartorial obsession with the women footballers in the Scotland–England match are merely a reflection of the moral reprobation of British patriarchal society towards the young socialites engaged in a male sporting practice – and in front of a male crowd, too. The hostility was such that the players, to protect themselves, used assumed names, with the organiser of this football tournament and goalkeeper for the Scottish team, suffragist activist Helen Matthews, calling herself 'Mrs Graham'.

Just a few days after this first match, the 5,000 spectators of a second women's England–Scotland clash in Glasgow staged a pitch invasion, putting an end to the game.

> At last a few roughs broke into the enclosure, and as these were followed by hundreds soon after, the players were roughly jostled, and had prematurely to take refuge in the omnibus which had conveyed them to the ground. Their troubles were not, however, yet ended, for the crowd tore up the stakes and threw them at the departing vehicle, and but for the presence of the police some bodily injury to the females might have occurred.[4]

A few weeks later, on 20 June, at another women's England–Scotland match in Manchester, a riot broke out in the stands, putting the daring female footballers in peril once more. Raising the ire of the British press, including the *Manchester Guardian* which spoke of the 'vulgar curiosity' and women 'attired in a costume which is neither graceful nor very becoming',[5] and leading to dangerous scenes in the grounds, these pioneering attempts to promote women's football by Helen Matthews were swiftly put on hold until the mid-1890s.

At the end of the 1880s, the popularity of men's football had spread rapidly through the working classes, with the first season of the professional Football League attracting over 600,000 spectators.[6] The same year, the Polytechnic Clubs were founded, London sports clubs that offered basketball, cricket and swimming to commercial employees and teachers in the capital. In girls' schools, football made a timid appearance at Brighton High School for Girls, Roedean School, and Girton College, Cambridge. But the practice was quickly prohibited by the governing body before the *British Medical Journal* proclaimed in December 1894 that 'football should be damned out of hand as dangerous to the reproductive organs and breasts because of sudden jerks, twists and blows'.[7] Robert Miles, an accomplished sportsman and player on the Oxford cricket team, hammered the sexist nail home claiming the same year that 'maternity is also a sport – woman's true sport'.[8]

It was into this hostile social and sporting context that the first women's football club in history stepped in late 1894: the British Ladies' Football Club, founded by Nettie Honeyball, a militant feminist whose real name was Mary Hutson, and Florence Dixie, political writer, war correspondent and daughter of the Marquis of Queensbury. In an interview with the *Daily Sketch* on 6 February 1895, club secretary Nettie Honeyball made no effort to hide their militant ambitions.

> There is nothing grotesque about the British Ladies' Football Club. I founded the association last year, with the fixed resolve of proving to the world that women are not the 'ornamental and useless' creatures men have pictured. I must confess, my conviction on all matters, where the sexes are so widely divided, are all on the side of emancipation, and I look forward to the time when ladies may sit in parliament and have a voice in the direction of affairs, especially those which concern them most.

On 23 March 1895 at Crouch End in Hornsey, North London, the British Ladies' Football Club held its first tournament opposing a team from the North of Great Britain – including the Scottish pioneer Helen 'Mrs Graham' Matthews – with a team from the South. Although it was attended by 10,000 spectators, the event was almost unanimously condemned in the press.[9] 'It is evident to the eyes of all, that girls are wholly unsuited to the rough practice of football', blared the weekly *Sketch* on 27 March. 'As an outdoor game, it is not to be recommended, and as a spectacle it is to be deplored'. The baggy knickerbockers worn on the pitch by the ladies were again viewed as the embodiment of moral depravity. The 'femininity' injunction found in all these reports was accompanied by a growing interest in a young footballer of just 14, Miss Nellie Gilbert, nicknamed 'Tommy' by the journalists. 'Her arrival sparked laughter, though it was more due to her size and boyish appearance than anything else', reported the London daily *Pall Mall Gazette* on 25 March 1895. 'In the first place, she looked ridiculously small to participate in a football game. On top of that, she was built like a boy and ran like the kids who can run very fast at the age of ten'. Unanimously seen as the best player of the British Ladies' Football Club, the gender ambiguity of Miss Nellie Gilbert was constantly hammered home by the media. 'He (or she) moved around the pitch like a young colt, and was often "on the ball", tackling with courage', wrote the *Paisley and Renfrewshire Gazette*. 'He (or she) was constantly alert, agile and energetic'.[10]

With a non-stop series of 150 matches played from 1895–1897, attracting thousands of spectators, the women footballers, despite their popularity, crystallised male anxiety at the questioning of the sexual hierarchy.[11] This focus on the moral danger represented by women's football was exacerbated by a national scandal involving the family of Florence Dixie, president of the British Ladies' Football Club. Her brother was the one who in 1895 publicly accused the writer Oscar Wilde of homosexuality, claiming he was romantically involved with Dixie's nephew, Alfred Douglas. After a trial that shook the nation, the playwright was imprisoned for two years.

Enjoying a scandalous reputation following matches won against men's teams – and for having fielded a black woman player, Emma

Clarke – the British Ladies' Football Club disappeared from the sports fields for almost six years. When in October 1902 the Football Association formally banned its affiliates from playing against women, the British Ladies' Football Club brazenly reappeared for three games against male squads. Their last official meeting, on 2 May 1903, was against players from Biggleswade in Bedfordshire. Having won the game 3–1, the score sheet of this final confrontation records that the ladies' team captain was a certain Miss Nellie Gilbert.

From the assembly lines to the green pitches

If 1903 marked the end of the footballing adventures of the female pioneers, it was also the year the Women's Social and Political Union was established under the leadership of Emmeline Pankhurst, a figurehead of the suffragette movement. Tumultuous demonstrations, hunger strikes, sabotage of lines of communication and even letter bombs: the fight for women's right to vote shook the British political landscape until the outbreak of the First World War.

It needed a global conflict for the winds of female emancipation to blow through English football. From 1914, industry underwent a total reorganisation. As part of the war effort, steel and textile mills were converted to assembly lines for weapons, shells and ammunition. They recruited many working-class women to replace the men called to the front. At the height of the war, almost a million workers produced 80 per cent of British military armaments, including 700,000 in the munitions industry alone.[12] Nicknamed the 'munitionettes' and also known as the 'canary girls' due to their yellow-tinged skin from exposure to TNT, these young women workers suffered physically exhausting working conditions. They worked twelve hours a day, handling explosives that put them at risk of accidents. However, from 1915 onwards, industrial employers set up various recreational and sporting activities within their factories with the aim of containing the workers who might be inclined to go on strike or free themselves of patriarchal bonds by heading to the pub after work.

With football already deeply embedded in the working culture of their fathers, brothers or husbands, the chance to play the sport themselves won over many munitionettes. At the company Armstrong Whitworth & Co., which ran factories across northern England, it was reported that: 'In every department of the factory, dancing and swimming were very popular, and almost every branch successfully ran a football team […] Women's football was perhaps most developed in the munitions factories'.[13] Becoming established in Lancashire and Cumbria as well as the industrial suburbs of London, women's factory football developed rapidly under the aegis of the social paternalism of industrial bosses. Between 1915 and 1918, more than 150 munitionette teams were established.[14] At Christmas 1916, the first official tournament was organised at Dragley Beck in Lancashire between a team from the neighbouring factory, the Ulverston Munitions Girls, and local athletes. A few weeks later, a new inter-factory meeting pitted a squad of female workers from the Swansea National Shell Factory against the Newport munitionettes.

The British Prime Minister David Lloyd George encouraged these 'valiant heroes' to fully express their patriotism by playing football in their spare time.[15] For the government, which introduced conscription in January 1916, it was a question of boosting the social image of the women workers devoting themselves to a healthy and fortifying national sport, one that enhanced their physical ability to replace the male industrial labour force now mobilised at the front. On the initiative of factory superintendents and hospital directors, a number of charity matches between teams of munitionettes were set up for the benefit of war charities. On 21 April 1917, a match between the Carlisle Munition Girls and the Workington Munition Girls, organised for the benefit of the Cumberland Prisoners of War Fund, attracted some 5,000 spectators to Lonsdale Park in Workington, Cumbria.[16] In total, around 40 such matches were held in this county alone during 1917, with the takings sent to the military hospitals, Soldiers' Comforts Fund or the Red Cross. 'Who could imagine, just two years ago, that women could play football. But times change and we change with the times', celebrated the factory magazine *The Bombshell* in June 1917. 'In their great and determined effort to save their country, women have not only taken on their shoulders the work of man, but his pastimes and recreations as well'.[17]

With the English football championship and the FA Cup suspended due to the hostilities, the charitable dimension of these matches between workers obliged the football authorities and press to show benevolence towards these women's teams, seen by the Football Association as a provisory and inoffensive phenomenon that would only last as long as the war. At first treated as a fun or even comical entertainment – some matches were played against men with their hands tied behind their backs, or amputee soldiers – women's football steadily acquired its own following with the public who appreciated the courage of these young workers on the industrial assembly lines, their charitable work, but above all their sporting performance.

Reputed for the quality of their play, the munitionettes team of Dick, Kerr Ladies from the industrial town of Preston, Lancashire, was founded in 1917. 'We used to play at shooting at the cloakroom windows', recalled the working footballer Alice Norris. 'They were little square windows and if the boys beat us at putting a window through we had to buy them a packet of Woodbines, but if we beat them they had to buy us a bar of Five Boys chocolate'.[18] An administrative employee of Dick, Kerr & Co., Alfred Frankland used to watch from his office as the players kicked the ball around during their lunch break, before taking them under his wing and persuading the professional club Preston North End FC to lend their Deepdale ground for a charity match. At Christmas 1917, the Dick, Kerr Ladies attracted 10,000 spectators to Preston for a match against the women players of the Coulthard foundry, to benefit the local Moor Park Military Hospital, raising the equivalent of £40,000 today.[19]

In parallel to the creation of the Dick, Kerr Ladies, some squads of munitionettes were supported logistically by local football clubs. The Blyth Spartan Ladies, who adopted the colours of the semi-professionals at Blyth Spartans AFC, were trained by the Royal Navy marines who came to the port of Blyth (Northumberland) to load the shells manufactured by these worker-footballers onto their warships before heading back to the front in Europe. Faced with this multiplicity of teams and the popular success of charity matches, the *Newcastle Daily Chronicle* announced on 20 August 1917 a women-only charity football tournament to begin that autumn, the

Munitionettes' Cup. Fourteen workers' teams participated, with the final played on 18 May 1918 in Middlesbrough between the Blyth Spartan Ladies and the Blockow Vaughan Ladies. Some 22,000 spectators turned up at Ayresome Park to attend this clash for the benefit of Teesside Medical Charities. Finally, the same year, international Scotland–England matches were organised, such as the one held on 2 March 1918 at Celtic Park in Glasgow, where the Scottish munitionettes of the Beardmore factory faced the Vickers Munition Girls from Barrow-in-Furness.

After the Armistice and the troops' return home, time was called on the war industry and its munitionettes. Between November 1918 and August 1919, 750,000 female workers lost their jobs,[20] as the factories returned to their pre-war production: Dick, Kerr & Co. went back to making railway tracks. However, the women weren't ready to hang up their boots: although a number of teams disappeared,* at the end of 1918 Great Britain still had around a hundred women's teams ready to fight it out on the grass.

'Much better hitters'

Finding jobs at the town hospital, the talented Dick, Kerr Ladies, still supported by their former factory and managed by Alfred Frankland, continued to enjoy popular enthusiasm through 1919. Proof that women's football had won a faithful following during the First World War was a match on 8 March 1919 between the Dick, Kerr Ladies and the Newcastle Girls that attracted 5,000 people and raised £179 for charity. A few weeks later the same billing gathered a crowd of 35,000 at St James' Park in Newcastle.[21] The following year, the Dick, Kerr Ladies played almost 30 official matches, recording 25 wins, 3 losses, 133 goals scored and only 15 conceded; as many or more than a male professional team of the period.[22]

On 26 April 1920, 16 French female footballers disembarked at Dover to play a series of four international matches against the Dick, Kerr Ladies for the benefit of the National Association of Discharged

* The women footballers were also decimated by the Spanish Flu pandemic of 1918. On 16 November 1918, for example, only two players from Armstrong-Whitworth Co. showed up for a tournament, the other nine having been struck by the influenza.

and Disabled Soldiers and Sailors. Mainly comprising players from Fémina Sport and En Avant!, two Parisian women's clubs, the French selection was captained by Alice Milliat, president of the newly created Fédération sportive française de sport féminin (FSFSF) [see Chapter 19]. However, women's football in France still being in an embryonic state, with barely ten clubs mostly from the Île-de-France region, the French press was overwhelmed by the euphoria of the 25,000 spectators who attended the first match at Preston: 'Exiting the first match was an odyssey, one great traffic jam', reported *L'Auto*.

> As for alighting from the car to cross the pavement and enter the hotel, it was unbelievable: stout English policemen tried to clear a passage they were powerless to keep free for more than a few seconds, and if the French girls emerged victorious from this crowd it was only by leaving scraps of their clothes behind.[23]

Right through to the final clash on 6 May at Stamford Bridge – the ground of prestigious London club Chelsea – the tournament was met with enthusiastic fervour by the English. 'We suffered with a smile the torture inflicted on us for over an hour by reporters and photographers upon disembarking from the train at London', recalled Alice Milliat.

> At each station of significance, we had to descend onto the platform or stand in the carriage doors for yet another photograph [...] It must be said that the welcome afforded by the whole population of the large town of Preston was most unexpected. The streets were lined with flags and banners with inscriptions in French; the mayor was standing on the steps of the town hall to welcome us as we went past.[24]

Five months after this sporting triumph, the Dick, Kerr Ladies crossed the English Channel to play a series of four matches against their French peers. The first, on 31 October, drew a crowd over 12,000 strong, as well as the British ambassador, to the Pershing ground in Paris.[25] The next day, in Roubaix, 10,000 spectators witnessed a 2–0 defeat of the English at Parc Jean Dubrulle. As they travelled across northern France, stopping in Le Havre and Rouen on 6 and 7 November, the footballers paused at the war memorials dotting their route, sealing the friendship between the nations forged in the First World War.

The high point of 1920 came with the traditional Boxing Day match, which saw 53,000 spectators crowd the stands of Goodison Park, Liverpool's Everton FC ground, to watch the Dick, Kerr Ladies defeat the St Helen's Ladies 4–0. The footballers needed a police escort to reach their locker rooms, and the huge crowd meant the vast sum of £3,115 was raised for the Unemployed Ex-Servicemen's Distress Fund.[26] The young footballer Lily Parr, just 15 years old, became the star of the team.

> There is probably no greater football prodigy in the whole country. Not only has she speed and excellent ball control, but her admirable physique enables her to brush off challenges from defenders who tackle her. She amazes the crowd wherever she goes by the way she swings the ball clean across the goalmouth to the opposite wing.[27]

The following year, the Dick, Kerr Ladies strung together sporting successes playing a total of 67 matches – or around two per week during the season, including a series of games in support of the widespread miners' strike sparked in April 1921 – before an average attendance of 13,000 spectators.[28] Impressed by the quality of the English women's play, and by the crowds they drew, the *Sport of Dublin* opined:

> If the players of the Irish league could play with as much skill and character as that shown by the Dick, Kerr Ladies at Windsor Park last week, there would be bigger crowds and more admissions. The women were as fast and skilled as the internationals the weekend before and much better hitters.

A return to the patriarchal order

With the Football League relaunching the professional English championship in the 1919–1920 season and the Football Association its FA Cup, the footballing authorities began to take a very dim view if not of the competition in terms of audience and sporting spectacle, then at least of the fact these women's matches were held in the grounds of its affiliated clubs. The large amounts of money generated by ladies' tournaments were also a cause for concern, calling into question the character of this women's football: was it simply a continuation of the charity matches between munitionettes during the First World War, or a popular sport that was becoming rooted in the United Kingdom?

Meanwhile, the social context of the 1920–1921 tournament no longer favoured the emancipation of women. While in 1918 the British Parliament had adopted the Representation of the People Act, authorising married women over 30 to vote, and Nancy Astor became the first woman MP in 1919, a reactionary and patriarchal wind was blowing across British society. Without doubt, the participation of women workers in the war effort had overturned the rigid division of the sexes for a time. But the emergence in the English cities of 'flappers' – young women who flaunted their sexuality, wore their hair short and consumed tobacco and alcohol – triggered a moral panic.

In these circumstances, women's football increasingly appeared as a vector in the crisis of gender identity and a challenge to the procreative role allocated to women. In early 1921, an open letter was published in the *Blaydon Courier* that purported to be from a woman addressing her younger football-playing sister:

> You mention something about the sacred cause of charity. Is charity the only thing that is sacred? Is there not a beautiful flower called modesty? Have you no respect for your sex? Dear, gentle Jennie, are you not aware that every time you enter the dressing room and discard your feminine attire for a pair of men's football knickers and a sweater you not only disgrace yourself, but lower your sex in the eyes of everyone with a sense of decency.[29]

In an interview published on 21 April 1921, the celebrated athlete Walter Goodall George spoke about women's football:

> We have to keep in mind the motherhood of the future and, as a nation, to make up our minds as to whether this forcing process in women's sport, which is associated with a new mentality, is beneficial or detrimental. This point, I am inclined to believe, calls for an official investigation, under Government auspices by medical authorities of the highest repute.

The desire to return to the patriarchal order meant the Football Association blowing the whistle on women in football. On 5 December 1921, the English federation officially prohibited its member clubs from lending their pitches to women's teams, together with any technical or refereeing support. Imposing heavy fines on Winchester City FC for having made its grounds available to the women's team of Plymouth and Seaton, it stipulated that 'the game of football is quite unsuitable for females and ought not to be encouraged'.[30] Meanwhile, the FA half-heartedly tried to justify its decision with allegations that not all the money collected for charity had been used for that purpose. Without doubt, the takings from these matches must have whetted the financial appetites of the managers of women's teams. However, although just as in the beginnings of men's professional football, the players received a discreet remuneration to compensate for the loss of their working days, the instigators of these meetings were more driven by the desire to develop women's football of high sporting quality than by purely mercantile concerns.[31]

The day after the shocking FA decision, the celebrated tennis player and promoter of physical education Eustace Miles expressed his approval:

> I consider football to be quite an inappropriate game for women, especially if they have not been medically tested first [...] The trouble is that the type of woman who wants to play football will not be medically examined first. The kicking is too jerky a movement for women (just as throwing is in contrast to bowling at cricket) and the strain is likely to be rather severe. Just as the frame of a woman is more rounded than a man's, her movements should be more rounded and less angular.[32]

The official position of the FA was relayed by the bosses at the professional clubs. Peter McWilliam, coach of Tottenham Hotspur FC, explained it in the columns of the *Hull Daily Mail*: 'I've watched one or two women's matches, and they have persuaded me that the game can only have damaging consequences for females'. The Arsenal coach, Albert Leslie Knighton, played the same tune: 'Anyone acquainted with the nature of the injuries received by men footballers could not help but think – looking at girls playing, that should they get similar knocks and buffetings their future duties as mothers would be seriously impaired'.[33] The political message sent by the sporting authorities was clear: football grounds should remain a temple of masculinity, and women should devote themselves to the regeneration of the nation.

One of the first direct consequences of this radical resolution is that a significant number of women's matches programmed for the season were cancelled due to the lack of available grounds. Of the 150 teams recorded at the end of 1921, only a score successfully continued to play over the following years.[34] Still availing of their notoriety, the Dick, Kerr Ladies set sail for a transatlantic tournament in September 1922. After a series of matches against men's teams in Baltimore, Washington and New York, they were shocked to learn that the games they had lined up in Canada had been cancelled, following a decision by the Canadian football federation. Disappointed, they returned to Liverpool on 17 November. An official celebration welcomed the players as they disembarked from the liner, with regional councillors in attendance. Yet the toasts to the glory of women's football rang false in the ears of the Dick, Kerr Ladies. A few sporadic games were played, but the France–England games of 1922 and 1923 no longer drew big crowds. Daily papers like the *Manchester Guardian*, the *Daily Mail* or *Times*, which had previously announced and reported on matches, barely referred to women's football after 1922.[35]

The collective memory of the popular enthusiasm in Britain for women's football and its working women footballers then gradually faded in favour of exclusively male football. In 1926, the Dick, Kerr Ladies even lost their name following the withdrawal of the manufacturer's backing. They were renamed the Preston Ladies, and the celebrated women's team disappeared altogether in 1965. As for the resolution of 5 December 1921, it would take exactly 50 years for the Football Association to reverse the banishment of women from English football.

5
Class against class

Working-class football in France, an extension of the field of struggle

> And when the Great Evening comes, we will bombard the enemy with footballs.
>
> *Le Socialisme*, 9 November 1912

> There are 15, 20 of them, perhaps more. Some wear the blue coat of the worker, others the jacket shiny around the elbows of the clerk [...] What to do before returning to work to be shut up until seven in the evening? Head for the football pitch. Four flat stones for goalposts. Placed wherever. The touchlines are two pavements and play is with a small rubber ball. This is association football [...][1]

This was the 1904 description by a sports journalist of lunch-hour football in Paris. The Tuileries garden was the first playing field for many Parisians while, on the edge of the capital, the Bois de Vincennes became a favoured space for football matches. Players carried wooden goalposts there on their shoulders and, each Sunday, 'all the lawns bristle with poles marking out the playing fields, the goals are raised and the unsuspecting passer-by is astonished by these clusters of stakes whose purpose he is unaware of'.[2]

While football was not yet a mass sport in France in this period – in 1906, there were around 4,000 footballers playing in 270 clubs, about half the number in Germany[3] – the 1901 law on freedom of association revitalised sports organisations. In a country undergoing rapid industrialisation, the sports club offered a convivial and accessible social structure for workers newly arrived in the cities. For the French football historian Alfred Wahl, the emergence of this sport

> announced a veritable revolution in modes of socialising and also represented a change in sensibility: a new aspiration for the return to a community way of life, a collective engagement. The conviviality woven around the game of football is bound up with many late 19th-century phenomena, characterised by a desire to recover a sense of association, in reaction to the breakdown of traditional communities and the consequences of urbanisation.[4]

With no proper pitches to practice their sport on, footballers were compelled to maintain a nomadic condition. Just as with pubs in Great Britain, the cafés played a leading role in the emergence of clubs. At the start of the 20th century, in the Seine department, 59 out of 140 official addresses for football clubs were cafés, brasseries, taverns or wine bars.[5] The Mollard brasserie on Rue Saint-Lazare became a social hub of Paris football, hosting the Racing Club de France, the White Rovers and the Stade Français.[6] The watering holes served as changing rooms, as a place to store equipment, and for players to organise their gatherings, general meetings of the association and Sunday post-match banquets, even if it meant drowning their defeats in alcohol, as the *Football Association* journal recalled in 1921:

> You missed a goal, you crossed behind the goals, you conceded a handball which cost your team a penalty. At the bistro, in return for a glass of cassis, you have plenty of time to justify yourself and to dismiss in advance the hurtful illusions that the journalists will seek to assign you the next day […][7]

Social phobia, martial values

As they became part of an increasingly dense network of associations, the football clubs were quickly taken over by secular bourgeois sports institutions and Catholic youth clubs seeking to supervise the sporting activities of young people. The Union des sociétés françaises de sports athlétiques (USFSA), the umbrella national sports federation that did its best to govern sports in the country, took a dim view of the arrival of football. Run by the aristocratic Georges de Saint-Clair and Pierre de Coubertin, the federation defended bourgeois amateurism tooth and nail and feared, with football's growing popularity, the import of British-style professionalisation.[8] In an attempt to nip the spread of the English model in the bud, in 1904 the Union backed the creation of the Fédération Internationale de Football Association (FIFA), which was initially shunned by the English Football Association because of French hostility to professionalism.

The restrictive amateurism of the USFSA also reflected a certain social phobia towards the working classes. The statutes of the federation established in July 1890 stipulated in their first article:

> No one may be admitted as a member of a society that is part of the Union who is not an amateur. An amateur is any person who has never taken part in a public race open to all comers, nor competed for a cash prize [...] nor engages in a working trade.

Founded by Pierre de Coubertin in 1890, *La Revue Athlétique* disparaged the practice of football by the less well-off and exhibited the highly aristocratic notion of fair play that reigned at the heart of the sports federation:

> Played by miners and workers in large factories, people not known for their chivalrous spirit, football is inevitably brutal and dangerous; played by well-bred young men, it remains what it is, an excellent exercise in skill, agility, strength and coolness which one can engage in without departing from the rules of courtesy.[9]

The Church, through its Fédération gymnastique et sportive des patronages de France (FGSPF) – a competitor to the USFSA – became the leading promoter of the game. On 14 April 1901, the Catholic federation organised its first football match at the Vincennes racecourse, and in 1904 it established a French youth club championship. By 1912, the FGSPF already had almost 1,000 football teams under its aegis, mainly in the northern half of the country.[10]

For the USFSA and for the Catholic youth clubs, football was a matter of strengthening the body and forming character with respect for authority, courage and endurance. In the eyes of the sporting leaders still traumatised by the country's defeat in the Franco-Prussian War of 1870, football had to prepare a new generation of soldiers for military discipline: 'The Republic is very pleasant in its politics, but on the football pitch, there is only one form of government that can lead a team to victory: Caesarism, in other words absolute power in the hands of the captain', as the magazine *Tous les Sports* put it bluntly in July 1901. While gymnastics had been the dominant sport in France until the end of the 19th century, the martial spirit that suffused the discipline spread to football. In the first French book dedicated to association football, published in 1897, Eugène Fraysse of the USFSA and the English player Neville Tunmer described the team as a military squadron under the orders of an officer:

> The many qualities a player must possess in order to be suited to the position of captain are the same as those of a general; his team is a small army he must know how to command, instruct and direct, and it must have unlimited confidence in him [...] A team that allows itself to discuss the orders and the manner of directing the game of its captain will never be worth anything.

Being a captain 'is a gift of nature; we are born a general, we do not become one, and the science of commanding is not given to all'.[11] In *Les Jeunes*, the federal bulletin of the sports federation of Catholic youth clubs, the articles on football were similarly stuffed with warlike metaphors:

> When an army wants to operate, it generally places its most active and mobile detachments at the head of the column [...] In a well-organised team, the forwards are a bit like hunters, scouts in the army [...] they are the ones who have to make contact with the enemy – sorry, the opposing team – and by the fervour of their attack decide the victory.[12]

While the French colonial empire was expanding in South-East Asia and in Africa, the Anglophile mania for the game among the bourgeoisie, which it saw as a moralising and disciplinarian tool at the service of the nation's interests, was reflected in the discourse of the sporting authorities. In 1894, Pierre de Coubertin summarised the conquering virtues of football as follows:

> If you later become a great businessman, a distinguished journalist, a hardened explorer, a wise industrialist, the shop counter you open far away, the news agency you establish, the improved product you launch, will all be victories for France. For such works, you must be a man of initiative, a good football player, not afraid of blows, always agile, quick-minded, while retaining sang-froid; you must (to use the beautiful Yankee expression) be *self-governed* [...] I would like you to have the ambition to discover an America, to colonise a Tonkin and to take a Timbuktu. Football is the forerunner to all these things.[13]

Play more to work more

If during the First World War rural France began to discover the joys of the ball game thanks to improvised matches behind the front lines, the emergence of a more corporate sporting movement after the war did a great deal to popularise football across the nation. Applying the (perhaps apocryphal) adage of Henry Ford, 'Make the workers play sports. That will stop them from thinking about unionising',[14] the large banks had their own football teams – such as the Cercles Athlétiques de la Société Générale – as did the industries. In the automobile sector, the Association Sportive Michelin was founded in 1911 at Clermont-Ferrand, while the Club Olympique des Usines Renault (COUR) was established in 1917. The mines of Drocourt formed their team in 1921 and the Société des Tréfileries et Laminoirs du Havre wire works set up the Union Sportive des Tréfileries in 1922. Overwhelmed by the rapid emergence of company clubs, the fledgling Fédération française de football-association (FFFA), founded in 1919, authorised them to take part in national competitions on the condition that the name of the company be removed from their club name.[15] The Saint-Étienne Casino group, which had established its corporate sports club in 1919 as the Amicale des employés de la Société des magasins Casino (ASC), therefore had to change its name to Amical Sporting Club in order to preserve the initials ASC, before becoming, in the 1960s, the legendary and popular AS Saint-Étienne.

Thanks to these company-led sporting activities, the *Bulletin des Usines Renault* claimed in January 1919, the workers 'acquire a taste for open struggle, become energetic men with an honourable ambition to improve their situation and that of their family, that is, to produce more. One who regularly practices sports has a very different life to one who spends all his free time in a café'.[16] Taking both a hygienist and paternalist view, the bosses anticipated that football would improve the physical constitution of their workers, increasing both the productivity of their labour and their identification with the company.[17] 'Company sports are good for the physical development of the individual, but also for the relationship between the employer and employee', stated the president of the Union Sportive des Tréfileries at a Cup presentation.[18] The make-up of the club management often mirrored the hierarchy of the company, with the director himself presiding and investing in quality sports infrastructure. 'Never has sport developed so rapidly in our region', stressed the Peugeot company newspaper in 1935. 'This is thanks to the spirit of understanding of their social duty and the generosity of Messieurs Peugeot, who see it as a source of physical and moral education'.[19] The factory bosses also saw in sport a useful tool of education in the new forms of industrial organisation. On the playing field, the intensive physical engagement of the players and the will to compete echoed Taylorism in production and economic competition.[20] The evocatively titled journal of the car manufacturer Berliet – *L'Effort* – even declared in 1920 that 'a well-organised factory should be like a football team […] where each puts himself in the place that best suits him, and where he fulfils his role, with pride, with joy, with all his heart'.[21]

Regardless, the Sunday football matches organised by the factory broke up the hard weeks of work and became a new space for workers to socialise: 'Monday morning, the chat at the sheet metal workshop was all about the previous day's matches: comments, criticisms and hopes for the next Sunday', reports a car factory worker in 1932. 'Production must have been affected by this on Mondays, but at the time it wasn't an obsession, like now'.[22] Practising on the turf the physical and disciplinary analogy between sport and industrial work, the footballing skills of the players became a factor in the recruitment of young workers. The Renault factory managers used their Club Olympique de Billancourt (COB) to hire new talent, as an unemployed carpenter-cabinetmaker explained in March 1931:

> I went to the ground of the Club Olympique de Billancourt, on Île Saint-Germain, and showed off my footballing skills to the trainer, a man by the name of Stutler. He was a former player at Red Star [a club from Saint-Ouen, near Paris] where I've played three seasons as a junior, on the second team and now as a reserve. It troubled me to leave a great club like Red Star but he won me over because he said that if I agreed to play for COB, then I'd be hired at Renault [...] At the end of the training, Stutler told me I'd passed the trial [...] And here I am, working as a carpenter at Renault![23]

The individual commitment to the company club and the sporting skills of each worker combined to establish a parallel social ranking within the factory, and even to boost internal promotion for the top performers. 'I'm in the stronghold of football, at the big factory, the sheet metal workshop', the Renault worker-footballer declares, a year and a half after his recruitment.

> The boss of this manufacturing sector is president of the football section of the COB; all the players and managers work there. So, I'm working in the sheet metal shop as a skilled worker [...] I'll do this mind-numbing work for a year [...] I'm constantly reminding my football managers I want to change jobs. I threatened to leave the COB; and finally I was offered a job at the central office, as a graphic designer. I have no idea what they do there.[24]

Inspired by its Italian peer Fiat, which managed Juventus in Turin, by the Dutch company Philips, which founded PSV Eindhoven and by the German industrial chemist Bayer, which established Bayer Leverkusen, Jean-Pierre Peugeot founded Sochaux Football Club in 1928. As the automobile group embarked on a plan for the overhaul and expansion of its factories, establishing a football team enabled Peugeot to boost the image of the company, while mobilising staff for its new commercial and industrial strategy. 'This team's task will be to acquire followers for our cause and to win over the crowds to the beauties of a sport which is becoming more and more popular', the group's leaders told the local press. 'It will raise high the banner of Peugeot automobiles throughout France at its matches with the top national teams, and to make this little corner of the Pays de Montbéliard better known and appreciated'.[25] The new team was to be the mirror-image of the company and its cars. Indeed, the sports press described FC Sochaux as a team with a 'perfectly regulated technique', playing a 'classic' and 'elegant game'. Jean-Pierre Peugeot asked his player-workers not to win but 'to always play correctly and provide sporting spectacles of the highest quality'.[26] With this in mind, he launched the Sochaux Cup in 1930, reserved for the best clubs in France, a tournament that would finally force French sports officials to establish a French professional football championship in 1932.

A new pitch for the struggle?

The escalation of workers' struggles led to the creation of the first French confederation of trade unions, the Confédération Générale du Travail (CGT), founded in 1895. Together with widespread strikes in certain industries, this led to improvements in working regulations in France in the 20th century. Among the greatest social advances of the period, the Millerand law adopted in 1900 limited the working day to eleven hours, and the 1906 law established a six-day week, thereby fostering the enjoyment of sports among industrial workers. However, the ideal of the sportsman promoted by the ruling classes aroused mistrust among the workers' movement. Imbued with workerism as a class culture and the general strike as a praxis of revolutionary struggle, the different components of the working left systematically rejected everything that demonstrated itself to be bourgeois in essence. Accused of diverting workers from the struggle for their own emancipation and of being an instrument of capitalism and militarism, sport was criticised by the anti-establishment press, which particularly took against English football whose clubs were described as 'business spectacles' and hubs of 'white slavery'.[27] More pragmatically, the unions pointed out that workers were hardly eager to indulge in physical exercise at the end of a day at the factory. This, at least, was the view of Léon Jouhaux, secretary of the CGT, in 1919: 'It was always hard to ask the worker, exhausted by his daily tasks and heading to uncomfortable lodgings, to perfect his education [...] As for asking him to play sports, that would be bitter derision, wouldn't it?'[28]

Yet more and more militants realised that the physical virtues of the sport could benefit the forces of the Left. In 1903, the socialist daily *La Petite République* published a piece by professor of physical culture Albert Surier asserting that 'sport for the people is indispensable to their intellectual and moral development [...] The proletariat of today is considerably inferior in physical strength to the middle bourgeoisie, which for some years now has devoted itself passionately to sports'.[29] *L'Humanité* regularly praised football for helping 'young men to learn the need for individual effort at the service of the collective'.[30] This did not prevent the daily founded by socialist Jean Jaurès from denouncing the sway that youth clubs maintained over a sector of the youth through sports, thereby keeping them away from militant recruitment circles:

> Secular and religious youth clubs alike are skilful and persevering. From school, they draw children on Thursdays and Sundays. When the child grows up, he is already apprenticed, and they keep hold of him by offering sports, gymnastics or music according to his tastes. The apprentice become a young man, they facilitate his securing a military aptitude certificate. They make him their soldier. They follow him into the regiment itself, especially the priests. He is their thing. As a man, they have every chance of keeping him for themselves. He is lost to us, most often because we didn't know how to prepare this child to become one of us.[31]

When the workers' movement unified under the banner of the French section of the Workers' International (SFIO) in 1905, some members of the party expressed openness to the idea that sport was a new front for class struggle and affirmed that as 'socialist sportsmen' they should 'fight capitalism in sport just as we fight it in political and economic life'.[32] Some SFIO militants, including Abraham Henri Kleynhoff, a sports journalist at *L'Humanité*, proposed in 1907 the creation of the Sports Union of the Socialist Party, a first milestone in independent French workers' sports. In November, these militants called a meeting in the 10th arrondissement of Paris to draft the statutes of this association which set itself the mission of 'developing muscular strength and purifying the lungs of proletarian youth', 'offering a palliative for alcoholism and bad company' and 'bringing young comrades to the Party'.

The next year the Fédération sportive athlétique socialiste (FSAS) was founded, a workers' sports organisation that initially brought together fewer than a dozen clubs. 'We want to create, in reach of the working class, centres of recreation that will develop together with the Party and which will also be centres of propaganda and recruitment', declared the founders.[33] The beginnings were modest: in 1914, the federation claimed 4,000 members, while the Catholic youth clubs had 150,000 and the USFSA 200,000. Football, however, came to the fore among the workers' movement as a 'true sport, socialist in character, in which players coordinate all their efforts and their will towards a collective action and result'.[34] In 1909–1910, eleven teams from six clubs took part in the first workers' football championship. Four years later, 40 teams, from 20 workers' clubs, participated.[35]

These red football clubs got by with limited means, mobilising militant volunteer efforts, worker sociability and family solidarity to organise as best they could. The team manager was often at once coach, referee and logistics coordinator, and his partner treasurer and administrator. At its creation in the early 1930s, the Club populaire sportif of the 10th arrondissement of Paris had no support from either federation or municipality. The footballers, who paid for their own jerseys, trained in the suburbs or at the Porte de Charenton on a pitch where 'it was harder to play at one end because of the slope'.[36]

'We had shoes and tracksuits that didn't fit', a former player recalled. 'We didn't even think about it. We were really happy. There was a good camaraderie'.[37] Despite the precarious material conditions, the warm ambience, the pleasure of playing together and the Sunday reunions turned the team into a 'band of pals'. 'Every week, no matter if we won or lost, there was no escaping sauerkraut at Jenny's. There were about thirty of us on match nights, which made for a very long table on the ground floor', reminisced another young footballer from the period. 'These were friendly gatherings, it was great'.[38]

The intense political debates that traversed the worker movement, above all in the wake of the 1917 Bolshevik Revolution, spilt over into the sporting sphere. To counter the bourgeoisie's stranglehold on sport, the Leninist current exhorted the federation to sharpen class consciousness and to warn 'young workers who play football with the bourgeois classes', as *Le Sport Alsacien* pointed out: 'We know that sport is a means of reducing social contradictions [...] Players dressed in sports attire that removes all differences between rich and poor, and who fight for the same colours, become friends for life'.[39] Likewise, influenced by the Soviet cultural movement *proletkult* and the sporting model of *fizkultura*, which believed that competitive sport should be abolished as part of a total socialist revolution,[40] the communists condemned 'competitions reserved for aces and not for the masses', even if this meant 'eliminating football championships that arouse so much animosity between teams'.[41] In the eyes of the revolutionaries, football had to become authentically proletarian.

The split between the French Left at the Tours Congress of 1920 into communists and socialists was reflected in the sporting world. Worker football divided into two organisations, the communist Fédération sportive du travail (FST), which joined the Red Sport International in 1923, and the Union des sociétés sportives et gymniques du travail (USSGT), founded by socialists in 1925 and affiliated with the Socialist Workers' Sport International.[42] For the larger FST, 'the local sports club is the anteroom to revolutionary organisations'[43] and had to adopt the 'class against class' strategic line dictated by the Comintern.[44] On its foundation in 1930, the Étoile sportive de Gentilly club proclaimed:

> The bourgeoisie uses sport to recruit young workers into the military and inculcate a jingoistic spirit. There is no neutrality in sport. Young workers! Reject these capitalist formations. Your only interest is in the physical and moral development of your class. Wherever you are, you must never forget that you are workers. This is why, in your own interest, and in the interest of all Gentilly workers, so many of you will join our club.[45]

Less inclined to this radical politicisation of sport, the USSGT upheld access to sports for all and endeavoured to disseminate through its clubs the 'principles of working-class sport' advocated by the Socialist Workers' Sport International, such as 'education in the field of solidarity, discipline and the spirit of sacrifice', or improving the 'state of health of the working class, which suffers from capitalist working methods and modern living conditions'.[46] Yet while cracks were appearing in the workers' movement, football was spreading like wildfire among working people. 'Football in France is a working-class sport, almost exclusively a working-class one', asserted *Le Miroir des sports* in 1926. 'It has deeply penetrated the masses. It is no exaggeration to say that it has won few followers among the bourgeoisie'.[47] In 1927, the FST could boast 160 teams, and the USSGT a further 40,[48] as well as clubs of immigrants and refugees in Paris such as the Ashkenazis of the Yiddischer Arbeiter Sporting Club or the Spaniards of Armonia Deportiva.

Ball at the feet, fist raised

In the Paris region, the universités populaires* and workers' cooperatives were important early supporters of workers' football. These self-managed organisations – in 1907 there were 41 workers' cooperatives and 30 universités populaires in Paris and its surrounding area[49] – set up their own sports clubs affiliated with the Fédération sportive athlétique socialiste (FSAS – prior to the split between the communist FST and socialist USSGT). The football team of the

* 'Folk high schools (universités populaires) are institutions for adult education that generally do not grant academic degrees, though certain courses might exist leading to that goal' (Wikipedia).

Club athlétique socialiste (CAS) of Bellevilloise, a workers' cooperative in the 20th arrondissement, was created in 1909 and organised a friendly with L'Union à Amiens team, the Club sportif de la coopérative, to celebrate New Year 1910.[50] Likewise, the Avenir de Plaisance in the 14th arrondissement of the capital, the Utilité Sociale in the 13th, the Égalitaire in the 10th and Progrès in Aubervillie all had their own football clubs aimed at the 'socialist comrades of these working-class districts'.[51]

The cooperatives also supported the association activities of these workers' football teams. The first 'red' club, the Union sportive du parti socialiste, celebrated its founding on 1 March 1908 in the events hall of the Égalitaire. The Utilité Sociale hosted the creation of the Socialist Youth's Club sportif in the 13th arrondissement, and served as the headquarters of the FSAS during the First World War. The CAS in Bellevilloise provided a presence every morning at the cooperative's refreshment room and the club treasurer held meetings there.[52] The workers' sports federation even employed the cooperative's orchestra to enliven its sporting occasions and organised meetings there to discuss its association policy.

The workers' cooperatives were careful to protect their political diversity, welcoming socialists and libertarians, communists and non-politicised workers. Some cooperative-based clubs regularly denounced attempts by the FSAS to force members to join the party. At a federal sports congress in 1913, the Étoile sportive socialiste of the Utilité Sociale proposed, unsuccessfully, that cooperatives and unions should sit on the management of sports clubs. The Égalitaire club, meanwhile, in order not to scare off 'young people taken with anarchist or libertarian ideas', suggested – to no avail – that the FSAS drop the term 'socialist' from its name.[53]

Following the communist and socialist victories at the municipal elections of 1925 and 1929 in the suburbs of Paris, as well as in Lille, Roubaix and Toulouse, many of the newly elected officials took an active role in the development of workers' football. As early as 1926, the communist Georges Marrane, new mayor of Ivry, called on his party: 'We must work with communist municipalities to build sports pitches in the suburbs. If young workers prefer the bourgeois clubs, it's because they have good pitches'.[54] The mayor established the Lenin stadium in his commune in 1926 and the Union sportive du travail d'Ivry, affiliated with the FST, received the support of the municipal team and grew from 39 members in 1925 to 450 in 1933.[55] The newspaper *Le Populaire* of 7 March 1930 enumerated the exemplary new sports facilities of the socialist municipality of Pantin, comprising two football pitches with 'water and dressing rooms in the grounds'. The Club athléthique ouvrier de Villejuif, meanwhile, a member of the FST, moved its headquarters from a wine bar to the newly communist town hall in 1925. The club leaders, who were all members of the municipal council, implemented the social policy of the city, facilitating membership for the unemployed from 1933, or organising matches in support of the workers' cause.[56]

The rise of workers' football offered a new space for militant distinction and affirmation on the sports and municipal scene. The red clubs deployed a series of solidarity practices for their members as well as for the entire working community. For example, the teams offered their young players on military service the 'soldier's sou'. Originally established by the CGT in 1900, this financial contribution, an anti-militarist collective action, meant sending a few francs to unionised workers in the army so that they could maintain contact with militant spheres.

Matches were also organised as benefits for the workers' struggle. For example, when the Union sportive ouvrière d'Halluin played the Jeunesse sportive ouvrière de Puteaux at the Vincennes velodrome it was in support of the major strikes of 1928–1929 in the textile factories of Halluin.[57] Others were an opportunity to extol political slogans: a 'turbulent' match with AS Roma at the Stade de Paris on 29 December 1929 was interrupted by some 200 communist militants and Italian political refugees who chanted 'anti-fascist vociferations' in the stands and some of whom were arrested for 'shouts hostile to the government'.[58]

The workers' clubs demonstrated their political affiliation in their names, with terms like 'star', 'proletarian', 'worker', 'work', 'popular' or indeed 'socialist', and through their jerseys, usually red, sometimes with black and often marked with a star. At matches, the stands would be hung with red flags, the players would sing the Internationale before the game and fans would chant 'Red Front!', 'Red Sport!' or 'Long Live the Soviets!'[59] The sporting anthem of the communist federation affirms that: 'The FST, a big family / Will welcome you, brother worker / Because his hammer and his sickle / For all the outcasts must shine'. In 1928, at FST-organised events at the Pershing ground in Paris, the tricolour badges, 'harmful symbols of brutal jingoistic teams', were torn down and replaced by the 'scarlet standards of workers' organisations'.[60] Before the match and half-time were the moments for mobilisation and political propaganda. In 1934, at Aimé Saunier stadium in Bobigny, communist militants spoke at half-time to urge people to fight fascism and imminent war. The same year, at the Unité stadium in Saint-Denis, a match between the Club sportif ouvrier dionysien and a London team was an opportunity for a leader of the FST to make a speech before 600 people, enjoining the workers to sign up to the sports federation.[61] Finally, as sports journalist and scholar of workers' football Nicolas Kssis-Martov underscores, the names of the tournaments drew on the memory of workers' struggle.[62] From 1920, a Jean Jaurès National Football Cup was established in memory of the Socialist Party leader, and the winner of the Steelworkers' Clubs Cup received the Benoît Frachon prize, named in honour of the communist trade unionist leader. In 1927, the CGTU Union of Trade Unions organised a Dzerzhinsky Challenge, named after the boss of the Cheka, the Soviet political police, who had died the previous year, and an inter-depot tournament was called Yves Maurice in memory of a driver killed during the taxi strike of February 1934.[63]

Towards an anti-fascist football

The affiliation of the two French workers' sports federations to Red Sport International (RSI), the communist organisation founded in 1921 by Comintern, or to the Socialist Workers' Sports International (SWSI), established in 1913, offered footballers the chance to take part in competitions under the seal of the international labour movement. In the summer of 1928, a delegation of FST athletes was sent to Moscow for the first international games sponsored by the Soviet Union, the Spartakiads. Bringing together a dozen countries, RSI conceived of this sporting event both as a demonstration of Soviet physical culture at the service of the revolutionary movement, and as a counter-rally to bourgeois sport (the 1928 Summer Olympics were taking place in Amsterdam).[64] Honouring working-class sportspeople and permitting the Soviet authorities to show off the factories and hospitals of the 'homeland of the proletariat' to foreign athletes between events, the Moscow Spartakiads were hailed by French Communists as striking proof of the 'appearance of a new race, created by the benevolence of an entire political system'.[65]

The Spartakiads also served as a staging post for the 'class against class' policy declared by the Comintern. While the SWSI had been organising workers' Olympiads since 1925, the Spartakiads were the chance, for the Soviets and their supporters, to mark their distance from the 'socialist-traitors'. Disparaged as 'lackeys of the yellow bourgeois groups',[66] the socialist sports societies, although invited, refused to go to Moscow in 1928. The second Spartakiad was held in Berlin, and organised in opposition to the workers' Olympiad that took place a week earlier in Vienna. Red Sport International then denounced the 'social-fascists' of the SWSI and argued that only the Spartakiads were the true banner of the 'struggle against impoverishment rooted in the capitalist system, against fascism and the threat of imperialist war, and for the defence of the Soviet Union'.[67]

In 1934, the Comintern nevertheless made a radical strategic change in response to the European political context. Mussolini had been in power for over twelve years, Hitler had taken over in January 1933, and Spain was being torn apart by nationalists and republicans. Moscow called on communists to form a united front with socialists against the fascist threat. In this light, the Spartakiad in the summer of 1934, held in Paris, was called the 'International Sporting Rally Against Fascism and War'. It was a time for both sporting and political unity and the FST, affiliated with the RSI and organiser of these games, invited the socialists of the SWSI via its French section, the USSGT, to participate. Some 3,000 communist and socialist athletes from 18 different countries inaugurated the anti-fascist sports rally at the Pershing stadium in early August before 20,000 spectators.[68]

Athletes from the FST and the USSGT marched under the same banner 'Red Sport, Red Front' to demonstrate the unity within the workers' sports movement.

Although the SWSI had been trying since 1932 to establish a European championship of workers' football – aborted once the German and Austrian sections disappeared with the arrival of the Nazis[69] – a Workers' Football World Cup was organised as part of this International Sporting Rally Against Fascism and War. In response to the official World Cup held two months earlier in fascist Italy, which served as a great propaganda tool for Il Duce, the Workers' Football World Cup sought to reject the national jingoism deliberately 'promoted by the bourgeoisie' and act as a showcase for international solidarity among peoples.[70] Twelve football teams, including the United States, took part in this global tournament between 11–14 August 1934. Due to the Nazi repression of the worker movement, Germany was absent from the contest. A team from Alsace and a team from Sarre were invited, however, as testimony to the organiser's pacifist aims. A Soviet squad was also invited, to the great displeasure of the French authorities, who disapproved of this revolutionary sporting tumult – on 10 August, there were violent clashes between communist players and the police at the Gare du Nord.

The Workers' Football World Cup also sought to propose an alternative model to the mercantile and nationalist tournaments organised by FIFA, one that rejected the separation, specialisation and apolitical character of different sporting disciplines.[71] Similarly, workers' football did not distinguish between levels of practice, with regional tournaments among local red clubs taking place at the same time as the Cup. The French players themselves took part in the smooth running of the tournament, finding accommodation for their comrades, sticking up posters in the street, and distributing 400,000 leaflets for the event on the city's buses.[72] The Workers' Cup didn't even schedule knock-out phases: each team invited an opponent through their links among sports federations. The matches had a political dimension, too. Two Dutch teams, affiliated to the RSI and SWSI respectively, played a match for the benefit of Ernst Thälmann, the secretary general of the German Communist Party, imprisoned since 1933 by the Nazi regime. The Cup was also an opportunity to display the territorial rootedness of red football: the pool games were played at the municipal grounds of Clichy, Saint-Denis and Ivry. As for the final, it took place at the Buffalo velodrome in Montrouge where – as proletarian supremacy dictated – the Soviet Union won against the Norwegians.

The budding unification of the global labour movement seen at the International Sporting Rally Against Fascism and War galvanised the dynamics of rapprochement between the FST and the USSGT. Beyond the Comintern's instructions to establish a united front, the international situation – marked by Hitler's accession to power through the ballot box – together with the political atmosphere in France raised fears that the divisions between socialists and communists would sow the seeds of an electoral victory for fascism in France. The anti-parliamentary riots of the far-right leagues in front of the National Assembly on 6 February 1934 – seen by the left as an attempted coup – and the counter-demonstration on 12 February where socialist and communist processions converged chanting 'Unity!', reinforced among working-class athletes the importance of joint action.[73]

Following the success of this united and anti-fascist summer of sport, militants saw in the merger of the FST and USSGT a full-scale test of the unity of the Popular Front which prevailed during the legislative elections of May 1936. On 1 November 1934, Raymond Guyot, leader of the Young Communists, declared that he saw in this sporting rapprochement a foreshadowing of the Popular Front that made it possible to 'stand before the workers of France with the specific example of a congress for the merger of the organic unit of a large organisation'.[74] It was with this heavy weight of expectation on its shoulders that the congress of red sporting unity, under a banner marked 'Forward for International Unity', brought together delegates of the FST (representing 12,000 members) and the USSGT (6,000) on 24 December 1934 at the Maison des Syndicats in the 10th arrondissement of Paris. During the public debates, Georges Marrane, the communist mayor of Ivry, said: 'The total unity of the working class still being impossible, we seek it wherever it is possible.

We don't want the unity of communist and socialist militants to be in concentration camps, like in Germany'.[75] Unanimously, hands were raised to create the Fédération sportive et gymnique du travail (FSGT). The charter of the new federation opened with an anti-militarist and anti-fascist profession of faith:

> Faced with the fascist menace and the threat of war, the workers' sporting organisations cannot prolong their division any more, nor ignore the lessons that emerge from the hard struggles that the working classes of other countries (Germany, Austria, Italy, Latvia) have had to wage against adversaries whose victory was only possible because of the division among workers.

Just a few months after its creation, the FSGT led a boycott campaign under the slogan 'Not a penny, not a man for the Olympic Games in Berlin!' The federation also prepared to participate in the People's Olympiad in Barcelona, an alternative to the 'Games of Shame' to which no less than 6,000 athletes signed up, including political exiles.[76] 'We fight for stadiums, playing fields, and support', declared *Sport*, the official journal of the federation, on 10 April 1935. '[...] We want our youth to be healthy and strong, but we don't want to deliver them up to militarists, jingoists, fascists. No sport at the service of arms dealers!'

Nevertheless, it was arms that put an end to these anti-fascist games in Barcelona. On the evening of 18 July 1936, the day before the opening ceremony at Montjuïc Stadium, General Franco launched a military uprising to overthrow the Popular Front, elected in February. A number of anti-fascist athletes took to the streets of Barcelona and were involved in the first battles of the Spanish Civil War, such as Emanuel Mink, a Polish Jewish footballer from Anvers who joined the International Brigades and remained in Spain until 1939. Others joined the Durruti column or the Thälmann battalion, declaring: 'We came to defy fascism in a stadium, and the occasion arose to fight it outright'.[77]

PART II

Attack

Assault on dictatorships

6

'A small way of saying "no"'

Italy, the USSR, Spain: stadiums under totalitarian regimes

Hey, keeper, prepare for the fight
You are a sentry in the goal
Imagine there is a border
Marked behind you.

Vassili Lebedev-Koumatch, song composed for the Soviet film *The Goalkeeper* (Вратарь, 1936).

The spectacle is not a collection of images, but a social relation among people, mediated by images.

Guy Debord, *The Society of the Spectacle*, 1967.

'You, athletes of Italy, have special duties', declaims Benito Mussolini before a disciplined crowd.

> You must be tenacious, chivalrous and brave. Remember that when you participate in a contest beyond your borders, your muscles and above all your spirit bear the honour and prestige of our national sport. You must therefore employ all your energy and all your will to win out in combats on land, on sea, and in the air.[1]

On this day of 28 October 1934, during an impressive sports parade celebrating the twelfth anniversary of his march on Rome, Il Duce was jubilant. Four months earlier, fascist Italy had triumphed before the eyes of the whole world, both hosting and winning the second Football World Cup.

Since he seized power in January 1925, Mussolini had made sport a political weapon like no one else before him. With the entrenchment of the dictatorship, sports institutions were purged of communists and Catholics and subjugated to the fascist authorities. All physical activities had to take place within state mass organisations, starting with the Opera Nazionale Balilla, for children, and the Opera Nazionale Dopolavoro, for adults. With its 15,000 sports clubs, in 1935 this latter was the largest recreational organisation in the world (ahead even of its Soviet equivalent).[2] Mussolini's sports policy was intended to prepare future soldiers to defend the fatherland and to bring about the emergence of a new man, the spearhead of a healthy and renewed nation. The physical dimension of the totalitarian ideology was embodied by Il Duce himself, who didn't hesitate to put himself forward as 'Italy's first sportsman', the robust physique of the autocrat reflecting the virility and warrior masculinity so beloved of fascism.

Black shirts and blue jerseys

Football didn't escape the fascist turn in sport. In 1926, Leandro Arpinati, a confidant of Mussolini, was put at the head of the Italian football federation. From 1932, the Fasci Giovanili di Combattimento – the youth organisations of the National Fascist Party (PNF) for 18–21-year-olds – were encouraged to take part in the amateur championship and, in 1935, football became one of the official disciplines of the Littoriali dello Sport, the 'Olympics' of the Mussolini university youth.[3]

The fascist hierarchy was suspicious of football's British origins, however, and decided to present it as the distinguished heir of *calcio fiorentino* – a popular ball game from Middle Ages Florence.* The name 'Football Club' was replaced with 'Associazione Calcio' and a number of clubs from the same city were merged to ensure better control over them. In Rome, for example, the Fortitudo, Roman and Alba Roma clubs became AS Roma in 1927. The Internazionale de Milan, too cosmopolitan an affair for the fascists, was renamed the Società Sportiva Ambrosiana in 1928, in homage to Ambrose,

* The fascism regime also attempted to popularise *volata*, an 'authentically fascist' team sport somewhere between football, basketball and rugby invented from scratch in 1928. It failed to win over Italians, and was abandoned altogether in 1936.

patron saint of the Lombardian city. Finally, the *campanilismo** or local pride of the football fans was deliberately manipulated by the regime to exalt the national character of *calcio* (literally meaning a 'kick' in Italian) and in the early 1930s the neologism *tifosi* (from *tifo* or typhus) appeared in reference to the 'fever' of the supporters.

With football's popularity rapidly expanding among the Italian working class, Mussolini had built over 2,000 stadiums by the end of the 1920s.[4] These in turn became propitious spaces for mass propaganda. Matches large and small were regularly accompanied by military music and chants glorifying the regime. The stands were festooned with giant portraits of Il Duce and banners proclaimed the arrival of the new man.[5] To entertain and to galvanise: these were the missions the regime assigned to *calcio*.

The expansion of newspapers and radio – there were barely 40,000 radio sets in the country in 1927 compared to almost a million in 1938[6] – also helped to transform football into mass culture. The players of the national team, the 'Azzurri', such as Giampiero Combi, Giovanni Ferrari and Giuseppe Meazza, were deified and vaunted by the media as soldiers of the new Italy. For the authorities, football's 'natural, supreme goal was honour, power and the greatness of the Fatherland',[7] with each victory by the national squad illustrating the strength and superiority of the fascist regime.[8]

In 1932, its dynamism in the sporting realm meant that FIFA saw Italy as the ideal country to host the second Football World Cup, which ran from 27 May to 10 June 1934. The impact of the first Cup, held in July 1930 in Uruguay, had been relatively modest since the international financial crisis had meant few European teams had made the onerous journey by boat. This partial failure had not discouraged FIFA: determined to counter the hegemony of the International Olympic Committee (IOC) over global sport, it relied on Italy, its modern stadiums and the public security ensured by its authoritarian regime to make the second World Cup a resounding success. For its part, the fascist power counted on using the symbolic power of football on the international stage to establish its suprem-

* *Campanilismo*, meaning the 'spirit of the bell tower', has its origins in the countless warring kingdoms and rival cities that once dotted the Italian peninsula.

acy. Two ambitions, sporting and political, came together in 1932. 'The ultimate aim of the tournament will be to show the universe what the fascist ideal of sport is, whose sole inspiration is Il Duce', bluntly asserted General Giorgio Vaccaro, the new president of the Italian football federation.[9]

Anticipating the media boost fascism would receive on the back of this global tournament, Mussolini went into overdrive. Eight large stadiums were built or renovated. The one in Rome was named the Stadium of the National Fascist Party, and the one in Turin the Mussolini Stadium, the largest on the peninsula at the time with a capacity of 70,000. Unprecedented millions of lire were spent on propaganda and on media relations.[10] Sixteen nations were expected and over 400 international journalists invited. Hundreds of thousands of copies of the event poster were printed, a football framed by fasces adorned every cigarette packet in the country, and a million commemorative stamps were issued. Some 7,000 Dutch, 10,000 Swiss and 10,000 French fans travelled across the Alps to support their teams.[11] The day before the first match was played, General Giorgio Vaccaro rejoiced: 'We need only think [...] of the vast crowds gathered around the loudspeakers, in each town and village of the sixteen nations [...] to understand that tomorrow will see more than a great spectacle: it will be a profoundly meaningful ceremony'.[12]

Between sporting spectacle and fascist spectacle

From the start of the tournament, nationalist effervescence was at its peak. The state-run newspapers vehemently flaunted their fascist ardour. 'Spirit and muscle, in the service of fascist discipline, will assure victory', spouted *La Nazione*. To certify in the world's eyes that the new Italy was competing with an authentic national squad, the players born in South America – Luis Monti, Enrique Guaita and Raimundo Orsi – were naturalised overnight. The Blackshirts, Mussolini's fearsome militia, were enlisted as stewards to contain any misbehaviour that might spoil the display.

Having crushed the United States 7–1 in the first round of the competition, the Azzurri met the talented Spanish team in the quarter-finals on 31 May 1934. Just minutes after kick-off, the away team began to display an unprecedented level of violence. Seven Spanish and four Italian players were badly hurt and carried off, and the match ended in a nil–nil draw. Penalty shoot-outs not yet having been introduced, the game was replayed the next day. This time the Italian squad carried it 1–0, but the Swiss referee René Mercet was so complacent – he subsequently received a lifetime suspension from his federation – that the special envoy from the French *L'Auto* reported: 'The referee managed affairs with such off-handedness that he frequently seemed to be Italy's twelfth man'.[13] The threats in the corridors of the hotels hosting the foreign teams, the pressure in the dressing rooms from fascist dignitaries, and more generally the total control by the fascist power over the event would lead Jules Rimet, the president of FIFA, to say 'during this World Cup, the true president of FIFA was Mussolini'.[14]

Yet the tournament itself was a victory for popular passion. The stadiums were bursting with fans and all of Italian society was won over by the footballing success of the Azzurri. Radio broadcasts of the matches in Czech, German and Spanish helped to generate a positive media image of the fascist regime across Europe. A few days before the final, General Vaccaro congratulated himself before the Italian press: 'We are putting on special trains and tourist caravans from abroad, so that the World Cup will come to a triumphant close in the presence of Il Duce, for the prestige of Italian sport'.[15] Everything was carefully orchestrated for the Cup final to become a consecration for Mussolini and to affirm the superiority of fascist Italy.

On 10 June 1934, the Stadium of the National Fascist Party in Rome was full to its 50,000 capacity for the final between Italy and Czechoslovakia, who had qualified by beating Nazi Germany 3–1. In the seats dotted with zealous Party militants, the *tifosi* chanted 'Italia, Duce! Duce, Italia!' In his purple-draped box, Benito Mussolini responded, his arms and chin outstretched to the crowd. 'When the Czechs ran onto the pitch, Il Duce stood up and applauded them, reported the *Berliner Tageblatt*. The stadium was in a frenzy. The atmosphere was already at its peak even before the start of the match.'[16] From the kick-off, the Azzurri played aggressively and quickly dominated possession, though the Czech squad resisted until half-time. The public sang *Giovinezza*, the official anthem of the National Fascist Party. On the restart, after a first goal from Czechoslovak Antonín Puč, the freshly naturalised Italian Raimundo Orsi scored the equaliser, in an electric atmosphere. The suspense ended in extra time when Bolognese striker Angelo Schiavio placed the winning goal. 'As the tricolour flag was raised on the highest pole in the stadium, the crowd felt the aesthetic emotion of having won world primacy in the most fascinating of sports', reported the Rome newspaper *Il Messaggero* the next day. 'And in this moment when the great victory is consecrated – the fruit of so many years of effort – the crowd offered Il Duce their gratitude'.

The coronation of fascism in the media was complete. Under the benevolent gaze of the FIFA dignitaries, Mussolini presented the winners with his own trophy, an imposing *Coppa del Duce* in severe bronze, in place of the traditional Cup. Vittorio Pozzo, the authoritarian Italian coach, declared to the press: 'Our success is a true reward for seriousness, for moral firmness, for the spirit of abnegation, for the determination of this team'.[17] Symbolising the blindness or even complicity of the foreign observers with regard to the political takeover of the tournament, the FIFA president pitifully saluted the fascist victory proclaiming: 'The Italian ball game federation [sic] and its team gave this example, if not this lesson, by organising and winning the 1934 World Cup. I congratulate them and admire the faith capable of stirring such virtues'.[18]

In the wake of this political and sporting triumph, Italy's football victories proliferated. The Azzurri carried the gold medal at the Olympic Games in Berlin in August 1936, while at the tournament held as part of the Universal Exposition of Paris in the summer of 1937, the Bologna team, already champions of Italy, defeated its French, Czech and English adversaries. Nevertheless, in parallel to the rise of fascism in Europe, the Mussolini regime hardened. In 1936, the Italian army invaded Ethiopia, satisfying the colonial desires of Il Duce who then sent, in concert with Adolf Hitler, military contingents to Spain to support Franco. In November 1937, Mussolini signed the anti-Soviet pact promulgated by Nazi Germany and the Empire of Japan and then, from 1938, decreed a series of anti-Semitic laws which would have repercussions even in football. Two Jewish-Hungarian coaches, Árpád Weisz (Bologna) and Ernő Egri Erbstein (Turin), were forced out of their positions in 1938 and 1939 respectively.[19]

It was against this turbulent international background that the third Football World Cup opened in France in June 1938. The Nazi armed forces had occupied Austria three months earlier, the Spanish Civil War was about to be won by the Francoists, and France was still shaken by the experience of the Popular Front, which came to a bitter end that spring. Arriving in Marseille for its opening match against Norway, on 5 June 1938, the Italian team was received at Saint-Charles station by 3,000 Italian communists and exiles, who were violently dispersed by the police.[20]

On the day of the match, the tension was at its peak in the Vélodrome stadium even before kick-off. The Roman salute of the Azzurri and the national anthem were thoroughly booed by the 10,000 anti-fascist protestors in the stands. Far from their usual crowd, in hock to pro-Mussolini propaganda, the team played under continual pressure from the anti-fascists who did their best to upset the match.[21] On 12 June, Italy and France disputed the quarter-finals in Parce des Princes, Paris. The two teams usually sported blue strips, but on this occasion the Azzurri wore black jerseys, a sinister fascist symbol personally ordered by Il Duce that caused uproar in the stands. As reported the following day by *L'Auto*: 'There was a moment of excitement when the Italian goal was bombarded with stones from the stands'.[22] Until their victory in the final against Hungary on 19 June, the Italian team played in a climate of hostility. Nazi Germany, meanwhile, was humiliated by Switzerland, which eliminated the Reich's team in the first round. From the seats, glass bottles and rotten vegetables rained down on the supporters from across the Rhine. Total war was already brewing on the green turf. Four years after the spectacle of the fascist regime was staged in the sporting arenas of Mussolini's Italy, it was in the stands that the first cracks appeared in the triumphal new order of totalitarian football.

An indomitable Soviet football

'It is essential to consider physical culture, not only from the point of view of physical education and health […] but also as a method for education of the masses in its own right'.[23] These were the austere objectives of *fizkultura*, 'Soviet physical culture', as defined by an official resolution of the Communist Party of the USSR dated 13 July 1925. The Bolshevik sporting model, which promoted the development of *Homo sovieticus*, ready to work and to defend the proletarian fatherland, was established in the 1920s in opposition to capitalist bourgeois sport. For supporters of an authentic proletarian culture – *proletkult* – the spirit of competition and professionalism in sport were to be banned, while football was seen as a decadent physical practice that risked injury to the worker, reducing productivity.

These aspirations to a purely proletarian sport began to fall by the wayside with the rise to power of Joseph Stalin within the Party. For the dictator, the USSR had to 'systematically outpace the performances of bourgeois athletes from capitalist countries'.[24] While Soviet propaganda instituted Stakhanovism, the cult of worker productivity, the review of Red Sport International announced in July 1935 that 'We work, and we should work with even more energy, for Soviet athletes to become the greatest in the world, so that in the coming years the USSR becomes the land of world records.'[25]

Soviet workers didn't wait for the approval of regime bureaucrats to find a passion for football. 'Take a large factory like the Orekhovo-Zuyevo or the industrial suburbs of Leningrad. We will see sport and especially football plays a key role in the leisure time of workers', reported the Soviet sport journal *Krasnyi Sport* in 1927. 'At the last Congress of Workers' Unions, it was noted that the matches attract so many spectators that the mines of Donbas were completely deserted'.[26]

From 1929 to 1933, the first five-year plan triggered a mass rural exodus due to the forced-march industrialisation of the country and the collectivisation of lands. Rapid urbanisation saw Moscow grow from 2.3 to 3.6 million people between 1928 and 1934.[27] For thousands of workers freshly settled in the suburbs, just as for their peers facing big-city anonymity in Western Europe and Latin America, football became a new form of male socialisation. Its popularity made itself felt from the late 1920s, as a Dynamo Moscow player reflected later: 'At the first light of the morning, during the weekends, a great ballet of trams began in Moscow, the players and the supporters travelling between the stadiums and the various grounds of the capital. On average, the best teams could already attract five to ten thousand spectators'.[28] The infrastructure was rudimentary: the largest stadium, the ZKS, offered just 5,000 seats on timber stands, and the terraces were filled with humble workers.[29] 'It was truly a working-class event, made up of workers', recalled Konstantin Beskov, professional footballer and coach from Moscow. 'They were dressed all the same, in simple Russian work smocks under jackets, with their trousers tucked into their boots'.[30] For the thousands of emigrants from the countryside, attending a football match provided a semblance of community. 'Head to the stadium, take a seat in the terraces and suddenly it's like you've known the person sitting next to you since childhood. You understand each other without a word [...]' reported *Krasnyi Sport* in 1938.[31]

While the Stalinist regime's obsession with productivity led to police crackdowns on disorder, football was proving to be a leading culprit. On the pitch, play was often rough or even violent, and fights between supporters were a regular event. In 1934 in Leningrad a football match was halted when it descended into a brawl on the turf. At Simferopol in Crimea, fans beat up the referee and a goalkeeper during a match, while drunken players faced off.[32] To the chagrin of the Communist authorities, instead of sport's official role of elevating the proletariat by instilling in it Soviet patriotism and discipline, it was becoming a source of disorder.

In light of the growing popularity of football and to quell the disturbances it caused, the Soviet state set about a wave of stadium construction. The 50,000-capacity Dynamo stadium was erected in Moscow in 1928, while sports arenas with over 20,000 seats were built in Leningrad, Tbilisi, Stalingrad and Kyiv through the 1930s. In total, 650 stadiums with at least 1,500 seats were built in that decade.[33]

Ensconced within these sporting temples to urban modernity, football rapidly developed into a true spectacle that served to stage the different bodies of Soviet society. The CSKA, the football club of the Red Army, promoted the image of the military forces on the turf, while Dynamo Moscow, created by the Ministry of the Interior in 1923 under the aegis of the GPU, symbolised the power of the political police. Generously financed by the Soviet state apparatus, these two Muscovite sports clubs nevertheless competed on the pitches with another team: Spartak.

Emerging from Presnia, a working-class district of Moscow, Spartak was founded in 1922 by the Starostin brothers. The eldest, Nikolai, who had studied business, and his three younger brothers Alexander, Andrei and Piotr, regularly organised games on patches of wasteland in the neighbourhood before founding the club without any support from the state or the Bolshevik party.[34] During the period of the New Economic Policy (1921–1928), the relative liberalisation of the Soviet Union allowed the Starostins to enjoy a certain level of financial independence. The club, then named Krasnaya Presnia, played around 30 matches per year and survived on ticket sales. A small, profitable family business, the club unearthed a sponsor in 1926, the Pichtchevik food workers' union, and then approached the Promkooperatsya, a cooperative organisation of independent craftspeople. Beyond these financial backers, the club manager, Nikolai Starostin, found a political institutional representative in Alexander Kossarev, head of the Komsomol, the youth organisation of the Party.[35] In April 1935 the club was renamed Spartak (Spartacus in Russian), in reference to the Roman rebel gladiator.

Financially independent of the regime, neither affiliated to the police nor the army, Spartak enjoyed growing popularity among Soviet workers. Living in a communal apartment (*kommunalka*) in the 1930s like so many workers in Moscow, Yuri Olechchuk, then a teenager and club fan, recalled:

> Our discussions [in the *kommunalka*] for the most part revolved around Spartak and sometimes other clubs. At the school it was the same. Why? Today I realise that Spartak was the club that best represented ordinary people. Why? The name made sense to us. All the kids and even the adults knew the name of the leader of the

> slave revolt in ancient Rome. The names of other clubs – Dynamo, CSKA, Lokomotiv or Torpedo – couldn't compete with this.[36]

The year 1936 saw the total and definitive seizure of power by Stalin through the adoption of a new constitution by the government of the Soviet Union. In May, the dictatorial regime regained full control of football by organising a Soviet league as well as a national championship – previously, matches were played between clubs from the same city or via interregional meetings. While the regime shifted towards totalitarianism and repressive terror, football became a Soviet passion that the Party had to control.

The professionalisation of clubs was semi-legitimised, as was an increase in competitive spirit. With the establishment of the national league, football became a mass phenomenon attracting 10 million supporters each year, or 20,000 spectators on average for a first-division match.[37] Dynamo Moscow and Spartak frequently topped the tables, followed by CSKA, Lokomotiv – the team of the Soviet transport companies – or clubs like Dynamo Kyiv, Dynamo Tbilisi and Torpedo, sponsored by the automobile builder ZIS. In an article entitled 'The Magic Sphere', the journal *Izvestia* remarked on the game's hold on the Soviet people: 'Thousands of people of all ages, sexes and occupations rise from their seats to stare in the same direction. Even citizens who are distinguished by their seriousness and serenity begin to move and gesticulate wildly under the influence of football'.[38]

The Spartak matches in particular aroused great popular fervour. At each match, the stadiums were the stage for chaotic scenes, with crowds of young people invading the stands after having queued to enter. 'Only a madman would have gone through the turnstiles alone', recalled Yuri Olechchuk.

> There was another, more collective way of doing things. It was a system that worked well: we called it 'the steam engine'. Thirty, forty or fifty of us without tickets formed a long queue before one of the entrances and, at an agreed moment, we all surged towards the gate. The ticket sellers could yell and try to hold us back, but it was impossible to stop us.[39]

With scoreboards or public address systems still uncommon, confusion reigned throughout the match, during which spectators threw objects of all kinds onto the pitch. The satirical writers Ilya Ilf and Yevgeny Petrov mocked the archetype of the Spartak fan in the pages of *Krasnyi Sport* as someone ready, in order to attend a match, to deploy the physical effort of a soldier in training: 'Race behind a tram / Jump on a moving subway train / Seventeen rounds of boxing at the entrance to the stadium / Carrying heavy objects (such as a child or a woman) / Military swimming (standing for two hours in the rain without an umbrella)'.[40]

'Down with the cops!'

While the feared and hated political police spread their reign of terror through Soviet society, the rivalry between the elitist Dynamo and the popular Spartak expanded. 'Relations between Spartak and Dynamo fans were a source of great conflict', a Muscovite recalled. 'Dynamo represented the authorities: the police, the state security apparatus, the detested privileged elites. They ate better than us, were better dressed, and didn't live in communal apartments like all of us workers did'.[41]

The 50,000 seats of the Dynamo stadium were regularly taken by storm during Dynamo–Spartak matches, with countless clashes in the stands. 'It was war on the pitch as well as in the stands', wrote Yuri Olechchuk. 'Fights between supporters were frequent. They were separated to prevent a riot. The Spartak supporters were at the East bend, where the seats are the cheapest, while Dynamo occupied the oligarchs' seats, on the North and South sides'.[42] The Red Army received similar treatment, given its status, as a *Krasnyi Sport* report on a match against CSKA on 30 October 1936 suggests: 'At half-time, the spectators who were behind the barriers launched a general attack on the turf. Thousands of people tumbled down like an avalanche and crowded around the pitch, giving the rectangular playing area an oval shape'. Spartak won the game 3–1, after one of the goalposts was torn up by the crowd.

The popular enthusiasm for Spartak and the wild excesses of the supporters nevertheless contain a political significance. 'In a communist country, the football club you supported was a community you chose to belong to [...] It was one of the rare moments when you were free to join a community and to express yourself there without constraints', explains the anthropologist Levon Abramian. 'In Moscow, there were many teams, each representing a social group, and most Spartak supporters were from the lower classes'.[43]

In a totalitarian, Stalinist society that afforded very few personal liberties, football offered a space where each could support their favourite team, to choose their own heroes rather than those designated by the state. In affirming their support for one club or the other, the men of the working class constructed a part of their social identity independently from the proletarian identity promoted by the regime. However slim, this freedom of choice was a chink of light in the gloomy daily lives of the working classes in the 1930s Soviet Union. 'Football was somehow separated from everything that happened around it and escaped the authorities', wrote Nikolai Starostin in his autobiography. '[...] For most people, football was the last hope of maintaining a semblance of humanity in their souls'.[44]

The rivalry between the two Moscow teams that dominated Soviet football was also between two cultural, social and physical models. On the pitch, Dynamo was a reflection of 'state rationalism' with an austere, mechanical and precise game, based on long passes. The club of the political police reflected the official values of *Homo sovieticus*: order, discipline, physical health, respect for authority. Spartak's playing style, by contrast, was described as 'romantic', being more unpredictable and improvised. In a patriarchal society where women had no place in the stands – and playing was forbidden because the dictatorship considered it 'harmful to the female body'[45] – the two clubs represented two models of masculinity. The white-collar Dynamo, which represented the archetype of the educated urban man, was juxtaposed with the rough, undisciplined crowd, which sings, yells, leaps the turnstiles and literally overflows the stands.

The foundation for a popular identity that hated the repressive state, Spartak also gathered around it a community of thousands that, for 90 minutes in the stands, could escape the omnipresent political police. In the tumult of the terraces, the anonymity of the crowd challenged police surveillance and permitted fans to safely insult an adversary who embodied their hatred of state repression and wealthy oligarchs. 'When Spartak confronted Dynamo or CSKA, the cries in the stands were "Down with cops!" or "Down with soldiers!"', recalls Boris Nazarov, another supporter of the Moscow team.[46] As historian Robert Edelman points out, in a society where three people gathering in a public space aroused the suspicion of the political police, supporting Spartak was 'a small way of saying "no"'.[47]

Without being either a social escape valve knowingly tolerated by the regime, nor a carnival-type spectacle, football became a phenomenon of the male urban working classes with a political dimension that escaped Stalinist power. The Party quickly realised, however, that the relative respite offered by the football grounds, where everyone expressed their rejection of the state, only lasted as long as the match and didn't lay the foundations of any real opposition to the regime.[48] In the end, it was neither Spartak's popularity nor its anti-authoritarian symbolism, but rather its sporting performance that would attract the wrath of the secret police.

In November 1938, the Georgian Lavrentiy Beria was named the head of the Soviet political police after leading the Stalinist purges in the Caucasus with an iron fist. As chief of police, Beria also became honorary president of the Dynamo sports club. A lover of football and supporter of Dynamo Tbilisi, his home city, he took to this role with élan. However, Spartak was at the peak of its popularity: already champion of the USSR in 1936, in 1938 it took the double. Its matches drew crowds of 53,000 (for comparison, English league champions Everton attracted 40,000 spectators at the time[49]), and the brothers Andrey and Alexander Starostin, who also played in the team, had become major celebrities. The team's victories, the ostentatious lifestyle of the Starostin brothers and the financial independence of Spartak began to seriously irritate the political police.

Having dominated the championship throughout the season, on 9 September 1939 Spartak won the semi-final of the USSR Cup against Dynamo Tbilisi 1–0. The score was contested by the Georgian team but Spartak qualified for the final, winning three days later against Stalinets Leningrad. To widespread surprise, the Central

Committee of the Communist Party announced a week later that it was invalidating the winning semi-final goal and the match was to be replayed. On 30 September 1939, before 80,000 jubilant supporters and police dignitaries including Beria himself, Spartak again defeated their adversary 3–2. In a rage, the sinister chief of the secret police stormed out of the stadium.

From that point on, irate at these consecutive defeats, Lavrentiy Beria became obsessed with putting the Starostin brothers in jail. The problem he faced was that Nikolai's son was the best friend of the son of Prime Minister Vyacheslav Molotov, who refused to sign the arrest warrant in late 1939. Three years later, during the 'Patriotic War' against Nazi Germany, the four brothers and their close circle were denounced and then arrested in March 1942 for anti-Soviet propaganda, corruption or for conspiring against Stalin.* The Starostin brothers were imprisoned in the grim security services headquarters, the Lubyanka, and then deported for a ten-year stretch in the Gulag.[50] Delighted to have these footballing celebrities in their grasp, the Siberian camp bosses exempted the brothers from forced labour and instead had them play in the inter-gulag championships, while training the other prisoners. 'Their limitless power over human lives was nothing compared to the power football exerted over them', Nikolai Starostin noted retrospectively.[51] The 'place they had kept in the fans' hearts' allowed the footballing brothers to overcome the appalling conditions of their captivity, with prisoners and even some of the guards supporting them.[52] Until their liberation in 1954, the Starostins survived the hell of the Soviet camps thanks to the immense popularity of Spartak and its 'small way of saying "no"', which even extended to the Siberian gulags.

Realpolitik

While the 1940s marked the twilight of Italian fascism and Nazi tyranny, in Spain they foreshadowed the rise of the Franco regime after three years of civil war. In order to better consolidate his hold on the Iberian Peninsula, on 22 February 1941 Franco created the

---

* More prosaically, it would seem that the Starostin brothers were involved in the black market.

Delegación Nacional de Deportes (DND), an institution close to the Falange – the Spanish fascist political party – with a view to subjugating sport in Spain to the nationalist regime. Yet the sporting ambitions of the Caudillo were more modest than those of Mussolini or Hitler. Economically exhausted and isolated on the global stage, Spain suffered from a severe lack of sports facilities and was nowhere near becoming a nation of great athletes.[53]

Aware nevertheless that its citizens were fervent football fans, in 1939 the government ordered the Spanish Football Federation to rename the Copa del Rey – the country's main tournament, named after the king – the 'Copa del Generalísimo'. The red jerseys of the national team were replaced by the Falangist blue, and fans were encouraged to sing the fascist anthem *Cara al sol* and to yell 'Viva Franco!' from the stands. One of the official newspapers of the regime, *Arriba*, championed the *furia española* – fury or virile exaltation – on the turf:

> The *furia española* is to be found in all aspects of life in Spain, more than ever since the 'war of liberation'. In sport, it is in football that the *furia* is best expressed, a game where the virility of the Spanish race can flourish, imposing itself at international matches against teams that may be more technical but are certainly less aggressive.[54]

Under the Franco regime, the leading representative of this *furia* at both Spanish and international stadiums was the Real Madrid Football Club. The Caudillo's favourite team, the 'Casa Blanca' – the club played all in white – embodied for regime and fans alike the unity of the Spanish nation and state centralism. Foreign ministers like Fernando María Castiella or Gregorio López Bravo acknowledged that they saw the Madrid squad as an 'ambassador of the regime' that offered an honourable image of Francoism on the global stage.[55]

The Argentinian Alfredo Di Stefano and the Hungarian Ferenc Puskás, both players at Real Madrid, became true popular icons for the *aficionados*[56] and in light of the catastrophic economic situation and the ponderousness of the dictatorship, football progressively became a mass phenomenon as well as a 'culture of escapism'.[57]

In the early 1950s, there were no fewer than 25 football weeklies, without counting the sports sections that became standard in all newspapers (first begun by the official daily paper *Marca*, with its circulation of 400,000).[58] While many Spaniards were still suffering from hunger, the football clubs, with little financial support from the DND, built giant stadiums that drew on the generosity of their *socios* – their corporate members, who held a stake in the club and were entitled to vote in major elections. The Deportivo de La Coruña opened the Riazor ground in 1944, with a capacity of 34,000. Meanwhile, Athletic Bilbao expanded its stadium from 35,000 to 47,000 seats, and Real Madrid opened the Chamartín in 1947, seating up to 70,000, and renamed the Santiago Bernabéu in 1955.

In the 1940s, Spanish society was 'trembling with fear at a new White Terror that extended even into language and culture', wrote historian Josep Solé I Sabaté, before adding: 'Sport was a space where people felt a greater sense of freedom, and FC Barcelona was both a refuge and cradle – fluctuating and diffuse though it may be – for Catalonian identity'.[59] Despite Franco's vicious repression, under the ashes of the Civil War the Republican and anti-fascist embers still glowed in Catalonia. To better bring the rebellious region – which had fought the nationalist troops until the end – into line, the vindictive regime organised, barely two months after its accession to power, a veritable humiliation of the Catalan people by playing the final of the first Copa del Generalísimo at the Montjuïc stadium in Barcelona. On 25 June 1939, before 60,000 spectators, a speech to open the match was delivered by the far-right ideologue Ernesto Giménez Caballero – an ardent defender of the linguistic hegemony of Castilian Spanish – in which he expressed his pride in the liberation of Catalonia from the claws of Republicanism. The players from the two finalists, Sevilla FC and Racing Club de Ferrol, greeted the senior Francoist officials with the fascist salute, while the loudspeakers played *Cara al sol*. The first touch of the ball was by the daughter of General José Solchaga, the nationalist dignitary who led the final bloody offensive on Barcelona.[60] In 1942, the Caudillo attended the same stadium in person, leading a monstrous parade of 24,000 Falangists and the release of a thousand white doves.[61]

Catalonia was seen as a bastion of Republicanism by the fascists because it refused to submit to the centralist vision of the Spanish nation imposed by the dictatorship. Determined to muzzle all forms of cultural difference and regional politics, the regime focused its repression on the Catalan community. The language was prohibited in public spaces – the street, cafés, teaching, newspapers – together with local cultural practices such as the *Diada*, Catalonia's national festival, traditional folk songs, place names and the Senyera, the flag of four red stripes against a gold field. FC Barcelona was renamed the Club de Fútbol Barcelona, its logo stripped of Catalan iconography, and the Francoist aristocrat Enrique Piñeyro de Queralt imposed as club president in 1940.*

Since its creation in 1899, the *Blaugrana* – 'blue and garnet' – club had become a sounding box for Catalan and Republican demands. At a meeting of *socios* on 27 June 1920, an official declaration was released: 'We are from FC Barcelona, because we are Catalan'.[62] In 1925, under the dictatorship of Primo de Rivera, the club was suspended for six months after thousands of Barça supporters wolf-whistled the Spanish national anthem. During the 1930s, FC Barcelona had an ever-growing presence on the Catalan political and cultural scene, with its official newsletter even noting in October 1932 that 'the popularity of our club is without doubt connected to our extracurricular activities'.[63]

In the early days of the Spanish Civil War, in July 1936, the Catalan capital rose up in response to the insurrection by the nationalist generals. The Esportiu Júpiter ground in the Poblenou district of Barcelona – in the hands of National Workers' Confederation (CNT) – became the rallying point for the anarchist forces. The libertarian militants, who were already taking advantage of the team's movements to transport pistols hidden inside footballs, transformed the stands at the Júpiter stadium into a clandestine arsenal. FC Barcelona, meanwhile, encouraged its players to join the anti-fascist front. Over the summer of 1937, Barça footballers also played a tournament in Mexico as ambassadors for the Republican

* The Basque club Athletic Bilbao was similarly renamed Atlético de Bilbao and placed under the management of the Francoist hierarch Eduardo Lastaragay.

struggle, raising money both for the club and the resistance.* The club president since July 1935, Josep Sunyol, a former deputy in the left-wing independence movement, disappeared at the start of the conflict: during a journey to Madrid on 6 August 1936 – presumably to deliver messages to the Republican government of the capital – nationalist militiamen stopped his vehicle in the Sierra de Guadarrama and, recognising the leader of the Catalan club, executed him in cold blood.

After the Civil War, with many Barça players in exile or suspended for playing solidarity matches abroad, the club stadium Les Corts officially reopened on 29 June 1939. Heedless of the dictatorship's aversion to FC Barcelona, the club carried off the Copa del Generalísimo in 1942. The semi-finals of the same tournament the following year saw them face their great rivals, Real Madrid. In the Les Corts stadium, the *Blaugranas* won 3–0 before Catalan supporters who no longer hesitated to publicly jeer a Madrid team that to their eyes represented the centralism and authoritarianism of the regime. In response, the shaken leaders decided to intimidate the Barcelona players at the return match in Madrid. 'The evening before the match, we had to change hotel, and we didn't move all night, sure we would be lynched in the street', recalls Angel Mur, team physiotherapist. 'During the match, our keeper was so scared of being injured by the projectiles being thrown at him that he spent most of the game well in front of the goals, allowing the Madrid players to score easily'.[64] After receiving a visit in their dressing rooms from José Escrivá de Romani, the sinister head of the State Security Service, FC Barcelona lost the match 11–1 before a crowd disgusted by this Francoist masquerade. Fearing that anti-regime incidents would increase, in December 1943 the General Directorate of State Security published a notice in the daily *Marca* threatening with internment anyone guilty of 'subversive acts' in the stadiums.[65]

* That same year, a Basque team played a series of matches to support the Republican cause across Europe, the USSR and Mexico. The Basque Country then being occupied by nationalist troops, these players became stateless political refugees who successfully played in Mexican and Argentinian sides.

The Camp Nou, a bastion of anti-Franco resistance

'In the 1950s, while Real Madrid was associated with state power, FC Barcelona began to stand out as a tool of socio-political resistance and became not only the club of the city but of all Catalonia', according to historian Josep Solé i Sabaté.[66] While Franco sought to use football as a tool to depoliticise the crowds and channel demands for autonomy, supporting Barça gradually became a form of popular anti-Francoism within reach of any Spaniard, regardless of their social category.[67]

Whenever the Catalan club played against its great Madrid adversary, the stands became a lightning rod for a whole society muzzled by the tyranny of Franco. 'Since you couldn't shout "Franco is a murderer!" in the street, people booed the Real Madrid players', reports Lluis Flaquer, a Catalan sociologist and Barça supporter. 'It's psychological: if you can't yell at your father, you yell at someone else'.[68] Beyond the symbolic dimension of resistance expressed by the Catalan club, FC Barcelona's draw was also its ability to act as a factor of social cohesion in a regime that sought to break down bonds of solidarity. Beginning in the 1950s, over 2 million immigrants from southern Spain moved to Catalonia as a result of the region's industrial boom.[69] From a Francoist viewpoint, this economic migration was a way of diluting the Catalan independence movement, and the sporting authorities counted on RCD Espanyol de Barcelona, standard-bearers for Spanish national identity in Catalonia, becoming the club of choice for the new arrivals. Yet FC Barcelona was such a powerful cultural actor that, to the contrary, the new arrivals saw it as the best way to integrate. 'Supporting Barça was the only way to feel a part of something that went beyond ordinary life, to immerse oneself in a greater world, to be able to laugh and cry without being punished', explains a supporter of the *Blaugranas*. 'It was also about thanking the Catalans for their welcome, because immigrants don't survive for long if they are seen as ungrateful. Thanks to Barça, immigrants could hold their heads up on Sundays and say, "I'm Catalan, even if I was born in Andalusia"'.[70]

Similarly, the anti-Franco dimension of the club grew in March 1951 following a series of workers' strikes – the first organised since the end of the Civil War – against tram ticket price increases in Barcelona. During a match between Barça and Racing de Santander, leaflets calling for a mass boycott of public transport were distributed in the stands of Les Corts. This provocation was all the more serious under the dictatorship, and after the match the Catalan supporters collectively refused to take the trams, instead returning home on foot as a sign of solidarity with the strikers.[71]

Around this time, FC Barcelona decided to build a new stadium on the scale of its sporting ambitions. After three years of work, the 93,000-capacity Camp Nou opened with great ceremony on 24 September 1957. Following a blessing by the city's archbishop, thousands of spectators together began to sing the *Himne a l'estadi*, a song newly composed by Adolf Cabané i Pibernat, before the city governor and an audience of astonished Francoist officials. The Camp Nou thenceforth embodied a new political arena, a symbolic refuge for resistance to the dictatorship and for Catalan identity. Normally confined to private spaces, Catalan was freely spoken on the terraces while anti-Franco pamphlets circulated, and the club membership cards were printed in the language. Sporadically, popular songs banned by the regime were sung in the Camp Nou, such as 'Els Segadors', a rallying song for the Catalan Republicans during the Spanish Civil War, or 'La Santa Espina', a *sardana* prohibited since the dictatorship of Primo de Rivera.[72] 'Catalan had no legal existence, it was forbidden to teach it at school and to use it in the media, but Barça supporters never stopped speaking it', says Joaquim Maria Puyal, a doctor in linguistics and pioneering journalist of match broadcasts in Catalan.[73]

Beginning in the 1960s, Senyera flags gradually began to appear on the stands, while supporters would shout 'Independencia' at precisely 17 minutes and 14 seconds into a match, in reference to the year 1714, the year Franco-Spanish troops entered Barcelona during the Spanish War of Succession. As repression by the regime grew harsher (in July 1963, attacks were carried out on the Security Service and Francoist Trade Union headquarters in Madrid), the Camp Nou inspired an unprecedented feeling of belonging among fans. A Barça *aficionado* in the 1960s recounted:

> In the city, fascism was highly visible – in street names, Falangist berets, portraits of Franco, flags – but in the stadium you were among the crowds and I felt – it may be that I imagined it, but I felt it all the same – that everyone around me was at bottom really anti-fascist.[74]

In 1968, for the first time since 1939, FC Barcelona finally had a manager who was not from the Francoist inner circle. Narcís de Carreras, elected by almost 50,000 *socios*,[75] made a public statement at his inauguration ceremony on 17 January, saying that Barça is *més que un club* – more than a club. This mythical phrase that foregrounded the cultural power of FC Barcelona became the club motto. Barça acquired such a level of political and sporting popularity that it progressively pushed back against the limits imposed by the regime: from 1972, announcements in the stadium were made in Catalan, provoking the ire of the city governor, and the following year, the club recovered its original name: Futbol Club Barcelona – the absence of the accent on the 'u' marking the distinction between Spanish and Catalan.

The Dutch player Johan Cruyff, one of the top internationals of his day, joined Barça at the start of the 1973–1974 season, to the detriment of Real Madrid, who coveted the genius from Ajax Amsterdam. The talented player breathed an unprecedented wind of freedom into Spanish football by taunting the dictatorship: he gave his son the banned Catalan first name Jordi, and dedicated a photograph to members of the Assembly of Catalonia imprisoned in Francoist jails. The arrival of Johan Cruyff also helped to revitalise a club that had not won the Spanish championship since 1960, unlike its Madrid rival which, over the same period, has been crowned champion of the country nine times. From October 1973, the Catalan team won a succession of victories and quickly climbed to the top of the rankings thanks to Cruyff's flamboyance.

On 17 February 1974, on the 22nd day of the championship, the *Blaugranas* travelled to Madrid to play their nemeses. From the off, the atmosphere in the Santiago Bernabéu stadium was electric, but the home fans were soon disillusioned. Before half-time, the visitors Juan Manuel Asensi and Johan Cruyff had both scored. As if to exorcise the humiliating 11–1 defeat they had suffered in 1943, symbolic of a Barça under the yoke of the regime, FC Barcelona went on to score a further three splendid goals, inflicting a historic 5–0 win over the Casa Blanca. Foreshadowing the fall of the Caudillo, this footballing earthquake in the heart of the Madrid ground signalled for many Catalans the 'true beginning of the political transition'[76] that would end with the arrival of democracy in 1975. A crushing result baptised '*la manita*' ('the little hand') and which retrospectively sounds like the five fingers of a hand giving a fateful slap to Francoist power.

7

Ball at the feet against the iron fist

Football's resistance to Nazi domination

> Because we, as working athletes, have faced and still face Capital and its brown-shirted lackeys in mortal combat […] be united in the fight against the Nazi sports leadership and the dictatorship, against the principle of authority and the actions taken to deprive us of our rights.
>
> Editorial for *Rot Sport*, the clandestine German workers' sport newspaper, 16 November 1934

An extraordinary 600,000 players were affiliated to the Deutscher Fußball-Bund (DFB) in 1936.*[1] The largest European football federation in terms of both clubs and members, the DFB rapidly became a tool of government and domination of the working classes upon Adolf Hitler's accession to power. In *Mein Kampf*, published in 1924, the Führer had already envisaged sport as a tool for training and shaping the bodies of the masses in the service of the Reich. 'Millions of bodies trained by sport, imbued with love for the fatherland and filled with a spirit of attack could be transformed, in the space of two years, into an army', he wrote.

Following Hitler's election as Chancellor in January 1933, German sports institutions were immediately subject to the doctrine of the National Socialist Party. SA officer Hans von Tschammer und Osten was appointed head of the Ministry of Sports as *Reichssportfürher*, and on 23 April 1933, Propaganda Minister Joseph Goebbels declared

* For comparison, in this same period the French equivalent had around 150,000 members.

that 'German sport has but one task: to strengthen the character of the German people, imbuing it with the fighting spirit and steadfast camaraderie necessary in the struggle for its existence'.

Maintaining political and racial unity and the health of the 'body of the German people' – the *Volkskörper* – while inculcating the values of obedience to the leader: these were the new missions assigned to football. Alongside paramilitary exercises, the game became a key sporting activity for the Hitler Youth, whose objective was to make young Germans 'lively like a greyhound, resistant like leather and hard like Krupp steel'.[2]

A new football for a New Germany

In common with the rest of German society, football had to be Aryanised and purged of its 'Judeo-Bolshevik enemies'. The working-class sports movements, the Kampfgemeinschaft für Rote Sporteinheit – KG, more commonly known as Rot Sport, 'Red Sport' – which was affiliated to the German Communist Party, and the Arbeiter-Turn- und Sportbund – ATSB, literally 'Workers' Gymnastics and Sports Federation' – which was socialist, were dissolved in 1933. With their 3,400 clubs and their 200,000 members, the militants of the KG were among the first targets of Nazi terror; leaders were arrested and assassinated, workers' premises and sports infrastructure were attacked and burned, and punitive raids were carried out. Representing a total of nearly 2 million members and more than 20,000 clubs, German workers' sport saw its patrimony confiscated – including 230 gymnasiums and 1,300 sports grounds – and its organisations dismantled by the Nazi authorities.[3]

The DFB, meanwhile, lost its autonomy and simply became the 'football section' of the National Socialist Federation for physical education, the new federal sporting organisation of the totalitarian regime.[4] Without missing a beat, hoping to maintain their financial interests,[5] football's governing bodies applied the new racial and anti-communist laws to their clubs. In April 1933, the federal football authorities announced that 'members of the Jewish race and individuals belonging to the Marxist movement are no longer authorised to occupy decision-making positions at regional organisations and clubs, which must swiftly take all appropriate measures if they have not yet done so'.[6] As a Jew, Hugo Reiss, treasurer of Eintracht Frankfurt, was unceremoniously dismissed from his club, while Kurt Landauer, president of Bayern Munich – which had many Jewish players and fans – was forced to resign in 1938 before being deported to Dachau, finally fleeing into exile in Switzerland. Dozens of professional Jewish players were banned from the federation. Julius Hirsch,[7] former star of Karlsruher FV and legendary left-winger in the German national team (the Mannschaft), was forced into exile in Alsace in 1933. Refusing to believe he was in danger given his glorious military past in the First World War and his marriage to a 'certified Aryan' Christian, Hirsch returned to Germany in 1939. The former international was deported to Auschwitz on 1 March 1943, where he was murdered.* His teammate in Karlsruher FV and the Mannschaft, Gottfried Fuchs, mythical goalscorer at the 1912 Olympic Games, barely escaped the hell of the camps, fleeing the country in 1937. Once the professionals had been excluded, it was the turn of Jewish amateur players to find themselves prohibited from sports in November 1938, after Kristallnacht. By the end of 1938, German football was officially decreed '*judenfrei*'.

Hitler detested football, seeing it as too urban and not German enough; he preferred boxing. But the popularity of the game among Germans was such that the Führer had to assimilate it into National Socialist doctrine. On the pitches both at home and abroad, footballers became proud ambassadors of the Third Reich, or even – in the eyes of the sporting authorities – worthy successors to German warriors. Jerseys adopted Nazi heraldry and players performed the Nazi salute and new national anthem – the *Horst-Wessel-Lied* – to perfection. The status of the professional player was expunged, leaving the 'purity of the amateur'. More noble in the eyes of the Nazis, amateur footballers were also easier to subordinate to state power. 'We had classes every Tuesday after training', recalls Herbert Moll, former player at Bayern Munich. 'We had to pass an official state exam and those who succeeded received a Nazi stamp for their

* Since 2005, the DFB has awarded a Julius Hirsch Prize to a personality or organisation working to tackle racism, xenophobia or anti-Semitism in sport.

"player passport", such as meal tickets, second-class train tickets, and a few Deutschmarks for each match'.[8] Football grounds were systematically occupied by the parastatal organisation responsible for recreation, the '*Kraft durch Freude*' or 'Strength through Joy', which offered reduced-price tickets for matches, distributed flags adorned with swastikas to supporters, and encouraged them to sing songs to the glory of the Reich.[9]

Some clubs, such as Schalke 04 from the industrial town of Gelsenkirchen, in the Ruhr, transformed themselves into showcases for totalitarian football. Very popular with the miners and steelworkers in the region, Schalke 04 dominated football in the country and lifted the national trophy six times under the Nazi regime. Hitler travelled to these industrial lands several times to salute the proletarian club and its vigorous players with their physical yet disciplined game. Representatives of the 'New Germany', Schalke 04 symbolised the conquest of the working-class sphere by the dictatorship.[10] The son of Polish immigrants, the Schalke 04 and national squad midfielder Fritz Szepan embodied this shift when he became a member of the Nazi party, declaring in 1938 that 'The enthusiasm of the fans in the stadiums of the Third Reich bears witness to the health and strength of our race. My eternal gratitude to the leader of the Germans for having safeguarded our future in sports and games. An ardent "Yes" to our Führer Adolf Hitler!'[11]

The Nazi regime also strived to exploit the sway football held over the population. Sports tournaments became a powerful tool for mass entertainment, but also for National Socialist propaganda. The Berlin Summer Olympics, held between 1–16 August 1936, marked the height of German athletics as spectacle. A compliant International Olympic Committee (IOC) allowed the Nazi authorities to transform the world's greatest sporting event into a mass spectacle that served to glorify the regime. Close to 4,000 athletes from 50 countries arrived at the Olympiastadion and – just like fascist Italy with its 1934 World Cup – Nazi Germany triumphed on the political and sporting field alike. The Reich's Olympic victories and the popularity of the Games were described by the official propaganda, as well as by many other observers, as final proof of the new totalitarian regime's superiority.[12] Albert Berdez, IOC secretary, wrote to Pierre de Coubertin on 8 August 1936: 'The organisation of the Games is perfect [...] The enthusiasm of the general population is beyond description'.[13] He reaffirmed the sentiment in a speech delivered at the closing ceremony: 'May the people of Germany and their leader be thanked for what they have accomplished'.[14]

Congratulating himself on the physical improvement of the German race that the Olympic Games had – in his view – just demonstrated, the Führer rejoiced: 'Sporting competitions, tournaments, and games harden millions of young bodies and show them more and more in a light not seen for perhaps a thousand years. A new human type, radiant with beauty, is growing'.[15]

A grain of sand in the propaganda machine

Yet it was also football that tarnished this symbolic representation of the arrival of the 'New Man', and abruptly brought Hitler's well-oiled propaganda machine to a halt. On 7 August 1936, the quarter-finals of the Olympic tournament saw Germany play against outsiders Norway. Never eager to attend a football match, the Führer nevertheless made the trip. According to his advisors, German victory was assured and his presence in the official box could only be beneficial to his image. Just seven minutes after kick-off, Oslo native Magnar Isaksen scored the first goal before the eyes of a furious Hitler. With 100,000 supporters in the stands, the Mannschaft failed to avail of its chances and Isaksen put home a second decisive goal in the 83rd minute, eliminating Germany from the competition. Wild with rage and without waiting for the final whistle, the Führer hastily left the stadium with Joseph Goebbels, Hermann Göring and Rudolf Hess, all of whom had accompanied him for what was to be a consecration of National Socialist football. A week after this encounter, which marked Adolf Hitler's first and last official appearance at a football match, fascist Italy won the gold medal against Austria, and dedicated their flamboyant victory to Mussolini.

Escaping the attention of the international media, German football's resistance to the Nazi dictatorship rapidly expanded across the country after 1933. Most of the 2 million working-class sportsmen joined the ranks of 'bourgeois' clubs, which were happy to win new followers.* While it remained difficult to create clandestine sports associations (since by definition the game requires a large number of players to gather outdoors), working-class footballers formed informal autonomous groups within clubs in order to maintain their sporting and militant camaraderie. Refusal to perform the Nazi salute at sports events, setting up solidarity funds for political prisoners, flyposting and handing out flyers (notably during the 1936 Olympic Games, with a leaflet entitled 'The World Record of Terror'), tearing up flags, and distributing the clandestine press were all resistance practices deployed by these left-wing sportsmen.[16]

Matches likewise became an opportunity for public displays of hatred for the Nazi regime. In October 1934 in Senzig, near Berlin, a group of local fans attending a premier division game manhandled the referee for repeatedly making Nazi salutes. The latter spoke to the newspaper *Die Fußball-Woche*:

> An unfortunate and ugly scene took place after the final whistle at the time of the German salute. A spectator punched me in the back of the neck with such force that I collapsed unconscious. The fugitive culprit was chased by a few Stern players, one of whom was seriously injured by onlookers. The solidarity of the other spectators, who prevented the culprit from being identified, shows that this 'prolo', who so virulently expressed his hatred of Nazi fascism, was not the only one of this opinion.[17]

In January 1935 in Berlin, the SC Olymp team – mostly comprising former working-class players – played its nationalist rival BFC Preussen, the favourites. In the eyes of both team and fans the match took on a political dimension. For the militants of SC Olymp it was a question of symbolic revenge over the ones they referred to as the 'Prussians'. As a working-class Berlin fan reported:

> The club is arrogant, reactionary and ethnocentric, claiming that Jews can't be 'Prussians'. The Olymp-Platz match saw a record

* Others working-class clubs 'camouflaged' themselves by altering their statutes and adopting names more in tune with national-socialist ideals.

> attendance, with the 'Prussians' fielding a shock team. The 'little yellows' received a hostile welcome because the two teams weren't meant to get along, what with the differences in living conditions and social status. The home advantage and the fans who egged on the Olymp players undoubtedly contributed to the 4–1 victory, with the two goals by our Helmut, the 'red player' being decisive.[18]

The next morning, the Gestapo arrested Helmut and his teammates, who were still drunk from celebrating their victory. Realising that the striker had taken part before 1933 in workers' sports meetings in the Soviet Union, Helmut was sentenced to a prison term.[19]

A paper man facing the iron regime

On 12 March 1938, two years after the Berlin Olympics, the Wehrmacht invaded Austria. The Anschluss gave birth to a Greater Germany that a 'referendum' held under military surveillance a month later claimed was supported by 99 per cent of the population of the two countries.[20] A week earlier, to celebrate the 'reunion' between the two German-speaking peoples, the Nazi leaders decided to organise a friendly match in Vienna between Germany and Ostmark – the new name for Austria now it had become a German province. The outcome of this pro-Reich propaganda match – which became known as the *Anschlussspiel* or 'Annexation Match' – scheduled for 3 April 1938 at the Praterstadion, was agreed in advance by the authorities. The match had to end with a 0–0 draw in order to satisfy both sides and embody the unity of the Reich in sporting equality. However, a waif-like Viennese player undermined the predestined outcome. Nicknamed the 'Mozart of football' or *Der Papierene* ('The Paper Man') for his slight build and his ability to slip through the defence, Matthias Sindelar was considered one of the best centre-forwards in the world.[21] A native of Moravia, the Austrian forward had learned to play in the winding streets of Vienna's rougher districts. He was a splendid captain of the Austrian national team which dominated European football at the time, earning it the name of '*Wunderteam*', the 'dream team'.

But Matthias Sindelar and his teammates were aware that the annexation of Austria was synonymous with an Anschluss in sports, meaning their team would no longer officially exist, but be integrated into an inferior German team. On 3 April 1938, minutes before taking to the pitch to play a farcical match to the glory of Greater Germany, Sindelar defied the Nazi authorities in the dressing rooms, demanding to play in the red and white jersey of the Wunderteam. After reminding them that it was forbidden to score a single goal, the organisers allowed the Austrians to wear their colours.

Before almost 60,000 spectators mechanically waving swastika-adorned flags, the match played out in a leaden silence. The first half was goalless, but no one in the stands was under any illusions. The Wunderteam demonstrated to the point of absurdity their technical superiority over the arrogant selection of their 'German brothers', showing unprecedented awkwardness and blunders whenever they approached the box. But in the 78th minute the grotesque display collapsed in on itself. Exasperated, Matthias Sindelar could not help himself from scoring, raising his clenched fists in victory.[22] A wave of dread ran around the stands when Sindelar and his teammate Karl Sesta carried out an insolent celebratory dance before the Nazi officials.[23] A few minutes later, any ambition of sporting equality between the two peoples vanished when, after a daring lob from a free kick at 45 metres, Sesta scored a fatal second goal.[24]

The very opposite of the Aryan physical archetype, the delicate 'Paper Man' and Karl Sesta, of Polish extraction and nicknamed 'the Fat', pulverised the totalitarian propaganda apparatus with their two goals. The Austrian players exulted, proud to have displayed their footballing talent despite the threats from Nazi dignitaries. A few skimpy Austrian flags passed around in secret were waved, celebrating the rejection of the sporting Anschluss by their team, but in the dressing rooms the footballers were trembling. Everyone knew that with this brazen humiliation of the Nazi authorities, Matthias Sindelar had signed his own death warrant. Yet the player's popularity among the Viennese was so precious in the Nazis' eyes that instead they chose to manipulate his public image. On the very day of the referendum on the annexation of Austria to the Third Reich,

10 April, the local edition of the *Völkischer Beobachter*, the official newspaper of the Nazi party, published a photo of Matthias Sindelar with the caption 'All footballers thank the Führer from the bottom of their hearts and call on people to vote "Yes"!'[25]

Two months later, for the 1938 World Cup held in France, the German coach, Sepp Herberger, included several former players from the Wunderteam to try and improve the technical level of the Mannschaft. The regime was ready to excuse Sindelar's irreverence if he joined the national team. But the Viennese forward refused to play, claiming a dodgy knee at his advanced age. He made his last public appearance on 26 December 1938, wearing the Austrian colours of Vienna, defeating Hertha BSC Berlin with his sole goal.

Matthias Sindelar was living a semi-clandestine life with his Italian Jewish companion Camilla Castagnola. Pursued by the police, they were listed as 'Jewish and Czech sympathisers and social-democrats'.[26] They were found dead in their flat on 23 January 1939. Officially, their death was attributed to carbon monoxide poisoning, but some believe it was suicide or a Gestapo assassination. Be that as it may, Vienna had its martyr. Under the watchful eye of the security apparatus and despite the ban on all public demonstrations of mourning by the authorities, 15,000 people attended the funeral of Matthias Sindelar, who had become a symbol of civil resistance to Nazi hegemony.*

The resentment towards the Germans – called 'Prussians' or *Piefke* – continued to be expressed through football until the fall of the Third Reich. During those dark years, the Viennese identified with the creativity of Austrian football, translating onto the pitch the *Wiener Schmäh* – the typically Viennese levity and sense of humour – which contrasted with the rough, imagination-free play of the Germans. The grounds filled up when a local team clashed with one from the occupying country, and the stands became a stage for 'anti-German chants, brawls, and stone-throwing by overexcited supporters', reported the secret police.[27] In November 1940, a match between Schalke 04 and Admira Wien turned into a riot after the

* The Vienna street the slender footballer lived on was renamed Sindelarstrasse.

German referee refused the Viennese two goals. The local authorities reported:[28]

> Result: the police were called in against the rebellious masses, the seats of the stands were destroyed and windows smashed, police officers were beaten and the limousine of district manager Baldur von Schirach ended up with flat tyres and broken windows, right in front of the stadium. A sporting event turned into a political demonstration.

They were perfectly aware that this type of spontaneous uprising against the 'Prussians' often concealed popular unrest with the Nazi occupation. The National Socialists knew how to take revenge, as when SK Rapid Wien dealt a humiliating defeat to Schalke 04 in June 1941: most of the Austrian club's players were unceremoniously packed off to the Eastern Front.

The 'Match of Death'

On 22 June 1941, the Third Reich launched Operation Barbarossa: the invasion of the Soviet Union. Kyiv fell to the Wehrmacht on 26 September, and *Generalmajor* Kurt Eberhard and his armed forces subjected the occupied city to a reign of terror. On 29 and 30 September, the Ukrainian capital became the scene of the largest Holocaust massacre carried out in the USSR: on the outskirts of the Babi Yar ravine, more than 33,700 Jews were murdered.

In the aftermath of the occupation of Ukraine by the armies of the Axis, all the national football teams were dissolved, like Dynamo Kyiv, the flagship club of the USSR founded in 1927 under the aegis of the Soviet political police. However, the Nazi authorities hastily organised a local football championship where teams from different military forces competed. At the beginning of 1942, Josef Kordik, manager of a Kyiv bakery and unconditional Dynamo supporter, happened to meet Nikolaï Troussevitch, former goalkeeper of his favourite club, on the ruinous streets of the capital. Called up to the front with his teammates and then captured by the armies of the Reich, Troussevitch had just been released from the Darnitsa camp and was wandering, starving, around occupied Kyiv. Kordik offered him a job in his bakery and, over the weeks, a crazy idea germinated: to reform a local team in order to raise the morale of the locals at the championship orchestrated by the Nazi authorities.

In the spring of 1942, Nikolaï Troussevitch managed to locate the winger Makar Gontcharenko and six more of his former team-mates from Dynamo, plus three players from Lokomotiv Kyiv. Some of them had just emerged from prisoner-of-war camps and were sleeping under bridges; Josef Kordik also took them on. The team looked shabby, but the footballing baker's boys pieced together red jerseys however they could and called themselves FC Start, as if to better channel this new beginning.

On 7 June 1942, FC Start played its first match and roundly defeated, 7–2, Rukh Kyiv, a team made up of Ukrainian collaborators. Over two months, the footballer-bakers won landslide victories in their ten meetings with the occupying forces. On 21 June, FC Start defeated a Hungarian garrison 6–2 and, a week later, won 7–1 against the team of a Wehrmacht artillery unit. On 12 July, it was the turn of the German workers to suffer an abysmal 9–1 defeat.[29]

This series of sensational successes began to seriously bother the Nazi authorities. Even more so when on 6 August FC Start subjected Flakelf – the team of prestigious Luftwaffe pilots – to a humiliating 5–1 beating. Fearing that this sequence of matches won by a team of starving bakers would sap the morale of the Axis troops and, above all, inspire the Ukrainians to defy the occupiers, the Nazi officials proposed a rematch.

Kyiv was covered with posters announcing this high-stakes match to be played on 9 August and on the big day, the Start and Flakelf players entered the Zenit stadium before 45,000 spectators.[30] Despite the presence in the stands of *Generalmajor* Kurt Eberhard and numerous officers from the occupying forces, the FC Start eleven refused to give the Nazi salute. From the kick-off, the aggressive Flakelf team tackled from behind and grabbed shirts before the eyes of a referee – an SS officer – who averted his gaze. The Germans opened the scoring when the keeper, Nikolaï Troussevitch, found himself flat on his back after being hit on the head. Ivan Kouzmenko,

Dynamo's giant centre forward, equalised and when the half-time whistle blew FC Start was leading 2–1. In the dressing rooms, the Ukrainian footballers received a visit from the Nazi officers, asking them to reflect carefully on 'the consequences' of victory.[31]

Despite these threats, FC Start was leading 5–3 at the end and, before the final whistle, Oleksiy Klymenko humiliated the Nazi team by dribbling past all of the defenders and the keeper, before turning around on the line and kicking the ball back up towards the centre circle. The SS referee blew the final whistle before full-time, leaving the *Generalmajor* and other Nazi officers mortified.

Not long after, the footballers were arrested in Josef Kordik's bakery and some of them were interrogated for 20 days by the Gestapo as suspected members of the Soviet political police. The player Nikolaï Korotkikh was tortured to death and eight further players were deported to the Syrets concentration camp, near the lugubrious Babi Yar ravine. Nikolaï Troussevitch, Ivan Kouzmenko and Oleksiy Klymenko were executed in cold blood in February 1943, in reprisal for an attack by the Ukrainian Resistance.

According to Soviet propaganda – which would name the clash with Flakelf the 'Match of Death' and largely rewrite the story of FC Start for its own benefit – the players were arrested and deported because of the final scoreline of their tumultuous match against the Nazi team. However, 70 years later, the winger Makar Gontcharenko would give a more humble yet equally poignant version of the death of his teammates. 'They didn't die because they were great footballers or players for Dynamo. They died like many other Soviets because of the clash of two totalitarian systems. They were victims of this vast massacre. The deaths of the players were not so different to those of many other people […]'[32]

Resistance in troubled waters

As the Nazi stranglehold tightened in Northern and Western Europe, football was less able to deploy acts of political resistance and turned to civil disobedience to combat Hitler's totalitarianism. In Norway, invaded by the armies of the Reich in April 1940, the sports boycott became popular in the world of football in order to challenge the occupier's control over the game. Indeed, the Reichskommissariat Norwegen, the civil administration responsible for bringing the country to heel, appointed a *Sportsführer* to better subjugate all sporting activities to National Socialist ideology. Reluctant to follow the recommendations of the authoritarian regime, Norwegian athletes collectively refused to endorse the restructuring of sports activities orchestrated by the Nazis. Some 800 members of FK Lyn, one of the most popular Oslo football clubs in the country, stopped renewing their membership of the club, already in the hands of the occupier. The largest sports centre in the capital, the Ullevaal stadium, with a capacity of 40,000 people, was literally deserted by the population. At the semi-final of the 1942 Norwegian Cup in Bergen, just 27 spectators could be seen in the stands.[33]

Asbjørn Halvorsen, a very popular pro footballer, was one of the leading figures in the sporting boycott. Having played in Germany as a defender at Hamburg SV until 1934, Halvorsen benefitted from his aura as coach of the Norwegian team – the one that had humiliated the Mannschaft at the 1936 Olympic Games. During the final of the Norwegian Football Cup in 1940, in his capacity as secretary general of the Norwegian football federation, he refused access to the official box to the *Reichskommissar* Josef Terboven and his retinue of Nazi dignitaries, asserting that they were reserved for the royal family, then in exile. Resisting the organisation of propaganda matches intended only to glorify the regime, a few months later Halvorsen resigned from his position in the Norwegian football federation, before converting their offices into the hub of the sporting boycott.[34]

The contempt for the Nazi occupier was such that Heinrich Himmler in person, Chief of the SS and Minister of the Interior, turned his attention to Norway after 1943 in order to assert the authority of the Reich. Beyond the popular insubordination in the face of the totalitarian normalisation of Scandinavian sport, some went so far as to set up clandestine football matches in rural areas to attract new recruits to the resistance networks.[35] Nazi repression fell hard on any athlete who persisted in taunting the Reichskommissariat Norwegen. Asbjørn Halvorsen was deported in August 1943 to the Grini concentration camp, near Oslo. Transferred to the Neuengamme camp in Germany, the former player of Hamburg SV met one of his ex-teammates, centre forward Otto 'Tull' Harder, who had meanwhile become camp goalkeeper with the SS rank of *Hauptscharführer*.[36] Towards the end of the war, suffering from pneumonia, malnutrition and typhus, Halvorsen barely survived the death camps. He lived until 1955, tenaciously continuing to fulfil his duties as leader of the Norwegian football federation.

In the Netherlands, meanwhile, from August 1941 the Nederlandsche Voetbal Bond (national football federation, NVB), under the yoke of the occupier, banned Jewish players and spectators from sports arenas. 'My Jewish father was a big supporter of Ajax Amsterdam, and we went to the stadium every Sunday', recalls Pelle Mug, a supporter of the Dutch team.

> After the prohibition of Jews, I went alone to the matches. It was awful. My father and I agreed that if Ajax won, I was to whistle the club anthem as I walked down our street. My father was always waiting impatiently at the window for news of the results. And when it was a defeat, he lost his appetite [...][37]

On 1 November 1941, Jews were excluded from all sporting practice and in Amsterdam five clubs with roots in the significant Jewish community shut their doors.[38]

A number of figures from the footballing world began to disappear, making the active anti-Semitism of the Dutch regime all the more visible. Hartog 'Han' Hollander, the first great Dutch sports radio commentator, was deported together with his wife and daughter to the Sobibor extermination camp in July 1943, where they were murdered.[39] Leo Horn, a renowned Jewish referee, went into hiding in 1941 under the name of Van Dongen, and joined the Stanz resistance army, taking part in a spectacular attack on a German munitions truck.

While the Dutch footballing world did not comprise an organised clandestine movement, a number of clubs engaged in activities of dissidence or resistance. Ajax Amsterdam, which took its name from the brave hero of the Trojan War, functioned as an 'informal network' that secretly brought assistance to people, Jewish or otherwise, who were threatened by the Nazis.[40] The bonds of solidarity within Ajax enabled players and supporters alike to escape the horrors of war. The Jewish Jaap Van Praag, at the time just a club member – though he became president of Ajax in the 1960s and 1970s – was protected by the player Wim Schoevaart and then hidden away for more than two years above a photography store (unbeknownst to the owner). During the artificial famine of the winter of 1944–1945, the players of Ajax Amsterdam pulled together by collecting their meagre food resources while the members clubbed together to send around 20 teenagers of the club to regain their strength on the farms of Friesland.

Unlike some footballers who, like Ajax's Harry Pelser, navigated the troubled waters of opportunistic collaboration and joined the NSB (the Dutch Nazi party), others clearly asserted themselves as anti-Nazi. Jan Wijnbergen, from Ajax's first team, became involved in the resistance movement in 1941. 'After distributing pamphlets calling for a general strike in February, [the communist Resistance] asked me to deliver packages or maintain contacts', he says. 'I was still playing at Ajax but it was becoming more and more incompatible. I regularly had to cancel training, however irritating it was for the club'.[41] He swiftly brought his playing career to an end when he became involved in a Jewish network for rescuing children, 'convinced that resistance activities were more important than playing football'.[42] As for Rein Boomsma, former player at Sparta Rotterdam and on the national team, he joined the 'army of shadows' at the start of the Occupation, and was arrested three times by the Gestapo before dying at the Neuengamme camp in May 1943.

The north Amsterdam football club De Volewijckers was one of the few Dutch sports associations to fully dedicate itself to opposing Nazi occupation. From 1941 to 1943, Gerben Wagenaar, midfielder and team captain, was head of Militair Contact, a communist Resistance organisation, then member of the Resistance Council until Liberation in May 1945. On top of that, his brother Douwe, club administrator, readily displayed his opposition to the Nazi authorities by dressing De Volewijckers in orange jerseys, the national colour, at a match on 3 August 1943, an act that led the Gestapo to imprison him for three days.[43] Douwe Wagenaar also organised travel enabling the club's supporters to fight physically in the stands with the fans of The Hague's ADO team, nicknamed 'Hitler's Eleven'. The resistance shown by the club extended to the turf, too. Initially in the third division, De Volewijckers rose to the premiere league of Dutch football in 1942 and went on to defeat their pro-Nazi rivals, the ADO, by ousting them from the top of the championship in 1944.

However, Dutch football withered away at the end of 1943. On top of the worsening food and material shortages and the ever more brutal Nazi repression, all able-bodied men between 17 and 40 were called to work in the German war industry. Football stadiums became dangerous places where the Nazi commandos carried out mass arrests to send men to the Reich's work camps. On 27 February 1944, following a match between PSV Eindhoven and TSV Longa, the Germans rounded up 20,000 spectators as they were leaving the stadium.[44]

In September 1944, when the southern part of the Netherlands was liberated by the Allies, the Dutch government in exile called for a strike by railwaymen in order to slow down the delivery of supplies and German soldiers to the front. The Nazi occupiers responded to the walkouts by blocking the transport of foodstuffs to the north-west of the country, causing the 'hunger winter' of 1944–1945. With travel impossible, all football matches were put on hold, but the De Volewijckers team, as national champions, continued to play a number of friendlies by journeying on horse-drawn carriages. Upon Liberation in the spring of 1945, the various footballing organisations – clubs, regional federations, professional leagues, etc. – underwent denazification. Leo Horn, the Jewish referee who went into hiding in 1941, became a guard at the internment camp for former members of the NSB. In a historical irony, one of his prisoners was Harry Pelser, the Ajax player who joined the Dutch Nazi party. Upon the latter's release, he declared: 'This period has created wounds that will never heal'.[45]

Clandestine football, weapons in hand

Following the signing of the armistice on 22 June 1940, subjugating France to the Third Reich, the Vichy government, via its General

Commissariat for General and Sports Education (CGEGS), made all sports federations subject to its policy of 'National Revolution' with the 'Sports Charter' law of 2 December 1940. The commissioner for sports, former tennis player Jean Borotra, and his successor Colonel Joseph Pascot, prohibited any football matches between French and German teams from August 1941, out of fear they would descend into anti-Nazi protests.[46] The Pétain regime also condemned professionalism in sport and in June 1941 imposed the 'Athlete's Pledge', which declared that 'I promise on my honour to practice sport with selflessness, discipline and loyalty to become better and to better serve my country'.[47] In July 1943, professional players became civil servants paid by the government. From a Vichy perspective, French footballers were called upon to serve the regime: 'France needs all its sons to harden their bodies and temper their souls to face the harsh duties imposed on them. Be the pioneers of physical and moral renovation', as the CGEGS put it.[48] Moreover, 1943 marked the intensification of Vichy France's anti-Semitic policy in sporting circles, notably with the far-reaching case of Alfred Nakache, a swimmer of Jewish origin and champion of France, arrested in November 1943 and deported to Auschwitz.

The workers' sporting movement, embodied by the Fédération sportive et gymnique du travail (FSGT) [see Chapter 5], was split between fighting either Pétain or the Nazification of French sport. When French men of fighting age were sent to the front on the declaration of war on Germany on 3 September 1939, a minority of socialist leaders of the Federation's executive committee met in October, and decided to ban from the FSGT any club that did not repudiate the German–Soviet pact signed two months earlier. Just a few weeks later, it was the turn of the communist officials to be excluded from the organisation's upper echelons, before the Federation was turned into a Union (UGST), and forced to conform to the Vichy directives.

Despite this eviction, ex-FSGT communists like Auguste Delaune (former secretary general), Robert Mension (former FSGT leader) and Aymé Radigon (goalkeeper for the Choisy team and the national team of the workers' federation) set up a clandestine network called

'Free Sport' in early 1941. The objective of this Resistance structure was to denounce the sports policy of the Pétainist regime by highlighting its anti-Semitism and collaborationism.

Free Sport encouraged militants to raise awareness among athletes at the grassroots level, within the clubs themselves. The Popular Sports Club of the 10th arrondissement of Paris (CPS X) thus resumed 'normal' operation from September 1941 in order to 'allow young people, students, high school students, to be able to meet and practice sport'.[49] Under the guise of sporting activities, some of its members actively joined the Resistance. 'We couldn't hide it, we couldn't accept the Occupation, it was a moral issue', recalls Albert Zandkorn, a member of the club. '[…] We started by receiving leaflets, to distribute on the stairs, either at cinema exits, or on café terraces. You had to throw them and run away immediately so as not to be caught. It lasted like that until May 1941'.[50] The young members of CPS X and other communist militants, including the illustrious Guy Môquet, 'met in the Bois de Boulogne under the pretext of organising football games. In reality it was to prepare actions against the occupier'.[51] Two members of the club, Georges Tompousky, one of its founders, and Bernard Grimbaum, its secretary, were nevertheless shot on 30 April 1942.[52]

On top of this activism on the ground, the Free Sport network circulated clandestine pamphlets each month calling for 'free sporting activities in a free France'. In these publications, the resisting athletes denounced the authoritarianism of the Sports Commissariat, in a 1943 tract entitled 'Storm over Football'[53] or called on their colleagues to rebel against the occupier, as another leaflet from the summer of the same year shows:

> Athletes of France, to help bring down the invader once and for all, there are many options. Above all, unite and uphold your own demands. Demand bread, better supplies, balls, jerseys, shoes, equipment […] Fight for the repeal of the Nazi Sports Charter; chase traitors like Pascot from your organisations. In this way you will support the French Resistance against the enemy.[54]

Upon the Liberation of Paris in August 1944, the Free Sport activists took over the headquarters of their federation, the FSGT, with weapons in their hands.

Outside of the Free Sport network, with many footballers remaining passive in the face of the Occupation, like the great majority of French people, a handful of professional players eagerly joined the armed struggle.* Étienne Mattler, former defender at FC Sochaux and on the national squad, fought for the Resistance in the Belfort region, before being arrested by the Gestapo and later participating in the Liberation.[55] The midfielder for the Girondins de Bordeaux, René Gallice, joined the ranks of the Free French Forces in 1940, taking part in the battle of Bir-Hakeim in Libya in 1942. Rino della Negra, a young fitter from Argenteuil and the son of Italian immigrants who played on the right wing for Red Star of Saint-Ouen, went into hiding in October 1942 and joined the Francs-tireurs et partisans – main-d'œuvre immigrée (FTP-MOI). As part of the Manouchian group, the young footballer participated in the execution of the Nazi general Von Apt in June 1943, and in the attack on the Parisian headquarters of the Italian fascist party. On 12 November 1943, he was injured and then arrested following an action against German money couriers. He was executed at Mont Valérien on 21 February 1944 at the age of 20, consigning his last words to his younger brother: 'Send my greetings and farewells to everyone at Red Star'.[56]

* Others, on the contrary, collaborated to the full, such as the former captain of the French national team during the 1930 World Cup, Alexandre Villaplane, who became a member of the French Gestapo and an *Untersturmführer* SS officer.

8

'Corinthian democracy'

Football and self-organisation against the Brazilian dictatorship

> To be a Corinthian is to dive
> In the ocean of hope, which drowns
> No matter the plan of fate
> Every match is a heart playing.
>
> Gilberto Gil, *Corintiá*, 1984

From 31 March 1964, when a military putsch overthrew President João Goulart, Brazil found itself under the iron fist of an oligarchy of generals, who raised the spectre of a communist threat to South America. Supported by the US government, the armed forces decreed a series of 'institutional acts' that suspended the constitution and abolished presidential election by direct and universal suffrage, together with the multi-party system.

Under the pretext of 'national security', a state of emergency was imposed: the military claimed the right to arrest and imprison anyone without legal process and embarked on a counter-insurrectionary war aimed at eliminating the 'domestic enemy'.[1] With all forms of cultural expression censured, the political police (SNI) terrorised the population and media outlets alike.[2] Trained in US military academies and employing techniques of repression developed by the French during the wars of decolonisation,[3] officers made systematic use of torture, with 434 people killed and 20,000 tortured according to post-dictatorship records.[4] Plainclothes SNI squads regularly abducted anyone suspected of opposing the regime. A sense of fear weighed on Brazil. Almost 10,000 dissident intellectuals, left-wing militants and artists – such as Caetano Veloso, Chico Buarque and Gilberto Gil – were forced into exile in Europe.

After many years of clandestine struggle and urban guerrilla warfare, Brazilian society's demands for a return to democracy emerged into the open. Starting in 1975, a widespread campaign for the liberation of political prisoners gathered strength and student protests multiplied.[5] While armed resistance declined, the left-wing opposition coalesced around the intelligentsia, worker and farmer social movements, and liberation theory-oriented priests. With the trade union leader Luiz Inácio 'Lula' da Silva at the helm, major strikes shook the metal industry in São Paulo in 1977. On 13 March 1979, 150,000 metalworkers occupied the pitch and stands of the Vila Euclides football ground in the industrial suburbs of the city. The following year they launched a strike that lasted 41 days. The workers' assemblies held at Vila Euclides were overflown by helicopters toting machine guns.

All this meant that when the former head of the SNI, General João Figueiredo, came to power in March 1979 he faced an unprecedented set of economic problems, compounded by the oil price shock and debt crisis impacting on countries in the Global South. Insolvent, the state was on the verge of bankruptcy, with inflation soaring. On 30 November 1979, during a state visit to Florianópolis in the south, Figueiredo was jostled by thousands of young protestors, angered by their living conditions as well as by the general's contempt: he had earlier declared 'I prefer the smell of horses to that of people'. With the military dictatorship on its last legs, Brazil entered recession in 1981.

Breaking with the established order

'In Brazil, football is more than a sport: it is also a tool of socialisation, a very complex system for the transmission of values and an inclusive territory for perpetuating cultural and ideological identities', the Brazilian anthropologist Roberto Da Matta wrote in 1982.[6] Ever since the Seleção won its first world title in 1958, football and Brazilian identity have been closely bound up [see Chapter 12]. A survey held after the 1970 World Cup indicated that, for almost

90 per cent of working-class Brazilians, football was connected to their idea of nationhood.[7] In this light, in the eyes of the military the game had to be kept under control – and at all costs could not become associated with the social unrest shaking the country. In 1981, the Brazilian Football Confederation was presided over by Admiral Helenio Nunes, one of the leading figures in Arena – the National Renewal Alliance, the political party of the military junta. The national championship, meanwhile, had since the 1964 putsch been little more than a tool in the hands of the military oligarchy to flatter regional pride and feed local corruption networks. Indeed, the manipulation of tournaments – the premier division comprised as many as 94 teams – and stadium construction served to maintain a semblance of peace even in the most far-flung states, as well as distributing lucrative contracts to public works companies. 'When Arena does badly, that's another club in the national championship; when Arena does well, that's also another club', Brazilians joked at the time.[8] However, while the bosses got rich on their backs, the living conditions of professional footballers left much to be desired. Vassals of their team thanks to a contract system that bound them to their club for life, infantilised by authoritarian managers, the vast majority of players received a miserable salary and were poorly fed, regularly suffering from dysentery.

While demonstrations against the dictatorship expanded in São Paulo, the city's most popular team, SC Corinthians, was stagnating in the second division and had not won a victory in the regional championship for three seasons. However, in November 1981 the club board was up for election. Longstanding fixture Vicente Matheus, a mining entrepreneur close to the ruling military, was forced to hand over the presidency of the club to Waldemar Pires, a businessman from São Paulo. Orlando Monteiro Alves, vice-president of Corinthians, convinced the new club president to appoint his son as sporting director.

A 35-year-old sociologist, Adilson Monteiro Alves had seen the inside of the dictatorship's prisons thanks to his leadership of student protests. Although he admitted to having little knowledge of football, the ten years he had spent on the club's board of directors provided him with an insight into the precarious daily lives of football professionals. Being parachuted into the post of sporting director was no reason to ignore his contentious views. 'The players are treated like slaves', he declared soon after he took up the position. 'The authoritarian model is being questioned all over the country, and football should be no exception'.[9] The evening of his swearing-in at the club, the defiant sociologist joined the players at dinner and told them straight out: 'The country is struggling for democracy. Even when it achieves it, football will take time to catch up [...] We're going to hold a dialogue. Tell me what's not working, take your destiny into your own hands, be aware of your power, and we will decide everything together'.[10] While many of the players were disconcerted by this initiative, which was the antithesis of the authoritarianism of previous sports directors, others were immediately receptive to this novel approach. Among them were Sócrates, Wladimir and Casagrande, three politically committed players.

An admirer of Franz Kafka and Gabriel García Márquez, the centre-forward Sócrates – nicknamed 'the Doctor' thanks to his medical studies – was a fervent opponent of the regime. A member of the Workers' Party since its foundation in February 1980,* he recalls that his political awakening came early: 'I witnessed a scene that had a powerful impact on me, and transformed my view of the world. I saw my father burning his most precious books after the coup d'état of 31 March 1964'.[11] The left-back Wladimir was a leader of the players' union in São Paulo. He defined himself as 'a worker of the ball', saluted the metalworkers' strikes and didn't hesitate to denounce racial segregation of black players.[12] The 19-year-old forward and fan of Brazilian radical rock music, Casagrande's political enlightenment had come two years before the club's change of direction, when he organised a demo demanding amnesty for political prisoners.

The promises of the young sports director rapidly came to fruition. Meetings with the players were held almost every day, and on the initiative of Monteiro Alves and some of the more politically aware footballers, direct democracy was introduced to the club's

* The Partido dos Trabalhadores (Workers' Party, PT) was founded on 10 February 1980, mainly on the initiative of Lula and Olívio Dutra. It defined itself as a 'democratic, mass party of socialist inspiration'.

decision-making process. 'Before he is a professional, the player is a citizen', asserted the dissident sociologist. 'Gone are the days when the student had to study, the worker had to work and only the politician had to play politics. Everyone must have the freedom to participate in decisions concerning their destiny'.[13] All deliberations were heard collectively and then voted on. Every employee of the club had a vote, whether they were players, trainers, bus drivers or groundsmen. The Corinthians voted first to redistribute ticket sales, sponsorship and television rights to all employees. 'We abolished the paternalistic process by which football managers rendered players helpless, not allowing them to behave as adults', Sócrates later said. 'Initially that created a certain anxiety among those who weren't used to expressing themselves or taking decisions'.[14] At the interminable meetings, where philosophy and politics were discussed and books were exchanged, a majority vote decided everything: training times and methods, dates and choice of transport for away games, teams and substitutes for each match, new recruits [...] 'We even voted to decide if a player who had just got married could leave Tokyo [where the team was to play] to see his new wife', joked Wladimir.[15] 'We decided everything by consensus', recalled Sócrates. 'It could be simple things, like what time we ate breakfast, and we'd all vote on three options, with the majority vote being accepted by all'.[16] He adds: 'We wanted to overcome our condition as simple player-workers in order to fully participate in the strategy of the whole club. That led us to reconsider player-manager relations'.[17] The footballers even turned to a psychologist in order to better work on their personal and collective development within the group, a totally absurd idea in the eyes of the conservative footballing authorities of the time.

Under the military regime, the resistance by the horizontal democracy of the Corinthians took on a more political dimension after 1982, when the players elected Zé Maria as their coach. As a player in the team – with the added aura of being a 1970 world champion – Zé Maria had also recently been elected city councillor in the first free local elections under the dictatorship. 'We went for a self-management solution by choosing one of our own players to coach the team', recalls Sócrates. 'Believe me, that led to all sorts of controversy. We suddenly had 80% of the press against us!'[18] Treated as 'anarchists' or 'bearded communists', the daily practice of direct democracy at SC Corinthians aggravated the government-controlled media. The hostility grew further when the players collectively decided to abandon the *concentração*, the disciplinary practice that takes its name from the assembly of troops in time of war and consisted of locking up the players the day before a game for fear of festive excesses or potential sexual escapades. For the Corinthians, this patronising treatment of players as irresponsible individuals revealed the ineptitude of the dictatorship that, in football as in wider society, preventively arrested suspects on the premise of maintaining order. As a journalist who followed the Corinthians wrote:

> From the perspective of those in power, football had to be the opium of the people, when it was much more than that, and they had to control the players as much as possible. As they could not have complete control during the matches, it was important to do so before and after them. The *concentração* was a way of denying their human value.[19]

After a year of heated debates and voting, the Corinthians abolished the practice. The players could spend time with their families the night before the match, or gather together at group barbecues. Sócrates and Casagrande had no compunction about being seen with a cigarette between their lips or a beer in their hands.

This radical break with sporting authoritarianism and moralism was reflected on the pitch, too. The Corinthians' game was strong on attack and artistry, aimed at catching the opponent off-guard. Sócrates became as ingenious at passing as he was at attacking, displaying an elegant and technical style and celebrating each goal with his fist proudly raised, in the fashion of the Black Power militants in the US. To the fury of the authorities, the Corinthians did not lose a single match between November 1981 and July 1982, allowing them to ascend to the premier division, winning fourth place in the national rankings in 1982, and carrying off the São Paulo Cup for two years running, a first for the team in 30 years.

'We exercised our profession with greater liberty, joy, and sense of responsibility. We were like one big family, with the wives and children of the players. Each match was like a party', Sócrates recalls. 'On the pitch, we fought for freedom, to change the country. The atmosphere gave us greater confidence to express our art'.[20] To Brazilian eyes, if the authoritarian regime of the generals was incarnated in lugubrious repression and violent poverty, the self-management of the Corinthians was expressed in sporting successes as spectacular as they were joyful. The footballers were a living embodiment of how sporting creativity on the pitch and organisational creativity at the club could shake up a political system.[21] 'These victories were fundamental to the movement', Sócrates continues. 'Initially, we sought to change our working conditions, then the country's sports policies. Then the country's policies full stop'.[22] With SC Corinthians having vindicated its founding in 1910 as 'the people's club' – in contrast to the wealthier São Paulo FC – the team furnished Brazilian society with a living example of how to tackle the established order, becoming a sounding box for the democratic hopes of a whole nation.

Anti-authoritarian jersey

According to the SC Corinthians club statutes, the governing council and the members of the club alternately elected its managing bodies. In 1982, it was the members' turn to vote, and club president Waldemar Pires and sports director Adilson Monteiro Alves both sought a new mandate. Washington Olivetto – a well-known Brazilian publicist who supported the team – and sports journalist Juca Kfouri suggested the duo call their list 'Corinthian democracy', a subversive formula that expressed in two words the self-management project of the club. Sócrates, meanwhile, publicly threatened to leave the game if Vicente Matheus, the former caudillo at SC Corinthians, were to return. On the day of the vote, 60 per cent of members backed Pires and Monteiro Alves: their support vindicated the anti-authoritarian militancy of the Corinthians. The mood of the opposition only grew stronger when their emblematic player Sócrates was named captain of the Seleção for the 1982 World Cup.

The same year, following tough discussions with the national sports council and the managers of Brazilian clubs, advertising on jerseys was permitted by the dictatorship. The team assembly decided to emblazon the players' backs with the words '*Democracia corinthiana*', surrounded by drops of blood in reference to the repression by the regime. From September 1982, their black and white jerseys became the standard of their resistance, and TV broadcasts of matches helped considerably to popularise Corinthian democracy.

Just two months later, under threat from runaway inflation and popular discontent, the junta was forced to implement new political openness, and the first direct elections of state governors were held on 15 November. In a last thumbs-down to the generals, at the final of the São Paulo championship held a week before the vote, the Corinthians entered the stadium with the inscription *Dia 15 Vote* displayed on their backs. This televised call to vote finally transformed SC Corinthians into a political identity all its own. Football became a weapon against the regime, which was powerless to repress the sport, on peril of fanning the flames of protest that were smouldering throughout the country. The team became the popular voice of the opposition movement and received the support of intellectuals and artists, creating a bridge between the protesting elites and the people. The architect Oscar Niemeyer, writer Jorge Amado, performers Chico Buarque, Tom Jobim, Toquinho, Os Mutantes and Gilberto Gil – who composed *Corintiá*, a song honouring the team – appeared alongside the footballers. 'It all took shape the way I dreamt it could', Casagrande exulted in 2014. 'Living and playing with the Corinthians was one and the same: going for a drink, attending a rock concert or a play, going on a march'.[23]

The wave of protest against the dictatorship continued to sweep the country. In January 1983, the deputy Dante de Oliveira filed a constitutional amendment that would allow the president of the nation to be directly elected by popular vote, provoking the ire of the junta. In March a huge campaign was launched, 'Diretas Já', or 'direct elections now'. Yellow was the colour of the movement, and assemblies were organised across the country, with 15,000 marching in São Paulo in November. Two months later, the numbers had risen to 300,000. Dazed, the regime declared a 60-day state of emergency to try to break the movement. The Corinthians took part in the demonstrations and, to support the campaign, the players wore the characteristic yellow of the movement on the field: in the armband of captain Wladimir, in the 'Justice' band in the hair of Sócrates, and on Casagrande's shoes.

The political climate was electric. With inflation rates running above 20 per cent, São Paulo saw riots on 3 and 4 April 1983: 200 businesses were ransacked and looted.[24] Despite the repression directed towards Diretas Já, the democratic process was unstoppable and the national press was now infatuated with the Corinthians. With his lanky physique and his hair and beard reminiscent of Che Guevara, the charismatic and educated Sócrates became the figure who embodied Corinthian democracy and Brazilians' thirst for freedom. Some of the team's players sang on stage with the psychedelic singer Rita Lee from Os Mutantes, while on the TV Globo channel a soap opera portrayed the adventures of a Vasco player from Rio de Janeiro who dreams of transferring to Corinthians in order to fight for democracy. As if this were a magic recipe for sporting success, other clubs like Palmeiras and Flamengo also began experimenting with direct democracy.

Outflanking the military junta

On 13 December 1983, the day before the national championship final against São Paulo FC, the Corinthians, as title holders, were nervous. The future of Corinthian democracy rested on their shoulders. A defeat would be interpreted as the failure of the club's self-management adventure, closely linked to the ongoing mobilisations against the dictatorship. Without doubt, the generals would use a loss to mock the democratic impulse that day by day was eroding the regime. Assembled for dinner, 24 hours before the final, the Corinthians feverishly discussed the slogan they would unveil when they walked out. The next day, the footballers took to the pitch in the Morumbi Stadium before 88,000 spectators. At 9 pm the Corinthians unfurled a huge banner before the TV cameras and the jubilant stands: 'Win or lose, but always in democracy'. The team, thus freed from the obligation to win the competition at all costs, unleashed all their footballing magic. Sócrates scored the winning goal and, at the final whistle, Casagrande burst into tears on the shoulder of the 'Doctor'. The Corinthians had successfully outflanked the São Paulo FC defence as much as it had the ruling junta.

At the start of 1984, Sócrates celebrated his 30th birthday. Considered one of the Corinthians' best players, and regularly selected as captain of the national team, the 'Doctor' drew the attention of the European football markets. He had turned down a contract with Roma in 1982, preferring to stick with the Corinthians' anti-dictatorship struggle, but was made a new offer – US$12 million – by Italian club Fiorentina. Aware this might be his last chance to play in Europe, Sócrates faced a political dilemma, exacerbated as the protests gripping Brazil continued to grow: Diretas Já exhorted the population to take to the streets to defy the regime. On 24 February 1984, 400,000 people gathered in Belo Horizonte. On 10 April, almost a million protestors assembled in Rio de Janeiro. On 16 April, a million and a half Brazilians marched through São Paulo to demand direct presidential elections. Sócrates, Wladimir and Casagrande were at the head of the procession. On the podium, he took the microphone to declare to the crowd that he would turn down the transfer to Fiorentina and stay in Brazil if the National Congress (the Senate and Chamber of Deputies) accepted the demands of Diretas Já. Besieged by tanks and machine guns, the deputies authorised, on 25 April, the holding of presidential elections – but by an indirect vote.

Disappointed, Sócrates bowed out and left for Italy, promising: 'I will return to continue our struggle for political democracy and social justice'.[25] At his first Italian press conference, he stunned sports journalists with his comments on the political situation in Brazil and the writings of Antonio Gramsci, the founder of the Italian Communist Party who died in Mussolini's prisons in 1937. Shortly after the departure of the 'Doctor', the striker Casagrande underwent a difficult meniscus operation. The performance of the team declined, and they lost the 1984 São Paulo championship. In parallel, the Brazilian political landscape was evolving: the opposition forces focused their energy on the presidential campaign, perceived as the final chance to overthrow the dictatorship. The sporting defeats, together with this strategic reconfiguration of the movement, contributed to the loss of momentum of the Corinthian democracy.

Still on the prowl, the old SC Corinthians cronies who had been expelled from the club management in the early 1980s took advantage of the situation. When the governing body came up for re-election in 1985, some 30 'Corinthian democracy' councillors were insidiously removed from the electoral lists and then prevented by the police from standing for the ballot. Despite the cries of protest from the members, the conservatives took back the reins of the club and wiped out three years of self-management experience. Adilson Monteiro Alves was removed from office, while Casagrande and Wladimir were sold to other clubs. But the footballers' spirit of protest continued to blow through Brazilian society. In January 1985, the opposition politician Tancredo Neves, a civilian who united all the elements of the opposition movement, was elected to the presidency by an electoral college, and in May the Congress revoked the last constitutional vestiges of the dictatorship. The twilight of the Corinthian social experiment was thus the dawn of Brazil's democratic transition. A political revolution in which the Corinthians were the creative protagonists, if not catalysts. Casagrande summed it up: 'For all those who fought since 1964, who died, disappeared, were tortured, imprisoned, exiled, Corinthian democracy has taken the penalty'.[26]

9

On the front line, Tahrir Square

Ultras Ahlawy fans at the heart of the 2011 revolution in Egypt

I was just a slave to the system,
and when the Revolution broke out,
we all took to the streets.
We have died for freedom,
and for the corrupt heads to fall.
We are not about to give up,
because the regime continues to strike.
The dogs of the police and injustice are all around.

Our Story, Ultras Ahlawy chant.

'The people want the regime to fall!' chanted hundreds of thousands of people gathered on Qasr al-Nil bridge on 28 January 2011. For three days, the Egyptian people had been taking to the streets to protest against the military regime of Hosni Mubarak. Police violence, mass unemployment, corruption and the permanent state of emergency had undermined the *Rais* (leader or chief) who had ruled for 30 years. When the government simply cut off the internet and mobile phones across the country, on this 'Friday of Rage' the police forces suddenly decided to charge the crowds on Qasr al-Nil bridge. The reason: the bridge leads straight to Tahrir Square, which the protestors had been trying to occupy in the previous days.

Under a rain of tear gas, the Ultras Ahlawy – identifiable by their red jerseys with a black eagle – threw the canisters into the water or back at the police. The supporters of Al Ahly SC, the most popular Cairo-based football club, formed a single block of resistance. After almost five hours of pitched battle, the police were defeated and humiliated, and were hastily replaced by the armed forces. Thousands of demonstrators rushed to Tahrir Square to begin an occupation which lasted weeks. The Ahlawys were jubilant, chanting one of their anti-regime songs which regularly resounded in the stadiums: 'Hey government! / Tomorrow the hands of the people will cleanse you. / Hey stupid regime! / When will you understand what I demand? / Freedom, freedom, freedom!'[1]

That evening, the headquarters of the National Democratic Party (NDP) was on fire. A symbol of the regime had fallen. Thanks to their know-how and courage in the face of police brutality, the Ahlawys became one of the spearheads of the Egyptian revolution that 28 January. This image was reinforced by Al Ahly SC's reputation as the 'club of the people', whose history was bound up with that of the country.

From anti-colonialism to guardianship

'Al Ahly victories, above all in its early days of playing against the British, were a source of patriotic pride', explains Alaa Sadek, author of a reference work on the club and a specialist in Egyptian football. 'These players were the first from Egypt and perhaps all of Africa to play in and to win international tournaments, including the footballer Hussein Hegazi at the Antwerp Olympic Games of 1920'.[2] In 1905, the lawyer and independence activist Mustafa Kamil founded the Students Club, bringing together young Egyptians excluded from the sporting infrastructure reserved for the elites and colonials. Two years later, the club officially became the Al Ahly Sporting Club – 'The National' in Arabic – and became a forum of encounter and militant activity for Egyptian students and trade unionists fighting British colonialism. In 1909 Saad Zaghloul Pacha, the charismatic leader of the Egyptian nationalists and a figurehead of the 1919 Egyptian revolution, became president of the Al Ahly board. While the first Egyptian club, Al-Sakka Al-Hadid (The Railway Club), was established in 1903 by British and Italian railway engineers, the Egyptian independence movement made Al Ahly SC a showcase for anti-colonialism, having seen football's popularity grow among Cairo residents.[3] The players wore red and white jerseys, the colours of the pre-colonial Egyptian flag. Likewise, having boycotted matches against British military teams since the first championship of the Sultanate of Egypt in 1916,[4] the board of Al Ahly decided in 1925, three years after the British protectorate had ended, to restrict membership of the club to players with Egyptian nationality.

After the Second World War, the popularity of the 'people's club' drew the attention of the Egyptian authorities, who interfered in its governing bodies. They saw the 'Red Devils' as an instrument to entertain the 'Egyptian masses' and to promote the regime. As soon as he took over the country in 1956, Gamal Abdel Nasser became the club's honorary president. During the rise of pan-Arabic nationalism, and following his election as Secretary-General of the Non-Aligned Movement in 1964, the Egyptian leader sought to maintain control over the club and its anti-colonial symbolism. In 1965, he ordered General Abdul Mohsen Kamel Murtaja to assume the management of Al Ahly and to improve the club's sporting performance, which was rather mediocre at the time and perceived as a possible cause of popular discontent with Nasserism.[5] After the crushing defeat in the June 1967 war against Israel, Nasser, who was looking for tangible excuses for this humiliation, decreed the suspension of all national football tournaments that year, considering them a harmful distraction for the Egyptian people.[6]

His successor, Anwar Sadat, declared himself to be a great fan of the Cairo club and supported the game for its ability to revive both patriotic fervour and his own popularity.[7] Al Ahly even lent a hand to the regime's foreign policy. After signing the 1978 Camp David accords with Israel, Sadat encouraged the club to recruit Palestinian players in order to restore the image of the regime in the Occupied Territories.* The renown of Al Ahly in Palestine grew to the extent that the British journalist Steve Bloomfield reported: 'When Hamas and Fatah fought each other for control over Gaza in 2007, the only day the guns fell silent was when Al Ahly took on Zamalek [a rival Cairo club]'.[8]

---

* The team's revered goalkeeper, Marwan Kanafani, went on to become spokesman and personal advisor to Yasser Arafat in the 1990s.

No leader was as attached to the game as Hosni Mubarak, however. With the growing power of the football business in the 1980s, the regime transformed the Egyptian championship into a vast financial resource at the service of the Mubarak clan. The national media that broadcast matches, the managing boards of the largest clubs and the supporters' groups were all close to the NDP.[9] During the 2005 presidential election, Mubarak boasted of his proximity to Al Ahly: he made televised visits to the training camp and welcomed players at the airport after their victory in the African Champions' League.[10] The Rais attended all matches played by the national squad, and the regime's propaganda machine endeavoured to distil slogans and patriotic songs at each major match to fuel national feeling.[11]

In 2009, while Egypt was in deep economic depression and the regime was facing growing unrest, the president attempted to weaponise the national team's defeat against Algeria which had excluded it from the 2010 World Cup. Following violence between fans of the two teams in Algeria and in Egypt, Cairo cried foul and recalled its ambassador. Alaa Mubarak, eldest son of the president and a wealthy businessman, called on Egyptians to rise up during a talk show: 'We have been humiliated and we can't remain silent after what has happened [...] Egypt must be respected. We are Egyptians and we hold our heads high. Whoever insults us must receive a beating'.[12] In reprisal, Algiers imposed a tax bill of over half a billion dollars on the Egyptian owner of the Algerian telecoms operator Orascom. The diplomatic quarrel only ended with the mediation of the Libyan leader Muammar Gaddafi.[13]

Just as the history of the Al Ahly club is closely bound up with that of contemporary Egypt, the rivalry between the Red Devils and their fellow Cairo team the Zamalek Sporting Club is a keystone of the Egyptian popular imagination. If Al Ahly is the club of the people, with anti-colonial origins, Zamalek was founded in 1911 by a Belgian lawyer, George Marzbach, who had come to Egypt to build the Cairo tram system. Zamalek promoted cosmopolitanism and sought to offer European and Egyptian elites in the capital a space to meet and socialise through football. Nicknamed 'The White Knights' due to the colour of their jerseys, the club became the pride of the country's middle classes and the favourite team of King Farouk I, who ruled from 1936 to 1952 (Zamalek was even renamed Farouk Al-Awal in his honour between 1942 and 1950).

Between the Reds (blood) and the Whites (purity), the Devils and the Knights, Nasser and Farouk, or indeed independence and elitist aristocracy, the rivalry between the two Cairo clubs is both one of the most violent in the world, and part of the bedrock of Egyptian social identity.[14] As an Al Ahly fan observed when asked by journalist and Middle Eastern football expert James M. Dorsey: 'It's like a religion. In most countries, you're born Jewish, Muslim or Christian. In Egypt, you're born Ahly or Zamalek. People will never ask you for your religion, they'll ask if you're Ahly or Zamalek'.[15] A match that saw Al Ahly humiliate Zamalek 6–1 during the 2002 Egyptian championship became mythical in popular culture. In her bestselling novel *I Want to Get Married!* Ghada Abdel Aal even referenced it, with a character exclaiming: 'It's a disaster! I'm lost! I feel as disgraced as Zamalek in the championship, mother!'[16] For the sports sociologist Michel Raspaud, this Cairo rivalry symbolises above all the 'duality of Egypt – a society that both incorporated and suffered the influence of certain aspects of British colonial society for almost half a century – between the popular "nationalist" club (Al Ahly) and the "cosmopolitan" club of the upper classes (Zamalek)'.[17]

An autonomous youth

The Mubarak regime's control over Egyptian football and the century-old rivalry between Al Ahly and Zamalek were shaken up, however, by the wave of the 'ultra' movement breaking over North Africa [see Chapter 15 on the birth of the ultras]. Influenced by the Italian and Serbian ultras seen online, the Tunisian supporters of the Emkachkhines, who supported the club Espérance de Tunis from 2002 onwards, were the first representatives of ultra culture in North Africa. These groups of fans are characterised by their radical engagement with the club they support, self-funding, solidarity among members, and above all their inventive displays in the stands at both home and away games. Impressing supporters from neighbouring countries with their passion for their club and the *tifos** they deploy at every encounter, the Emkachkhines ultras spread to Tunisia, to Morocco (the Ultras Askary Rabat have supported FAR Rabat since 2005) and Algeria (the Ultras Mega Boys of MC Saïda or the Ultras Verde Leone of MC Alger were founded in 2007). In Egypt, the Ahlawy Ultras or UA-07, some of whom had met the Emkachkhines, were created in 2007 by members of the Ahly Fans Club. Eternal rivals, the Ultras White Knights (UWK or Zamalkawy) emerged the same year, made up of Zamalek supporters.

In a country where freedom of association or to protest do not exist, the Ultras Ahlawy quickly assembled some 4,000–6,000 young men aged between 15 and 25, almost all from the working and middle classes.[18] Across North Africa, in the conservative Muslim and Arab societies living under authoritarian regimes, football grounds have become one of the rare spaces that function as an escape valve: young fans come in search of a weekly dose of freedom and excitement, often consuming drugs and alcohol. Faced with widespread unemployment and the tight grip of their families, many young people take to ultras groups as a second family, where the collective power allows them to escape the struggles of everyday life: 'The Ultras Ahlawy are like a family, which is why we're so careful about who we accept as a member, in order to keep that family atmosphere of the group'.[19]

When compared to the social, religious and moral straitjacket of Egyptian society, the ultras offer a completely different lifestyle, tinged with individualism, raw pleasure and the romanticism of dissent: 'What we expect from an ultra is for them to throw flares onto the pitch despite the CCTV cameras, despite the police around the pitch and the plainclothes officers who've infiltrated the stands and arrested anyone with a flare', the Ahlawy say. 'It's when you're eating, thinking about a new chant, when you're drinking, thinking about a new idea for a *tifo*, when you're out with your friends, thinking about ways to bust the Zamalek guys the next time you run into them [...]'[20]

Beyond this intoxicating fraternity interspersed with self-financed group trips across the country, the ultras have developed a culture all

* Visual display of a large-scale motif that can fill a whole stand.

of their own, free from the traditional, patriarchal and authoritarian structures that circumscribe Arab youth. Each new football season is punctuated by the release of free online music albums that gather the latest stadium chants of different ultras groups. Insults addressed to rival clubs, songs glorifying their own club, denunciations of police violence, exaltation of their freedom and their lifestyle: these are the recurrent themes of this rich and varied musical genre. In the stands, the ultras of Egypt stage dramatic spectacles with smoke bombs and homemade rockets that can last an hour, and group choreographies called *dakhalat*. They abound in visual creativity, deploying vast frescos of fabric (*qomesh*), large banners that are unrolled to form an image (*sharayat*) – or even squares of fabric lifted by each supporter to reveal a message (*galads*).[21] Finally, two prominent slogans in English bring together under one banner the teenagers, students and ordinary workers who are members of the Al Ahly ultras: 'Together forever', signifying the solidarity among Ahlawy, and 'We are Egypt', indicating the social diversity of the fans. The ultras' ethic is also characterised by their total dedication to the group, before all else: studies, work, and love life.

> We chose the name ultra because it best described what we feel towards our club, which is our life and death, our mother and father, our wives, our children and our religion. You wake up in the morning thinking about Al Ahly, you go to bed dreaming of Al Ahly and the *tifo* you will perform at the final. The ultra mentality is a way of life and a state of being.[22]

Egyptian ultras groups are organised around individuals who, because of their seniority, 'sponsor' others, but also around internet forums and social networks. Each group is self-financing through membership fees and the sale of fan materials to its own members. This organisational and financial autonomy allows them to assert a fierce independence with regard to their club, any political party or institution, as well as to display their 'anti-media', 'anti-football-business', and 'anti-police' attitudes.[23] The distrust of the media is reflected in the anonymity of their members and absence of identifiable leaders.

They see themselves as the true owners of their clubs, the managers being merely the puppets of the regime, and the players mercenaries. Since its foundation in 2007, the Ahlawy have not been acknowledged by the official club authorities, and have staged mass protests against the cost of match tickets, which they claim only serve to swell the hidden accounts of the NDP bosses.[24]

Representing an autonomous segment of young people who refuse to bow to political and religious powers, the ultras have become a major challenge to the Egyptian regime. Stadiums have become increasingly militarised, with the pitches impenetrable zones surrounded by barriers and security. Truncheon blows in the stands, degrading searches, arrests of supposed leaders, systematic beatings at the police station: conflict with the authorities erupts each week and leads to prolonged urban disturbances. In the eyes of the ultras, the security forces embody the armed wing of an authoritarian regime that harasses them in order to maintain its monopoly over public space. Since 2007, the Ahlawy have organised direct confrontations with the police, with stones, Molotov cocktails and other homemade weapons. 'The ultras were the first group in Egypt to respond with violence to the violence and intimidation of the Ministry of the Interior', says Ashraf el-Sherif, political analyst at the American University in Cairo.[25]

The reputation of the Ahlawy was quickly dirtied, with sports media referring to them as 'atheists', 'drug addicts', 'communist hoodlums' and 'sexual deviants'.[26] Police violence, media discourse and hatred of the government in turn radicalised the ultras groups in Egypt. When no one was daring to openly criticise the regime, the Ahlawy and the Zamalkawy were the first to boo Hosni Mubarak en masse in the stadiums. 'I was against corruption, against this regime, and pro-human rights', declared Mohamed Gamal Bechir in April 2011. 'Radical anarchism was my credo. The ultras live outside the system [...] Our power lies in our capacity for self-organisation'.[27] Thanks to their autonomy and determination to stand up to the repression of the regime, they were seen – together with the Muslim Brotherhood – as the most robust groups when it came to escaping the control of the NDP.[28] As Assad, an Ahlawy group leader, commented ironically in 2012: 'The two largest political parties in Egypt are Al Ahly and Zamalek'.[29]

Although a segment of the 'masterminds' of the Al Ahly and Zamalek ultras call themselves anarchists, the groups are not ideologically homogenous. They bring together Egyptians who are simply fans of the game together with secular and Islamist militants, left-wingers and followers of the Muslim Brotherhood. Only the passion for the club unites them, undermining the efforts of Egyptian political organisations. 'Football is greater than politics', explains Assad.

> It's all about escapism. The typical Al Ahly fan is a guy who lives in a one-room flat with his wife, his mother-in-law and his five kids. He earns minimum wage and has a shitty life. His only good time is those two hours on Friday when he goes to the stadium and watches Al Ahly play. People suffer, but when Al Ahly wins, they smile.[30]

This popularity of the Red Devils has led to multiple branches of Ultras Ahlawy becoming established across the country. Wherever the 'people's club' plays, the ultras are there to challenge the forces of order. By 2011, just four years after it first emerged, the Ultras Ahlawy movement numbered tens of thousands of unemployed youths who were sworn enemies of Hosni Mubarak and his security forces.[31]

Everyone to Tahrir!

A few weeks before the self-immolation of Mohamed Bouazizi in Sidi Bouzid in December 2010 triggered the Tunisian revolution, the ultras of the Espérance Sportive de Tunis clashed violently with the police forces of the Ben Ali regime. From their earliest days, the Tunisian ultras had formed a close relationship with Takriz, an anonymous, militant cyber-network founded in 1998. The young Tunisian activists were attracted by the ethic and the rebellious spirit of the ultras, and helped them develop secure internet forums so that they could escape the surveillance of the security services. This alliance between football fans and radical militants turned into street battles in early 2011 that hastened the departure of Ben Ali: the Takriz ultras formed the hard core of protestors on the front line.

Ten days after Ben Ali went into exile on 14 January 2011, the Egyptian ultras took their cue from their Tunisian equals. The day before the first major anti-government protest on 25 January, named the 'Day of Rage', the Ultras Ahlawy and the Ultras White Knights of Zamalek stated on their Facebook pages that their members should feel free to take part in the demonstrations. In private, some were more direct: 'We have fought for our rights in the stadiums for four years', one wrote after the events. 'All of that was only preparation for this day. We told our members that this protest was a decisive event for us. Losing was not an option'.[32]

On 25 January, the Ultras White Knights headed up a procession of 10,000 people that broke through the seven security barricades leading to Tahrir Square, where they were joined by the Ultras Ahlawy and other protestors. Some of the ultras fought violently to break through the police blockade protecting the Egyptian parliament. 'We were on the front line', recounted a youth from the Ultras White Knights. 'When the police attacked we called on everyone to stand firm. We began to throw flares. People summoned their courage and joined us. They knew we were suffering injustice and loved that we were fighting against the devil'.[33]

Repelled from Tahrir Square that night, the revolutionaries organised the 'Friday of Rage' three days later, recovering the square thanks to the street fighting acumen of the ultras. Tahrir became the epicentre of the protest. The army was called in to replace the police. On 2 February, or horse and camelback, partisans of Mubarak supported by the *baltageya* or regime men charged the protestors with batons and knives, seeking to clear the square and put an end to the uprising. Before the cameras of Al-Jazeera, the ultras, with Ahlawy to the fore, protected the occupiers and sent the pro-Mubarak forces packing. The confrontations left three dead and hundreds injured.[34] Rivals in the stadiums, Al Ahly and Zamalek joined forces on that decisive day that would become known as the 'Battle of the Camels'. Ahmed Radwan, one of the founders of the Ultras Ahlawy, recalls:

> All of us were on the front line of the protests against the police, and it was so violent that I astonished myself with my courage. But we ultras have experience of fighting against the police forces. We are used to fighting them in the stadiums, and we were able to mobilise thousands of people in Tahrir.[35]

Faced with the protests in Tahrir Square, Hosni Mubarak left power on 11 February.

During the occupation of the square, the ultras gradually became full participants in the Egyptian revolution. Their experience of confrontation with the forces of order, their bravery and their solidarity with the protestors were respected and indeed admired by the anti-Mubarak activists. Their creativity, artistry and the rhythmic sound of their chants were a powerful influence on the revolutionary slogans and songs. 'In Tahrir, it often felt like we were at the stadium, above all when Mubarak announced he was stepping down', recalls Ashraf el-Sherif.[36] The ultras patrolled the square, setting up checkpoints and allocating responsibilities: stone throwers, specialists in turning over cars and setting them on fire for defensive purposes, projectile-making teams, improvised rescuers on mopeds circulating among the clouds of tear gas. In the words of one head of a medical post in the occupied square: 'They go where the ambulances won't, and we've saved at least a dozen lives'.[37] Mohamed Nagy, a Youth for Freedom and Justice militant, says: 'Without them, none of it would have been possible, because they do what no one else can do [...] They showed us that it was possible to hit back at the dictator's cops'.[38] The image of the ultras completely changed, as Céline Lebrun, a sociologist working on the Cairo groups sums up:

> In the process of creating a new ideal type of the 'revolutionary' youth, the young ultra became a model embodying strength, courage and determination [...] The stereotypes associated with the ultras radically changed following the uprising of 25 January 2011. The image of the violent and depraved thug gave way to the romantic image of a brave young person, a 'fearless' hero or even a 'guardian of the revolution'.[39]

The Supreme Council of the Armed Forces (CSFA), the military body responsible for ensuring the transfer of power in Egypt, took over the reins on 12 February, the day after the resignation of Hosni Mubarak. But the anti-authoritarian embers kept alive by the ultras were still smouldering under the ashes of the occupation of Tahrir Square. In September, during an Egyptian championship match, 7,000 Ahlawy relentlessly waved Tunisian, Libyan and Palestinian flags and chanted slogans attacking Mubarak and the former Minister of the Interior, Habib el-Adly.[40] In the eyes of the Ultras Ahlawy, the pair were responsible for hundreds of deaths resulting from the repression of anti-government protests. By the end of the match, the violent clashes with the security forces had left 130 injured (including 45 police officers), and a score of ultras were arrested.[41]

'Tantawi, the people will come for you!' demonstrators threatened on 18 November 2011, taking to Tahrir Square once more. After Mubarak stepped down, the people demanded that Marshal Mohamed Tantawi, chief of the CSFA, cede power to civilians. Ahlawy and Zamalkawy supporters were again united in mass protest against the military regime and leading the defence of Tahrir Square and Mohammad Mahmoud Street. The latter links the square with the Mounira district, home to government offices including the Interior Ministry. 'We are ordinary people. We love our country, our club and our group', declared an ultra member taking part in the street battles. 'What we have in common with revolutionaries is that we're fighting for freedom. We have dedicated our ideals and feelings to the revolution'.[42]

Mohammad Mahmoud Street was the scene of the heaviest fighting against the military sent by the government to support the overwhelmed riot squads.* Walls along the thoroughfare were soon covered with depictions of martyrs, anti-CSFA slogans, giant 'ACAB' slogans and frescos in honour of the ultras groups. By the end of the month, around 50 protestors were dead and thousands injured: November 2011 was the bloodiest month of the Egyptian revolu-

* Since the clashes, the street has been nicknamed *Sharei' uyuun al-huriyyah*, the 'Street of the Eyes of Freedom', in reference to the many demonstrators who lost an eye to police gunfire.

tion.[43] In parallel to the anti-military protests, the chants of the ultras and their calls to overthrow the regime became increasingly vindictive. In the stadiums, the Ahlawys unfurled a giant banner showing a 'vampire' Field Marshal Mohamed Tantawi at every match, chanting: 'The CSFA are all dogs / And so are the police!'

'Oh, Council of Bastards'

On 1 February 2012, an Egyptian championship match was played in Port Said between the local team Al Masry and Al Ahly. After the final whistle blew on a 3–1 victory over the Red Devils, the Port Said ultras – known as the Green Eagles – suddenly invaded the pitch for no apparent reason. After trying to attack the players, the Green Eagles began to climb the opposite stands, armed with stones, knives and bottles, taking on the Ultras Ahlawy.

'It's not football, it's a war, people are dying before our eyes!' screamed the Al Ahly player Mohamed Abou Treika into his mobile phone. Speaking live to the club's channel, the footballer was desperate: 'The security forces abandoned us. They didn't protect us. One of our fans was killed in front of me'.[44] The Ahlawy were thrown from the stands, stabbed, strangled and trampled. Shortly after the attack began, the stadium lights suddenly went out and the exit doors were locked for about 20 minutes. As for the security guards, they remained almost impassive. The attack turned into a massacre: 74 people were killed and nearly 200 seriously injured.

For the Ahlawy, this carnage was obviously revenge on the part of the CSFA for having acted as the armed wing of the revolution and the protests against the military government. The supporters of the Red Devils also noted the date: the Port Said massacre was the anniversary of the Battle of the Camels one year earlier. 'The Minister of the Interior never got over that humiliation', says Ahmed Radwan of the Ultras Ahlawy. 'This is what they wanted to tell us: "You thought you were stronger, well no, we're going to break you". This was their revenge!'[45] This tragic event shook international football as much as it did the Egyptian people and ultras groups in the country. On hearing the news while their team was playing Ismailia, the White Knights Ultras turned over their banner, a powerful gesture in ultra symbolism. 'I have a hard heart', swears Ahmed Radwan, who was in Port Said. 'Of course I lost a lot of friends but we can't retreat. We want a country that respects us, we are fed up with the "sons of" and the privileges, we want the military to leave'.[46]

The Ahlawy were enraged, covering Cairo with ACAB slogans and portraits of the slain supporters, and organising demonstrations to demand justice and reparation for the 'Port Said martyrs': in their eyes, Mohamed Tantawi was responsible for the massacre. At the end of every match and at every rally, Ultras Ahlawy and White Knights supporters chanted: 'The Ministry of the Interior are thugs', 'I hear the call of the martyr's mother' or 'Down with the military regime'.[47] While waiting for the Port Said events to go to trial in early 2013, they didn't let up the pressure: blocking the Cairo train station, surrounding the Stock Exchange and the Central Bank, barricades on the roads delaying the return to the United States of John Kerry, emissary of the Obama administration. A new song was added to the Ahlawy repertoire, 'Oh, Council of Bastards', to denounce the death of their fellow supporters:

> In Port Said the victims saw treachery just before they died / They saw a regime that brings only chaos / This regime thought that its hold would make it untouchable / And bring the revolutionary people to their knees in the face of martial law / […] I will never trust you and let you control me one more day! / […] Oh AFSC bastards, what is the price of a martyr's blood?[48]

In 2013, after the initial verdict, 21 Al Masry supporters were condemned to death. The Red Devils fans, disgusted at the acquittals of seven police officers, set the Egyptian Football Association offices on fire. In total, 70 detainees were accused of homicide, including nine police officers and three employees at the Port Said stadium.[49] In June 2015 a second trial was held that saw half of the 21 supporters condemned to death. But the ultras denounced a trial where the real instigators of the tragedy were absent: the senior officers of the CSFA, led by Marshal Tantawi.

Lost causes

Seeking justice for their martyrs did not prevent the Ahlawy and other ultras from joining in the revolution. In June 2012, Mohamed Morsi, the Muslim Brotherhood candidate, was elected president of the Egyptian Republic. On 23 November of the same year, a red wave broke over the Qasr al-Nil bridge, heading towards Tahrir Square. Al Ahly supporters joined thousands of demonstrators to commemorate the bloody month of November 2011 while protesting against the Morsi government. The ultras demanded a thorough reform of the police force and an end to their presence in the stadiums. They demanded the resignation of all Egyptian football officials, seen as corrupt and too close to the former regime. Under pressure from fans, Al Ahly president Hassan Hamdy was banned from travelling abroad and had his fortune, estimated at US$82 million, frozen by the authorities on suspicion of corruption.[50]

However, following the military coup against Morsi in July 2013 and the seizure of power by Marshal Abdel Fattah al-Sissi, repressive measures were directed towards the ungovernable ultras once more. This time it was the turn of the Zamalkawy. On 8 February 2015, at an Egyptian championship match the police violently dispersed the Ultras White Knights with tear gas and buckshot. The Zamalkawy had gathered outside the 100,000-capacity Cairo Army Stadium, where the authorities had assigned them just 5,000 places. The police violence against the fans, who were trapped between the fences and a stadium entrance, resulted in 20 deaths. The president of the Zamalek football club, Mortada Mansour, accused the White Knights of being responsible for this tragedy, describing them as a 'criminal phenomenon that must be eradicated'.[51] After Mansour filed a complaint against them, in May 2015 an Egyptian court ordered the dissolution of all the ultras groups, accusing them of being 'terrorist organisations'.[52] Despite the court ruling and the heavily guarded matches, the Egyptian ultras continued to chant and insult the police and the government. Angered, the director of the Al Ahly football club, Abdel Aziz Abdel Shafy, said in December 2015: 'We [Al Ahly SC] apologise to the men of the armed forces whose work we appreciate. Field Marshal Mohamed Hussein Tantawi has suffered a lot and, in his great wisdom, we ask him to forgive us'.[53]

On 2 February 2016, the Ahlawy commemorated four years since the Port Said massacre at the grounds of their own club, the Mokhtar El-Tetch Stadium. The portraits of the 74 martyrs were hung in the stands and on the crammed pitch, framed by an immense banner reading 'Never Forget'. The gathering swiftly became a great anti-government demonstration since, in the view of the ultras, Abdel Fattah al-Sissi was implicated in the killings as a CSFA member at the time. The very next day, al-Sissi challenged the Ahlawy on live television to send ten of their members to join a committee charged with examining the circumstances of the Port Said aggression. Seen as an authentic call for dialogue, this TV broadside revealed the official recognition by the authorities of the ultras groups, even though they were banned by the courts. On their official Facebook page, the Ahlawy refused to accept: 'Ultras Ahlawy demand reparation from the government and the president for the martyrs of the Port Said clashes, and for all those involved in this tragedy to stand before justice, including the senior officers responsible for security at the time'. A few days later, alongside the traditional 'We are Egypt' and 'Together for ever', the Ahlawy displayed a new banner in English in the stands and on the street: 'Ultras never die'.

As a result of the balance of power they had established with the authorities since 2011, the ultras regularly attracted the interest of Egyptian political organisations. The three largest ultras groups in Egypt – the Ahlawy, the White Knights and the Blue Dragons – amounted to nearly 20,000 active individuals and could mobilise over 50,000 people between them.[54] They hotly contested any attempt at political organisation, however: 'Ultras in the stadium, there is no such thing as ultras outside the stadium', they liked to assert.[55] They found any suggestion of forming links with a party or a union absurd, as the ultras claimed to represent the diversity of the Egyptian people, in all its contradictions. 'Just like Egyptians, they are divided', explains the Egyptian football journalist for Reuters, Osama Khairy.[56]

Despite having embodied the figure of the brave young hero who breaks the barrier of fear, and then the archetype of the martyr, the ultras have not become an integral part of the revolutionary movement. For one thing, certain groups, such as the Union of Independent Egyptian Women, reject their male-oriented culture and patriarchal vision of society. It is true that some ultras refused to mingle with women at occupations or even asked them to go home at night. 'The ultras' attitude to human rights is the flip-side of the exploitation of football's patriarchal values by neo-patriarchal regimes in North Africa and the Middle East', in the view of journalist James M. Dorsey. '[…] the protestors, despite their revolutionary spirit, were often incapable or unwilling to fully throw off the patriarchal values they held'.[57]

Meanwhile, having suffered such heavy losses, the ultras groups were gradually withdrawing to their footballing origins. 'I lost ten of my close friends at Port Said', recounts Al Ahly ultra Ahmed Radwan. 'If you lose ten friends you ate with on a daily basis, that's a huge trauma. And you lose hope. You stop caring about who will take power. You just think: I want my life back'. He adds: 'We lost our friends on Tahrir Square and in Port Said, we fought against the police and the army, but the revolution did not achieve its goals […] After three years, we needed to return to the stadiums'.[58]

Despite this recent distancing between militants and ultras, Amr Abderrahmane, a member of the Socialist Popular Alliance – a left and far-left coalition that emerged from the revolution – recalls that:

> This generation born under Mubarak, with access to the internet, was capable of creating a new, anti-middle-class identity and provoking the prevailing morality. They are a side of the revolution that everyone would like to forget: the side of rage, of anger. Not the neat, flowery side of the polite youth: the anti-social, anti-family, anti-institution, anti-moral side.[59]

PART III

Dribble

Outmanoeuvring colonialism

10
The Algerian Independence Eleven

A liberation struggle in football boots

> They rule us with their rifles and machines.
> But face to face, on a football pitch, we
> can show them who is really the strongest.
>
> Ferhat Abbas[1]

> It was only when playing for a team as a young man that I experienced that powerful sense of hope and solidarity which used to accompany the long days of training before a match, won or lost. And really, what little morality I have learned, I have learned on the football pitch or on the stage, both of which remain my true universities.[2]

This footballing soundbite uttered by Albert Camus during a TV interview in 1959 has passed into posterity. A goalkeeper for Racing Universitaire d'Alger in the 1930s, Camus' writings occasionally evoke his memories of a multicultural Algerian football that was symbolic of a fraternal *entente* between the Muslim, Jewish and European communities of the Maghreb. As the Algerian historian Abderrahmane Zani nostalgically recalls: 'Whether their names were Mohamed or Marcel, they sweated in the same jerseys, supported the same club and chanted the names of Salva or Haddad [celebrated Algerian players in the 1940s]. This is the other face of Algeria, the everyday one shared by *pieds-noirs* and Muslims'.[3]

However, such reminiscences of Algerian football breaking down ethnic boundaries conceal the true role of the sport in the culture of a territory that had been under French rule since 1830. The most popular sport among all sectors of the Algerian population, in the eyes of the colonial authorities football was a tool of social control aimed at the cultural integration of the 'natives'.[4] While strengthening ties with metropolitan France, football was to be a social peacemaker at the service of the colonial order. This aspiration was made clear in 1936 by General Henri Giraud, then at the head of the Oran Division: 'Sport must be the bond that brings together French and Muslims in a joint desire for performance and noble aspirations, while eliminating all rivalry based on religion and race'.[5]

Football and national liberation

Nevertheless, the 1920s saw the emergence of the first wholly 'native' Algerian football teams in the local leagues (Oran, Algiers and Constantine). Beginning in the 1923–1924 season, there were no fewer than ten 'Muslim' teams in the Oran league (out of a total of 40), four in Algiers and the same number in Constantine.[6] Despite their community character, these 'native'* teams enjoyed the benevolence of the colonial authorities as long as they remained neutral with regard to French rule and confined themselves to their recreational and social hygiene-related objectives.[7] What is more, the Algerian football pitches began to operate as recruiting grounds for the big professional clubs in the metropole. Following the example of the industrial sector, which drew extensively on the Maghreb for its workforce, the first professional Algerian players – such as Ali Benouna, recruited by FC Sète, or Abdelkader Ben Bouali, a brilliant defender for Olympique de Marseille – played in the French championship from the early 1930s.

During the interwar period, two parallel movements helped to make football a vector for anti-colonial politicisation: the growing popularity of the sport, both in France and Algeria, and the emergence of the first organisations supporting Algerian independence (the Étoile Nord-Africaine was founded in 1926, and the Algerian People's Party in 1937). Football pitches were transformed wholesale into sites of conflict between communities, and the 'native' teams

---

* The Jewish community of Algeria also set up its own sports organisations, such as the Olympic Football Club of Oran.

came to embody the embryonic desire for independence from France. Numerous incidents involving supporters or players occurred in the Constantinois region, leading the governor-general of Algeria to decide on 20 January 1928 to forbid matches between European and 'native' teams.[8] However, the regional football associations paid little attention to this prohibition, which in any case was difficult to enforce locally, and inter-community clashes on the pitch continued. In the Djidjelli district these caused the prefect to raise the alarm with the governor-general on 22 December 1937 about a series of 'demonstrations that are unfortunately likely, given the circumstances, to represent a risk to public order'.[9] In an attempt to weaken the assertion of Algerian identity through football, a circular was issued by the colonial authorities obliging Muslim clubs to accept a quota of three, and later five, European players per team. Just like the previous ruling, this incongruous administrative decision was applied in a haphazard manner that reflected the power struggles between the various football leagues and the municipalities, until it was revoked altogether in 1945. However, the growing independence movement associated with football was becoming harder to keep in check. In December 1945, the Tlemcen police reported an incident during a match between the USM Témouchentoise team and the Europeans of Béni-Saf: 'The song taken up by the Muslim team of Aïn Témouchent went by the name of *Min Djibaline* ("In my mountains") and included the words "I love the free men who lead us to independence"'.[10]

After the Second World War, the growing aspiration for national liberation was met with a brutal military repression. In Sétif, on 8 May 1945, thousands of Algerians were murdered by French troops and colonists following an independence march. Yet across the globe a process of decolonisation was underway. The Egyptian revolution of 1952 and the pan-Arab policy of Nasser, together with the debacle of the French forces at the Battle of Diên Biên Phu, Indochina in the spring of 1954, aroused great hopes among Algerian separatists. On 1 November 1954, the National Liberation Front (FLN) launched an armed insurrection, committing a series of attacks. In response, France unleashed terror upon the Algerian people, believing it could stamp out the thirst for independence.

As Algeria was plunged into a dirty war, football became one of the fields of battle. In the spring of 1956, the final of the North African Cup set two clubs from Sidi Bel Abbès against each other: SC Bel Abbès, a team of *pieds-noirs*, and the Muslim Sporting Union of Bel Abbès. However, a controversy broke out around the status of a player on the SC Bel Abbès team, who had officially been suspended. Morocco and Tunisia had just won their independence in March, the political climate in Algeria was like a tinderbox, and this dispute over a football match triggered a wave of popular protest across the country. Fearing the situation would degenerate, the governor-general cancelled the match, arousing the anger of the FLN, which from that moment on obliged all Muslim clubs to boycott their games. A number of players and club managers joined the independence struggle, following the example of Mohamed Benhamed of the Muslim Sporting Union of Oran, who became the leader of the FLN in Morocco, and several members of the Muslim Sporting Union of Bel Abbès, who became guerrilla fighters.

During the Battle of Algiers on 10 February 1957, the independence organisation carried out two bomb attacks on the El-Biar and Belcourt stadiums, causing terror among the *pieds-noirs* supporters. Three months later, the FLN took action in France itself: during the final of the French Cup, on 26 May the loyalist deputy Ali Chekkal was assassinated by an FLN gunman as he left the Colombes stadium, having watched the game alongside French President René Coty. Meanwhile, the French government continued to employ football as a tool to assert its colonial authority. A number of Algerian stadiums were designated by the French Football Federation (FFF) as hosts for French championship games. On 4 March 1956, the quarter-finals between Havre Athletic Club and OGC Nice were played in the Monréal stadium in Oran, before the same city was chosen to host the World Military Championship in 1960.[11]

However, until the autumn of 1957 the liberation war waged by the FLN received little coverage in France, with the media under pressure to characterise it merely as internal 'incidents'. On the military front, money and weapons were sorely lacking, while on the diplomatic front, the United Nations was slow to acknowledge Algeria's right to self-determination. In order to raise the profile of the separatist cause and bolster political agitation, a plan emerged among the FLN leadership to contact professional Algerian sportsmen living in France and invite them to join the struggle, becoming the flag bearers of Algerian liberation. A leading member of the French section of the FLN, Mohamed Boumezrag – a former player at the Girondins de Bordeaux and coach of the Le Mans team – proposed creating a football team from scratch, one with the official stamp of the liberation organisation.

In fact, the establishment of a 'native' team had already been mooted three years earlier – but on the initiative of the French authorities. On 7 October 1954, the FFF had organised a charity match for the benefit of the Algerian town of Orléansville (Chlef), damaged by an earthquake the previous month. At Parc des Princes, the French national reserve team had played against a selection called 'North Africa' which comprised, alongside Tunisian and Moroccan players, talented Algerian footballers like Mustapha Zitouni, Abdelaziz Ben Tifour, Abderrahmane Boubekeur and Abdelhamid Bouchouk. In front of 90,000 fans, the North African team won 3–2. Taking place just days before the outbreak of the Algerian War, this match would, in retrospect, become deeply symbolic.

In early 1958, on FLN orders, Mohamed Boumezrag was tasked with spiriting a handful of professional players out of France and bringing them to Tunis, headquarters of the Provisional Government of the Algerian Republic (GPRA), in order to form the flagship team of the revolution. During the 1957–1958 season, some 40 professional Algerian players were playing in the French championship.[12] Several of them already paid the FLN a 'revolutionary tax' of up to 15 per cent of their salary.[13] Boumezrag would approach them individually as they left training, at the end of a match, or after a night out, and try to convince them to join the independence struggle. After months of work, the FLN militant persuaded twelve footballers to leave France in secret.

The great escape

Early in the morning of 14 April 1958 Rachid Mekhloufi, a young striker for AS Saint-Étienne, leaves hospital with a bandaged head, still dressed in his pyjamas. The night before, during a lame excuse for a home match against Béziers in the Geoffroy-Guichard stadium he had an unfortunate collision with his teammate Eugène N'Jo Léa. As soon as he emerges, he leaps into a waiting car with two men inside: Mokhtar Arribi, former player for RC Lens and now Avignon coach, and Abdelhamid Kermali, winger for Olympique Lyonnais. Two days earlier, they had persuaded Mekhloufi – like them a native of Sétif – to join them in their independence adventure. Recalling the painful memory of the Algerians machine-gunned near his family home during the Sétif massacres in 1945, he hadn't hesitated for long before choosing exile in Tunis.

The trio take off for Switzerland, with a pit-stop in Lyon to pick up Abdelhamid Bouchouk of Toulouse FC, and cross the border just as the first radio dispatch is reporting the desertion of the Algerian players. A few days earlier, five Algerian footballers from the first division, including the popular Mustapha Zitouni, had abandoned France in secret. The information has not yet reached the border guards, who recognise the Saint-Étienne scorer Mekhloufi and congratulate him on his recent exploits. They make it to Lausanne without incident, where Toulouse FC striker Saïd Brahimi and mastermind Mohamed Boumezrag await them, ready to board a train for Rome, and from there they travel by plane to Tunis.

The next day, of the twelve footballers recruited, two are missing. Mohamed Maouche of Stade de Reims was stopped at the Italian border and Hassan Chabri of AS Monaco was arrested in Menton and imprisoned.* Even so, the operation reverberates across the moribund Fourth Republic like a thunderclap in the worlds of politics and sports alike. By the morning of 15 April, the disappearance of the Algerian players is already on the front page of *L'Équipe*. The magazine *France Football* devotes four pages to this earthquake. A week later, *Paris Match* publishes a long, excruciating article under the headline 'French football stars revealed as Fellaghas'. Beneath a photo of the rebels clinking champagne glasses in the Nice bar owned by fellow player Abdelaziz Ben Tifour, the magazine's caption reads: 'Now they are drinking water in the land of veiled women'.[14] At

* Both would later join the FLN team.

once furious and scandalised, the French Football Federation issues a cruelly patronising press release: 'The faith in the future of football in our beloved North African provinces reaches all the way to their leaders [...] The native players eagerly feed on the football bread we distribute to them'.[15]

The date chosen for the defection was no coincidence, and nor were the identities of the ten rebel Algerian players. On 16 April the French national team was to play a warm-up match against Switzerland in advance of the World Cup to be held in Sweden in June. The dissident Mustapha Zitouni of AS Monaco was a key defender in the French team. Rachid Mekhloufi, French champion with AS Saint-Étienne and world champion with the French military team in 1957 (he signed up to the Joinville Battalion), had also been pre-selected to play in the World Cup. Others among the group, like AS Monaco player Ben Tifour or Toulouse FC's Saïd Brahimi, had already donned the blue jersey on numerous occasions.

By weakening the French team on the eve of a high-status game, the FLN hoped to have an impact on public opinion in metropolitan France. This act of sporting war also aimed to demonstrate that professional football stars were ready to embrace the cause of Algerian independence. On 15 April, the FLN released the following communiqué:

> The National Liberation Front is pleased to announce that a number of Algerian professional sportsmen have just left France and Monaco in response to the call of Algeria [...] Welcomed by the FLN, our brothers expressed their joy to be among us. They explained to us at length that, at a time when France is waging a merciless war against their people and their homeland, they refused to play a role in a tournament of such importance.[16]

The organisation ended its statement asserting its intention to create an Algerian Football Association and join FIFA. 'Few French people knew what was happening in Algeria', recalls Rachid Mekhloufi. '[...] The French realised when we left that there was a war in Algeria, a war of liberation'.[17]

Two days after their arrival in Tunis, Ferhat Abbas,* the head of the GPRA, visited the exiled players. 'There is no question that this team is of enormous importance to us', he explained, 'because through its appearances abroad it will present the image of a people fighting for their independence'.[18] On the shabby pitches of the Tunisian capital, the subversive ten players immediately began training under the leadership of Boumezrag and Arribi. An Algerian defender playing at Stade Tunisien, Hammadi Khaldi, completed the team.

The first match of the squad that became known as the 'Independence Eleven' was played on 9 May 1958 against Morocco at the Chedly Zouiten stadium in Tunis, as part of the North African Djamila Bouhired tournament (named after the Algerian political prisoner). The FLN team won 2–1. 'The stands were full of Algerian fighters', Rachid Mekhloufi recalls. 'When I saw our flag raised, heard our anthem resound around the stadium, and the resistance fighters firing their weapons all around the pitch, I was overcome by a great emotion'.[19] Two days earlier, under pressure from the French Football Federation, FIFA decided to suspend the fugitive players and to sanction any association or team that agreed to play against them.

The political commitment demanded from the footballers, who had undergone a transformation in status from French sporting stars to clandestine players unrecognised by the official bodies, was total. While each enjoyed a furnished apartment in Tunis and a small salary, the players of the Independence Eleven nevertheless made major sacrifices. The young Saint-Étienne prodigy Rachid Mekhloufi not only had to renounce the dream of playing in the World Cup in Sweden; as a soldier he also risked court martial for desertion. But all the players suffered from abandoning their first-division French championship clubs for exile in Tunis. They had to leave behind a relatively comfortable lifestyle, sporting fame and popularity along with their career, family life and friendships. Mekhloufi, for example, was unable to attend his mother's funeral in September 1959. Yet years later, looking back at this period, he regretted nothing:

---

* A football player in his youth, Ferhat Abbas was for a time president of the Muslim Sports Union of Setif.

> Our departure demonstrated that the whole people of Algeria were behind the FLN, that they weren't just bandits or mercenaries. We were doing fine in France, we had good positions, people loved us. We weren't against France but against colonialism, against the people who are in Algeria and who have monopolised its resources.[20]

Football Fellaghas

After the first sporting successes of May 1958 – among other wins, the FLN team crushed the Tunisian selection 6–1 – the ambassadors of Algeria's independence cause made their international debut. With their white and green jerseys, the revolutionary squad set off in June of that year for Libya, where it soundly defeated the teams of Tripoli and Benghazi. Proof that not all their French colleagues had turned their backs on them came when Mustapha Zitouni received a friendly postcard from Sweden, sent by Les Bleus players Raymond Kopa, Just Fontaine and Roger Piantoni. Over the course of that summer, more rebel players came to expand the ranks of the FLN selection until they numbered 32, including such star recruits as Abderrahman Ibir, goalkeeper at Olympique de Marseille, and the brothers Mohamed and Abderrahmane Soukhane from Havre AC.*

Braving FIFA's censure, the FLN team played over 80 matches across 14 countries before Algeria won its independence in 1962.[21] There were three major international tournaments in particular that proved to be as much political events as sporting ones. Following a series of six tumultuous matches in Iraq in the winter of 1959, between May and July of that year they toured Eastern Europe, playing 20 matches in Bulgaria, Romania, Hungary, Poland, the Soviet Union and Czechoslovakia, where they were warmly welcomed by spectators in packed stadiums. For the FLN, these illicit international matches between its team and those of friendly countries laid the ground for the future diplomatic relations of independent Algeria.

In order to remain in FIFA's good graces, the national associations that agreed to play them camouflaged their teams in the strips of local clubs, or as company or trade union teams. Regardless, every

---

* Not all Algerian players in France responded to the FLN's invitations, such as Kader Firoud of Nîmes Olympique or Khenane Mahi of Stade Rennais.

match was intended to throw the spotlight on the Algerian revolution, meaning the team had to represent the future independent nation. The FLN leaders – notably Mohamed Allam, the political commissar who oversaw logistics – ensured that the Algerian flag was hoisted and the *Kassaman*, the national anthem, was played, though neither were in any sense official. In Warsaw, having accommodated the Algerian players in grimy rooms, the Polish authorities at first refused to bring out the flag of independence, for fear of offending their French counterparts and being excluded from FIFA. After a vigorous altercation, both anthem and colours emerged. Rachid Mekhloufi recalls the time:

> When we travelled to Eastern Europe and Arab countries, the politicians were up to date on the war, but not the local people. Our role was to inform these populations. We weren't just playing football! We visited factories, talked with people, explained what was happening in Algeria. We were the footballing arm of the Revolution. What's more, our results and our playing helped us enormously. People asked themselves 'Who are this team? Where do these devils come from?' We had a dream team.[22]

On the pitch, the Independence Eleven expressed through their football the Algerian people's aspirations for emancipation. Their game became very offensive, with a total occupation of the space on the pitch. The ball passed back and forth constantly between players, each displaying full freedom of improvisation, and the selection scored on average four goals per match. 'At the tactical level, there was one constant: attack as part of the spectacle', Mekhloufi recalls. 'With our different backgrounds, we had no trouble in integrating because we were living together, sharing our joys and our sorrows. These are perfect conditions for a team game'.[23]

In October 1959 the footballers travelled to South-East Asia for a tournament lasting several weeks that saw them play some ten matches in China and North Vietnam. Once the Algerians had defeated the various local teams, General Giáp of Vietnam, architect of the victory at Diên Biên Phu against the French coloniser, assured the FLN team: 'You succeeded in defeating us, so logically you will gain your independence'.[24] Rachid Mekhloufi later reflected: 'This odyssey opened up new horizons for me. It shaped me politically. We played the role of emissaries among the players, coaches, managers and athletes of Afro-Asian countries. At a human level, the experience was as exciting as it was painful'.[25]

While the adventures of the Algerian footballers schooled their political awareness, the players were also getting exhausted. Travel and accommodation conditions were often basic, and their weariness started to show as they played less talented teams. Tensions within the squad regularly broke out as the FLN general staff gradually lost interest in their flag bearers on the pitch. The last big outing for the Independence Eleven was set for March to June 1961, with 20 matches in Yugoslavia, Bulgaria, Romania, Hungary and Czechoslovakia. At the Red Star stadium in Belgrade on 29 March that year, Mohamed Allam burst into the locker room to warn the players that the French Ambassador was in the stands. With a knot in their stomachs and a rage for victory, the footballing Fellaghas recorded a 6–1 victory against a flamboyant Yugoslavian national team. Before the game was even over, the ambassador slipped away while the Belgrade fans chanted 'Free Algeria!' in solidarity with the independence struggle.

The Évian Accords between the French government and the Provisional Government of the Algerian Republic were signed on 18 March 1962, opening the way to independence for Algeria, declared on 5 July the same year. As for FIFA, it immediately recognised the Algerian national team. With the French clubs anxious to recover their star players as quickly as possible, the suspension against the rebels was lifted. Eight players from the FLN team, including Boubekeur, Mekhloufi and Zitouni, joined the new Algerian selection formed in 1963, while most of those who had previously played in the French championship returned to metropolitan France.[26] Before their departure, Ferhat Abbas, aware of the role of the Independence Eleven in the internationalisation of Algeria's national struggle for liberation, confided to them: 'You have brought the Revolution forward a decade'.[27]

11

When Palestine occupies the pitch

Football as a political weapon in the hands of the Palestinians

> We will be a people when the Palestinian remembers his flag only in stadiums [...]
>
> Mahmoud Darwich[1]

Jibril Rajoub is no longer picking up his phone. Broad-shouldered and with a balding head, the imposing 50-something moved heaven and earth over six months to organise the first official international football match in Palestine. Two days before the match, however, the Israeli authorities detained their prospective opponents – Jordan's national team – at the Allenby Bridge border crossing between Jordan and the West Bank.

While headlines were appearing in the local media about the 'historic event', as the day of 26 October 2008 approached Jibril Rajoub refused to give way to despair: 'I am a Palestinian fighter. Whatever the situation, I find ways round it and prepare a plan of action'.[2] He's not the kind of man to give in easily. At the age of 17, he was sentenced to life in prison for throwing a grenade at a bus full of Israeli soldiers. Freed after 16 years behind bars, he was deported to Lebanon after he participated in the first Intifada of 1988, and then joined the upper echelons of Fatah, becoming the head of National Security in the West Bank. His house was bombed by the Israelis, but he escaped unscathed before being elected head of the Palestinian Football Association in 2008.

Rajoub's forceps diplomacy paid off. On 26 October, the friendly match took place in the brand new Fayçal Husseini ground in

Al-Ram, a stone's throw from the separation wall. The match ended in a draw, one goal apiece, under the glaring portraits of Yasser Arafat, Mahmoud Abbas and King Abdullah II of Jordan. Three years later, it was the turn of the Palestinian women's team to play their first international fixture at home, also against Jordan. The result mattered little to the fans. 'A team coming to play on our land means recognition of the Palestinian state', according to player Murad Ismail Said. 'It is as important to Palestinian sport as it is to our cause'.[3] Welcoming the Jordanian women's team was far from insignificant. Many Jordanians have a parent or family member born in Palestine, and for periods the capital Amman hosted the Palestinian squad, long prevented from playing at home by the Israeli government. One of the most popular Jordanian clubs in the kingdom, Al-Weehdat SC, itself emerged from the Palestinian refugee camp of the same name. In the 1970s–1980s, the team was one of the few sporting embodiments of the Palestinian people, leading Yasser Arafat to say: 'On days when we no longer had a voice, Al-Weehdat was all that was left'.[4]

Restrictions on movement

The first Palestinian national team, the 'Lions of Canaan', was formed in 1946 before disappearing in the limbo of the Arab–Israeli War of 1947–1948. It was not until the Oslo Accords were signed in 1993 that the foundations of a Palestinian league were laid (1995)[5] and the Palestinian Football Association joined FIFA (1998). This meant that FIFA became the first international organisation to recognise Palestine as an independent state (it was not until November 2012 that it joined the UN as a 'non-Member Observer State'). Recognised by international bodies and represented by a national team ready to carry its cause beyond its borders, Palestine entered the football arena in the early 2000s. 'Through this team, we hope to achieve a political goal, to show that we deserve a state and that we have built our institutions, despite the occupation, the separation between Gaza and the West Bank and the war against us', acknowledged the team coach Ahmed al-Hassan in 2015.[6]

This means that football has become both a prolongation and a distorting mirror of Israeli–Palestinian tensions. The restrictions on movement imposed on all Palestinians by the Israeli authorities have repercussions on the footballers who need to move around according to the calendar of the Palestinian championship matches. Fixtures are regularly cancelled, with players or the referee held up at one of the check points that divide the Occupied Territories.

The same goes for the national squad, formed of footballers from the West Bank, Gaza, Israeli dual nationals or the diaspora. This geographical fragmentation means that the players need to travel a lot, a fact the Israeli state takes advantage of to restrict their freedom of movement. 'For the 2006 World Cup qualifiers, the team had to train in Ismailia, Egypt, and play its "home" games in the stadium in Doha, Qatar', recalls Palestinian coach Izzat Hamzeh. 'In order to make up for the absence of those players prevented from leaving by the Israelis, we even selected Chilean players of Palestinian heritage'.*[7] The final straw came in June 2004, when not a single Gazan footballer was permitted to play in Uzbekistan for 'security reasons'. Deprived of some of its best players, Palestine lost 3–0 against a weak Uzbek side, its dreams of playing in the World Cup vanishing with it.[8]

In October 2007, the Israeli authorities again refused to provide visas to 18 footballers and officials living in Gaza for a 2010 World Cup qualifying match against Singapore, obliging the Palestinians to forfeit the game. For the first leg, held in Doha, the team was missing four of its regulars, including its captain. 'It's a complex job', sighs Mahmoud Jamal, coach for the 2012 selection. 'I never know which players will be available [...] What I do is plan for three potential teams, and then we see which one of them we can put together'.[9]

The national team depended on the goodwill of the Israeli government. Tel-Aviv is well aware that the game is one of the keystones of Palestinian identity and a bond uniting Gaza, under the control of Hamas, and the West Bank, in the hands of Fatah. The Israeli authorities even hassled local football teams. In 2012, they temporarily shut down Silwan FC from East Jerusalem, accusing it of financial links to Hamas. 'We are sportspeople like any other, not terrorists', pro-

* The Palestinian community in Chile is 300,000 strong. In Santiago, the jersey of Palestino, a football club founded in the 1920s, still bears the colours of the Palestinian flag.

tested Nadim Barghouti, a young Silwan player. 'Palestinian players struggle to move around and after every match we know that we can be harassed or detained on our return by Israeli soldiers. Israeli players travel without problems or restrictions. It's discrimination. It's oppression'.[10]

The Israeli authorities are sometimes even more coercive. On 12 July 2012, the Gazan footballer Mahmoud Sarsak was freed after three years of administrative detention and over 90 days on hunger strike. He was arrested at the Erez crossing point to the Gaza Strip for representing 'a danger to Israel'.[11] The professional player was heading for the West Bank to train with the national team and to sign a contract with a Nablus club. The militant solidarity networks, together with prominent figures like Eric Cantona or the UN Special Rapporteur for Palestine, Richard Falk, mobilised to demand his release. In a statement released on 12 June, FIFA's otherwise apathetic president Sepp Blatter encouraged the Israel Football Association to intervene on behalf of Palestinian players 'held in apparent violation of their human rights and their personal integrity, apparently without right to trial'. Upon leaving prison, Mahmoud Sarsak declared: 'For a Palestinian, playing football has become an act of resistance in the eyes of Israel'.[12]

Finally, many footballers have fallen victim to Israeli military offensives. During Operation Cast Lead in January 2009, three Gazan players, including international Ayman Alkurd, were killed. On 10 November 2012, during the 'Pillar of Defence' offensive, the Israeli armed forces knowingly bombed a stadium in Gaza and killed four young footballers aged between 16 and 18, leading to expressions of outrage from some 60 European professional players. Two 19-year-old footballers, Ahmad Muhammed al-Qatar and Uday Caber, together with the Palestinian legend Ahed Zaqout, lost their lives in air raids during the 2014 Gaza War. Another episode of violence occurred on 31 January 2014 when Israeli soldiers in a control post opened fire without provocation on 19-year-old Jawhar Nasser Jawhar and 17-year-old Adam Abd al-Raouf Halabiya, two new recruits to Palestinian football returning home from training at the Fayçal Husseini ground. Having been shot several times in the feet and then savagely bitten by police dogs, the two young hopefuls will never play football again.[13]

The obstacle course

The repression of Palestinian sports dates back to the first appearance of football in the region, during the British mandate. First brought over by English missionaries and Jewish immigrants – HaRishon Le Zion-Yafo, the first Jewish football club in Palestine and forerunner to Maccabi Tel-Aviv, was established in 1906 – the game spread rapidly across the former Ottoman region through the 1920s. In July 1928, Yosef Yekutielo, a Jewish immigrant from Belarus, founded the Palestine Football Association, bringing together both Jewish and Arab clubs as well as those of the British colonial forces. Joining FIFA the following year, the association soon began to discriminate against Arab teams. By 1931, the administrative body was dominated by Jews. Hebrew was made the official language, the colours of Israel were incorporated into the logo,[14] and only the British national anthem and that of the Zionist movement (*Hatikvah*) were played at the start of matches.[15] 'From 1934, the Arab clubs no longer had a say in the functioning of the association, even though Arabs constituted more than three-quarters of the Palestinian population', says the Palestinian sports historian Issam Khalidi. 'Dominating sporting activities, marginalizing the Arabs and cultivating cooperation with the British were the key traits of Zionist involvement in sport'.[16]

This takeover of the Palestine Football Association by elites who favoured the creation of a 'national home for the Jewish people' reflected their desire to move forward with the elements needed for a future Jewish state.[17] Promotion of the Zionist project and the institutionalisation of sport in Mandatory Palestine were therefore closely linked. Yosef Yekutieli was also among the founders of the Maccabiah, the sports Olympiads organised locally since 1932 by Maccabi, a sports organisation that emerged from the civic and liberal wing of the Zionist movement. Meanwhile, the Histadrut, the powerful socialist union of Jewish workers in Israel, was developing a whole network of clubs in the territory through Hapoel, its sports association. The various clubs affiliated with Maccabi or Hapoel served both to unify new Jewish immigrants to Palestine through physical activities and to recruit athletes for military self-defence groups.

Together, Zionist sports bodies helped to represent Mandatory Palestine as a fundamentally Jewish state at regional and international levels. Just two years after its creation, the Palestine Football Association sent a team named 'Palestine – Land of Israel' and comprising six Jews and nine Brits to a tournament in Egypt.[18] Likewise, the association failed to include a single Arab player in its team for the qualifying rounds of the 1934 and 1938 World Cups.

However, the repeated attempts by the Zionist movement to marginalise or even exclude Arabs from sports ran up against growing Arab-Palestinian national sentiment. A few months before the Palestinian revolt of August 1929, the pro-independence newspaper *Filastin* reported frequent incidents between Jewish and Arab supporters around grounds, the latter angered by the Israeli flags and Zionist chants.[19] Two years later, in March 1931, a national Arab team was raised to play against the American University of Beirut,[20] and immediately afterwards the Arab Palestine Sports Federation (APSF) was created in response to the ethnic segregation of the Palestine Football Association. From then on, some players no longer hesitated to assert their Arab identity, like the Palestinian footballers who left the Salesian Club of Haifa in September 1934 to found a new club with a more assertive name: the Shabab al-Arab (Arab Youth). Football matches under the aegis of the APSF strengthened the links between the various Arab-Palestinian teams and neighbouring countries, consolidating their membership of a single Arab community. When Jaffa Orthodox Club played an Egyptian team, *Filastin* praised the Palestinian performance: 'The Egyptian University team came to Palestine and played Jewish teams, but no Arab team dared to compete with them, except the Jaffa Orthodox Club [...] We can proudly demonstrate that there are Arab teams in Palestine that play this game just as well as the British and Jewish teams'.[21]

Tired of British colonial oppression and the growing scale of Jewish immigration, a major Arab-Palestinian revolt shook the country in 1936. Young Palestinian footballers and other sportsmen were at the forefront of the uprisings, organising logistics and care for the injured during the anti-British demonstrations.[22] The uprising did not end until 1939 after a long series of strikes, sabotage, urban guerrilla warfare and targeted assassinations. The relentless reprisals by the British forces and the Notrim – a Jewish police force set up in 1936 – resulted in the arrest of 200 senior Arab-Palestinian leaders and the dismantling of Palestinian institutional structures, including the Arab Palestine Sports Federation, which ceased all activity in 1937.[23]

In the eyes of young Arab activists who aspired to independence, the Palestinian authorities had – unlike their Jewish equivalents – underestimated the role sport could play in building national identity and resistance to colonial oppression.[24] In May 1944, the Arab Palestine Sports Federation rose from the ashes, its new regulations stipulating that: 'members solely comprise Arab and non-Jewish clubs and institutions in Palestine'. Its leaders had clearly learned a lesson from the Jewish sports organisations, in forming an autonomous Arab-Palestinian sports body capable of asserting itself on the international stage.* From this point on, Palestinian urban elites would see football as a political weapon in their independence struggle. 'Football teaches us to obey the coach and the referee, to submit to rules and to justice', explained a *Filastin* editorial of 11 March 1945. 'Obedience is one of the most important qualities of a soldier on the battlefield, and war is not won without obedience'.[25] A few pages further on in the same issue, Muhammad Tahir Pasha, an Egyptian politician, promoter of Olympism and founder of the Mediterranean Games,** lamented: 'The East has neglected sports for too long. This is one of the reasons, if not the main reason, for its decline'. From this point on, the Palestinian authorities no longer hesitated to take part in major fixtures, and on 3 June 1945 the senior official Ahmed Hilmi Pasha attended the final of the first Arab-Palestinian football championship between the Islamic Sports Club of Jaffa and the Orthodox Club of Jerusalem. Before kick-off and as a gesture of pan-Arab solidarity, two minutes of silence were observed by the

* However, some Jewish footballers did play for teams affiliated to the Arab Palestinian Sports Federation.

** Olympic-style competition founded in 1951, bringing together athletes from some 20 Mediterranean countries every four years.

10,000 fans in honour of the victims of war in Syria and Lebanon.[26] By the following year the Palestinian sports federation comprised some 50 clubs throughout the country, and a national team, the Lions of Canaan. With the support of the Lebanese and Egyptian federations, it requested FIFA membership, which was rejected on the basis that a Palestinian federation had already been a member since 1929.

A contested pitch

However, the 1947–1948 civil war that led to the independence of Israel halted this trend in its tracks. No Arab sports institutions survived the conflict and the resulting organisational void benefited the Palestine Football Association, now known as the Israel Football Association (IFA). In the 1950s and 1960s, the wholesale confiscation of their lands and their dependence on the Israeli economy led to drastically reduced incomes for the Palestinian population.[27] Many young workers from Arab-Israeli towns asked the Histradout (the national trade union organisation) to set up sports infrastructure. Hapoel and Maccabi both worked hard to establish dozens of Arab clubs that were *de facto* affiliated to the IFA. For the authorities, supporting sports in Arab communities was a means of keeping Palestinian youth under surveillance, to prevent them from turning to nationalist militancy, and to prevent the creation of independent clubs that might become bases for activism.

However, the rise of the Palestinian resistance movement, marked by the creation of the Palestine Liberation Organisation (PLO) in May 1964 and the outbreak of armed struggle by Fatah in January 1965, loosened the state's hold over Arab football in Israel. In March 1964, a match between the Arab Hapoel Bnei Nazareth and the team from the neighbouring Jewish village, Hapoel Migdal HaEmek, ended in a generalised confrontation between players and fans of both sides. The next day, hundreds of Arab workers went on strike, refusing to go to work in Migdal HaEmek. Two months later, Hapoel Bnei Nazareth celebrated their entry into the second division in style, crushing the Jewish team Kiryat Shmona 8–0. Thousands of Palestinian fans invaded the pitch and paraded the Nazareth players on their shoulders through the city, celebrating a team that for over 15 years would be the leading Arab team in the Israeli championship.[28] That same year, the Israeli state dissolved a network of teams that was trying to establish an embryonic Arab championship between the towns of Tira, Qalansawe, Kafr Qassem and Taybeh. One member of this footballing adventure, writer and activist Sabri Jiryis, described the Israeli authorities' chokehold over Palestinian football: 'They are the only ones permitted to set up clubs in Arab villages, and only they are authorised to form football teams, and only once these are clearly established can we decide how to organise games and with who'.[29]

In the decades following the June 1967 war and the subsequent military occupation of Palestinian territories, the Israeli football championship became both a tool of integration for young, marginalised Israeli Arabs and a space for affirmation of Arab identity. Numerous players were elevated to the rank of heroes in Palestinian popular culture, such as Rifaat Turk, the first Israeli Arab player selected for the national team in 1976,* or Najwan Ghrayeb, who scored one of the two winning goals in a match against an outstanding Argentinian team on 15 April 1998. 'For Israeli Arabs, football was a contested pitch between two concurrent tendencies: an opportunity for integration into Israeli Jewish society and acceptance by the Jewish majority, or a form of political protest and national pride', according to sociologist Tamir Sorek.[30] With the multiplication of Arab teams playing in the Israeli championship – eight in 1976–1977 versus almost 40 in 2000–2001[31] – in May 2004 an Arab team, Bnei Sakhnin FC, won the Israel State Cup for the first time, provisionally becoming a symbol of reconciliation between Jews and Arabs in Israel.

In occupied Palestine, although makeshift national squads represented the nation in sporadic fashion – notably at the 1953 Pan-Arab Games in Alexandria and the 1965 Pan-Arab Games in Cairo – it was thanks to international solidarity that Palestinian football truly emerged from Israeli oversight. While the Palestinian Football Association was founded in exile in 1962, the PLO's Youth and Sports

* Hassan Boustouni, who played for Maccabi Haifa from 1963, was the first Arab player in the Israeli professional league.

Council established relations with European sports federations, notably in France via the Fédération sportive et gymnique du travail (FSGT) [see Chapter 5]. In May 1982, under the slogan 'Recognition and solidarity with Palestinian sportsmen and women', several matches were organised between Palestinian and French teams in Vigneux, Arcueil and Le Havre. 'For us, it was an opportunity to publicise the situation of Palestinian sportsmen and women, to promote the Palestinian cause through non-violent struggle', recalls Anouar Abou Eisheh, then president of the Association of Palestinian Students in France. The arrival of the Palestinian team also meant the Palestinian flag was officially raised for the first time in French stadiums.[32] Three years later, in July 1985, an FSGT football team toured the Occupied Territories.

It was not until 8 October 1993, just three weeks after the Oslo Accords were signed, that the Palestinian national team was able to play a match on its own soil. At that time, peace seemed within reach, and under the aegis of the PLO, a Palestinian squad welcomed France's Variété Club to Jericho, a team formed of past stars like Michel Platini, Serge Blanco and Yannick Noah. In a stadium crammed to the gills – 20,000 spectators occupied stands built for 5,000[33] – and on a ravaged pitch, the Palestinian players put on a rather clumsy show before dozens of foreign TV cameras. The match was less of a sporting than a media spectacle, but the winning goal put home by Mahmoud Jerad that day underscored more than ever the words of Eric Hobsbawm: 'The imagined community of millions seems more real as a team of eleven named people'.[34]

Anti-apartheid red card

With the official recognition of the Palestinian Football Association in 1998, the establishment of a Palestinian league and the construction of a dozen stadiums with financial assistance from FIFA, many Israeli Arab players, fed up with the racism endemic to the Israeli league, were attracted to professional clubs in the West Bank. Rifaat Turk, the first Arab player in the Israeli national team, still remembers the warnings of his coach Ze'ev Segal after he joined Hapoel Tel-Aviv:

> An important rule. We live in a racist country. They will curse you, they will curse your mother and your sister. They will spit on you. They will try to cut you off. You'll have to be pretty smart about it and know how to handle it well. You can't respond to provocation. You have to stay focused. If you are smart, then you will survive.[35]

Indeed, fans of some Israeli football clubs are notorious for their openly racist and Islamophobic chants and slogans. Fans of Beitar Jerusalem, one of the most popular and successful teams in the country, and in particular members of its ultras group, 'La Familia', are regularly singled out for their physical violence against Muslims and for the slogans they chant in the stands ('Death to the Arabs', 'May your village burn', etc.).[36] The club, which was founded in 1936 during the first Palestinian uprisings by Betar – an extreme right-wing Zionist youth movement – has nevertheless enjoyed the benevolence of the Israeli sports authorities.

This anti-Arab racism and the restrictions placed on Palestinian players prompted the Palestinian Football Association to file a motion with FIFA in 2015 calling for the exclusion of the Israeli association from the international body as long as the Jewish state continued to impede their freedom of movement.* The FIFA president's response was merely to propose a 'peace match' between Israel and Palestine, but Palestinian Football Association President Jibril Rajoub fulminated, stating the obvious: 'All we are asking for is respect for our fundamental rights'.[37] Many activists in the BDS (Boycott, Divestment, Sanctions) movement, which seeks to put pressure on the State of Israel to change its policy towards Palestinians, decided to support the motion brought by Jibril Rajoub. But the goal is ambitious: to be accepted, the motion must receive three-quarters of the votes of the 209 voting FIFA members.

Initiated in 2005 by Palestinian civil organisations, the international BDS coalition was inspired by the political struggles against apartheid in South Africa from the 1960s to the 1980s and pro-

* One year after the 1973 Arab–Israeli war and under pressure from the belligerent Arab countries, the Israel Football Association was excluded from the Asian Football Confederation. It joined UEFA, the European federation, in 1994.

motes a boycott – particularly of sports – as an additional means of international pressure to denounce the Israeli occupation.[38] A BDS campaign called 'Red Card Israeli Racism' focused specifically on football: 'The football establishment should uphold the highest values of anti-racism', said Geoff Lee, a British activist involved in the campaign, arguing that the Israeli state should be boycotted 'until it respects the human rights of all Palestinians and complies with international law'.[39]

Before the vote on the motion, scheduled for 29 May 2015 at the FIFA Congress in Zurich, the international solidarity movement with the Palestinian Football Association intensified. On 15 May *The Guardian* published an article signed by, among others, linguist Noam Chomsky, writer John Berger and filmmaker Ken Loach. Recalling that FIFA had suspended South Africa for 30 years and Yugoslavia between 1992 and 1994, it accused the Israel Football Association of complicity with the 'murderous Israeli regime'.[40] On the eve of the congress, the *New York Times* published a plea by the Gazan player Iyad Abou Gharqoud, describing both the travel restrictions and the Israeli association's passivity in the face of the anti-Arab excesses of Beitar Jerusalem supporters.[41] In the Israeli press, Gershon Baskin, a peace activist and former Israeli negotiator with Hamas, emphasised:

> Whether or not the Palestinians win this vote is secondary, because what we are witnessing is the first diplomatic effort by the Palestinians to impose sanctions on Israel. This is not really about football or the freedom of movement of footballers [but about] the continued occupation and Israel's refusal to recognize Palestinians' right to self-determination in an independent state next to their own.[42]

Two weeks before the fateful ballot, the Israeli daily *Haaretz* revealed that Israel had exerted intense diplomatic pressure on the sports ministries and heads of football leagues in some 100 countries, asserting that many Palestinian professional footballers were involved in terrorist activities.[43] As a result of these intimidations and behind-the-scenes dealings under the auspices of FIFA, the Palestinian Football Association gave up the idea of putting Israel's suspension to the vote, in exchange for the formation of a monitoring committee to ensure the free movement of Palestinian players. At the congress, Ofer Eini, the president of the Israeli Football Association, was in a celebratory mood: 'Let's leave politics to the politicians while we play football as best we can'.[44]

Just three months later, the final of the Palestine Cup was in the news because the Israeli authorities refused permission to travel for four players from Gaza's Chajaya team, which was to play Ahli al-Khaleel of Hebron in the West Bank. In July 2016, it was the turn of six players and the coach of the Shabab Khan Younis team to be confined to Gaza during the final of the Palestinian Cup. Meanwhile, the administrative detentions of footballers resumed in earnest: two players from Al-Samou Youth FC in Hebron, Sami Fadil al-Daour and Mohamed Abu Khwais, were 'preventively' imprisoned in Ashkelon in March that year.

Despite these challenges, FIFA became a political arena for the Palestinians. In late 2016, the Palestinian Football Association, supported by some 60 MEPs, approached the international body with complaints about six clubs based in Israeli settlements in the West Bank and affiliated to the Israel Football Association. The Palestinian authorities asked why the clubs in these settlements were members of the Israeli association, when these settlements were illegal under international law. The Palestinians also pointed out that FIFA regulations prohibit a national association from hosting a club from a foreign territory. 'By allowing the IFA to organise matches inside settlements, FIFA is engaging in a commercial activity that supports Israeli settlements, an activity that is contrary to its human rights commitments', a Human Rights Watch report denounced in September 2016. 'Settlement clubs provide part-time jobs and recreational services to settlers, making the settlement more sustainable, and perpetuating a system that is based on serious human rights violations'.[45] In the NGO's view, these six clubs were blatantly ignoring international law while legitimising, with FIFA's blessing, the illegal occupation of the Palestinian territories. Among many other examples, Human Rights Watch reported that the club of the Giv'at Ze'ev settlement organised matches under the auspices of the IFA at an approved ground that had been expropriated from two Palestinian families in the neighbouring Arab community of Beitunia, 'agricultural land to which they have been denied access since the construction of the village in 1977'.[46]

Meanwhile, the UN Security Council condemned the Israeli colonisation of the Occupied Territories and demanded that it 'immediately and completely cease' these illegal settlement activities. This amounted to greater international pressure on FIFA to put an end to these violations of international law. As Sari Bashi of Human Rights Watch puts it, 'the resolution clearly stipulates that the settlements have no legal validity. [FIFA must] establish a distinction between Israel and the Occupied Territories'.[47]

Gazan football from the sidelines

While the Palestinian authorities were putting pressure on FIFA, a series of initiatives were launched in solidarity with the players. In 2015, Sevilla FC rejected a sponsorship deal worth US$5.7 million for advertising on its jerseys promoting Israeli tourism. Meanwhile, Hapoel Katamon Jerusalem, the Israeli club set up by militant supporters in 2007, launched its 'Equal Team' programme to promote mixed football squads including young players from its own training centre and the Beit Safafa football academy in the Palestinian suburbs of Jerusalem.

Before kick-off at the Wales–Israel qualifying match for Euro 2016 on 6 September 2015, thousands of supporters showed their support for the Palestinian people in Cardiff. Members of the Easton Cowgirls, an amateur women's team from Bristol that had played a series of matches in the West Bank, were at the demonstration. 'What we saw really affected us, how they are restricted in their movements, the daily oppression they are subjected to', said Isabel O'Hagan, the team's midfielder. 'We promised when we came back we'd share their story'.[48]

Finally, following a Champions League qualifying match in August 2016 between Celtic and Israeli club Hapoel Be'er-Sheva, members of the Green Brigade, one of Celtic's main ultras groups, were heavily fined by UEFA for waving dozens of Palestinian flags in the stands, which the European body considered 'a political message unrelated to the sporting event'. The Green Brigade had earlier called on Facebook for Celtic fans to bring out the flags to 'show their opposition to Israeli apartheid, colonialism and the countless massacres suffered by the Palestinian people'.[49] To protest this sanction, the Scottish club's ultras launched the hashtag #MatchTheFineForPalestine on social networks, raising tens of thousands of pounds for the organisation Medical Aid Palestine and for the Lajee Centre, a Palestinian cultural centre for the children of a refugee camp in Bethlehem.

This football-based solidarity also resonates with the emergence of new forms of expression combining political protest and football within Palestinian society. As a true act of resistance to the restrictions on their freedom of movement, the Gazans organised their own World Cup during the 2010 World Cup in South Africa, the Gaza World Cup, under the slogan: 'If you can't go to South Africa, the World Cup will come to you'. For a fortnight, 16 teams from the Gaza Strip – including 14 professional clubs – were renamed 'England', 'Brazil', 'Italy' and so on, and participated in the World Cup by proxy. The final was played on 15 May between 'France' and 'Jordan' in Gaza's Yarmouk stadium, broadcast live on Al-Jazeera, and the winners received a trophy made by local craftsmen from metal recovered from buildings bombed by the Israeli army. 'We wanted to draw the world's attention to our isolation and show that there is life in Gaza', says Tamer Qarmout, one of the event's organisers. 'The young people here should have the right to leave, travel and take part in cultural and sporting events like anyone else'.[50]

Caught between the economic blockade imposed by Israel and Egypt on the one hand, and the religious conservatism of Hamas and the corruption of the Palestinian Authority on the other, football remains a rare collective escape for Gazans. Surprising as it may seem, the most popular club among them does not play in the Palestinian league but is none other than FC Barcelona. The footballing standard-bearer of the Catalan independence cause [see Chapter 6] has a particular resonance for the Palestinian population.[51] 'We identify with the Catalans whose fight against the great power of Madrid reminds us of our fight against Israel', a young Palestinian

Barça supporter explained in 2012.[52] 'FC Barcelona arguably brings more joy to the Palestinians than any other institution in the world', adds Jon Donnison, BBC correspondent in Gaza and the West Bank.

> Whenever the Catalans play, you'll be hard-pressed to get a table in the bars of Ramallah and the cafés of Gaza City. On match days, a myriad of traders sell Barça's blue and garnet jerseys on the sly at Qalandia, the always-congested Israeli military checkpoint that separates Ramallah from East Jerusalem.[53]

During a FC Barcelona–Real Madrid *clásico* on 7 October 2012, the Catalan team announced that it had accepted a request to be invited to the stands from Gilad Shalit, a former Israeli soldier captured and held by Hamas for more than five years. This gesture was not to the liking of Gaza's football clubs which, in an open letter to FC Barcelona, declared:

> The Palestinians of Gaza support Barcelona more than any other club [...] As shown by the effective boycott of sports teams from the South African apartheid regime, sport and politics cannot be separated. We ask you not to show solidarity with the army that oppresses, imprisons and kills Palestinian sportsmen and women in Palestine.[54]

In response to this rebellion, Barça decided to also invite Jibril Rajoub, the indomitable president of the Palestinian Football Association, as well as Mahmoud Sarsak, the Gazan footballer released four months earlier after three years of administrative detention in Israel. However, the latter declined the invitation, affirming, as a sign of respect for the Palestinian prisoners, that he did not want to 'play at symmetry between the "coloniser and the colonised"'.[55] On the day of the match, former prisoners wearing FC Barcelona and Real Madrid jerseys decided to kick a ball around a patch of wasteland in Gaza to protest against the presence of Gilad Shalit in the stands. 'Football is a sport that carries a message of freedom and love, but not when a soldier is invited because it puts the victim and his executioner on an equal footing', Yasser Saleh, who spent 17 years in Israeli jails, told the press.[56]

Recalling that the negotiations to free Gilad Shalit had led to the release of over a thousand Palestinian prisoners, Hamas urged Palestinians not to watch the match, before awkwardly announcing that it would censor future television broadcasts of FC Barcelona matches. This declaration, which *de facto* expected Palestinians to renounce their fervour for the Catalan club, immediately rebounded in their faces. In a society locked down by the Islamic organisation and the Israeli security forces, 'watching the match' represented a rare opportunity to defy the Gazan authorities and to voice widespread discontent with a disastrous economic situation and the stalled Israel–Palestine talks. On the Sunday evening of 7 October 2012, Gaza's cafés were packed with supporters in blue and garnet in front of television sets, just like usual. Regardless of the drawn match, children wearing counterfeit Barça jerseys ran up and down the maze of alleys in the Palestinian enclave, while swarms of honking cars were fuller than ever with passengers waving their Palestinian flags to the sky. That evening there was football, and neither the soldiers at the Israeli checkpoints nor the Palestinian caciques could take it away from the Gazans.

12

Dribbling the ball, a decolonial art

Afro-Brazilian identities and indigenous resistance in football

In a single transport the contrite crowd
In an act of death rises up and cries
in unison their song of hope.
Garrincha, the angel, listens and answers: GOOOOOL!
It's pure image: a G that kicks an O
Into the goal, an L.
It's pure dance!

Vinícius de Moraes
'O Anjo das Pernas Tortas'

Greetings and a football that, like in dreams, flies very high.

Subcomandante Marcos, letter to Eduardo Galeano, July 1996

'Those of us who have a certain position in society are obliged to play with workers, with drivers [...] Playing this sport is becoming an agony, a sacrifice, never a pastime'.[1] This complaint was made by the footballers of Rio de Janeiro to the review *Sports* in 1915. First introduced in 1894 and rapidly adopted as a leisure activity by the urban bourgeoisie of São Paulo and later Rio de Janeiro, football was a reflection of Brazilian society: elitist and racist. Slavery had only been officially abolished in the country in 1888, and black, mixed-race and indigenous people were initially excluded from championships – as were less well-off whites. The amateur character of sports practice preached by the Anglophile Brazilian elites was a pretext for cultivating bourgeois segregation. Each match was punctuated by festivities typical of the English way of life. Singing British songs, drinking whisky and attending matches in top hats or lace dresses were all ostentatious marks of social distinction that relegated the few Brazilian fans from the lower classes who ventured into the grounds.[2]

Far from the snobbish stands of Brazil's white aristocracy, a different kind of football was developing in parallel, one that was socially and racially mixed. In Campinas, a small working-class town in the state of São Paulo, the Ponte Preta club was founded in August 1900 by non-white railway workers. Every time they played, spectators greeted them with monkey calls, but Ponte Preta dealt with the racial stigma by adopting a primate as its mascot, together with the nickname 'Os Macacas'. Meanwhile, in the suburbs of Rio in 1907 the club Bangu AC, which grew out of the local textile factory, also opened its doors to black workers – and was immediately excluded from the Carioca championship. Rio's big football clubs were overtly racist, banning not only black players but spectators too. In 1914, when the first mixed-race footballer, Carlos Alberto, joined Fluminense FC, he bleached his skin with rice powder before taking to the pitch.[3]

'Something like dancing'

The gradual appearance of Brazilians of mixed African heritage in football teams was a source of social and racial tension.[4] In 1919 the national squad scored its first international win at the South American Football Championship – forerunner of the Copa América. Yet the man who forged the Brazilian victory and highest goalscorer was a source of embarrassment for the country's elites. The centre-forward Arthur Friedenreich was the son of a rich German businessman from São Paulo and a black-skinned Brazilian washerwoman. Despite his higher social status, the player, who tried to conceal his Afro-Brazilian roots by straightening his kinky hair, felt the referees' racism on the pitch. During play, the whistle never blew for fouls against him, forcing Friedenreich to develop subtle feints with his body to dodge his opponents' violent charges when he pulled away with the ball. 'This is how the dribble was born in Brazil', says journalist and writer Olivier Guez.

> As a ruse and survival technique used by the first players of colour, dribbling avoided contact with the white defenders. The black player who winds and sways escapes a beating, both on the pitch and from the spectators at the end of the game; no one can catch him; he dribbles to save his skin.[5]

With this technical skill, Friedenreich laid the foundations for a Brazilian football distinct from its British alter ego, while performing the condition of the downtrodden who, simply in order to exist, must dodge the violence of those who tread on them.

The following year, once again against the backdrop of the South American Championship, the mixed-race players in the Seleção were subjected to racist insults from Argentine spectators, while the Uruguayan press caricatured them as monkeys or referred to them as 'macaquitos'. These events pushed the Brazilian president, Epitácio Pessoa, to issue in 1921 a 'whiteness decree' to ensure that the national team would henceforth only accept 'the best of our footballing elite, the sons of our best families, the lightest skins and the straightest hair'.[6]

In 1923, the Carioca championship was won by CR Vasco da Gama, to widespread astonishment. Founded by Portuguese immigrants, the club proclaimed itself to be democratic and popular, with a black, white and red jersey that represented the African, European and Amerindian identities of Brazil. The team it fielded was composed of white drivers and black workers. A real affront to the four big clubs of Rio, Fluminense, Flamengo, América and Botafogo, which, together with the whiteness of their players, tried unsuccessfully to prohibit players who were illiterate or day labourers.

As if to challenge these attempts at racial and social discrimination, Vasco da Gama carried off the Rio championship for the second time in a row in 1924. In affirming its diversity, the club helped break down the barriers of segregation. At the first World Cup of 1930, played in neighbouring Uruguay, the Seleção fielded Fausto, a black midfielder who was spotted by Bangu AC and then recruited by Vasco da Gama. The technical prowess of the Afro-Brazilian footballer captivated international sports writers, who nicknamed him the 'Black Wonder'. Two years later, at the Copa Rio Blanco, a mixed-race Seleção beat the world champions Uruguay 2–1 on their own turf. The Brazilian novelist José Lins do Rego wrote: 'The men who won in Montevideo are a portrait of our social democracy, where Paulinho, the son of a good family, joined forces with the black Leônidas, the mulatto Oscarino and the white Martim. Everything was done in the Brazilian style'.[7]

It would take the arrival of professional football to Brazil in 1933, however, for the first signs of real democratisation to reach the sport. The competition between the big São Paulo and Rio clubs for the best players effectively levelled the playing field when it came to racial or social status. In 1936 Flamengo, previously so quick to denounce the Afro-Brazilian background of Vasco da Gama players, hired Fausto, Leônidas da Silva and Domingos da Guia, three of the top non-white players of the period and who had long been acclaimed by the working classes. Clubs no longer hesitated to recruit players from the lower segments of society, helping to bring new audiences to the stands from the poor districts of the country's big cities. The first fan associations – the *torcidas organizadas* – flourished, with elements of Afro-Brazilian culture bringing the Carnival to the stadiums with flares, firecrackers, samba orchestras, *tamborims*, *caixas* and other percussion instruments.[8] Brazilian football was 'tropicalised' in the stands as well as on the pitch, giving rise, in the words of Uruguayan writer Eduardo Galeano, to a football 'made of hip feints, undulations of the torso and legs in flight, all of which came from capoeira, the warrior dance of black slaves, and from the joyful dances of the big-city slums'.[9]

While it is true that professional football offered mixed-race, black or indigenous Brazilians an unprecedented social lift and official recognition as full citizens for the first time,[10] these footballers of modest origins who were paid to play the game continued to be seen as outsiders due to Brazil's deeply rooted racial prejudices. When he refused to sign up for the renowned club América, Leônidas da Silva, aged just 18, was attacked by a virulently racist press campaign and accused of stealing a necklace from a white woman from the Carioca bourgeoisie.

The 1938 World Cup in France was Brazil's first chance to emerge from the shadow of the prestigious Argentina and Uruguay teams. The sole South American representative that year (Uruguay and Argentina having withdrawn due to the cost of the Atlantic passage), the Seleção took third place before spectators fascinated by their playing style. The journalist and former professional footballer Lucien Gamblin described his experience of watching them train: 'They never stopped laughing, juggling the ball, dribbling endlessly and making complicated passes to get the ball in front of the goal [...] Brazilian players are perfect artists with the ball, controlling it with great ease'.[11] A striking antithesis to the 'scientific' and 'rigorous' style of European football, the spectacle they offered nevertheless displeased some sporting commentators like Maurice Pefferkorn: 'The public exclaim and applaud in response to their repeated short passes, which sometimes leave their adversaries embarrassed. But at bottom it is inefficient and unproductive play'.[12] As for the official press of Mussolini's Italy, it celebrated the Brazilian defeat in frankly absurd terms: 'We salute the triumph of Italic intelligence over the brute force of the Negroes'.[13]

Despite this second consecutive victory of fascist Italy in the World Cup, the two universally recognised stars of the tournament were Brazilian.[14] The centre-forward Leônidas da Silva, alias the 'Black Diamond', popularised the 'bicycle kick'– an athletic move to kick the ball overhead in mid-air – in the host country's football grounds, and was crowned top scorer in the Cup with seven goals. The mixed-race defender Domingos da Guia, meanwhile, won fans' hearts with his *domingadas*, which saw him take the ball out of the defensive area by carefully dribbling past his opponents.[15] In the words of journalist Gabriel Hanot in *France Football*, 'He doesn't attack, doesn't break, doesn't halt brutally, nor even with force; he doesn't strike; he doesn't clear: he intercepts, diverts, subtly deflects, and escapes, without hitting or rushing the ball. Domingos is a footballer of finesse, flexibility and astuteness'.[16]

The racial mix of the 1938 Seleção illustrated the success of football's democratisation in that country. The Brazilian style of play, meanwhile, became a vector of popular collective identity, an expression on the pitch of a mixed kind of football, both artistic and creative, wholly emancipated from its English and aristocratic origins.[17] In the words of Gilberto Freyre, a leading Brazilian intellectual of the period:

> Our way of playing contrasted with the European style thanks to a combination of characteristics: surprise, cunning, skill, enthusiasm and – I would say – spontaneity and individual talent, which expresses our mixed background. There is something of dance and capoeira in Brazilian football that softens and rounds out this game invented by the British, played so sharply and angularly by the Europeans – all of this seems to express [...] the flamboyant and ingenious mixed character that can be detected today in all things Brazilian.[18]

Under the authoritarian and populist regime of Getúlio Vargas, which ruled from 1937–1945, football became a mass culture that cemented the nation's different social and racial components. As part of a vast programme of industrialisation and urbanisation, the state pursued a stadium-building policy. President Vargas personally opened the 70,000-capacity Pacaembú stadium in São Paulo in April 1940. Ten years later, timed to host the 1950 FIFA World Cup, the giant 180,000-seat Maracanã stadium opened in Rio de Janeiro, a world record for size at the time. A material expression of Brazil's claim to be a modern, industrial nation, the concrete vessel was a national monument, built with terraces – *gerais* – to ensure even the poorest could attend matches standing.

The Brazilian team was by far the favourite at that World Cup, and the Maracanã was seen by all as the setting for the assured victory, symbol of the country's unity. For the first and only time in the history of the Cup, the winner was determined by a mini-tournament between the four teams that won their respective groups. Thus, Brazil, Spain, Sweden and Uruguay played each other over a series of six matches. To the delight of Brazilian fans, the Seleção first crushed the Swedes 7–1, before going on to defeat Spain 6–1. The atmosphere was euphoric. 'In the stands, tightly-packed spectators overflowed into the surrounding areas despite the interventions of the police', reported a French journalist at the time. 'Planes flew over the stadium. An infernal din, to which music and 60 loudspeakers contributed, made it impossible to concentrate. There were 155,000 spectators, the largest crowd ever massed in such a small space'.[19]

The third match, Brazil–Uruguay, was the one that was to crown the Seleção world champions. It seemed to be a formality, as the Brazilians were already ahead and only needed a draw to carry the Cup. The evening before the game, headlines in local papers already reported proudly on the future winners, the players were each given a gold watch engraved with the words 'For the World Champions', and the finishing touches were confidently being put to the upcoming celebrations.[20] On 16 July 1950, in a feverish Maracanã, the mayor of Rio opened the final match with these words for the team: 'You, the players who in less than two hours will be hailed as champions by millions of compatriots! [...] You, who I already salute as victors!'[21] The kick-off whistle blew in front of a colourful and excited crowd, and although the Seleção only managed to open the scoring in the second half, the mood was still celebratory when Uruguay equalised 20 minutes later.

The crowd was left stupefied and commentators speechless when Uruguayan right-winger Alcides Ghiggia scored a surprise second goal ten minutes from full time. A great wave of dread rolled around the stands at the end of the game and the Uruguayan players did not seem to believe in their victory themselves. After an interminable silence, the Brazilian spectators burst into tears, while others remained immobile, as if stunned by a violent blow. Confusion reigned in the stadium and the winners' ceremony was aborted. FIFA president Jules Rimet hastily handed the trophy to the Uruguayan captain Obdulio Varela. The grounds had become a tomb.

The defeat was experienced in Brazil as a national tragedy, a historic trauma that became known as the *Maracanaço*, the 'shock of Maracanã'. The failure of the Seleção reflected the fiasco of an entire nation that sought to construct a collective, multi-racial identity through football. Considered the main culprit of this humiliation, the black keeper Barbosa was ostracised, accused of bringing bad luck and condemned to live as an outcast in his own country.* The *Maracanaço* immediately aggravated existing racist prejudices in Brazilian football. Accused of being insufficiently aggressive on the pitch, the black players were further suspected of being unable to withstand the mental pressure of a World Cup. In 1956, an official report by the Brazilian Football Confederation stated that 'Negro players lose a great deal of their potential in world competitions'.[22] For the proponents of a European-style game, the intricacies of *futebol arte* had to end and the national team had to be 'whitened' by discarding the Afro-Brazilian footballers more inclined – according to racist cliché – to spectacular technical displays than to strategic rigour.

Dribbler Social Club

The arrival in power of President Juscelino Kubitschek, democratically elected under the slogan '50 years of progress in 5 years', marked Brazil's entry into an era of prosperity. The country enjoyed an economic and urban boom that had repercussions on football. The mass rural exodus made the impoverished districts of the great metropolises a hotbed of young talent, while the big clubs, fuelled by the flow of money from economic development, increased their recruitment efforts.[23] In 1958, the Brazilian Football Confederation elected João Havelange as its head: the wealthy owner of Brazil's leading transport company and a businessman specialising in financial speculation, arms sales and life insurance – who later became FIFA president from 1974–1998 – he sought to secure the financial and material means for his nation to win the 1958 World Cup in Sweden.

The 28 players who flew to Scandinavia that summer formed a team of both veterans, such as Nilson Santos, who had witnessed the *Maracanaço* from the subs' bench, and players at the peak of their sporting glory, such as the Afro-Brazilian midfielder Didi. But it was two young recruits selected by coach Vincente Feola, Garrincha and Pelé, who attracted fans' greatest curiosity.

* In 1993, Barbosa was refused entry to a Brazilian national team training session, prompting him to declare: 'In Brazil, the maximum sentence is 30 years, but I have been paying for 43 years for a crime I did not commit'. It wasn't until the 2006 World Cup that another black goalkeeper, Nélson 'Dida' de Jesus Silva, joined the Seleção.

Born with a congenital anomaly – his legs, one of which was 6 centimetres longer than the other, bowed outwards – Garrincha (real name Manoel Francisco dos Santos) was the fifth child in a poor Amerindian family from the working-class city of Pau Grande. His childhood was free and wild, making him both reserved and joyful and earning him his nickname, after the small wren-like bird with an elegant song that dies as soon as it is caged. Illiterate, he was employed very young as a textile worker, then recruited for the factory team at the age of 15. His physical deformity made his dribbling unpredictable and his feints devastating. Spotted by the great Carioca club Botafogo, at 19 years old he became an indispensable right winger for his team. His modest origins, his lack of affectation and his dribbling skills quickly made him a popular idol with whom fans could easily identify.

Meanwhile, Edson Arantes do Nascimento, alias Pelé, became the new young prodigy of São Paulo's Santos FC at the age of just 17. Son of an Afro-Brazilian player who had to give up his career following repeated injury, the legend tells that, seeing his father crying on the day of the *Maracanaço*, he swore to him that he would win the World Cup in his honour.[24] Far from a mere game, for Pelé football was a profession, a status that allowed him to escape the social and racial chains of Brazilian society. He spent all his free time training intensively to become an all-round athlete.

Young, talented, inventive: Garrincha and Pelé reflected a Brazil with a promising future. For the managers, however, they remained non-white players first. Still traumatised by the 1950 defeat and gripped by debate over the whiteness of its players, the federation sought to discipline the Seleção and keep a strict watch over their physical and psychological condition. The footballers regularly visited medical centres, revealing their malnutrition and poor general health.[25] Upon arrival in Sweden, the players were confined to their hotels. Their diet, movements, family life and sex life were closely monitored, and the female hotel staff were hastily replaced by men.[26] The psychologist João Carvalhaes, called in by the technical committee to select the players most mentally fit to compete, judged Pelé 'unquestionably child-like'. He added: 'He lacks the necessary fighting spirit, and doesn't have the sense of responsibility that is essential for any team game'.[27] Garrincha, meanwhile, was judged to have a lower-than-average IQ and not suited to high-pressure games because of his lack of aggression.

These sordidly racist views kept Vincente Feola from fielding the two players in the first two games, against Austria and England. Yet in light of the nil–nil draw against the latter, the coach decided to introduce Pelé and Garrincha to the Swedish turf as an offensive duo to combat the formidable USSR team. From that moment on, the Seleção was transformed into a winning machine. Garrincha tortured the Soviet defender Boris Kouznetsov with his twisting dribbles, to the great entertainment of spectators, while Pelé scored the winning goal in the quarter-finals against Wales, before chalking up a hattrick in the semis against France.

Inventor of the *folha seca* ('dry leaf'), a swerving shot that applies topspin to the ball to create a slight boomerang effect, Didi, together with Pelé and Garrincha, developed the artistic, aerial game that became known as the *jogo bonito* – the beautiful game – as spectacular and attacking as it was a creative riposte to the austere European style of play. Having reached the final, the Brazilians were to play the Swedes on 29 June at the Råsunda Stadion on the outskirts of Stockholm. International media played up the symbolic character of the match: 'The Swedes are large, angular, pale, homogenously blond. The Brazilians are a mixture – but for the most part smaller, rounder, darker [...] The Old World against the New World, advanced industrialisation against delayed development, consensual democracy against febrile populism'.[28]

The Scandinavians opened the scoring in the fourth minute, but Vavá swiftly put home two goals, followed by Pelé who scored in the 55th minute with a spectacular sombrero* over the last Swedish defender. Garrincha wowed the crowd with his dazzling tackles that literally knocked the Nordic giants off their feet. At full time the Brazilians had won 5–2. Amazed by their flair, Sigge Parling, the defender marking Pelé, said: 'By the fifth goal, I wanted to applaud him myself'.[29] 'They showed football as a different conception; they

* Shot made by passing the ball over the head of an opponent while dribbling.

killed the white skidding ball as if it were a lump of cotton wool', wrote a British journalist for the *Times*. '[...] Didi, floating about mysteriously in midfield, was always the master link, the dynamo setting his attacks in motion; and besides Didi with Vavá and Pelé a piercing double central thrust, they had one man above all the others, to turn pumpkins into coaches and mice into men – Garrincha'.[30]

Before ascending the podium, the players offered the match ball to their most faithful supporter, Américo, the team's black masseur. A few days later, Didi was voted best player of the 1958 World Cup. The Seleção's international triumph overcame the curse of the *Maracanaço* and showed all Brazilians that young, non-white players could not only 'withstand the pressure' of a high-profile match but also exalt the racial diversity of an entire people. For the playwright Nelson Rodrigues, this sporting consecration symbolised the advent of Afro-Brazilian pride:

> With the 1958 victory, Brazilians even underwent physical changes. I remember right after the Brazil-Sweden match, seeing a petite, black-skinned woman. A typical favela resident. But she was transformed by the win. She marched along the pavement with the assurance of a Joan of Arc. The same went for the black men who – attractive, dazzling, splendid – recalled the fabled princes of Ethiopia.[31]

The Brazilian triumph over the Old World endorsed the *jogo bonito* as a collective form of expression with a decolonial dimension. The *futebol arte* became a kind of body language in its own right, one that established cultural mixing as a fundamental feature of Brazilian identity.[32] This inventive hijacking of a sporting practice symbolising European cultural hegemony also rehabilitated a popular mythical figure: the *malandro*. A hedonistic and seductive ruffian who flouts the established order, the *malandro* is embodied in the stadiums by a Didi or a Garrincha with devastating footwork – the *ginga*, a word that refers both to a favela tough's swinging gait, and a capoeira move. 'A classic figure in minority and oppressed cultures, half-crook, half-dandy, with no lord nor master, the *malandro* relies on his cunning alone to ascend into the ranks prohibited to him', according to journalist Olivier Guez.[33] 'The *malandro* walks and dances, feints and conceals, on the edge of good and evil, of the licit and the illicit', the musician Chico Buarque wrote in a musical play dedicated to the legendary scoundrel. 'Bluffer, provocateur: he is a social dribbler'.[34]

Garrincha and Pelé nevertheless heralded two diametrically opposed popular models of Brazilian identity: on the one hand, the *malandro*, the elusive and ungovernable indigenous man, and on the other the man who wanted to assimilate, to adopt the national motto of 'Order and Progress' as his own. From adolescence, Pelé had led an ascetic life, abstaining from tobacco, alcohol and nightlife. His sporting rigour made him a model footballer, as humble as he was obedient, as technical as he was physical. A rare practice at the time, Pelé very early on invited an agent to negotiate his contracts and a manager to combine football and business. Pelé's name was registered as a trademark before the footballer signed lucrative advertising contracts. While black international sports figures such as Muhammad Ali became the standard bearers of Black Power, King Pelé embodied a more consensual black consciousness, reassuring the football establishment.*

While Pelé carefully managed his future, Garrincha preferred to live in the moment. Nicknamed 'Alegria do povo' (the 'Joy of the People'), the footballer liked to return from the stadium on victory days with vans of supporters and celebrate his success by drowning in alcohol. For the fierce bird was also a night owl, regularly arriving late for matches due to his nocturnal adventures marked by sexual conquests. At the 1962 World Cup in Chile, Garrincha was at the peak of his career – he was voted best player – and despite Pelé's absence due to injury, the Seleção won their second world title against Czechoslovakia. Back home, Garrincha appeared in the arms of Elza Soares, an Afro-Brazilian samba star, causing a scandal. Regardless, the people worshipped him and the poet and musician Vinícius de Moraes dedicated a poem to him, 'O Anjo das Pernas Tortas' ('The Angel with Twisted Legs'). While the Botafogo continued to pay him a pittance, the 'Joy of the People' sank inexorably into alcoholism. By the 1966

* Pelé was also named Sports Minister in 1995.

World Cup in England, Garrincha was a shadow of his former self: the angel with the twisted legs had already burned his wings.*

In 1970, the World Cup was broadcast in colour for the first time, enhancing the *auriverde* (green and gold) of the Seleção under the Mexican sun. Defeating an outflanked Italy 4–1 in the final, Brazil rose above the competition, while Pelé went down in history as the first and to date only player to raise the trophy three times. With the country under the yoke of military dictatorship since 1964, the Brazilian president, General Emílio Médici, turned the victory to his advantage, consolidating his authoritarian regime. Posing for photographers with the trophy, the military cacique even attempted a few headers. On TV and huge posters paid for by the government, a Pelé in mid-flight was plastered with the slogan 'Nothing can stop Brazil now'.

The stranglehold of the military junta over football, together with the 1970s economic miracle in South America, led *futebol arte* to gradually disappear from Brazilian turf. Gone was the art of the beautiful game invented during *peladas*** and matches on the beaches of Rio, popular laboratories for footballing innovation. A driver of social calm and national unity, under the regime football no longer tolerated dribblers with a political dimension. The teams trained by Telê Santana with top players like Sócrates or Zico for the 1982 and 1986 World Cups still symbolised a collective and emancipated football, a country in the throes of rediscovering democracy. But they were the last gasp of the *jogo bonito*, which made way for a more 'realistic' game, better aligned with the profitability requirements of the football business.[35] Following the example of the Brazilian star Ronaldo, top scorer at the 2002 World Cup won by the Seleção, creative individuality in the service of the collective and spectators' enjoyment was transformed into an individualism that exalted the market value of players. The 'social dribbler' so dear to Chico Buarque became a liberal dribbler.

---

* On 20 January 1983, eaten away by osteoarthritis and alcohol, Garrincha died alone at the age of just 49. His body was exhibited at the Maracanã, where 100,000 Brazilians came to pay him a final tribute.

** Informal football games in which players focused on improving their displays of technical flair [see Chapter 22].

The Amerindian gap

Far from the economic concerns of globalised football, the impact made by the non-white Brazilian players of the 1950s–1960s and in particular by Garrincha's indigenous origins carved out a furrow for football with an indigenous identity on the continent. The Amerindian struggle would burst onto the international sporting scene most spectacularly during the 2014 World Cup held in Brazil, the event providing unprecedented visibility to the resistance of Brazilian indigenous groups.

The Amerindian protests, which began to gain momentum more than a year before the start of the Cup, started in a derelict colonial-period building that previously housed the National Museum of Brazilian Indians. Located opposite gate 13 of the Maracanã stadium, which was then undergoing major renovations, the building had been occupied since 2006 by a hundred or so Amerindians from different communities (Guajajara, Guarani and Tukano peoples). Renamed Aldeia Maracanã, the place was being self-managed as a cultural centre, offering Amerindian language courses, and conferences on the memory of the struggle against colonial expansion and on traditional ceremonial practices. This living example of Brazil's indigenous struggles had plans to become a people's university built by and for Amerindians. Nearby, a huge advertising poster for Coca-Cola, the official sponsor of the World Cup, showed the image of a smiling Amerindian, wearing a traditional feathered headdress, with the slogan 'Everyone is welcome at the World Cup'. However, in the eyes of FIFA and the Brazilian government, the display of indigenous demands on the doorstep of the Maracanã stadium, symbol of Brazil's unity around football, was not at all welcome. The occupants of the Aldeia were violently evicted on 22 March 2013 by the police forces, fobbed off with promises of rehousing.

Yet the indigenous movement did not lose heart at this expulsion and determined to add its voice to the wider social activism directed against the hosting of the World Cup. 'We will join forces with the social movements of Rio de Janeiro, those in the favelas and in the heart of the city, those of the Gypsies, those of the Blacks, we will all unite to organise our protest', declared Carlos Pankararu, a spokesman for Aldeia Maracanã.[36] People's committees were set up in each of the twelve cities hosting the tournament to denounce the expropriation of property due to World Cup-related construction works, as well as the vast public funds channelled towards the event.[37] On 17 June 2013, millions of protestors descended on the streets chanting the slogan *Não vai ter Copa* ('There'll be no Cup') and 'Brazil, wake up, a teacher is worth more than Neymar!' Such a rebellion had previously been unthinkable in a country that imagined itself the homeland of football. Pelé and UEFA president Michel Platini publicly called for an end to the demonstrations, prompting an outcry from the protestors.

Protest was on the rise again in a nation ranked among the world's top ten economic powers but also as one of the ten most unequal countries in the world.[38] In May 2014, outside the Arena Corinthians stadium in São Paulo, 2,000 people occupied a field on the outskirts of the stadium. 'We called our occupation the *Copa do Povo* (People's Cup) because we came to see that the World Cup would transfer billions from the public coffers to enrich businesses and the mayor's friends, giving nothing to the people, who can't even afford a match ticket. This was not our Cup', explained Fabio, a Brazilian militant involved in the occupation.[39] Bia, a young teacher from a striking school, added: 'The World Cup only laid bare the inequality and violence of a country that squanders millions to organise a mega-event while treating the population like cattle'.[40] On 27 May, in Brasilia, the police charged a demonstration by thousands of Amerindians and homeless workers around the new Garrincha national stadium after they took over the headquarters of the company that owned the building. In Recife, hundreds of supermarkets were looted and two Brazilian league matches were cancelled. Official ceremonies to present the FIFA trophy were regularly interrupted by demonstrators, while strikes by transport workers, teachers, and hospital workers spread throughout Brazil's major cities.

On 12 June 2014, during the World Cup opening ceremony, a young Guarani boy, a white boy and a black girl released a dove, a symbol of peace between peoples, in front of millions of television viewers. As they left the field, the 13-year-old Indian boy suddenly took out of his pocket a frail red banner with the word 'Demarcação' ('Demarcation') written on it. This was an allusion to the Amerindians' struggle to persuade the government to demarcate ancestral Indian lands that are under pressure from land speculators, in defiance of constitutional law. The protest was swiftly censored, the live broadcast switching its digital gaze to the stands.

Beyond these attempts at political appropriation of the World Cup, Indian peoples across Latin America have also seized on football to assert and even revive their indigenous identity. In Brazil, the country's first professional Amerindian team was created in 2009. Hailing from the Amazon basin, Gavião Kyikatejê Futebol Clube plays in the first division of the state of Pará and dreams of playing in the Brazilian Cup. The slogan 'Indigenous people are struggle and resistance' on the club's wall reminds Gavião's star striker, Aru, of his early days in the professional league: 'I suffered a lot of prejudice. Players would tell me: "go back to your tribe", "go and play with your arrows", "go and run in the forest instead, this is not for you"'. Zeca, the club's founder, adds: 'We Indians have never had a place in the white world. I had the idea to set up a professional team so that we could claim our own place and show our talent'.[41] Before taking to the pitch in a qualifying match for the 2014 Brazil Cup, Aru's body is painted in the colours of the leopard, the fastest animal in the Amazon forest, while a woman from the Kyikatejê community motivates the footballers: 'We have been excluded from society for 500 years. 220 peoples, 180 languages [...] Remember that you are not just a football team, you are the dream of a whole people'.[42] The team did not qualify in the end, but the defeat did not discourage Aru: 'When I head out onto the pitch, I feel proud to represent my people [...] My style? To get into the opposing half and slip through to score!'[43]

The number of teams founded by indigenous communities has exploded in recent years. In 2003, for example, Mushuc Runa ('New Man' in Quechua), a club now in Ecuador's top division, was born with the support of a micro-credit cooperative set up by the native farmers of Pilahuín, Chibuleo and Quisapincha. 'This project is not only based on football or [having] a stadium and [obtaining] publicity', says Luis Chango, a backer. 'Football is a way for us to make a big impact in Ecuadorian society. It aims to show that indigenous people can access all levels of society'.[44]

Since 1995 Ecuador has also hosted an indigenous 'Mundialito' or Mini-World Cup, combined with the traditional Quechua flower festival held in Otavalo, bringing together a dozen Indian teams from across the region. The trophy is a bronze replica of the World Cup and a Golden Shoe, in this case a painted indigenous sandal. In Peru, near Lake Yarinacocha, another indigenous Mundialito is held every year with 22 men's and women's teams from the Shipibo, Ashaninka, Yines and Kakataibo communities in the Peruvian Amazon. 'The goal has always been to unite peoples, communities, youth and to promote the value of solidarity through sport', in the words of Alejandro Ruiz Lopez, one of the organisers.

> At the same time, the tournament has ancestral roots, having replaced the Ani Sheati, the great festival of the Shipibo nation that used to assemble all the communities each year to make sacrifices and hold initiation ceremonies for young women into adult life. Today, this annual event has become an occasion for communities to meet and for relatives who live far apart to see each other, to be all together again.[45]

Zapatista footballs and indigenous rebellion

The best example, however, of football and indigenous struggle coming together in the popular imagination is in Chiapas, in south-east Mexico. In December 1994, the Zapatista Army of National Liberation (EZLN), which first emerged in Tojolabal, Tzeltal and Tzotzil villages in the region in the 1980s to assert the self-government of indigenous peoples, announced the formation of 30 'rebel Zapatista autonomous municipalities'. Football, the most popular sport among the indigenous peoples of Chiapas, developed particularly within these self-managed communities where the Indian populations experimented with autonomy outside of any state control. The game became a key element in the political life of the EZLN and played an important symbolic role in the zigzagging path taken by the Zapatista movement towards the recognition of indigenous rights.

On 16 February 1996, the dialogues between the EZLN and the Mexican government gave rise to the San Andrés Accords, the first step towards self-determination for the indigenous peoples of Chiapas. In July of that year, spokesperson Subcomandante Marcos wrote Eduardo Galeano a letter entitled 'Poetic tribulations of a footballer on the defensive':

> Olivio is a young Tojolabal boy, not yet five years old and therefore not yet out of the deadly age bracket in which so many indigenous children die here. The probability that Olivio will die of a curable disease before he reaches five is the highest in this country called Mexico.
>
> But Olivio is still alive. He is proud to be a friend of Major 'Zup' and to play football with Major Moisés. Well, it's too much to say playing football. In reality, the major just kicks the ball far enough away to get rid of Olivio, who, like any child, considers that the most important job of Zapatista soldiers is to play with children. I watch them from a distance. Olivio kicks the ball with a determination that gives you the chills.[46]

This is followed by a detailed description of the child playing football and imagining himself on real turf surrounded by packed stands. But the ball is only a small plastic one, and the turf a modest muddy field where Olivio dribbles between dogs and tree stumps before hitting a goal made of a pile of weeds.

Through this exchange of letters about an informal children's game of football, Subcomandante Marcos illustrates the precarious living conditions of indigenous people in Chiapas, a marginalised population in what is one of Mexico's poorest states.[47] He depicts the EZLN soldiers living among the autonomous communities, showing that the Zapatista army is both popular and indigenous in character, countering the federal government's claim that it is a terrorist group that manipulates the indigenous people. With no illusions about a

Zapatista armed struggle that is more symbolic than effective, the Subcomandante concludes his letter with this admission:

> It will not escape anyone that I am trying to give you an image of the tender fury that makes us soldiers today, so that tomorrow military uniforms will be reserved for fancy-dress parties, and if we have to wear a uniform at all, it will be the one we wear to play football.

Just six months after this letter, the negotiations between the Zapatistas and the Mexican authorities abruptly ended, President Ernesto Zedillo being persuaded of his ability to crush the uprising by military means. The government orchestrated the arming in Chiapas of paramilitary groups that unleashed a low-intensity war against the Zapatista communities. Forty-five Tzotzils, most of them women and children, were murdered on 22 December 1997 in the Chiapas village of Acteal, and many of the autonomous municipalities were violently dispersed in the spring of 1998.

A year later, during national consultations with Mexican civil society on the rights of indigenous peoples, an EZLN delegation was sent to Mexico City. Taking advantage of their visit to the capital, a football match was organised on 15 March 1999 at the Jésus Martinez Palillo stadium, between a Zapatista team and a team assembled by Javier Aguirre. Aguirre, a former Mexican international and coach, rallied former professional players – including Raúl Servín, Rafael Amador and Luis Flores – to the cause. With Commander Tacho as their captain, the eleven Chiapaneco footballers took to the field wearing their usual balaclavas – a symbol of the anonymisation of their struggle but also a way of avoiding police identification – before asking the public to lend them football boots to replace their usual guerrilla ones. Under a blazing sun, Javier Aguirre's team won 5–3, prompting Subcomandante Marcos, designated 'technical director of EZLN FC', to declare: 'In reality we didn't lose, we just ran out of time to win'.[48]

Harshly repressed by the Mexican government, and well aware that the military balance of power did not favour them, the Zapatistas diversified their militant tactics to popularise their cause. Their growing interest in football was a part of this. Though their struggle was local, they saw in the game a 'universal language' capable of arousing new forms of solidarity and conveying their message both within their country and internationally.

In May 1999, a European football team, the Easton Cowboys and Cowgirls, an amateur club rooted in Bristol's punk scene, played a series of matches in Zapatista territory to support the cause. Six months later, it was the turn of Lunatics FC, a militant team from Anvers, to make the journey. In January 2001, the 'Zapatista' footballers from Bristol returned to Chiapas with the street artist Banksy as their goalkeeper, who also created a Zapatista football mural in the Caracol de la Realidad* with the slogan 'A la libertad, por el fútbol' ('To freedom, for football'). In parallel, the Zapatista resistance had formed close ties with the prestigious professional club Inter Milan. At the end of the 1990s, the captain of the 'Neroazzurri', the emblematic Argentine international Javier Zanetti, embraced the indigenous cause and mobilised his teammates to establish a programme of solidarity with the Zapatista communities. Delegations of Milanese footballers were welcomed in the autonomous municipalities, and gradually Inter Milan jerseys and shiny official Italian footballs appeared on Chiapas' makeshift pitches. 'We believe in a better world, a world that is not globalised but enriched by the diversity of the cultures and customs of each people', said Javier Zanetti. 'That is why we want to support them in their struggle to maintain their roots and in their fight for their ideals'.[49] The Milanese club sent medical supplies to the free micro-clinics set up by the Zapatistas, and co-organised annual football training sessions for Chiapas high school students.

On 25 May 2005, one month prior to issuing the 'Sixth Declaration of the Lacandon Jungle', the Zapatistas' appeal to Mexican civil society to set up a new Constituent Assembly, Subcomandante Marcos sent a lengthy letter to Massimo Moratti, president of Inter Milan, proposing a series of matches in Mexico and in Europe. With

---

* The *Caracoles* ('snails' in Spanish) are the five political and cultural entities that together coordinate the rebel Zapatista autonomous municipalities.

his trademark self-mockery and irony, the insurgent called on the Milanese club to come and face the EZLN in a 'Pozol de Barro Cup', named after a traditional drink made from corn. The matches would be refereed by Diego Maradona, commentated by Eduardo Galeano and cheered on in the stands by the LGBT community. As for the EZLN team, it would be mixed gender and boosted by the presence of Maribel Domínguez, known as 'Marigol'. A brilliant Mexican forward who had played for FC Barcelona, the footballer became a celebrity when her contract with the professional men's team Atlético Celaya was rejected by FIFA under the pretext of 'maintaining a clear division between men's and women's football'.[50] 'As there are not only two sexes and there is not only one reality, it is always desirable that those who are persecuted for their differences share joys and support each other without giving up being different', the Subcomandante writes in his letter.

The letter goes on to outline the utopian trajectory of the football games that could be played on an international scale in support of the Chiapas indigenous groups, Latino and African migrants, and political prisoners. Finally, the EZLN spokesman explained that his team would be travelling to Genoa for the return matches in Italy. The city was the scene of fierce protests during the G8 in 2001, and the Chiapanecan activists would like to

> paint little snails [the symbol of the Zapatista movement] on the statue of Christopher Columbus (note: the probable fine for defacement will have to be paid by Inter), and bring a flower in remembrance of the place where the young anti-globalisation activist Carlo Giuliani fell* (note: the flower is for us).

The matches of this fantasy Pozol de Barro Cup, as imagined by Subcomandante Marcos, would be opportunities to weave bonds of solidarity in advance of the great movement that the Zapatistas would call for a few weeks later.

---

* Carlo Giuliani, a 23-year-old Italian student and activist, was killed by the police on 20 July 2001 during an anti-G8 demonstration in Genoa.

The circulation of the Sixth Declaration of the Lacandon Jungle was accompanied by a series of political communiqués, stories for children, and philosophical and poetic texts published by the Zapatista movement. It was in this context that *The Uncomfortable Dead*, jointly written by Subcomandante Marcos and crime writer Paco Ignacio Taibo II, appeared in 2005, first in the form of chronicles and then as a book. In the course of a chapter, this detective story depicts a football match at the Caracol de la Garrucha between a Zapatista team and a team of international observers (both male and female). 'What happened was that in one of the games our side had two huge Danes, about six-foot-six and terribly good at soccer. Their height, plus their extra-long strides, left the Zapatistas far behind, 'cause they're smaller and have shorter legs',[51] remarks one of the book's protagonists, who becomes the goalkeeper of the observers' team for a match. But in the face of the physical and sporting domination of the internationals, the local players were strangely passive:

> After our second score all the Zapatistas moved back to defend their goal. They left the whole field to our huge Danes, who were happily rushing back and forth. But with all those people on the Zapatista side, the field became a mudhole. The ball would stick, like in cement, and you needed several internationalist kicks to even make it roll. 'They're going to stall', I thought, 'so they don't get stomped'.[52]

However, from the second half onwards, the foreign team become physically exhausted and gradually get bogged down in the mud until, as one man – or woman – the Zapatistas overrun and then overwhelm their opponents, scoring no less than seven goals in 20 minutes.

Forged by 500 years of asymmetrical warfare against the coloniser, the indigenous people have learned both to retreat in the face of repeated onslaughts by their better-armed enemies, and to be stubborn. While football is all about moving constantly to occupy the opposing side, the Zapatista players thwart the physical domination of their opponents by patiently staying close to their goal, while employing their keen knowledge of the terrain to wear down the rival team. Symbolising the struggle of the indigenous rebels in Chiapas, the match described in *The Uncomfortable Dead* is also a footballing metaphor for the Zapatistas' overall strategy in dealing with the Mexican state: they have shunned the political game imposed by the federal government, preferring to build autonomy locally rather than attempt electoralism or the seizure of power by force.[53]

The same political tactic was used in 2006. While the Mexican authorities were preparing for the election, the Zapatista movement launched 'La Otra Campaña' ('The Other Campaign'), a long peregrination throughout the country to meet the poorest communities in order to build collectively, 'from below and to the left', a broad Mexican social movement. The initiative was the target of bloody police repression but gave rise to the constitution in 2013 of a vast informal planetary network of anti-capitalist struggles called *La Sexta*. Gathered around a first 'World festival of resistance and rebellion against capitalism' held in December 2014 in Mexico, the Sexta organised its own mixed tournament of 'rebel football' in support of the National Indigenous Congress* as if to celebrate the political relevance of the game among Zapatistas and to embed it in the history of indigenous resistance.

From Garrincha, the 'social dribbler' of Amerindian origin, to the autonomous football of Chiapas, in the past 50 years the game has become a popular decolonial practice. A language as physical as it is metaphorical, indigenous football has adopted different political masks, the better to dribble past the multiple faces of deadly neo-colonialism, allowing the indigenous peoples to recover their dignity, a principle elegantly defined by the Zapatistas as 'that murmur of the heart that doesn't care what blood makes it beat, that rebel irreverence that mocks borders, customs and wars'.[54]

---

* Founded in October 1996, the National Indigenous Congress brings together several hundred representatives of Mexican indigenous communities who work in support of their fundamental rights.

13

Sending colonialism off

Football and emancipation struggles in sub-Saharan Africa

In opposition to historical becoming, there had always been the unforeseeable.

Frantz Fanon, *Black Skin, White Masks*

To constitute a 'Black force'. Inspired by this credo of General Charles Mangin, who led the 'Senegalese riflemen' at the beginning of the 20th century, the French colonial authorities wanted to physically educate the 'natives' in the aftermath of the First World War in order to support the military power of the metropole and to create a docile workforce.[1] With this in mind, the colonial administration in French West Africa (AOF)* set out to develop physical activities for African youth. These would offer them the 'stimulus capable of giving these races the ardour and vitality they lacked', according to a physical education manual published between the two world wars.[2] In charge of physical and sports education in the French West Indies between 1923 and 1933, the colonial infantry commander Sergent wrote: 'The native needs, more than any other, a physical culture associated with an appreciable rise in the standard of living that will make him the normal man towards whom the efforts of French colonisation must first be directed', before adding that 'gymnastic and sporting events have their rightful place in the entertainment of the black peasant and must progressively replace the traditional and ancestral customs, some of which are too much of a hindrance to the

* A colonial entity that existed from 1895 to 1958 and included Mauritania, Senegal, Mali, Guinea, Côte d'Ivoire, Niger, Burkina Faso and Benin.

evolution of individuals'.[3] Throughout West Africa, gymnastics and military exercises were imposed from a very young age on pupils in colonial schools. Modern sports were reserved for the white elites. In AOF football was treated as a sign of social and racial distinction, and beginning in 1913 competitions were regularly organised in Dakar for the colonists.[4]

Nevertheless, as football's popularity swept the metropole in the 1920s and 1930s, Africans gradually fell in love with the game, discovering it through contact with expatriate railway and mining workers, European sailors and soldiers. Despite the reluctance of local notables, the colonial authorities saw in sport a means of 'civilising the African masses' by inculcating in them the virtues of obedience, respect for rules and individual control of the body.[5] 'We believe that sports, even in the popular ranks, must be encouraged both in the indigenous population and in the government', Baron Pierre de Coubertin confided in 1913. 'Sports are, in short, a vigorous instrument of discipline. They encourage all sorts of positive social qualities, hygiene, cleanliness, order and self-control. Is it not better for the natives to be in possession of such qualities, and will they not be more manageable than otherwise?'[6]

The club, a hotbed of protest

Just like in the metropole, where the Fédération gymnastique et sportive des patronages de France (FGSPF) had become a major backer of football [see Chapter 5], in AOF the Catholic missions and youth organisations served to popularise the game. For religious organisations, football continued the civilising mission of the Church, and the first clubs to include African players saw the light under their patronage. These included the Jeanne d'Arc de Dakar club, founded in 1921 by Father Lecoq, and Jeanne d'Arc de Bamako, established in 1939 by Father Bouvier. Secular sports clubs also emerged, directly run by colonists or by members of the African urban elite, such as the Union sportive indigene de Dakar in 1929 (its football team was threatened with excommunication by Father Lecoq), and the Union sportive de Gorée, the Athletic Club de Cotonou, and the Étoile filante de Lomé, all formed in the early 1930s.

Matches remained segregated, on the turf and in the stands alike. A perpetuation of the racial divide that silently reflected the authorities' fear of witnessing a symbolic win on the pitch of the 'natives' over the coloniser, and a threat to the colonial order. In 1912, Pierre de Coubertin was already warning: 'A victory – even for entertainment – of the subjected race over the dominant one would take on dangerous significance, and risk being exploited by local opinion as an encouragement to rebellion'.[7]

In French Equatorial Africa (AEF),* football and colonialism similarly went hand-in-hand. From 1929, informal teams of Congolese players met in Brazzaville to set up their own football ground. 'For six months, every Sunday and throughout the holidays, rain or shine, office employees and workers armed with hoes, shovels, rakes and machetes, cleared the bush, pulled out roots and stumps, levelled and marked out their pitch', recalled a schoolteacher who lived in the town at the time.[8] But the enthusiasm and collective initiative of these 'natives' troubled the colonial authorities, who decided to formalise black football and bring it back under their control. Barely two years later, Brazzaville was home to a dozen or more clubs, a regional championship and a 'native' sports association, all closely managed by the Europeans.[9]

In neighbouring Belgian Congo, sports apartheid was also the order of the day. In May 1911, a Katanga football league reserved for whites was established in the mining town of Elisabethville (today Lubumbashi).[10] Football for the 'natives' was actively promoted by the Flemish priest Raphaël de la Kethulle de Ryhove, who later explained: 'A well-organised football team was an excellent educational tool; it often meant the Negroes had to curb their innate passion for fighting'.[11] In his view, the game offered 'an opportunity for the missionary to establish contact with adult Negroes, and it could even be said that several conversions were achieved by this means'.[12] Known locally as Tata Raphaël, in 1919 the missionary priest founded the Association royale sportive congolaise, aimed at 'promoting indigenous football',[13] followed by Daring Faucon, a

* Between 1910 and 1958, AEF comprised what is now Chad, Gabon, the Republic of Congo and the Central African Republic.

club that still exists today under the name Daring Club Motema Pembe. It was also he who, in the 1930s, built the 25,000-capacity Queen Astrid stadium in Leopoldville (Kinshasa).

Finally, in French Cameroon, 'native' sports unions appeared from 1932, with each neighbourhood club reflecting the ethnic divisions of the territory. The Caimans d'Akwa represented the Douala community, while the Canon of Nkolndongo and the Tonnerre de Mvog Ada represented the two Ewondo districts of Yaoundé. For the French administration, this 'tribalisation' of football was an additional tool of control over the indigenous people and, as the historian Catherine Coquery-Vidrovitch points out, it made it possible to 'classify and fix these shifting populations whose names, languages and customs seemed as numerous as they were confused'.[14]

Gradually, though, football escaped the control of colonial authorities. As president of the AOF Central Committee of Physical Instruction and Military Training, Colonel Bonavita expressed concern in 1938 at the proliferation of 'native' sports clubs that were becoming ungovernable through their 'sheer number'.[15] This trend only accelerated after the Second World War. Weakened by conflict and indebted to its colonial empire, which played a decisive role in the country's liberation, metropolitan France loosened the colonial stranglehold over its overseas territories by embarking on a cautious social reform. The *Code de l'indigénat* (laws and regulations applied only to native peoples) and forced labour were officially abolished, and the colonial administration promoted an associationist policy in which urban African elites would henceforth form an interface between the colonial power and the indigenous inhabitants.[16] African civil servants, doctors and teachers began to appear on the boards of sports clubs. Moreover, the extension of the law on freedom of association to the colonies* in 1946 led to an explosion of the associative sports movement. The number of clubs created in AOF increased from 184 in 1943 to 438 in 1957, and the number of registered football players doubled between 1952 and 1957, to over 10,000.[17]

---

* More specifically, AOF, AEF, Madagascar, the French Somali Coast, the French Establishments of India and Oceania, Guyana, New Caledonia and Dependencies, Togo and Cameroon.

An AOF football league, dependent on the French Football Federation, was set up in Dakar in March 1946 and an AOF Cup was scheduled the following year. While this trophy was initially reserved for Senegalese teams, competition fever spread to clubs from Abidjan, Conakry, Bamako and Cotonou, who enrolled in large numbers for the tournament. The number of participating teams, from all over AOF, increased from year to year, rising from about 50 in 1948 to more than 300 in the 1958–1959 season.[18]

This competitiveness reflects the emergence of anti-colonial sentiment that prefigured the independence movements of the 1960s. For the football historian Paul Dietschy, even if 'native' football teams espouse the religious, ethnic or linguistic divisions consciously maintained by the coloniser, they also constitute a federative and popular point of focus that crystallises aspirations for self-determination.[19] And, with the rise of liberation movements, the anti-colonialist scope of football was consolidated. The post-war AOF was in fact riven by growing social unrest, which quickly led to a desire for political independence. In October 1946, the Rassemblement démocratique africain (RDA) was founded in Bamako, a pan-African political grouping which initially aimed to achieve socio-economic equality in the colonies. Virulent anti-colonialist urban demonstrations and widespread strike movements in the French West Indies, particularly by railway workers between 1946 and 1948 and by the civil service from 1954 onwards, regularly shook up the colonial system.[20] Fuelled by the Afro-Asian conference held in Bandung in April 1955, which encouraged further decolonisation, winds of independence began to blow over French-speaking Africa.

Though the colonial authorities saw sports associations as a means of distracting the 'natives' from political activity, the Africanised football clubs in fact became hotspots of protest against colonial domination. For historians Nicolas Bancel and Jean-Marc Gayman, this appropriation of football 'marks a double movement: it testifies to the gradual emancipation of the colonised, but also to a process of acculturation through these imported cultural practices'.[21] The stadiums gradually became a vast sounding board for independence claims, and the pitch a space for confrontation with the colonist.

In the Belgian Congo, a first official match between a white team, the visiting Beerschot Athletic Club of Antwerp, and a mixed local team made up of six Africans and five Europeans, was organised in June 1953 in Leopoldville. On the eve of the match, the Brussels press unabashedly spread racist prejudice against the Congolese players. 'Whoever has not seen four or five dozen Negroes playing against five dozen other Negroes [...] does not know what a bullfight is', said the newspaper *La Dernière Heure*.[22] However, to widespread surprise and before an audience of 70,000, the victory of the first-division Belgian club was far from convincing. The Antwerp team won 5–4, and everyone in the stands could see for themselves that the six African players had dominated the game. Robert Van Brabant, football coach in Leopoldville, was present that day and felt that an all-Congolese team would have produced an even worse result for Beerschot. 'It wasn't an experiment to be repeated', he said. 'If Beerschot had been beaten, their defeat might have had repercussions outside of sport'.[23]

Four years later, on 16 June 1957, a football match was played between the Brussels team Union Saint-Gilloise and the all-black Association royale sportive congolaise. Union won the game 4–2, yet the partisan refereeing that overturned two Congolese goals led to violence in the segregated stands. The white crowd was booed by the Congolese, who called them 'Flemish monkeys', 'dirty little Belgians' and invited them to 'go back to Belgium'. Fifty cars were damaged as they left the stadium and some 40 people were injured.[24] While, for the local daily, 'these matches are not appropriate because they take on a much deeper oppositional character than a simple ball game',[25] in the eyes of historians, these tumultuous events presaged the January 1959 revolts in Leopoldville, which marked a decisive turning point in the colony's accession to independence in 1960.[26]

Anti-colonial pressure

While football catalysed anti-colonial sentiment throughout Francophone Africa, it was even more evident in British colonies. Indirect rule, the colonial regime deployed by the British Empire in most African territories, whereby the colonial administration relied on indigenous leaders, was also applied in the world of football. At the same time, the values of sports education dear to Muscular Christianity [see Chapter 2] were inculcated from the beginning of the century in the local African elites, who formed the first football clubs composed exclusively of 'natives'. In Southern Rhodesia (now Zimbabwe), for example, the African Welfare Society was authorised to promote football in the Bulawayo district in the 1930s, and in 1941 organised a football league with 16 local teams.[27] Startled at this display of initiative, in 1947 the British suspended the modest league, provoking anger from the black population. Benjamin Burombo and Sipambaniso Manyoba, trade union leaders and independence supporters from Bulawayo who were also captains, respectively, of the Matabele Highlanders and Red Army football teams, launched a mass boycott of official matches.[28] A year later, also on the initiative of the anti-colonialist unions, a general strike paralysed Bulawayo, and the hard-won wage demands were combined with the chance to found an autonomous African football federation, established in 1949 as the Bulawayo Football Association.[29] 'Native' football clubs and embryonic associations independent of the British colonial authorities also sprang up in Nigeria, the Gold Coast (Ghana) and Tanganyika (Tanzania). 'The people recognised themselves in the identities clubs projected because they were rooted in the districts where they lived', in the view of sociologist Ossie Stuart. '[…] So, several decades after it was first introduced, football was fully embraced by Africans. It was part of a shared experience for those living in Bulawayo, Johannesburg, Lagos and elsewhere across the continent […] Football expressed defiance of the state and emancipation from colonial oppression'.[30]

Educated in the colonial school system, and nourished by the Anglo-Saxon sports culture, the young independence leaders of the 1930s and 1940s glimpsed in football a powerful recruiting tool for anti-colonial militancy among the working classes in Africa. Arriving in Lagos in 1915 at the age of 11 to study at the Wesleyan Boys' High School, Nnamdi Azikiwe, a Nigerian independence figure and the country's future first president, was trained in the tough, virile football of the English public schools.[31] An accomplished sportsman, he became general secretary of the Diamond Football Club, a black

1. *The Foot-Ball Play*, Alexander Carse, circa 1830. A popular game of football in rural England in the early 19th century.

2. Frenzied game of *soule* in Lower Normandy. *L'Illustration*, 28 February 1852.

3. The English working-class team of Blackburn Olympic (Lancashire) in 1882.

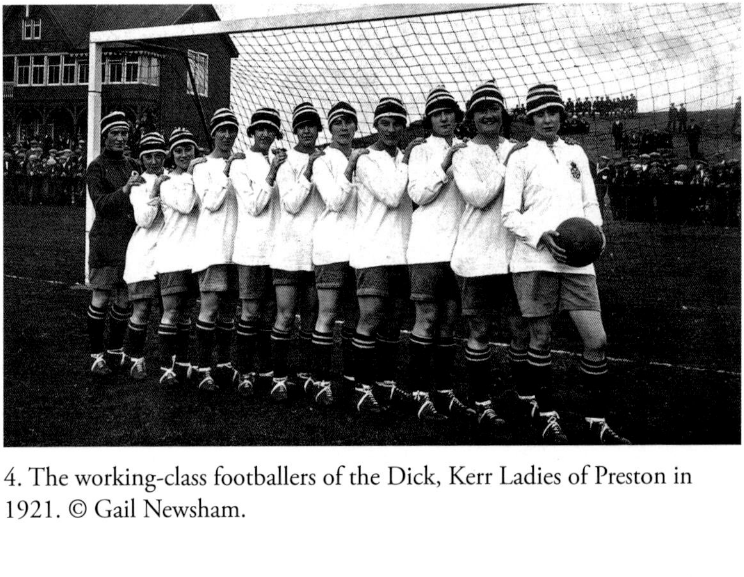

4. The working-class footballers of the Dick, Kerr Ladies of Preston in 1921. © Gail Newsham.

5. The stands of the Dynamo stadium in Moscow in the early 1930s. The stands were one of the few public spaces where it was possible to escape the surveillance of the Soviet political police. © DR.

6. Viennese striker Matthias Sindelar, nicknamed *Der Papierene* (the Paper Man), opposed the annexation of the Austrian team by the Nazi regime. © FIFA Museum.

7. During the occupation of the Netherlands by the German army, Dutch footballer Jan Wijnbergen, from the first team of Ajax in Amsterdam, joined the Resistance in 1941 before participating in a rescue network for Jewish children. © Jan Wijnbergen – © Jan Wijnbergen – Collection Dutch Resistance Museum.

8. The South African Wanderers team in 1956. From the township of Chatsworth, near Durban, the Wanderers are considered the first Black club in South Africa. © Archive Faouzi Mahjoub / FIFA Museum.

9. The Algerian National Liberation Front (FLN) football team in 1961. Rachid Mekhloufi is the fourth crouching player from the right. © Archive Faouzi Mahjoub / FIFA Museum.

10. The national team of Ghana celebrates its second African Cup of Nations after beating Tunisia 3-2 in the final, November 1965. Baptised the *Black Stars*, the team was both the standard-bearer of Nkrumah's pan-Africanism and the best African squad of the day. © Archive Faouzi Mahjoub / FIFA Museum.

11. Nicknamed 'the joy of the people', Brazilian footballer Garrincha alongside an English policeman during a tournament in Liverpool, July 1966. © Sport Archive / FIFA Museum.

12. Zapatista team from Caracol de La Garrucha (Chiapas, Mexico) at a match with the Easton Cowboys of Bristol, 1999. © R. S. Grove.

13. Diego Maradona escorted by the police on June 29, 1986, just after Argentina's victory against West Germany in the 1986 World Cup final in Mexico City. © Sport Archive / FIFA Museum.

14. Occupation of the headquarters of the French Football Federation on Avenue d'Iéna in Paris by the Footballers' Action Committee in May 1968. © DR.

15. Banner of a fan of FC United of Manchester, a club founded in 2005 by a cooperative of supporters who contested the acquisition of Manchester United by American billionaire Malcolm Glazer. © Mark Lee.

16. 'St. Pauli supporters against the right', legendary sticker produced by supporters of FC Sankt Pauli in Hamburg since the 1990s. © DR.

17. The Beşiktaş Çarşı ultras in the streets of Istanbul during the demonstrations of May 1, 2014. © Guillaume Cortade.

team that won the local championship in 1923 against the hitherto undefeated European club Lagos Athletic Club.[32]

Following a stay in the United States, where he was struck by the important role occupied by sport and the mass media in society, in 1937 Nnamdi Azikiwe set up an anti-colonialist press group, launching the daily *West African Pilot.* In April of the following year, he created the Zik Athletic Club (ZAC), open to 'sportsmen and women of any race, nationality, tribe or social class resident in Nigeria'. The multi-ethnic sports organisation embodied Nigerian urban modernity and Africans' capacity for managing their own affairs.[33] With the earnings from his media group, Azikiwe built his club a multipurpose stadium on the outskirts of Lagos, while in 1942 the team defeated colonial squads to win the Lagos League and the War Memorial Cup.

In 1941–1942 Nnamdi Azikiwe and the best ZAC players held a tournament across the country with the aim of raising funds to contribute to the British war effort against the Axis powers. After each game, however, Azikiwe launched into virulent anti-colonial diatribes before 5,000 to 10,000 fans, pointing out the hypocrisy of the British who claimed to be fighting for 'freedom and democracy' while the Empire oppressed its African subjects and denied them the right to self-determination.[34] A second football-cum-political tour was organised the following season in support of Nigerian prisoners of war, with Azikiwe bringing his independence rhetoric to ever larger crowds.[35] Building on the network of 'native' football clubs, in 1944 Azikiwe's political machine gave rise to the first Nigerian independence party, the National Council of Nigeria and Cameroon (NCNC).

From 1951 onwards, the Jalco Cup, a tournament financed by a car dealer, pitted a Nigerian team against the Gold Coast* every year, strengthening the sense of national identity in each of the British colonies.[36] The famous Ghanaian player Charles Kumi Gyamfi recalled his team's first victory in Accra in the 1953 Jalco Cup:

---

* With Accra's Hearts of Oak, Ghana's first football club founded in 1911, and Asante Kotoko, a team of the Ashanti people, known for their stubborn resistance to the British in the 1880s, the Gold Coast is also a land of football.

> We were crazy that day. We had to score and there were only a few minutes left in the game. And I scored. The crowd went wild and I was lifted up, thrown in the air. I scored a lot of goals but what happened that day in Ghana I will never forget in all my life.[37]

The proliferation of clubs formed by and for Africans, the creation of sports associations independent of colonial power, and the first African football tournaments all served as fertile ground for liberation struggles. With Ghana winning independence in 1957 and Guinea in 1958, a broad wave of sub-Saharan decolonisation kicked off in 1960. From football as a 'civilising' force to an emancipatory one, the game became an instrument of popular mobilisation at the service of post-colonial regimes. During Nigerian independence celebrations in October 1960, Nnamdi Azikiwe did not forget the debt he owed to the sport, organising a football match. In Guinea, Ahmed Sékou Touré, a big football fan, made the Syli National team (the National Elephants) a buttress of his Marxist revolution. Ghana's first president, Kwame Nkrumah, named the national team the Black Stars – a reference to the Black Star Line, a transatlantic shipping company for African-Americans set up by pan-African activist Marcus Garvey in the early 1920s. The Black Stars were both the flag bearer of Nkrumah's pan-Africanism and the leading African team of the day (they won the African Cup of Nations in 1963 and 1965). Finally, the first Jeux d'Amitié or Friendship Games, organised in Abidjan in 1961 and Dakar in 1963, which brought together thousands of French-speaking African sportsmen, and the African Games in Brazzaville in 1965 (with 22 countries playing football) served as a catalyst for national sentiment and contributed to the international recognition of the newly fledged African states.

Considered the first pan-African organisation, the Confederation of African Football (CAF) was founded in 1957 on the initiative of Egypt, Sudan, Ethiopia and South Africa. All the newly formed national teams jostled to sign up. At the presentation in 1962 of a CAF Cup – by then some 40 associations strong – Kwame Nkrumah declared: 'It is encouraging to observe how, in the progress made towards achieving economic and social unity in Africa, sporting and cultural activities have greatly contributed to creating a peaceful atmosphere for African unity and full independence'.[38] Two years later – still led by Nkrumah – the African federations that were members of CAF boycotted the 1966 World Cup. Alarmed by the politicisation of CAF, FIFA allocated only a single place to the entire Africa–Asia–Oceania zone for the World Cup qualifiers, compared to ten places for European countries and four for South America.

However, this 'African unity' would crumble in the mid-1960s. Post-colonial football, feeding on pan-Africanism, gradually succumbed to manipulative propaganda and the control of those in power. This was the case in Ghana, where the national football federation fell under the yoke of a Central Organisation of Sports, of which Kwame Nkrumah – paranoid after two assassination attempts – had become leader for life. A similar development was seen in Zaire (the name of the Democratic Republic of Congo from 1971 to 1997) where President Mobutu made the national team, the Leopards, a showcase of his dictatorial regime. After winning the African Cup of Nations in 1968, the flamboyant Zaire won the trophy for a second time in 1974, becoming the first sub-Saharan nation to qualify for a World Cup in the same year. But in the first round, the Leopards offered a tragic spectacle, losing to Scotland (2–0) and being humiliated by Yugoslavia (9–0) before facing Brazil on 22 June. Terrorised by Mobutu's threats not to lose by more than three goals, and deprived of their match bonuses, the players were soon trailing the Seleção 2–0. In the 78th minute, as the Brazilians were about to take a free kick from 20 metres out, Zairean defender Ilunga Mwepu, on the referee's whistle, suddenly sprang from the wall, ran towards the ball and cleared it with a powerful kick before the stunned eyes of players and spectators. It was as crazy as it was surreal. Mwepu became the laughingstock of commentators, rekindling racist prejudice against black footballers. It was only many years later that the significance of this shot as a protest was understood, lifting for a moment the weight of the Mobutist regime bearing down on the Leopards, and marking, in the civilised surroundings of the World Cup, the end to the bright football of African independence.

Township football against Afrikaner soccer

As liberation movements spread inexorably throughout the sub-Saharan region, one last bastion of segregation remained: South Africa. Apartheid, instituted in 1948 by the newly elected nationalist government, reinforced the bitter racial divide in South African sport. While whites preferred to play rugby and cricket as a means of exalting their Afrikaner identity, football was largely the domain of the country's black, mixed-race and Indian communities, who learned the joys of the game from British soldiers and European merchants in the early 20th century.

The urbanisation of South Africa and the proletarianisation of black people at the turn of the 1930s and 1940s encouraged the development of an informal football culture in the townships. Playing football barefoot and on makeshift pitches, adopting Zulu or Xhosa warrior nicknames, black ghetto footballers formed clubs, giving rise to the African Wanderers from the Chatsworth township near Durban, and the Moroka Swallows and Orlando Pirates from the townships of Soweto. The Johannesburg Bantu Football Association, one of several local associations for non-whites, gathered over 10,000 spectators for its matches every Sunday from the 1940s onwards.[39] The Orlando Pirates were one of the most popular clubs among black South Africans, thanks to their sporting success (they reached the top division of the Johannesburg Bantu FA in 1944) but also to their attacking, artistic style of play, which borrowed from marabi, a musical culture born in the underground bars of the black suburbs (the shebeens). Early star players, such as Eric 'Scara' Sono of the Orlando Pirates, emerged as folk heroes of this football scene, with whom their fervent supporters felt 'amathe nolimi' – a Zulu proverb meaning 'like saliva and the tongue'.[40] 'The important weekend games are discussed on buses, on the pavements at lunchtime, in the long queues where Africans wait for hours in the morning and afternoon', described the South African social worker Bernard Magubane in the early 1960s. 'Daily chores are temporarily forgotten. Conversations range from the fitness of players, to the likelihood of winning the next game, to assessments of previous matches. All these footballing preoccupations alleviate the difficult living conditions'.[41]

A first step towards challenging white dominance of football was taken in September 1951 with the creation of a multi-racial federation, the South African Soccer Federation (SASF), which was the result of a merger between the three pre-existing major black, mixed-race and Indian football organisations. By 1956, the breakaway sports body had 2,700 clubs and more than 45,000 players across the country, four times as many as its all-white counterpart, the South African Football Association (SAFA).[42] Although there was no South African law prohibiting racial mixing in sport, the Minister of Home Affairs, Theophilus Dönges, threatened: 'There will be no travel opportunities or government assistance for non-European sports organisations with such subversive intentions'.[43]

In parallel, the anti-apartheid struggle expanded to international football. The first black South African players were bought by the big European clubs, with Stephen Mokone recruited by Coventry City in 1955 and Albert Johansen by Leeds United in 1961, giving visibility to the existence of quality black football in the country. Meanwhile, the Confederation of African Football suspended the membership of the white association – since renamed the Football Association of South Africa (FASA) – when it made clear its intention to submit an all-white team to the 1959 African Cup of Nations.

Nevertheless, it took the Sharpeville massacre for public opinion to really become aware of the abomination of racial segregation. On 21 March 1960, in the township of this name in Vereeniging, a peaceful anti-apartheid demonstration was brutally repressed by police. Sixty-nine people were killed and some 200 injured. A year later, faced with international indignation and the explicit refusal of the South African association to prohibit racial discrimination in its clubs and in football grounds, FIFA suspended the country on a temporary basis.[44] Despite this banishment from the global football community, segregationist practices continued. The FASA established a National Football League reserved for whites, and in 1962 cynically organised an interracial match between the Black Pirates and the whites-only Germiston Callies in an attempt to return to FIFA's bosom (the suspension was lifted in 1963).[45]

While the rebellious SASF had organised an interracial cup every two years since 1952, in August 1959 *Drum* magazine, aimed at a black South African readership, asked: 'Remember that for whites, football is just another sport. Rugby attracts the crowds and football picks up the crumbs. But football has become *the* national sport for non-white South Africans [...] So why don't we set up our own interracial professional football league?' In October 1960, on the initiative of non-white clubs such as the Cape Town Ramblers and the Durban Aces United, the South African Soccer League (SASL) was founded, a professional league bringing together black, mixed-race and Indian players for the 1961–1962 season. Transvaal United, a club from a Soweto township, won the first SASL title and, from 1962, the first black women's teams appeared in the league, such as the Orlando Pirates Women's Football Club and the Mother City Girls. In those dark years of apartheid, the proximity of the football clubs to their supporters and families in the ghettos meant that the League's match calendar was a focal point for the festive and cultural life of the townships.[46] The SASL was a success and each match brought crowds to the dilapidated municipal stadiums of Johannesburg, Durban and Cape Town.

However, the Pretoria regime and the FASA took a dim view of the autonomous development of interracial football. After unsuccessful attempts to take legal action to stop the games for violating the state's racial segregation laws, the government authorities succeeded in forbidding municipalities from lending their grounds to the SASL.[47] On 6 April 1963, thousands of fans in Johannesburg found a municipal decree pasted to the gates of the Natalspruit Indian Sports Ground cancelling that day's match between Moroka Swallows and Blackpool United. Defying the ban, players and fans climbed over the barriers and replaced a pair of goalposts that had been removed. The game was played in front of 15,000 people in a feverish atmosphere, but after this brazen action several SASL officials were sacked and all league matches were banned. The SASL was finally dissolved in 1967.[48]

The apartheid policy of Afrikaner Prime Minister Hendrik Verwoerd was accompanied by a relentless crackdown on township-based activist organisations. In April 1960, following the Sharpeville massacre, the two main black liberation parties, the African National Congress (ANC) and the Pan Africanist Congress (PAC), were declared illegal. Many activists from both organisations were sentenced to life imprisonment on the infamous Robben Island – including Nelson Mandela, imprisoned for founding the ANC's armed wing, the uMkhonto we Sizwe. Like most black South Africans, the anti-apartheid prisoners were keen on football – Albert Luthuli, ANC president from 1952 to 1960, was head of the Durban and District African Football Association and later of the Natal Inter-Race Soccer Board – and after three years of protests and petitions they were allowed to play football within the prison walls. In 1966, five political prisoners, Lizo Sitoto, Sedick Isaacs, Sipho Tshabalala, Mark Skinners and Anthony Suze, launched the Makana Football Association, named after the Xhosa rebel leader Makana Nxele, who had been interned on the island in the 19th century.

Conceived as a fully-fledged amateur football league, the Makana FA adhered to official FIFA rules and was structured into three divisions, with real coaches and rigorous refereeing. The prisoners built the goals and nets, drained the pitch, hand-carved a wooden trophy, and wore different colours to distinguish between teams. The Makana matches took place over a nine-month season and the organisation of the league, run by hundreds of inmates, gave a rhythm to the harsh monotony of life on Robben Island. From Monday to Wednesday, prisoners discussed fouls during previous matches; Thursday and Friday were devoted to the formation and strategy of each team in preparation for the match on Saturday.[49] Until 1973, tournaments were closely followed, with flagship prisoner teams such as Manong FC playing in brown and yellow or the Black Eagles in blue. Over the years, about 1,400 prisoners were involved in the Makana FA as players, coaches, administrators or referees.[50]

Beyond the recreation and chance to escape from the difficult prison conditions, Makana FA became a tool for political education and learning about democratic culture. By applying the universal rules of football and the collective organisation of sport in a context of material scarcity, the militant prisoners of the ANC and the PAC learned to transcend their deep political divisions by uniting to better assert their autonomy in the face of the prison administration. The game enabled the Robben Island prisoners to prepare themselves politically for the post-apartheid era of the 1990s, and to better understand football's pre-eminent role in the history of resistance to racial oppression.

The anti-segregationist struggle in sport initiated by the SASL continued in South Africa through the 1970s and 1980s. Following the bloody repression of the Soweto uprising of 16 June 1976 against the imposition of the Afrikaans language in schools, FIFA definitively excluded the South African Football Association.* Similarly, while the Pretoria government continued to ruthlessly persecute black activists – Steve Biko of the Black Consciousness Movement was abducted and murdered by the police in 1977 – township football matches were used to clandestinely finance black liberation parties that were still outlawed. In the 1980s, flags bearing the colours of the ANC appeared more and more openly in the stadiums, a sign that the segregationist regime was weakening.

Formed in January 1970 by Kaizer Motaung, a former star player for the Orlando Pirates in the United States, from 1974 onwards the Kaizer Chiefs of Soweto flew above black South African football. At the height of the apartheid repression – Ariel Kgongoane, captain of the team, was killed by a stray bullet during the Soweto uprising – the charismatic Kaizer Chiefs, with their 'Love & Peace' slogan and their 'Glamour Boys' nickname, offered a new image of black professional football, one that was less confrontational but also more lucrative. The sporting successes and financial resources of the club in the ochre yellow jerseys even attracted the first white professional player in 1978, Lucky Stylianou, who would be followed by Peta Bala'c, Jingles Pereira and Jimmy Joubert. Open to white teams from the same year, the National Professional Soccer League – which in 1985 became the openly multi-racial and anti-apartheid National

* At a peaceful demonstration by some 20,000 students from townships against the obligatory use of Afrikaans as the teaching language in black schools, the police fired real bullets causing hundreds of deaths. Following the massacre, the UN voted for an embargo on arms sales to South Africa and a widespread political and cultural boycott of the country was imposed until the end of apartheid.

Soccer League – was then won in 1979, 1981 and 1984 by the Kaizer Chiefs who, transcending racial barriers, become the most popular team in the country by far.

The progressive dismantling of the apartheid policy after 1990 saw the liberation of political prisoners from Robben Island and the end of racial segregation in football. On 8 December 1991 a single, multi-ethnic South African Football Association was established, joining FIFA and CAF in 1992. South African football began to gain worldwide media acclaim. In the wake of the Springboks' victory at the Rugby World Cup, the national, multi-racial team known as the Bafana-Bafana ('The Boys' in Zulu) won the Africa Cup of Nations in 1996 on its home turf, with captain Neil 'Makoko' Tovey becoming the first white player to lift the African trophy.

Yet, at the turn of the new millennium, the trajectory of South African football, freed from the spectre of apartheid, took a bitter turn. Winning unprecedented continental pride, the country was selected to host the first football World Cup on African soil in 2010. While many predicted logistical chaos, the South African organisation of the sports event was unanimously considered a success. However, it was later tainted by scandals of corruption and embezzlement. In 2015, courts in the United States revealed that bribes were paid to FIFA for the decision to award the country the event and that millions of dollars were misappropriated for the personal enrichment of officials at the international body.[51] Barely twenty years after having readmitted the South African federation into its ranks, FIFA had succeeded in transforming the first African World Cup into a tarnished symbol of a game that has definitely become 'amathe nolimi' with the financial windfalls of the football business.

PART IV

Support

Collective passions and popular cultures

14

'You'll Never Walk Alone'

Hooliganism and subcultures in British stands

Some people believe football is a matter of life and death.
I can assure you it is much more important than that.

Bill Shankly, Liverpool FC coach 1959–1974

He was a sweet and tender hooligan, hooligan,
And he swore that he'll never, never do it again,
And of course he won't, oh, not until the next time.

The Smiths, 'Sweet and Tender Hooligan'

> There were many thousands at Shrewsbury on Easter Monday, and the concomitants of betting, drinking and bad language were fearful to contemplate, while the shouting and horseplay on the highways were a terror to peaceful residents passing homewards.[1]

So reported an observer of the aftermath of a match in 1899. In the late 19th century, crowds of workers would gather each Saturday in the grounds of the industrial cities to cheer on their club. In the 1888–1889 season, over 600,000 spectators attended English league matches. Ten years later, this number had risen to 5 million.[2] The Victorian bourgeoisie, meanwhile, remained largely absent from grounds, aghast at the unseemly behaviour of the working class. The popular passion for the game and the accompanying tumult in the stands dismayed the 'old-guard defenders of an upper-class amateur [...] game', notes the historian Rogan Taylor. The latter 'vented their spleen at the take-over of football by the industrial workers of the north by depicting them as dirty, fickle and degenerate'.[3] By contrast to the phlegmatic gentleman, who acts with restraint and is imbued with the ethos of fair play, the working-class spectator supports his team with heart and soul, while the players often come from the same factory or a family in his neighbourhood. Embodying a sense of pride and belonging, the local football club underpinned a shared culture. Pub toasts to both victories and defeats, factory conversations around the team's performance, or tales about the most popular players: all served to unite a working-class community around a club.

As the rivalries between the various football clubs were honed with each match – particularly between the London teams, as with West Ham United and Millwall – threats and insults aimed at the opposing team became a way of expressing attachment to one's club. While 'Gi'it some clog!' was one of the most popular injunctions in the stands, the fervour of the supporters quickly spilt over into violence.[4]

In 1885, after a friendly between Preston North End and Aston Villa, supporters described by the press as 'howling roughs' attacked the Preston players with sticks and stones, leaving one unconscious.[5] The following year it was the turn of the Preston and Queen's Park fans, who fought each other in a railway station. Between 1895 and 1914, the daily *Leicester Mercury* recorded 137 football-related incidents nationwide, while the Football Association noted 116.[6] Pitch invasions, punches thrown in the stands following contentious refereeing decisions, impromptu brawls at the stadium gates: the proliferation of such clashes among fans scandalised the conservative British press, who began to call them 'hooligans', after a late 19th-century London gang, the Hooligan Boys. The name belonged to an Irish family from a working-class district of the city renowned for their violence, popularised in 1899 by Clarence Rook's novel *The Hooligan Nights*, which recounted the nocturnal adventures of a young criminal in the capital's rough areas.[7]

In 1903, the authorities recommended installing fences around stands and digging tunnels to protect players from the missiles raining down on them.[8] Two years later, several Preston North End supporters – including a 'drunk and disorderly' 70-year-old woman – were sentenced for 'hooliganism' during a match against Blackburn Rovers.[9]

However, it was in Scotland that hooliganism would become a mass phenomenon of particular violence. In April 1909, the final of the Scottish Cup was played between old rivals Celtic and Rangers, from the Catholic and Protestant communities of Glasgow respectively. A 6,000-strong crowd invaded the pitch, tearing out the goalposts and the gates of Hampden Park and setting them on fire. All the streetlamps in the district were destroyed by fans, and 54 police officers were injured, including three stabbings.[10]

A respectable public

The First World War brought about deep changes in the British working class, reshaping the social composition of sports events. After the major strikes that shook Great Britain in early 1910, working-class trade unionism reached the apex of its power in 1914 with the formation of the Triple Alliance, combining the redoubtable forces of the mining, railway, and transport unions. The First World War caused an irrevocable split in the working left, torn between pacifist and pro-war positions. When the conflict ended, the Alliance imploded: on Friday 15 April 1921, the rail and transport union leaders failed to call on their members to support a major miners' strike. To this 'Black Friday' was added the disaster of the May 1926 general strike. Initiated by the miners' union, the uprising was snuffed out by the Trades Union Congress, which chose to play the card of moderation and negotiation. Worker agitation was neutralised by the entry into force, one year later, of the Trade Disputes and Trade Union Act, which proscribed general strikes altogether.

Abandoning the strategy of direct action and reneging on its solidarity with revolutionary militants, the workers' movement then tried the path of parliamentary representation and rapprochement with the industry bosses. Trade unions became institutionalised, developing the art of compromise and seeking practical changes from bosses. Together with the Labour Party, they won social benefits that enabled large sectors of the working class to significantly increase their standard of living. The interwar period thus saw the emergence of a so-called 'respectable' working class, more concerned with their regular wages, their union and their homes than with the rough-and-tumble spirit perpetuated in the pubs and on the streets by the poorer working classes.[11]

Having benefited from a reduction in working hours and an increase in wages, this 'respectable' sector came to form a large part of the crowd in football grounds after the war. Faithfully attending the Saturday afternoon match became the family recreation activity par excellence. The FA Cup final in 1923 broke attendance records: 250,000 spectators crowded around Wembley stadium; 126,000 of them managed to watch the match. In 1935 the traditional England–Scotland derby attracted over 200,000 fans.[12] Incorporating the values of fair play and self-control favoured by the ruling classes, embodying the prosperity and dignity of a working class that had succeeded in extracting itself from poverty, these 'respectable' crowds were less prone to the lack of discipline and the fighting in the stands of the 'roughs'. Reports of 'hooliganism' declined in this period and the many working families attending games with their children made for quieter stands.[13]

> It was a very mixed crowd. There were a lot of old blokes, and women, even some elderly women. You all stood there together. You knew everybody. You never saw 'em between games. But we always stood roughly in the same place and we knew the forty or fifty people around us 'cos they were always there.[14]

The 'rough' working-class way of life had not disappeared altogether. Left out by the great social compromise between the Labour Party and the conservative forces, many unqualified and unemployed workers failed to integrate into interwar British society. The ideals of fighting spirit and resourcefulness, the use of violence in defence of the group and the primacy of the law of the street over the law of the state had endured in marginalised corners, notably among the dockers and others living off illicit activities in Liverpool or London's East End quays.[15] Passionate about football, these 'rough' supporters' natural home was the terraces: the cheapest, standing section of grounds. Surrounded by working-class families, however, they maintained their propriety.

After the Second World War, the creation of the Welfare State enabled the respectable working classes to benefit from the fruits of economic growth and to buy their own homes for the first time. In parallel, reconstruction and rehousing policies focused on building large housing estates and renovating working-class suburbs that had been destroyed by bombing.

This intensive restructuring of the urban realm, which saw the displacement of the poorest people to the suburbs of the large industrial cities, as well as a significant improvement in the living conditions of skilled workers, destroyed a whole set of community links specific to working-class neighbourhoods. Until the 1950s, these working-class communities, firmly anchored in a particular urban area, constituted a world rich in social relations, networks of solidarity and mutual support, which were key to the survival of the working classes in the face of social insecurity. For the sports sociologist Patrick Mignon,

> you were first of all from a neighbourhood and then you were Geordie, Mancunian, Scouser, or Cockney,* before you were English or even a member of the working class; that is, belonging to a social class was only conceived on the basis of this local experience.[16]

In addition to this territorial and social uprooting, the arrival of the consumer society contributed to the erosion of working-class social life. The traditional weekend, with its Saturday afternoon football match, Sunday pub lunch, brass bands, greyhound breeding and pigeon racing, disappeared in favour of more individualised, family-centred leisure activities such as cinema, gardening and shopping.[17] With the explosion of television – by the early 1960s, four out of five households had a television set[18] – and the first television broadcasts of matches, the respectable working-class man, who no longer saw football as a part of his social life but as a simple entertainment to be enjoyed in his living room, gradually disappeared from stadiums.[19] Between the late 1940s and the late 1980s, the number of fans in the stands halved.[20]

---

* Residents of Newcastle, Manchester, Liverpool or London, respectively.

Unburdened by the scrutiny of respectable spectators, the rough-and-tumble crowd were resurgent. Between 1948 and 1958, the Football Association and the Football League recorded more than 238 acts of public disorder.[21] In 1954, for example, a match between Everton and Bolton Wanderers' reserve teams was marred by incidents: fireworks were thrown from the terraces, a linesman was assaulted and several hundred fans invaded the pitch. During the following season and until 1959, trains were regularly vandalised by Liverpool FC and Everton fans.[22] By the 1960s, it is estimated that annual recorded hooliganism incidents had doubled in 25 years.[23]

A crowd to overthrow the world

The resurgence of hooliganism went hand in hand with the growing number of young people. The post-war period saw the arrival of the first teenagers as a distinct cultural designation. Generational outcasts, the unruly Teddy Boys – school dropouts and rock'n'roll fans – appeared in 1950s London. These young, rebellious proletarians, recognisable by their Edwardian-inspired clothes, brought the 'rough' fighting spirit back into fashion, before being supplanted in the early 1960s by the mods and rockers. Rejecting the gentrification of the working class, playing on their adolescent virility and making a counter-culture out of organised violence, these juvenile gangs took over the stadium stands abandoned by working-class families. In the eyes of these new hooligans, attachment to a local territory and the affirmation of a certain 'hardness' were the two constitutive elements of working-class identity they wanted to perpetuate. Like the 'rough' workers who defended the honour of their working-class community and their neighbourhood at all costs, these teenagers made support for their club a symbolic substitute for the old working-class communities. The terraces become a new territory to be jealously defended.[24]

In view of the resurgence of incidents in grounds and the falling attendance, footballing institutions tried to modernise the game to make it more palatable to family consumption. Ceilings on player salaries were abolished and transfers were opened up, while match broadcasts were sold to the highest bidder. Stadiums progressively turned into commercial arenas with the arrival of VIP stands, vast advertising hoardings, and the hiring of hospitality staff.

At the same time, the stands became more and more segregated. Each team's most ardent fans gravitated towards a particular 'end' – the cheaper seats behind the goals – where they could keep apart from each other. Older spectators preferred the side stands where they could best enjoy the spectacle. The desire of clubs to attract spectator-consumers to the stands, the difficulty in identifying with new players who were more like stars than 'local lads' (such as the flamboyant George Best, striker at Manchester United from 1963 to 1974 and nicknamed 'the Fifth Beatle') and the erasure of a popular and local football culture in favour of football business only increased the rage of young hooligans.

In the mid-1960s, a genuine hooligan culture began to emerge at the 'ends'. The most zealous fans gathered in the 'Kop', a term first used at the Spion Kop, one of the two ends at Liverpool's Anfield Road.* 'Taking an end', i.e. invading the stand of the opposing supporters, became a popular activity in British stadiums.[25] In a society where recognition was now won by individual success, collectively charging the rival Kop, capturing their banners and flags and then occupying their end became, in the eyes of these young people, a way of establishing the prestige of their group while remobilising the social codes of the original 'rough' working class: courage, virility, solidarity, camaraderie and communion through alcohol.

Taunts, insults and other verbal provocations directed towards opposing fans were elevated to an art form, while songs reinforced hooligan culture on the terraces. Supporters of Oxford United had a repertoire of over 250 chants,[26] while the Liverpool Kop adopted the chorus 'You'll Never Walk Alone'** as its anthem, from the pop song by local group Gerry and the Pacemakers. The music and dress of hooligans became more sophisticated, not only to distinguish differ-

* Spion Kop is the name of a hill in South Africa that saw a vicious battle in January 1900, during the Boer War. Despite their defeat, the soldiers from Liverpool were recognised for their heroic resistance.

** This song was originally written in 1945 for the US musical comedy *Carousel.*

ent groups of supporters but to mark them out from the middle-class cultural trends then in fashion, such as hippy culture.

In 1969, at the crossroads of the 'hard mods' and the Jamaican 'rude boys', the first skinheads appeared on the terraces of London's East End, caricaturing the attributes of the dock workers: Doc Martens, braces and work trousers, shaved heads and tattoos. The Fred Perry polo shirt was as much about not sweating in soul music clubs as about subtly cultivating one's difference as a supporter: blue piping for Millwall fans, burgundy for West Ham. For these young people from the East End confronted with the closure of the docks and the major urban restructuring of their neighbourhoods at the end of the 1960s, football enabled them to revive a semblance of community culture and territorial solidarity. The skinheads developed the hooligan spirit in the grounds while merging it with the violent gang culture inherited from the hard mods and rockers. In the late 1980s, pioneering Leicester University researchers in the sociology of sport wrote:

> With the influx of the skins, 'gangs' began to take precedence over the game [...] The distinctive aggressiveness of the skins, the degree of organisation skinhead crews helped to bring to the football ends and the sense of unity that their style helped to give to young goal-terrace fans, all contributed to an intensification of the territorial preoccupations of rival factions. No greater disgrace, no greater loss of masculine pride could local fighting crews endure from the end of the 1960s onwards than to 'surrender' the home end to visiting fans.[27]

As well as leading to a veritable 'war of the ends' between supporters, away trips helped to forge a culture of collective travel at lower cost among young, broke hooligans. In his book *Among the Thugs*, US writer Bill Buford is told by Mick, a Manchester City supporter, that 'being on the jib means never spending money. That's always the challenge. You never want to pay for Underground tickets or train tickets or match tickets. In fact, if you're on the jib when you go abroad, you usually come back in profit'.[28] Travelling on the jib, beyond simple transport fraud, also involved thefts from supermarkets and luxury shops, a practice notorious among Liverpool FC hooligans that – much to the chagrin of European clubs who played the Reds – brought hooligan culture to the attention of their home fans.* The Liverpool hooligans, used to living on their wits to survive and with the strength of their 18,000 supporters in the Kop,[29] also developed the technique of 'bunking in', which consists of rushing the entrance to the grounds en masse to force their way through the police blockade and avoid paying for tickets. The principle asserted by travelling 'on the jib' and 'bunking in' is simple: 'Everyone – including the police – is powerless against a large number of people who have decided not to obey the rules. Or put another way: with numbers there are no laws'.[30]

While this anti-authority crowd may appear crude and homogeneous, hooligan groups were cunningly organised to achieve the best possible support for their team. Some specialised in creating slogans, making banners or stealing smoke bombs, while the 'hard men', the experienced supporters of the 1960s, launched the chants and displays of the Kop on the 'frontline', at the front of the stands. The youngest supporters, the scouts, were responsible for spotting the police and rival supporters.[31] Sociologist Stuart Hall studied the hooligan movement in the 1970s:

> Their own collective organisation and activities have created a form of analogy with the match itself. But in their case, it becomes a contest which takes place not on the fields but on the terraces. They have created a parallel between the physical challenge and combat on the field in their own forms of challenge and combat between opposing ends [...] Similarly, the chants, slogans, and songs demonstrate support for the team and involve an effort to intervene in the game itself, by lifting and encouraging their team and putting off the opposition [...] The violence between the sets of fans is part of this participation in the game – part of the extension of the game on the field to include the terraces too.[32]

* Hooligan culture was spread in this way to Dutch and Belgian *siders* and then to Eastern Europe and the former Yugoslavia.

The display of aggression, expressed in threats made against other supporters, in the punches during a fight to 'take an end', or even by a general brawl on leaving the stadium, is also one of the cardinal values of hooligan culture. Just like the ritualised violence of pre-industrial *soule* games [see Chapter 1], the violence staged by hooligans is largely symbolic. It is less about committing aggressive actions than about maintaining an atmosphere of violence, an attitude in its own right that hooligans call 'aggro'.[33] Ridiculing rivals, threatening them, charging the opposing end, stealing from a shop with flair: these are all manifestations of the aggro style which, rooted in the popular tradition of mockery, channel these violent impulses.[34]

Actual fights between hooligans, while rare, are seen as rites of male socialisation that allow them to display their physical courage to their opponents. Although the honour and prestige of one's community are at stake in these attacks, the risk of serious injury remains minimal.[35] Despite the appearance of chaos during confrontations in stadium ends or on the street, violence is rarely celebrated for its own sake, as hooligans seek above all a symbolic victory that causes the rival to flee in humiliation. Moreover, brawls only take place between those who are willing to fight. As for the blows used, they are strictly codified: pulling hair or hitting the crotch is prohibited, while harassing individuals or using weapons are (theoretically) prohibited.* 'If, for example, a supporter brings a knife, that's kind of cowardly', says one hooligan. 'There aren't many people who have the killer instinct. I mean once you knock him down and kick him a few times and he's bleeding, well that's it [...] on average that means you lose a tooth or two or you go home with a black eye or a gash'.[36]

Getting drunk, invading the other team's ends, letting off steam together, screaming at the top of one's lungs, dressing up as a bestial and aggressive individual, forming a mob to break down authoritarian shackles, insulting the referee – the embodiment of the law on the pitch – and opponents, and erasing for a time any social hierarchy by adorning oneself with the colours of the club or the dress codes of

* Certain objects such as flagpoles, darts and sharpened 50 pence coins, were later sometimes used. In the 1970s, the Millwall hooligans used the *Millwall brick*, a block of compressed and stiffened newspaper.

one's gang: these are all transgressive social practices specific to hooliganism culture. Hooliganism asserted itself like a Dionysian catharsis at the very heart of the mid-20th-century leisure industry. In the view of Patrick Mignon,

> For hooligans, football has a carnival dimension: a match is a moment for turning the world upside down. You turn it upside down noisily, by singing, by being obscene and drunk, but also by invading the pitch, not only because you think that this will cancel the game that your team is losing, but because it transgresses the laws of the game, imposing the presence of the people before the club authorities or the association. It is a form of rebellion.[37]

The English disease

While television was partly to blame for the decline in stadium crowds, the broadcast of games also made visible the chaos in the stands. In 1961, a brawl broke out between fans before a live audience of millions at a Sunderland–Tottenham match following an equalising goal.[38] The fervour of the ends, the banners and other displays in the Kops were now under the scrutiny of the cameras, inviting fans to compete through the screens for a nationwide audience. Drawn by this spectacle, in the 1970s British tabloids began to make rankings of the most dangerous hooligan groups, while relishing the chaos they caused. 'Off – To a Riot' was the headline in *People* on 2 August 1970. 'Scandal of Soccer's Savages – Warming Up for the New Season', wrote the *Daily Mirror* on 20 August 1973. The media coverage of the fans only fuelled the one-upmanship.[39] In 1967, a Chelsea fan appeared in court for bringing a razor to the stadium. In his defence, he said he had 'read in a local newspaper that the West Ham lot were going to cause trouble'. Manchester United's Stretford Enders, dubbed the 'Red Army' by journalists, went so far as to display a banner in their end reading: 'We're famous hooligans, read about us in the press!' They had made headlines for 'taking the ends' – not without a ruckus – at Arsenal in 1972 and Chelsea in 1973.

The constant media reporting, amplifying the feats of arms of the hooligans, kept up the moral panic around hooliganism. In 1974, the Stretford Enders, in first place in the 'League of violence' established by the *Daily Mirror*, invaded the ground a few minutes before the end of a match against Manchester City, which they were losing. The event having provoked the ire of the president of the Football League, who called them 'wild animals',[40] the club was relegated to the second division and the supporters were herded behind high fences. Crammed in like cattle, treated like fairground animals by journalists, the Stretford Enders chanted in anger from the terraces: 'We hate humans!'

The press sensationalism went into overdrive. 'Thugs', 'caged animals', 'mindless morons' and even 'sub-humans' were all contemptuous 1976 headlines in the *Sun* or the *Daily Express*.[41] 'They should be herded together preferably in a public place', the *Daily Mirror* fumed in April 1977. 'That way they could be held up to ridicule and exposed for what they are – mindless morons with no respect for other people's property or wellbeing. We should make sure to treat them like animals – for their behaviour proves that's what they are'.[42] Like the 'We hate humans!' of Manchester United, most hooligans appropriated the stigma attached to them by deliberately playing with their aggressive image or by making fun of it, like the Millwall fans who spontaneously came up with a new refrain: 'No one likes us, we don't care!'

The obsession of the British press with what they called 'the English disease' forced the government to commission a detailed report on the phenomenon from the Sports Council and Social Science Research Council. The conclusion of the 1978 report, however, is striking:

> It must be considered remarkable, given the problems of contemporary Britain, that football hooliganism has received so much attention from the Press. The events are certainly dramatic, and frightening for the bystander, but the outcome in terms of people arrested and convicted, people hurt, or property destroyed is negligible compared with the number of people potentially involved.[43]

At the peak of the hooliganism wave, between 1975 and 1985, numerous other studies agreed that the problem of football violence was overestimated.[44] A 1977 study by Strathclyde Police reported an increase in criminality of 1.7 per cent during football matches for the previous year. 'Concern expressed by the media about hooliganism is out of proportion to the level of hooliganism which actually occurs at these matches', remarked the authors.[45]

In May 1979, Margaret Thatcher came to power promising to radically reform a country hit hard by the industrial crisis, and to stamp out social discontent, restoring 'law and order'. By putting an end to welfare state policies and liberalising the industrial sector, the Iron Lady brutally plunged the British working class into a precarious existence. The poverty rate exploded and unemployment rose from 5.5 per cent in 1979 to 11.3 per cent in 1986.[46] Liverpool was considered the poorest city in Northern Europe with an unemployment rate above 25 per cent in 1987 – climbing to 96 per cent among young people in the suburb of Croxteth.[47] 'For a long time, Liverpool was the forgotten city of the North', according to John Aldridge, Liverpool FC forward in the 1980s.

> The docks were abandoned after 1972, Margaret Thatcher wanted to wipe us off the map, we were told to leave, to go live further south, or further inland. When things were bad, when the whole country looked at us with pity or disdain, locals only had the football club to defend their honour.[48]

In the face of this sharp rise in social and economic inequality, in 1981 riots broke out in working-class districts of Liverpool (Toxteth) followed by London (Brixton). Many hooligans were on the front lines of the confrontations with the police. They also provided reinforcements to the miners during the 1984–1985 strikes against the closure of a score of coal mines.[49]

Though football supporters sometimes showed solidarity with struggling immigrants or miners fallen prey to the ravages of neoliberalism, young hooligans were more likely to withdraw to their neighbourhoods and uphold their white identity.[50] In a fragile British society, the territorial dimension of hooliganism, embodied in the defence of one's community and the rejection of 'adversaries' (supporters of rival teams, workers who aspire to bourgeois respectability, inhabitants of wealthy neighbourhoods such as Chelsea, etc.), could quickly tip over into a rejection of 'outsiders' and provide a breeding ground for xenophobia, particularly against Pakistani or Caribbean populations settled in Great Britain.

As early as the 1930s, the British Union of Fascists had tried to seduce young working-class football fans into joining its militia.[51] In the 1950s, the White Defence League sold its *Black and White News* around London grounds. In the media spotlight in the 1970s, hooligan groups were particularly attractive to far-right activists. For the latter, the terraces offered a powerful political platform – one that was furthermore relayed on television – and a space for recruitment among increasingly marginalised underprivileged youth. From 1977 onwards, the Youth National Front's newspaper *Bulldog* devoted a separate section to football, entitled 'On the football front', and encouraged hooligans to compete 'for the most racist terraces in the country'. Chelsea, Leeds United, Millwall, Newcastle United, Arsenal and West Ham's ends teemed with radical activists from the British Movement, the National Front, the British National Party or the neo-Nazi groupings close to certain skinhead fringes.* Monkey noises made at black players, sexist obscenities and anti-Semitic chants became increasingly common in the stands and further damaged the image of hooliganism.

Against a backdrop of mass unemployment and the relegation of the working class, the 'hardness' and violence of fans also increased, as if in response to the social violence of Thatcherite politics. Hooliganism gradually became detached from sporting issues and violent acts were increasingly premeditated. Quasi-military operations in grounds were carried out by firms, small, highly organised gangs such as the Inter City Firm, an aggressive group of West Ham supporters created in 1975, which was soon imitated in the early 1980s. The Leeds United Service Crew, the Arsenal Gooners, the Millwall Bush-

* After running out of steam in the early 1970s, the skinhead movement saw a resurgence after 1977, particularly around the Oi! scene, whose slower rhythm than punk music meant it could be sung in the stands. West Ham United fans, The Cockney Rejects, an Oi! group from London's East End, sing 'War on the terraces' or play a lively version of 'I'm Forever Blowing Bubbles', the club's old fan anthem.

wackers, the Chelsea Headhunters and the Leicester Baby Squad were among the most notorious firms that sprang up around the country.

These gangs were formed by new groups of hooligans who distanced themselves from the skinheads. Known as casuals, they erased all signs of belonging to their team or to the working class. Mostly in their 30s, they neither joined their club's end nor travelled with other hooligans, preferring to mix with the ordinary supporters to evade police surveillance, the better to attack rival fans.[52]

The casual movement first emerged in 1978–1979 in Liverpool, where they won a reputation for stealing branded clothing and luxury jewellery. They cultivated a certain dandyism about their attire, wearing polo shirts by big sports brands (such as Lacoste, which was particularly popular with Liverpool fans), Stone Island coats, Burberry caps and Aquascutum scarves. The casual lifestyle came to reflect the triumph of 1980s Thatcherite liberalism. With the atomisation of the working-class world, hooliganism became a space of self-representation, asserting a hedonistic and individualistic lifestyle based on the logic of appearances.[53] Disconnected territorially and socially from the terraces, pure violence became a lifestyle, a search for immediate fun and adrenaline through virile confrontations organised outside the stadium, in car parks or discos. The match calendar merely signalled the opportunities for confrontation.[54]

A former Mansfield Town casual recalls the period:

> During the early 1980s I was to my shame very much involved with the organising of firm versus firm match ups. It was seen at the time to be 'the thing to do' and coming from a mining background the working week was always a hard one and the release of all the pent-up anger from the week peaked at the weekend where you could vent your spleen whilst having a bloody good laugh about it [...] This was their two hours where the rules were theirs and theirs alone. A sense of belonging is what most people crave and at football you are amongst several thousand people who share the same feelings as yourself, they have the same mentality for those few hours at the match.[55]

Some casuals even went so far as not to drink in order to improve their fighting performance, and had no compunction about carrying razors and blades to defend the prestige of their firm. In 1985 the *Daily Mirror* published the photo of a 'traditional' hooligan alongside that of a casual. Underneath the police line-up-style image, the caption reads:

> Can you tell the violent thug from the true soccer fan? The bovver-booted model on the left looks ready for a punch-up but the casually dressed model on the right is wearing the new disguise. And he is the real villain. His £300 outfit may look smart but tucked in the pocket of his Italian jacket could well be a lethal Stanley knife.

The Heysel turning point

The mid-1980s marked a turning point in the history of British hooliganism. On 11 May 1985, at the Valley Parade ground in Bradford, an accidental fire in the wooden stands that started a few minutes before half-time in a match between the local club and Lincoln City led to the death of 56 fans. Broadcast live on regional television, this dramatic event revealed the dilapidated state of many English stadiums and the lack of investment by the government and football institutions in sports infrastructure. In its editorial of 19 May 1985, the weekly *Sunday Times* proclaimed: 'Football is a slum sport played in slum stadiums increasingly watched by slum people, who deter decent folk from turning up'.

Ten days later, Liverpool played Juventus at Heysel stadium in Brussels in the European Cup final. Some 60,000 spectators, including a number of free-riding Liverpool hooligans, were crammed into the dilapidated ground. In the overcrowded stands, spectators were squeezed between security gates and overwhelmed police. A few minutes before kick-off, a hundred English hooligans charged the adjacent stand filled with Turin *tifosi* and Italian-Belgian spectators. Unaccustomed to this British practice of 'taking the end', the panicked spectators retreated, pressing up against the containment wall. The police, meanwhile, pushed back the fans who tried to escape from this terrible trap across the pitch. The low wall collapsed under the pressure of hundreds of crushed spectators, causing a general stampede. Thirty-nine Juventus supporters were killed, crushed by the wall or trampled by the crowd, and almost 500 were injured. The removal of the bodies was broadcast live, yet the football authorities insisted the match be played, to avoid unleashing thousands of furious supporters into the Belgian capital.*

The finger was quickly pointed at the savagery of the English hooligans. The European media let rip on 'these young men without rules, without laws, without order' and denounced the Belgian police for allowing 'the fury and rage of drunken brutes to escalate in line with their cowardice'.[56] English clubs were banned from European competitions for five years, while Liverpool's banishment would last six years. The Heysel trial, which began in October 1988, showed that seats reserved for Belgians had been sold on the black market to *tifosi*. These seats, originally intended for 'neutral' spectators, were also located close to the English ones, with the two stands separated only by a flimsy fence and a narrow no-man's-land. While 14 English supporters were sentenced to three years in prison, the police captain Johan Mahieu, former secretary general of the Belgian football association Albert Roossens and UEFA Secretary General Hans Bangerter also received suspended prison sentences of several months.

Two months after the Heysel tragedy, Leon Brittan, UK Home Secretary, announced: 'people also have the right to protection against being bullied, hurt, intimidated or obstructed, whatever the motive of those responsible may be, whether they be violent protestors, rioters, intimidatory mass pickets or soccer hooligans'.[57] For Margaret Thatcher's Conservative government, football supporters, miners, trade unions and young immigrants all belonged to this turbulent working class that had to be subdued. The European media interest in the 'English disease' was the perfect excuse for turning the repressive and legal arsenal on hooligans.

---

* Michel Platini, scorer of Turin's winning goal, didn't hesitate to joyfully celebrate his achievement on the Heysel pitch just a few hours after the tragedy, a controversial gesture which scandalised football fans.

By 1982, the criminalisation and repression of hooliganism had been facilitated by the creation of a new custodial sentence for minors, as well as by increasing the police presence at matches and installing fences to segregate supporters. In 1985, the Sporting Events Act specifically targeted hooligans, prohibiting the consumption of alcohol in and around grounds, banning fireworks and flares, and expanding police stop-and-search rights. But after the Heysel disaster the Thatcher government went on to pass the 1986 Public Order Act, the 1989 Football Spectators Act,* and the 1991 Football Offences Act that cumulatively imposed a whole series of security measures against supporters and introduced new specific offences such as pitch invasion and throwing a projectile. The fight against hooliganism became a laboratory for new police practices, and football grounds sites of experimentation for preventive crowd management and the targeting of 'suspect' individuals. The installation of surveillance cameras in sports venues became widespread. The first banning orders, or even bans on travel abroad, were issued, even if this meant violating the right to free movement of persons within European Community member states. A Portsmouth supporter recalled bitterly:

> Football fans in the UK also face banning orders the most sinister of which is the civil banning order where police forces can and have apply to the courts for an individual to be banned and surrender their passport during international games regardless as to if they have NEVER been convicted of a criminal offence, football related or not. Any other group in the country this would be seen as a breach of human rights but football fans are fair game.[58]

Databases in the UK and later Europe were created to keep a close watch on hooligans. Police officers filmed outbreaks of violence in the stands with their own cameras, allowing them to identify and

---

* The Football Spectators Act provided for the introduction of a compulsory computerised identity card for spectators, before the measure was withdrawn following the 1990 Taylor Report (see below). Meanwhile, Ken Bates, chairman of Chelsea FC, proposed the installation of electrified fences around the stands.

come down hard on troublemakers. Adopting the same infiltration strategies as in Northern Ireland against the IRA, plainclothes officers operated undercover to mix with supporter groups. In September 1989, Thatcher's Home Secretary Douglas Hurd announced the creation of a new police information department, the National Football Intelligence Unit.[59]

In response to this wave of repression and wholesale attack on their freedom, hooligan groups organised. After the Heysel tragedy, they formed the Football Supporters' Association in Liverpool, a fan defence organisation. In the Liverpool Kop, the chants and slogans became more vindictive, while the crowds gleefully sang 'We're Gonna Have a Party when Maggie Thatcher Dies!' or 'We Shall Not Be Moved', an African-American spiritual popular with the civil rights movement in the United States, and with trade unionists. Tired of their poor image among media and politicians, fans also took on the racism that plagued many ends. Multiple autonomous anti-racist groups were set up to combat the influence of far-right activists, such as Leeds Fans United Against Racism and Fascism, created in 1987, or the Supporters' Campaign Against Racism in Football (SCARF), founded in 1991 to counter the resurgence of the British National Party in the Scottish terraces.

Post-Heysel, a profusion of fanzines also appeared, offering a positive, militant and anti-business vision of English football. A genuine hooligan discourse emerged through these homemade publications, which had roots in the punk scene. With humour, irreverence and self-mockery, the fans criticised the Thatcher government's security measures and the business aims of their clubs' directors. Each end produced and distributed its own photocopied fanzine: *An Imperfect Match* at Arsenal, *The End* at Liverpool FC, *When Skies Are Grey* at Everton, *The Square Ball* at Leeds and *A Love Supreme* at Sunderland. Fanzines also appeared with a wider circulation and not affiliated to a single club, such as *Off the Ball* or *When Saturday Comes* (created in London in 1986, this remains the leading independent English football magazine), as well as more militant publications, such as *The Football Pink*, which defends the LGBT cause within the game, the anti-racist *Marching Altogether* and the women's football fanzine *Born Kicking*. By 1995, this counter-cultural movement had grown to over 2,150 titles, some of which still exist today.[60]

Gentrify to pacify

Four years after the Heysel disaster that was blamed on Liverpool's hooligans, on 15 April 1989 a match was played between the Reds and Nottingham Forest at Sheffield's Hillsborough stadium. Ninety-five Liverpool fans – including 39 under the age of 20 – were crushed to death when crowds surged into an entrance gate. A huge outpouring of emotion was triggered by the tragedy and the images of fans using advertising placards as improvised stretchers played constantly on TV. Disgust with supporters and class contempt returned to the front pages of British newspapers, which accused Liverpool's 'unemployed' and 'drunken' crowd of their usual mass entrance fraud and a deadly stampede when they arrived after kick-off. *The Sun* notoriously ran a police officer's testimony – later shown to be untrue – that drunken Liverpool fans had robbed and urinated on bodies.

As early as August 1989, a report commissioned by Lord Peter Taylor established that it was the negligence of the police, unable to manage the influx of supporters, and the installation of fences at the front of the ground to prevent pitch invasions, that were responsible for the tragedy.* The Taylor Report also called for improvements in safety and hospitality at the top two tiers of UK sports grounds, the majority of which – 70 out of 92 – were built before 1914.[61] The authorities launched a major programme of renovating sports arenas, one of the key measures being the replacement of terraces with all-seater stands. Many fans – believing that supporting your team is something that you do on your feet – considered this development to be heresy: would the audience at a punk concert be forced to remain sitting down? In the summer of 1992, Manchester United's legendary Stretford End and the North Stand of Arsenal's stadium were demolished, and seats were installed. Two years later, the leg-

* It was not until April 2016, following a damning independent investigation of the police, that they were found responsible for the tragedy and of giving false evidence to the courts.

endary terraces of Liverpool's Spion Kop and Aston Villa's Holte End disappeared.

Two new turns were made to the neoliberal and security screw, first with the launch of the Premier League in 1992, and second with England's hosting of the European Championship (Euro 96). Influenced by press magnate Rupert Murdoch, owner of the BSkyB satellite TV network, the first division of English football was reconfigured to include the country's top 20 clubs and renamed the Premier League. Massive sponsorship deals and eye-watering sums paid for broadcast rights (mainly by BSkyB) boosted the clubs, which became powerful financial machines obsessed with maximising profit. Five years later, 17 Premier League clubs, including Manchester United and Tottenham Hotspur, were listed on the stock exchange.

The security of Euro 96 was directly planned and coordinated by the National Football Intelligence Unit, which, since 1990, had already amassed 6,000 names of suspected hooligans, whose photographs were held on a database.[62] This system of police records made it possible to ban the most unruly hooligans from grounds for the duration of the competition. A 'hooligan hotline' was set up for spectators to anonymously report incidents. An armada of spotters, plainclothes police officers specialising in identifying fans, was also deployed in the stands. The event was an opportunity to launch the 'Hooliganism Programme' under the impetus of the European Forum for Urban Security. The aim was to set up an international network for the 'exchange of preventive or security technology' for managing hooliganism in football grounds.[63] The general public, meanwhile, were largely excluded from Euro 96 due to the staggering ticket prices and the pre-booking by the football authorities of seats intended only for corporate customers. As many as 14,000 corporate guests attended the England–Scotland match at Wembley Stadium in London on 15 June 1996.[64]

The anti-hooligan strategy and the gentrification of stadiums that began with the disappearance of standing terraces were followed by a drastic increase in ticket prices, resulting in a radical metamorphosis in the social composition of British stands. Between 1990 and 2011, the cost of the cheapest seats at Manchester United's Old Trafford and Liverpool's Anfield increased by 454 per cent and 1,108 per cent respectively.[65] A ticket to a Premier League match cost an average of £4 in 1990 compared to £35 in 2012[66] and the cheapest season tickets for Premier League clubs in 2015 ranged from £450 to £1,360, i.e. around four times more than for other major European clubs.[67] This high pricing allows clubs, in addition to financing stadium renovations, to keep fans from lower income backgrounds out of the stands, heralding 'an American-style scenario where stadiums are for the wealthy and the working classes watch sport on television'.[68] While the median age of supporters in the Stretford End at Old Trafford was 17 in 1968, it had risen to 40 by 2008.[69] According to the Football Supporters' Association, the average English fan today is in his 40s and spends on average £100 per match, travel and ticket included.[70] The days of groups of young, broke hooligans travelling 'on the jib' and 'bunking in' to grounds were long gone.

The entrepreneurial strategy of football clubs to transform the fan into a consumer and to attract a new, more affluent and older clientele also profoundly changed the atmosphere in Premier League stands. The arrival of season tickets – whose astronomical cost dissuades fans from taking the slightest risk of being expelled from the stadium for any offence – together with over-zealous stewards, the proliferation of VIP boxes and private company lounges, and the preventive architecture of new sports facilities, designed with police intervention in mind, are all intended to pacify and control fans' behaviour.[71] Between the 1988–1989 and 1998–1999 seasons, the number of arrests at football matches in the top two divisions fell by 58 per cent and, in 2000, less than 20 per cent of supporters who had attended the Premier League claimed to have witnessed a projectile thrown or any other hooliganism-related incident.[72] 'Many English fans remain loyal to the lower leagues. The third, the fourth division. Not to fight, no, but because it makes sense', says Cass Pennant, the notorious black leader of West Ham United's Inter City Firm and the first hooligan to be sentenced to prison. 'They travel together, they sing, they eat. Now, in the Premier League, that's all over. It's become all "sit down, give me your money, don't smoke, drink your beer in a plastic cup". It's all about business'.[73]

Proud of the security measures deployed against hooligans, Bryan Drew, a British intelligence officer with the National Criminal Intelligence Service, remarked:

> There's a nasty, ugly and anti-social element in society that clings to football that just won't give up. What became the 'English disease' is no longer characterised by the mass terrace affrays and running street battles of the 1970s and 1980s. But, like other infections, new strains of football hooliganism are developing that are clever, resilient and increasingly threatening.[74]

The violence inherent in British hooliganism became limited to sporadic incidents in the vicinity of pubs, subject to heavy police surveillance during certain matches, such as the high-risk Chelsea–Millwall games or European tournaments. So, in order to immunise any 'hooligan risk', the 2,181 hooligans banned in 2016 from British stadiums[75] were forced to leave their passports with the authorities before the European Championship, held that year in France. This did not prevent 200 English fans from causing a media scandal by fighting ultra-violent Russian hooligans in the streets of Marseille, on the sidelines of the England-Russia match on 11 June 2016. Similarly, during the Champions League final in Cardiff on 3 June 2017, a new electronic facial recognition system scanned the faces of thousands of fans around the stadium and fed them into a huge police database to target anyone who might be guilty of 'anti-social behaviour'.[76] As the English writer John King put it in his celebrated novel *The Football Factory*, 'Football violence is dead and buried. Society is much better balanced these days. The Tories have eradicated the class system'.[77]

With the wildest fans controlled, registered, excluded from the stands or imprisoned, the imagery of hooligan culture of the pre-Taylor era has been recycled by novelists or fans who have turned the sensational narrative into a literary genre of its own in England – Phil Thorton's *Casuals* (2003), Cass Pennant's *Terrace Legends* (2003), Ian Hough's *Perry Boys* (2007) and Dave Hewitson's *The Liverpool Boys Are Back in Town* (2008), to mention only the best-known works – while the film industry has sadly adopted the 'bad boy' clichés of hooliganism with big-budget commercial efforts such as Lexi Alexander's *Green Street Hooligans* (2005) or Nick Love's films *The Football Factory* (2004) and *The Firm* (2009). As for the casuals themselves, while there are still a number of firms kept under close watch by the police, they mostly dissolved into the acid house cultural movement at the turn of the 1990s. In 1989, the formidable members of West Ham United's Inter City Firm created Centreforce, a pioneering pirate radio station key to the emergence of house music, and thanks to their ability to mobilise and outwit the police, they organised the first major underground raves in London. Another way of perpetuating the rebellious tradition of the hooligans.

15
The twelfth man
The Italian ultras movement: from political militancy to supporter autonomy

> Football is the last sacred representation of our time. Basically it is a ritual, although it is also an escape. While other sacred representations, even the mass, are in decline, football is the only one left to us. Football is the spectacle that has replaced the theatre […] a spectacle in which the real world, of flesh, in the stands of the stadium, is measured with the real protagonists, the athletes on the field, who move and behave according to a precise ritual.
>
> Pier Paolo Pasolini, *L'Europeo*, 31 December 1970

On Piazza Castello in Turin, almost half a million people gathered that sad morning of 6 May 1949.[1] A seemingly never-ending funeral procession bore the coffins of 18 Torino FC players and their managers. Two days earlier, following a friendly match against Benfica in Lisbon, the plane taking the team back to Turin crashed into the Superga hill, a short distance from the Piedmontese city. The sudden disappearance of its 31 passengers – all the Torino footballers, the managers, the coaches, the trainer, three sports journalists and the crew members – triggered an outpouring of emotion across Europe. The tragedy was amplified by the fact that Torino FC was the most talented team in Italy at the time (winning the Italian championship four times in a row), and many of its players were on the national squad. With their innovative, rational and technical game, Torino's successes also symbolised the triumphant reconstruction and economic modernisation of industrial Italy just four years after the end of the Second World War.[2]

A rare source of optimism in a city that was occupied by the Germans before being heavily bombed by the Allies, the Torino team was mourned by the working class. The team was the popular rival of Juventus, a club with a more elitist image that was owned by the Agnelli family, founders of the Fiat car industry. The Turin edition of *L'Unità*, the press organ of the Italian Communist Party, described Torino's players as 'authentic representatives of the proletariat and of progressivism'.[3]

After the air disaster, a new team was set up, but the golden age of the 'Grande Torino' was definitively over. The 'Toro', the nickname of the club with a bull as its emblem, had broken legs. In the 1949–1950 season, Juventus topped the Italian league while Torino finished in sixth place. Another tragedy for Toro fans.

From spectator to supporter

In those difficult times, the most fervent *granata* fans – the nickname refers to the garnet colour of the Torino jersey – supported the downgraded and battered club by systematically attending every match to encourage the newly hired players and bail out the impoverished club. Seeking to do more, in 1951 the *tifosi* founded the Granata Supporters' Group in the back room of a popular restaurant in Porta Palazzo, the first organised supporters' association in Italy. For Toro supporters, it was about getting involved in the club's rebirth, but also about 'meeting frequently, in the cafés in the centre or on the outskirts, to give free rein to [their] passion'.[4] As early as December 1951, at a derby against Juventus, the Torino stand was 'dressed as if for a day of celebration', and filled with 'hundreds of flags and placards'.[5] This was a first in a European stadium where visual demonstrations were almost non-existent and spectators were content to show their support with applause, a few scattered cheers and spontaneous outbursts of emotion – the *sfogo*.

Gradually, the Supporters' Group established itself as a representative body for fans who wanted to influence the sporting and political life of Torino. It used its newsletter, *Toro*, to address players directly so that they would start each match with 'one single beat in their hearts, one single will': for Torino to win.[6] With the existence of their great club threatened by poor performance and budget difficulties, the Group became the guardian of *granata* identity. In August

1956, when the club's management was considering a merger with the black-and-white-shirted enemy, Juventus, the group renamed itself Fedelissimi Granata ('The most loyal garnets') with the aim of 'uniting in a single association all true *tifosi* of Torino [...] and defending the club's existence against a merger'.[7] Two years later, they called for the dismissal of Torino's management when the club president, Mario Rubatto, sought to turn the club's financial fortunes around with an advertising contract that involved renaming the team Talmone-Torino (after a chocolate bar) and printing a white 'T' on players' shirts.

From their headquarters on Via Carlo Alberto, the Fedelissimi raised funds to purchase garnet-coloured flags and took care, in close coordination with the club administration, of the sale of tickets. In March 1959, they hired a special train for 400 fans to travel to Bologna in support of their team. Even though Torino was relegated to the second-division Serie B, their support did not waver. In 1963, Torino took over new a ground at the Stadio Comunale, and the Fedelissimi appropriated one of the two *curve* behind the goals, where tickets were cheaper, making the *curva* known as 'Maratona' the gathering place for the *tifosi* faithful.

By the end of the 1950s, standards of living for Italians were noticeably improving, making matches more accessible to the working class. Between 1953 and 1963 attendances rose by over 30 per cent.[8] Inspired by the unwavering loyalty of the Fedelissimi, who compensated for their team's weakness by intensifying their support, other *tifosi* associations were created at the instigation of club directors, such as the Gruppo Simpatizzanti Juventus di Torino ('Juventus of Turin Sympathisers Group') or the Moschettieri ('Musketeers') of Inter Milan, both founded in 1960. With a view to controlling these fan groups, federations of associations such as the Centro Coordinamento Torino Clubs, founded in 1965, or the Associazione Italiana Milan Clubs in 1967, were set up to coordinate the dozens of small *tifosi* organisations that were sometimes based far from the home city of their team.[9] The large-scale migration of workers in that period also dispersed supporters to every corner of the country and beyond its borders. Fedelissimi Granata chapters were formed in Rome in

1971 and Pesaro in 1976. The Milan Clubs Association, meanwhile, assembled 1,300 fan clubs from across the country (and a dozen abroad) by the end of the 1980s.[10]

With their thousands of members – the *soci* – these supporters' associations have established close relations with the clubs' governing bodies, who see this cooperation as a guarantee that their stands will be filled at every match. The supporters' associations also act as neighbourhood houses or, abroad, as community centres for emigrant Italian workers, either in a bar or on their own premises. They regularly offer festivities: post-match meals, club anniversaries, celebrations of a major victory, and so on, while promoting the club's image more broadly by providing venues for social activities outside of football, such as family outings, Christmas tree building, card games and various neighbourhood charities. Men of all ages are involved, with boys often accompanying their fathers. As for the women, they are confined to administrative tasks – selling tickets and merchandise, updating membership fees, managing travel – or preparing the festive meals.

At important matches, the *soci* usually commission a banner with the name of their association, sponsored by a local shopkeeper. In the stands, they wave flags and scarves bought from the supporters' club, while outside they wear a *distintivo*, a brooch in the colours of their team. At the end of the 1960s, the *curve* of Italian stadiums became the territories of choice for *tifoseria*. At Turin's Stadio Comunale, Torino FC's Curva Maratona clashed with Juventus' Curva Filadelfia on the south side, while at Rome's Stadio Olimpico, Lazio's Curva Nord faced off with AS Roma's Curva Sud.

Left turn

The year 1968 marked the beginning of a period of intense political unrest in Italy. The social discontent was expressed both by students shaking off the shackles of the older generation, and by workers freeing themselves from the ideological weight of the Italian Communist Party (PCI). Known as the *Maggio strisciante* or 'creeping May' for the way events stretched out over several months, the movement began in Rome on 1 March 1968 with the battle of Valle Giulia between the police and students attempting to occupy their university. The revolt quickly spread across the country and close links were forged between students and workers, notably in Turin, home to the Fiat car factories. They soon turned violent. On 2 December, the police killed two striking farm workers in Avola, Sicily. On 9 April 1969 two more were shot down in Battipaglia (Campania), during a demonstration against factory closures. On 3 July in Turin, trade unionists at the Fiat plants in Mirafiori declared a day of general strike against the rise in rents. The march was joined by students and descended into ten hours of street fighting with the police.

The social movement hardened and became increasingly autonomous from the trade union leadership or the hegemonic PCI. New radical left-wing organisations emerged, notably *Lotta continua* ('Continuous Struggle') and *Potere operaio* ('Workers' Power'), while Unitary Base Committees (*Comitato Unitario di Base*, CUBs) sprang up in factories.[11] Three months of spontaneous and wildcat strikes followed without interruption, a combative period called the *Autunno caldo* ('Hot Autumn'). The Turin workers of the Fiat factories went on strike after strike, and on 9 October a general strike was declared in Friuli and the Julian Veneto. Ten days later, the inhabitants of the shanty towns of Via Latina in Rome set fire to their own shacks as a sign of revolt. On 25 November, chemical workers began a general strike, then on 28 November, metalworkers from all over the country converged on the capital. 'City by city, district by district, workers were laying the structural and cultural foundations of a vast network of power, which continued to operate for much of the following decade and would profoundly transform Italian society', noted Nanni Balestrini and Primo Moroni, writers and activists at the time. 'The political climate was boiling, the streets were continually invaded by tens of thousands of workers and students in rebellion'.[12]

This unprecedented militant, anti-authoritarian effervescence also spread to football grounds, since the protestors were in fact the same people as those who attended matches. In Milan, while the city was shaken by the uprising, the youngest Milan AC fans met before each match at gate 18 of the club's San Siro grounds to take up a position behind the older *tifosi* in a firmly left-wing Curva Sud.[13] In 1968, political events led them to found a small independent supporters' group, the Fossa dei Leoni. Inter Milan's own Boys San – neo-fascist in inspiration – was formed the following year, while youths from the Sestri Ponente de Gênes district who followed Sampdoria became known first as Ultras Sant' Alberto before changing their name to Ultras Tito Cucchiaroni, in honour of a popular Argentinian player on their team.

These new groups, the first to use the term *ultras*, meaning 'extremes', stood apart from other *tifosi* for their methods, inspired by those of radical political organisations and cells. Like the workers who broke free of the Communist Party-linked trade union offices to self-organise in CUBs, the ultras took a distance from their original supporters' associations, which they saw as overly friendly with the club management and not demanding enough towards footballing institutions. They also held that commitment to a cause – in this case, backing their team – should be total, and organised in the same way as a social movement.

At the crossroads of the association culture of their parents' supporters' clubs and the organisational model of extreme left-wing cells, the ultras formed highly structured groups in which decisions are taken collectively and in which a few heads, the *capi*, or even, for the largest groups, a *direttivo*, the equivalent of a 'political bureau', emerged, depending on the greater commitment of certain members.[14] They were also fascinated by the hooligans of Great Britain. The *tifosi* of Inter Milan confessed to being so overwhelmed by the fervour of the Liverpool Kop during a semi-final match of the European cup in May 1965 that they felt seasick at the constant waves of colour unleashed by the scarves of the English fans.*[15] Being an *ultra* meant an active militancy that for the duration of a match took the form of loud expressions of support with drums, rhythmic clapping and chorused slogans, together with visual displays comprising scarves held high, banners and flags on poles. The aim was to collectively generate the best possible atmosphere in the stands

* During the 1976–1977 European Cup final between Liverpool FC and Borussia Mönchengladbach at Rome's Stadio Olimpico, the fervour of the English Kop impressed the Roman ultras, who took advantage of the opportunity to study their displays closely.

and in the most creative way possible. In the days leading up to a match, the ultras would meet to plan and prepare the *tifo* together, forging bonds of friendship and consolidating the group unity, contributing in turn to the collective fervour. Gabriele, a member of the Leoni della Maratona, an ultra group that split from the Fedelessimi Granata in 1977, recounts the 'immense joy' he feels when Torino FC wins: 'I have wet eyes, goose bumps and the feeling of a fair return, of courage and hard work rewarded'.[16] Meanwhile, an AC Milan fan describes: 'As an ultra, I identify with a particular way of life. We are different from ordinary fans because of our enthusiasm and excitement. This means, of course, rejoicing and suffering much more than everyone else. Being ultra means exaggerating feelings'.[17] An ultra supporter of Atalanta, from Bergamo, put it this way: 'The love and passion I have for the team, in my case Atalanta, is not a rational thing. It can't be explained in words, it's something you feel inside. If you feel it, you can stay in the stadium for seven hours singing and shouting'.[18]

There are also similarities between the ultras in the stands and the demonstrators on the streets. The ultras go to the stadium in a procession, gather behind a banner bearing the name of their group and, like in a demonstration, a *bandierone* delimits their territory in the stands in order to form a 'block'. Similarly, the audio-visual displays are led by the *capo* who, in the manner of an orchestra conductor, motivates and coordinates his troop with a megaphone, his back to the match. These autonomous groups of young supporters swiftly proliferated in Italian stadiums: with the Ultras del Napoli, Forever Ultrà del Bologna, and Ultras Granata at Torino FC, a real 'ultra movement' took shape in 1970s Italy.

In the same period, the political context was being pushed to the limit. The 'hot autumn' concluded with the bombing of Piazza Fontana in Milan on 12 December 1969, which left 17 dead. The police accused railway worker and militant anarchist Giuseppe Pinelli; the protest movement blamed the attack on the far right. While intensifying police and judicial repression, the Italian state allowed neo-fascist groups to fuel a climate of tension, justifying the repression of extreme left-wing movements and precipitating the return of an authoritarian regime.

Certain radical left-wing fringe groups decided to take up arms against the fascist cells and police, a self-defence strategy that bordered on insurrection. Several different clandestine armed organisations emerged, such as the Brigate Rosse (Red Brigades) in 1970, the Nuclei Armati Proletari (Armed Proletarian Cells) in 1974, and the Prima Linea (Front Line) in 1976. An unprecedented wave of political violence struck cities. Bombings, targeted assassinations, *gambizzazione* (kneecappings), kidnappings and exchanges of shots at demonstrations became commonplace. From 1969 to 1980, more than 12,690 attacks resulted in 362 deaths, most of them attributed to the far right, which was committed to carrying out large-scale, indiscriminate strikes to instil terror.[19]

The landscape of the revolutionary left was notable for the emergence of Autonomia Operaia (Worker Autonomy), a vast radical and horizontal political movement that sought to break the authoritarian shackles of Italian society, and into which many extra-parliamentary groups dissolved in 1973. Social protest then spilt over from the universities and factories to city districts, where alternative practices proliferated (free radio, large-scale autoreductions, squatting, etc.). From February 1977, 23 universities went on strike and initiated a plural movement marked by political radicalism and counter-culture. Urban riots, prison escapes, strikes, armed attacks against representatives of industrial employers and the judiciary, feverish assemblies – the climate of spring 1977 was explosive, and the police repression was bloody.*

The political violence that shook Italian society in the 1970s had repercussions on the embryonic ultra movement. The supporters groups that flourished in the stands made direct reference to far-left armed groups in Italy, Palestine and Latin America.** The Commandos Rossoblù emerged in Bologna in 1969, and the Brigate Rossonere

* Like on 13 March 1977, when tanks entered Bologna to quell the social movement that had flared up after the death of a young Lotta Continua activist.

** Between 1970 and 1982, more than 500 acronyms of far left-wing revolutionary groups were recorded in Italy.

and Settembre Rossonero appeared in 1974–1975 in the stands of AC Milan. The Commando Ultra Prima Linea was created in 1978 in Cosenza, the Commandos Fedelessimi at Torino, the Venceremos and Autonomia Bianconera at Juventus and the Fedayn and Tupamaros at AS Roma.[20] The *curve* were taken over by a committed youth who wanted to make the stadium into a theatre of anti-authoritarian expression. Several leaders of the Fossa dei Grifoni of Genoa, formed in 1973, did not hide the fact that they were former Autonomia Operaia activists.[21] Giò, a 21-year-old ultra from Torino and a Fiat worker, stated in 1977 that 'at the moment the *curva* is mostly left wing but it's a bit confused because it's made up of members of the PCI, Lotta Continua and Autonomia',[22] a view supported by Massimo, a young ultra from Juventus, who asserted that 'what unites us is the fact that we are all left-wing'.[23]

Effigies of Che Guevara, yellow or red stars, raised fists: all were to be found on the flags and banners of the *tifosi*. And, as in the processions, the ultras arrived at the stadium with their faces masked by a scarf, wearing a balaclava or a helmet, giving the players a standing ovation by holding up three fingers of one hand, a salute used by the autonomous militants that symbolises the P38 pistol, the favoured weapon of the left-wing armed groups. Some professional footballers were also involved, either on the pitch or on the political scene, like Paolo Sollier, a centre-forward at Perugia from the Val di Susa, who greeted his fans with a raised fist, and was active in Avanguardia Operaia, a small extra-parliamentary left-wing organisation, and published a book in 1976 reflecting on his life as a footballer-worker and revolutionary activist.[24] When signing his professional contract with Perugia, the player successfully inserted a clause that for each of his goals, the club had to take out two subscriptions to the *Quotidiano dei lavori*, the newspaper of the Avanguardia Operaia organisation.

Previously unseen in Italian football grounds, more used to spontaneous shouts of encouragement and the somewhat soporific '*Alè, alè* […]', the chants and slogans sung together by the ultras expressed the close links between militant culture and football activism. Valerio Marchi, a sociologist specialising in fan culture, speaks of a 'reworking of political slogans by the ultras'.[25] From 1969, at Turin's Stadio

Comunale, the local ultras intoned an anti-bosses slogan to rail up Juventus. Owned by the Agnelli family, 'Juve' was associated with the Fiat factories, which also belonged to them and were a major hotbed of the current ferment: 'It's Monday, what a disappointment / Back to the factory / To serve the boss / O black Juve, go wash the feet / of the Agnelli family!'[26] That same season, the first slogan ever sung in the Bologna stadium was sung by the Commandos Rossoblù when they encountered Inter Milan's Boys San: 'Boys, Carrion, Go Back to the Sewers'. The refrain was inspired by the most popular anti-fascist slogan in the political marches of the time: 'Fascists, Carrion, Go Back to the Sewers'.[27] From 1975 onwards, AC Milan's Brigate Rossonere took up the tune of the song 'Per i morti di Reggio Emilia', written by Fausto Amodei in homage to five communist militants murdered by the police at a demonstration in July 1960. The lyrics were adapted by the Milanese *tifosi*: 'Red and black tifosi, Milan tifosi / Let's hold hands in these sad days / Again in Marassi, again there in Comunale / Red and black *tifosi*, we have been taken to hospital / Blood in the stalls, blood in the stands / We have been taken but we are not defeated / It's time for revenge, it's time to fight'.[28] Finally, the Vicenza ultras sang in the direction of their stadium's presidential box: 'Red, red, red Vicenza / Red Vicenza / Bastard bourgeois […] / You'll end up like Aldo Moro', in reference to the leader of the Christian Democracy assassinated in 1978 by the Red Brigades.[29]

Meanwhile, in Turin in 1968 the protestors sang '*Il potere dev'essere operaio*' ('Power Must Belong to the Workers'), while a decade later the city walls were inscribed with graffiti paying homage to Juventus: '*Il potere dev'essere bianconero*' ('Power Should Be Black and White') – the colours of the Turin club.[30] The same club's Armed Black and White Cells not only took their name from a far-left group but adopted the motto: 'For continuous struggle, an ever-stronger army'. This circulation between political and football vocabulary was not illogical for some ultras. 'Shouting slogans in the stadium that echo left-wing political demonstrations is something that comes to us spontaneously, because they're catchy slogans you can chant together – it's normal, right? It's natural to shout the same things that we do in the street', said Gianni, an 18-year-old member of Juventus' Fossa dei Campioni in 1977.[31] This recycling of political slogans was all the more obvious since Gianni, like many other ultras, was committed to the Autonomous movement:

> We, or at least some of us, were sympathisers with Lotta Continua at the end of 1976. In recent times there has been an evolution, a maturity that has emerged from our discussions. Yes, we are supporters of Autonomia Operaia. We told ourselves that we had to believe in something more radical [...] Responding to a police force that uses live ammunition is completely normal, it is 100% a just and legitimate form of struggle, because we live in a police state.[32]

However, the conflict on the streets between clandestine armed groups, the forces of order and neo-fascist cells spread into the grounds. The verbal and physical violence towards police and rival ultra groups, both seen as 'enemies', reached unprecedented heights between 1974 and 1979.[33] At a match between Juventus and AC Milan in February 1975 the Fossa dei Leoni and the Commandos Tigre continually fired flares and smoke bombs at the opposing players, before a Juve ultra was stabbed and a riot broke out between youths in balaclavas armed with flag poles. In March 1977, a pitched battle with knives between Inter Milan ultras caused a number of serious injuries. And on 28 October 1979, 33-year-old Lazio *tifosi* Vincenzo Paparelli died when a smoke bomb thrown by Roma supporters struck him on the head.

The dissident left saw these stadium clashes as a symbol of the social tensions inherent in Italian society. The newspaper *Il Manifesto* – born from a split in the PCI in 1969 – analysed a match between Catanzaro and Juventus in 1976 as a political encounter revealing the arbitrary violence of power.[34] It described Catanzaro as a modest team from the poor, rural province of Calabria that played against the rich, multi-talented Juventus, the symbol of the industrial bosses in the north of the country. *Il Manifesto* focused not on the performance of each team but on a Catanzaro fan who ran onto the pitch to protest against the assault of a player from his team by Juve footballers. The *tifoso* was: 'a teenager of about fourteen years old [...]'

He is skinny, with a long yellow and red scarf around his neck, the colours of his team, which has never won anything. He runs onto the pitch in a clumsy, wobbly manner, like all southerners malnourished for generations. After being hit on the back of the neck with a truncheon, the young supporter fell to the ground before being beaten by eight policemen. The other Catanzaro *tifosi* tried in vain to pull the poor man from the clutches of the police, but were rudely repressed as 'the boy was dragged by his feet, just below the stand where the *Avvocato* [Gianni Agnelli, owner of Juve and head of Fiat] was sitting [...] Some shouted "Fascists, fascists!" [...] But long, hearty applause was directed to the cops amid shouts of "Well done!"'[35] For *Il Manifesto*, police repression of the working classes occurred in the street and stadium alike, and the *tifoso* represented a new revolutionary subject just like the worker or the sub-proletarian.

Despite this politicisation of the *tifosi*, the ultras kept football apart from the militant sphere. The progressive disappearance of revolutionary culture from the stands coincided with the dampening down of social unrest after the spring of 1977 and the crisis that followed the assassination of Aldo Moro by the Red Brigades on 9 May 1978. The brutal government repression launched in April 1979 put an end to the political turmoil: over 6,000 militants were imprisoned and almost a thousand went into exile.[36] 'We now do a Roman salute, with a P38 in the other hand, and that's it!' said Claudio, an 18-year-old Juventus fan in 1979. 'We've excluded politics because it only serves to pit us against each other, whereas it's better to stay united. We've ruled out any political discourse'.[37]

Calcio dell'arte

At the dawn of the 1980s, the number of ultras groups expanded rapidly. However, while before they were largely left-wing, now far-right ultras, such as the Gioventù Bianconera at Juve and the Granata Korps at Torino, became increasingly visible. The *curve* were polarised, with the ultras of Bologna, AC Milan, Torino, AS Roma and Livorno trending more left-wing, and those of Lazio, Inter Milan, Verona or Ascoli more right-wing. The names and iconography of the new ultras borrowed more from pop culture than from politics, while invoking irony or provocation: Nuclei Sconvolti (Nuclei of the Crazy) in Cosenza, Brianza Alcolica (Alcoholic Brianza) at Inter Milan and Drunk Company Veneto Alcool at AC Milan, or more soberly Ragazzi della Maratona (The Maratona Boys) at Torino. Marijuana and beer mugs replaced red stars, while cartoon characters such as Asterix or Andy Capp replaced Che or Geronimo. Youths from the *borgate* (the shanty towns and illegal districts of the Italian metropolises), high school students from the residential districts, young immigrant workers from the Mezzogiorno, smartly-dressed middle-class students: the ultra groups – unlike the British hooligans who came from the most marginalised fringes of the working class – brought together all social backgrounds and became an inescapable 'mass phenomenon' among Italian youth.[38] In 1987, more than 32 per cent of *tifosi* were between 14 and 24 years old.[39] Moreover, with the travel of Italian supporters abroad and through television images (particularly on the occasion of Italy's victory in the 1982 World Cup), the ultra style was exported and emulated throughout Europe: the Biris Norte of Sevilla appeared in 1975, the Diabos Vermelhos of Lisbon's Benfica in 1982, the Commando Ultra of Olympique de Marseille in 1984, and the Bad Blue Boys of Dinamo Zagreb in 1986.

This densification of the ultra network gave rise to a shifting web of alliances (the *gemellagi*, a kind of 'non-aggression pact') and rivalries between the groups, which sharpened inter-supporter hostilities. These alliances were initially based on political affinities, but were also fuelled by traditional antagonisms between northern and southern Italy, by *campanilismo* (the parochial pride that remains so strong in Italy) or by ancient hatreds (originating in a particularly memorable match or historic clashes between *tifosi*). The Inter Milan ultras are thus allied with those of Lazio and Varese, while being rivals of AC Milan, Napoli and AS Roma. Torino's ultras have a long-standing *gemellagio* with Fiorentina based on their shared dislike of Juventus, while AS Roma's *tifosi* have affinities with the Greek ultras of Panathinaikos of Athens, and those of Lazio with their Spanish counterparts from Real Madrid.

The grounds hosting the traditional derbies between the three great industrial cities of northern Italy, Genoa, Milan and Turin, each of which has two teams, are key sites of conflict between ultras. Symbols of the wealthy classes, Genoa's Sampdoria, Milan's Inter and Turin's Juventus – collectively known as 'SAINJU' – wear sober black, white or blue colours, and embody openness (they were often adopted by the new immigrant working-class populations of these cities), innovation, elegant play and a disciplined and distinct fan culture. Meanwhile, Genoa, AC Milan and Torino – 'GEMITO' – with their red or garnet shirts referring to the working-class tradition, celebrate the local roots, loyalty, spirited play and warmth of their supporters.[40] The competition between the great clubs of the Peninsula was further exacerbated in the 1980s when they welcomed brilliant international players who made the Italian championship particularly attractive: Diego Maradona at Napoli, Michel Platini at Juventus, Sócrates at Fiorentina or Arthur Zico at Udinese.

The proliferation of the ultra movement in Italian and then European stadiums led to the emergence of a *mentalità ultrà*, while heightening the warrior rhetoric used by the pioneers of the movement. Visual displays developed from waving large, rudimentary flags to increasingly elaborate and imposing *tifos*. On 23 October 1983, for example, AS Roma's Commando Ultra Curva Sud unfurled a 60-metre-long, 20-metre-high flag to send a message to their team: '*Lo amo*'.[41] The same year, Sampdoria's ultras covered their entire stand with a giant tarpaulin. Pyrotechnic devices first appeared in the stadiums of port cities before becoming a widespread and essential part of ultra culture. The *striscioni*, simple banners on a black or white background, sent messages from the stands to their opponents (or the club's leaders) or referenced current events (homage to a deceased ultra, denunciation of a decision by the football federation, etc.).

A gigantic shirt or a sail in the club's colours is unfurled from the bottom to the top of the *curva*, foghorns sound and smoke flares are lit, confetti is thrown, jumps and movements are rhythmically performed under the guidance of the *capo* at certain moments of the match (kick-off, second half restart, goals scored): everything is intended to offer a total, creative spectacle. Finally, with the help of coloured squares, small flags, strips of paper or balloons, veritable *coreografie* – choreographies – are performed in the stands when the players enter the pitch. Begun in 1986 by the AS Roma ultras, these ephemeral artworks, which last mere seconds, require weeks of preparation and complex visualisation.[42]

In the eyes of the ultras, it is no longer a matter of going to the show, but also of producing the show, regardless of the team's performance. More than creating 'an exceptional moment of festive expression of collective life',[43] a match within the match takes place in the stands. 'I believe in it and at the same time I don't believe in it', explained a Ragazzi della Maratona ultra in the early 1990s. 'For me, going to the stadium means creating a show with banners and everything else. Then you see who is the strongest; there is a ranking. If you do something beautiful, the television picks it up and shows the other clubs what you are capable of'.[44] A visual battle between ultras, one that leads them to be more concerned with the reputation of their group than with their club's score.

In addition to this *tifo* rivalry, which is independent of the team's performance, there is a verbal joust between the *curve*. The love of the club, the attachment to the city and the dedications to the players feed the slogans and the songs of the supporters. International hits ('Sloop John B' by the Beach Boys), opera arias (Verdi's 'Triumphal March'), traditional protest songs ('Bella Ciao' or 'Bandiera Rossa'), popular hits ('Sarà perché ti amo' by Richi e Poveri), film music, folk-lyrical variations in local dialect are all sources of inspiration for the ultras to compose their vast vocal repertoire. But they also know how to use their imagination to insult their opponents, giving rise to an outrageous bidding war of offence – sometimes sexist and homophobic – that fuels confrontation. The Juventus ultras don't hesitate to invoke the Superga tragedy to denigrate Torino fans with the slogan 'Grande Toro, please: if you take the plane, we'll pay for it'.[45] Meanwhile, the *tifosi* of northern Italy, especially those of Hellas Verona, harangue the Neapolitans with stigmatising phrases such as: 'Welcome to Italy', 'Earthquake, come back' or 'No to vivisection, let's use the Neapolitans'.[46]

This antagonism increases the dramatic intensity of each match, making it all the more exciting and passionate. Rejecting the ethics of fair play advocated by the football authorities,[47] in the eyes of the ultras the match is combat where everything goes to discredit the opponent: exhibition of coffins in the colours of the opposing clubs, symbolic death notices, heckling outside the players' hotel to disturb their sleep on the eve of the match, not to mention the mobilisation of *scaramanzia* (superstition) where the *jettatore*, the spell caster, is called upon to go around the stadium banging his cymbals to ward off the evil eye.[48]

Unity of place (the stadium), of time (the 2 x 45 minutes of the match) and of action (the entire match takes place in front of all the spectators): football as a sporting drama offers a new scenario at each match which plays out simultaneously before our eyes. Whether it is drama, *commedia dell'arte* or tragedy, the nature and quality of the spectacle depends on the performance of the 22 actors on the stage and the arabesques traced by the ball. Yet with their intensive commitment to supporting their team, the ultras break with the conventions of the performance, where the audience is confined to the role of spectator. As the 'twelfth man', they try to influence the outcome of the match by interacting with their players, destabilising the opponents and conjuring fate. A twelfth man with real weight, because, at the beginning of the 1980s, Italian Serie A (first-division) clubs were winning games on average three times less often away than at home.[49] The impact of the public on sporting performance was such that the directors of Torino FC went so far as to retire the number 12 jersey from the *granata* team and officially assign it to Curva Maratona.

At the turn of the 1990s, the ultra movement in Italy was at its peak. Groups like Milan FC's Fossa dei Leoni or Juventus' Drughi had 10,000–15,000 members in 1988.[50] In Naples, the Commando Ultra Curva B, founded in 1972 under the guidance of the mythical *capo* Palummella, comprised 6,000 youths, printed 10,000 copies of its journal *Napulissimo*, and boasted its own weekly TV show, *Un'ora in curva B*.[51] All-women ultras groups also began to appear in the *curve*, such as the Ladies Napoli, the URB Girls in Bologna and the Ultras Girls in Sampdoria. In Bologna, 22 per cent of ultras were young women between 22–24, while in Turin 18 per cent of supporters under 24 were women.[52] In certain groups, notably Milan's Curva Sud or those playing in the second division such as Reggio Emilia, the role of *capo* often went to women.

The *direttivo* of each ultra organisation is efficiently structured to divide tasks: ticket sales, travel, sale of merchandise (scarves, badges, etc.), collecting fees, publishing the fanzine, coordination of *tifos* and so on.[53] Independence and autonomy are fiercely cultivated, evident in the self-financing of the group and an emphasis on anonymity. The blocks in the *curve* also became territories where a sense of common belonging is anchored behind the *bandierone* of one's group. The stadium ends offer transgressive spaces free from public authority, where drug consumption is tolerated and a police presence is unthinkable. Above all, they are places rich in socialisation, mutual support and solidarity between *tifosi* united by the unconditional love of their club.[54] They might pay for the ticket of someone who can no longer afford to come to the stadium at the end of the month, or offer a room to a young member of the group who can't find anywhere to live. 'All the profits are pooled and are available to those who are part of the group, for travel, or for those who need to pay for a lawyer [for ultras arrested by the police]', says an Atalanta ultra.[55]

As the ultra movement evolved, the symbolic warfare with visual spectacles and vocal performances was increasingly waged with fists. Acts of violence between ultras and against the police multiplied: whereas in the 1970s there were about ten clashes each season in the first two divisions of the Italian league, 72 were counted in 1988–1989.[56] In addition, railway and metro stations, bars and parks close to stadiums became, like the *curve*, exclusive territories to be defended from enemy ultras and marked with tags, graffiti and stickers.

These urban spaces have become the scene of intermittent confrontations – *scontri* – between supporters, where physical violence serves to rekindle rivalries after a match, but also a ritual in which the youngest demonstrate to their peers their courage and their commitment to the ultra identity.[57] The intensity and duration of these ritualised fights, which take the form of ambushes with a few punches and projectiles thrown, are closely monitored by the oldest and most respected ultra leaders, in order to avoid any serious injuries to their own, or their opponents. First and foremost, such virile confrontations serve to reinforce the social cohesion of the group and to maintain the basic idea of the 'enemy' so intrinsic to the ultra identity.[58]

Police everywhere, freedom nowhere

With the Italy 1990 World Cup around the corner, the intermittent misbehaviour of the ultras drew renewed attention from the footballing and public authorities. Between 1987 and 1990, the San Paolo stadium in Naples, the Olympic stadium in Rome, the San Siro stadium in Milan, the Renato Dall'Ara stadium in Bologna and the Luigi Ferraris stadium in Genoa were completely renovated. Numbered seats were installed in all the *curve*, and the first pens, fences and Plexiglas barriers around the pitch appeared. In December 1989 Law No. 401 on public order at sports events was enacted, introducing a stadium ban of six months to three years for any supporter engaging in violence. After the Cup, far from losing momentum, the mobilisation of the forces of order increased: between 1994 and 2002, the number of police officers in stadiums doubled.[59]

The 1990s were also marked by neoliberalism's arrival in Italy, with Silvio Berlusconi taking power in May 1994. The electoral campaign of his party, Forza Italia, relied on the supporters' association of Milan AC, which the magnate had bought in 1986. Football, politics and business went hand in hand more than ever. In Italy, as in other European countries, the football landscape was changing radically. The free movement of professional footballers within the European Union, confirmed in 1995 with the Bosmand ruling,* gave rise to a lucrative international market for players, the *mercato*, and led to footballers being hired by the highest bidder. The staggering inflation of match rights – Berlusconi was also the majority shareholder of Mediaset, the company that owns the country's three main private channels – made clubs dependent on the financial windfall provided

---

* In 1990, Jean-Marc Bosman, a Belgian professional player from RFC Liège at the end of his contract, was prevented by his club from transferring to USL Dunkerque in France. Bosman took the matter to court and in 1995 succeeded in suspending the existing transfer system (which obliged a player at the end of his contract to ask his club for permission to leave, in return for a transfer fee) and in ending the quota rule, which prohibited clubs in the EU from having more than three players from other EU countries.

by television and sponsors. 'They want people to stay at home instead of going to the matches, and to watch the game on pay-TV', says an Atalanta ultra. 'That way, they avoid the police, they can build smaller stadiums [...] It's all about business and profit'.[60] The cultural identity of each club was gradually diluted by marketing: the club's name became a brand, the crest a vulgar logo, the jersey an advertising space and the ground a commercial complex with an antiseptic atmosphere where the fan is just a customer with money, obliged to consume.

Feeling dispossessed, the ultras sought to counter this forced commodification of the *calcio* and defend a people's football, with its community, its history, its rites, its seasonality and its territory. 'Against modern football' became one of the most common slogans of the Italian and European ultras. They believe that the days spent organising *tifos*, the weekends sacrificed to support the team in the stands rain or shine, the miles swallowed up in a van to get to away games, and the loyalty they show regardless of poor results, give them the right to criticise the club's policy. They openly vilify certain players or coaches whom they perceive as mercenaries with indecent salaries and protest against decisions they consider to be erroneous or guided only by profitability.

For the ultras, football is not a financial industry in the hands of advertisers and the sport's authorities, but a public good and a democratic space, one where they adopt the stance of a trade union. As a 'social partner', they vehemently defend their interests as fans – for lower ticket prices, or against the transfer of a popular player. They don't hesitate to threaten to go on strike, for example, by halting the displays in the stands, or, like a unified trade union action, by joining forces with different ultras groups for shared causes (for example, to oppose changes to match times to benefit broadcasters). Lastly, asserting themselves as a factor of social cohesion in their own right within Italian society, ultras regularly organise family events in their neighbourhoods, fundraising campaigns for associations, tournaments for refugees or disadvantaged youths, or collections for the poor. The ultras of Atalanta and Livorno, for example, distinguished themselves after the 2009 L'Aquila earthquake by travelling to the region to help with the relief efforts and raising funds for the victims.

Despite this power of protest, police and legal repression, as well as the ageing and non-renewal of the *capo* leaders, led to the fragmentation of the *tifoserie* and the declining attractiveness of the historic ultras groups. Within the Curva Maratona of Turin, for example, the Leoni della Maratona suspended their activity in 1994 following the arrest of three figures in their group, including their *capo* (they would not reappear until ten years later). The prominent Raggazzi della Maratona self-dissolved in 2003 after clumsily allowing their tarpaulin to be stolen – the ultimate humiliation – by the Juventus Fighters. Italy's first ultra group, AC Milan's Fossa dei Leoni, also chose to end its activities in November 2005 after its *bandierone* were stolen by Juve ultras.

In an Italian society that was becoming increasingly right-wing – Berlusconi was again president from 2001 to 2006 and then from 2008 to 2011 – some ultras became radicalised through contact with extreme right-wing militants, in particular Forza Nuova, a neo-fascist party set up in 1997 and well-established in football grounds. Sometimes more as provocation than real ideological adherence, racist and anti-Semitic slogans as well as flags adorned with swastikas or Celtic crosses began to appear in the stands of Inter Milan, Lazio or Verona. The disappearance in 1999 of the left-wing Commando Ultra Curva Sud tilted the politics of AS Roma *tifos*. Out of 529 ultras groups registered in Italy in 2007, 72 were considered extreme right-wing, and only 35 extreme left wing.[61]

Some ultras organised a response to the growing racism. Since 1997 and under the aegis of the socio-cultural association Progetto Ultrà and the Unione Italiana Sport Per tutti, an annual Anti-Racist World Cup has been organised near Bologna, bringing together around 200 teams of European supporters and anti-racist activists every summer, in a festive spirit. More radical and political, the ultras of Livorno, Ancona and Terni founded in the new millennium the anti-fascist collective Fronte di Resistenza Ultra, while a number of Antifa ultra groups, like the Rude Boys of Sampdoria, the Antifa Bergamo of Atalanta and the Rebel Fans of Cosenza, joined the Alerta Network!, an international network to fight fascism and racism in the stands set up in November 2007 by the Sankt Pauli ultras of Hamburg and Munich.

The fragmentation of the stands and the disappearance of the flagship groups also broke the transmission of the ultra movement's implicit rules, particularly those relating to physical violence. A new phenomenon rose from the ruins of the historical groups: the *cani sciolti* – 'stray dogs' – young supporters who gravitated towards the ultras but who systematically fought with knives. On 29 January 1995, Vincenzo Spagnolo, a 24-year-old Genoa supporter, was stabbed to death by an 18-year-old AC Milan ultra, the prelude to a sinister spiral of violence that several ultras groups tried in vain to quell. Under the aegis of the Brigate Neroazzurre Atalanta, the latter published a joint declaration entitled '*Basta lame, basta infami*' ('Stop the blades, stop the disgrace'). But hostilities between *cani sciolti* continued and the number of people injured in and around stadiums tripled between 1995 and 2000.[62]

A legal arsenal specifically targeting supporters, arbitrary arrests, beatings: unprecedented police repression descended on the ultras with the turn of the millennium, using them as guinea pigs in new strategies for maintaining order. In 2001 and 2003, Law 401 on stadium bans, first introduced in 1989, was reinforced. Conditions of access to stadiums were tightened and, based on the principle of 'delayed evidence', a person could be arrested on the basis of video or photo evidence up to 36 hours after the match.[63] Officials could cancel a match or ban visitors from the stadium. From 2003 onwards, more than 8,000 police officers and carabinieri were mobilised every week in and around sports venues.[64]

With pyrotechnics officially banned in the stands, *tifosi* now needed permits to bring banners and other visual material into the stadiums. A new anti-violence law enacted in August 2005 reinforced stadium security with video surveillance in the stands and named ticketing. Any person interrupting a football match became liable to between one month and three years in prison.[65] After the death in February 2007 of a policeman during clashes with Catania *tifosi* and the death nine months later of a Lazio supporter (Gabriele Sandri, shot by the police), the Ministry of the Interior prohibited collective travel by any group of supporters considered a potential threat to public order.

Yet this repressive and legal escalation only served to fuel the 'anti-cop' attitude of the ultras and to keep fans away from the stadiums. In 2001, a Serie A match attracted an average of 30,000 supporters, compared to fewer than 18,500 in 2007.[66] At the same time, '*Ultra Liberi*' ('Freedom for ultras') and 'ACAB' ('All cops are bastards') became the most popular protest slogans, with national demonstrations organised against the new measures in October 2001, and again in April and June 2003. The ultras also declared a 'sacred union' in response to the repression. In 2005, following the stadium ban on *capo* Claudio 'Bocia' Galimberti of Atalanta, their formidable local rivals, the Brescia ultras, called for his release in a communiqué entitled: 'Bocia, our faithful enemy, don't give up!' Meanwhile, Lazio and Roma groups joined forces to attack police barracks in Rome in late 2007 following the death of Gabriele Sandri.

From the 2009–2010 season onwards, the Ministry of the Interior attempted to put the final nail in the coffin of ultra agitation by deploying a new security device: a 'supporter's card' (*tessera del tifoso*). Introduced under the pretext of better ticketing management and excluding the most violent supporters, the *tessera* functions like a bank card that contains the supporter's personal data as well as a microchip that allows the *tifoso*'s journeys between football grounds to be traced. Made compulsory in 2010, this powerful control tool has united the ultra movement, which considers it an attack on individual freedoms and a perfect embodiment of the football business: part commercialism, part police surveillance.

On 15 November 2009, an anti-*tessera* demonstration in Rome brought together 5,000 ultras.[67] From rival teams, ultras from all over the country marched dressed in white in order to underline their solidarity in this common struggle. From the refusal to cheer the team to the strike in the stands and the *striscioni* insulting holders of the new cards, the protests became progressively more radical. Napoli's ultras published an online guide to falsifying the *tessera*, while a nationwide campaign not to renew stadium season tickets was launched by three Sampdoria ultras, who declared in a press release in April 2010:

> We see no other solution, no matter how much harm we have done, than to sacrifice our beloved season ticket rather than submit to measures that we have long fought against for their absurdity [...] It is not normal that in order to attend a match, which until proven otherwise remains a public spectacle, we have to register (including children) as if applying for a gun permit! [...] We have never asked for permission to display our banners and we will not ask for permission to enter a stadium.

In July 2010, under the banner '*No alla tessera del tifoso*', 400 representatives of some 60 ultras groups put aside their historical rivalries to meet in Catania and coordinate their anti-*tessera* action. Asserting that 'a stadium without a *tifo* is even sadder than a stadium without a football match', they threatened the Italian football authorities with 'a general, open-ended strike in the stands'.[68] A month later, Atalanta's ultras disrupted a meeting of the Northern League – a regionalist, xenophobic political party – to which the Minister of the Interior, Roberto Maroni, was invited. While a handful of them infiltrated the rally armed with firecrackers and smoke bombs, 500 others caused a riot in the neighbourhood and set fire to several police vehicles.

The 1977 Parma Boys, for their part, harangued the Ministry of the Interior directly in November 2011: 'This card, with its fees, has shown itself in reality to be a credit card, a banking product, something totally unrelated to football and security, serving only to collect data'.[69] Finally, in February 2013, a few days before the Italian general elections, a thousand Neapolitan ultras went so far as to burn their voting cards after having called, along with ultras groups in Rome and Genoa, for a boycott of the elections. The *curve* inexorably emptied out and the stadium security vaunted by the promoters of the *tessera* ended in a resounding failure after two seasons. Banned from entering the visitors' stands because they did not have the supporter's card, some fans bought individual tickets for other areas of the stadium and found themselves mixed in with the local *tifosi*, only increasing hostilities between groups at away matches.

Following the plural and stubborn resistance of the ultra movement, the *tessera del tifoso* was finally abandoned by the authorities in 2013 in favour of a supporter's card managed by each club and not associated with a payment system or a system for tracking the supporter. By appealing to unity and mutual aid, two pillars of the *mentalità ultrà* that are too rarely emphasised by the media, the supporters thus won a hard-fought victory that demonstrated that the much-maligned ultras are above all watchdogs against the growing security order and defenders of football as a 'common good'. 'For those who have forgotten, football belongs to everyone and for generations has united Italians: even today, football is the only real social phenomenon in our country capable of bringing together young people from all over Italy', recall Ultras Tito Cucchiaroni of Sampdoria, a mythical group that pioneered the Italian ultra movement.

> By becoming a business, football has lost its skin, its beauty, its poetry and its credibility [...] Passion, the *tifo*, faith, the desire for freedom, the roar of the stands cannot and will never be reduced to a simple budget line. Football does not belong to those who profit from it, but to those who love it.[70]

16

'God and the devil'

Maradona, between popular passion and fan cult

> One fine day the goddess of the wind kisses the foot of man, that mistreated, scorned foot, and from that kiss the football idol is born.
>
> Eduardo Galeano, *Football in Sun and Shadow*

'I grew up in a deprived district of Buenos Aires [...] deprived of water, of electricity, and of phone lines', reflected Diego Armando Maradona in March 2004, during a visit to Bolivia. Among the stream of provocative, egocentric or disturbing statements made by the famous footballer, reminiscences of his modest childhood in Villa Fiorito, a shantytown in the southern suburbs of Buenos Aires, emerged from time to time. Until the sun went down, the young Diego, nicknamed 'Pelusa' ('Fluffy') because of his tuft of hair, spent most of his time outside playing football on the *potreros*, those bits of wasteland where children like to play.

In 1971, aged just 11, the small, dark-skinned left-footer was noticed by Francis Cornejo, a scout for the Argentinos Juniors, the top club in Buenos Aires. With its working-class origins – it was originally known as the 'Martyrs of Chicago' in homage to the anarchists killed in the 1886 Haymarket Square massacre – the club took Maradona into its junior team, the Cebollitas. Crowds quickly admired the devastating dribbles of the talented *pibe*, the 'kid' from the streets. The fascination with the sporting prodigy meant he was already giving television interviews within a year.

Hired as a professional player at 15, he went on to shine for Argentinos Juniors, taking the club to the top of Argentina's premier division. A few months later, in February 1977, he pulled on an

Argentina shirt for the first time against Hungary before winning the 1979 Youth World Cup and being voted best player. The *pibe* from Villa Fiorito was baptised the '*Pibe de Oro*' by the press – the Golden Kid – before being bought for a fortune by Boca Juniors, the mythical Buenos Aires club.

In a country crushed by the military dictatorship imposed by General Videla in 1976, the young Maradona breathed winds of freedom and footballing joy into the Argentinian championship. In 1978, Argentina, which was hosting the eleventh edition of the World Cup, caused international controversy and calls for a boycott in order not to endorse an event manipulated by a junta that shamelessly executed its opponents.* Despite the horrors of the dictatorship, the *Pibe de Oro*, in the blue and yellow jersey of Boca Juniors, set the overcrowded stands of the mythical Bombonera stadium ablaze by helping his team win the national championship and humiliating his Buenos Aires enemy, River Plate.** The great fervour felt for him by Boca Juniors fans conquered the hearts of the entire Argentinian people at the turn of the 1980s. With his passionate football and his social origins, the 'Golden Boy' expressed on the pitch the very essence of the nation's collective identity.

The *criollo* agitator

Introduced to Buenos Aires in the 1870s by English immigrants, Argentinian football was dominated until the turn of the century by amateur clubs of British expats who played a rough and physical, disciplined and mechanical football. In contrast to this 'Britishness', an authentically 'Argentinian' style of play emerged, called the *criollo* – literally 'creole' – style, in the lower-class districts of the capital, influenced by the waves of working-class immigration from Italy and Spain.[1] Individualist, lively and creative, the *criollo* style affirmed its place on the pitches when in 1913 a team without any British

* The anti-World Cup campaign in 1978 was led in France by the COBA (Committee for the boycott of the organisation of the World Cup by Argentina). Under Videla, an estimated 10,000 to 30,000 people were murdered or disappeared by the regime.

** The atmosphere of the Boca Juniors stadium is legendary. Some spectators even go so far as to spread deceased fans' ashes there during matches, to respect their last wishes. The sheer amount of ashes damaged the pitch, and a special cemetery was set up in 2006.

players, Racing Club de Avellaneda, won the national championship for the first time.[2]

In a cosmopolitan metropolis like Buenos Aires, where over 60 per cent of inhabitants were immigrants in 1914,[3] *criollo* football became a social cement and a means of cultural distinction from both Europeans and rival neighbour Uruguay.[4] The Argentinian *criollo* style was honed on the *potreros*, those urban gap sites that had survived the industrial rationalisation of the city undertaken under the guidance of the British. Like the tango, which reflected the lifestyle of those who survived by scavenging in the streets of the slums of Buenos Aires, feinting and cunning, victory not by force but by deception, became characteristic features of Argentinian football – *la nuestra* ('ours'), as the fans called it.

The game's power of attraction was phenomenal: in 1930, the best clubs would draw up to 40,000 fans to their grounds each weekend.[5] Passionately supporting one's team from the stands became one of the rare shared experiences in a country of fragmented identities and cultures. Football gradually became a catalyst of social unity, crystallising a new imaginary for all Argentinians. In 1948, at the height of the Peronist regime, the film *Pelota de trapo* ('Rag Ball') by Leopoldo Torres Ríos was an enormous popular success. In this production, a working-class Argentinian football star by the name of Comeuñas discovers after falling ill on the pitch that he has a serious heart condition. In his final match, a Copa America fixture against Brazil, one of his teammates pleads with him not to continue the game, but the hero refuses: 'There are many ways to give your life for your country, this is one of them', he says. After scoring a decisive goal, Comeuñas is rewarded for his service to the nation.[6]

Both inventive and unpredictable, the *criollo* game played by Diego Maradona swiftly turned the young virtuoso into the very embodiment of Argentinian football. Similarly, his modest origins, his small size – he was barely 5ft 4½" (165cm) tall – and his enthusiasm on the pitch were interpreted by fans as distinctive features of the *pibe*, a popular cultural figure in the country that evokes a child raised on the streets, outside of social conventions.[7]

For the 1982 World Cup in Spain, Maradona fully assumed his role as a rebellious *pibe*. To the surprise of the Europeans, this further reinforced his popularity among Argentinians. On 2 July 1982, the Albiceleste team (so called for their sky blue and white jerseys) faced the Brazilian squad for the second time in the tournament. From the first whistle, Maradona was targeted by defenders who tackled him whenever he approached the goal. Exasperated by the previous encounter with Italy, where he had been harassed by defender Claudio Gentile, and dominated by a Seleção leading 3–0, the *Pibe de Oro* cracked and kicked the Brazilian player Batista in the stomach, five minutes before full time. Maradona was immediately sent off by the referee, before the Argentinian selection was eliminated from the World Cup.

The reputation of the temperamental player became entrenched thanks to another violent incident. Transferred to Barcelona in 1982, Maradona was constantly tormented by defenders in the Spanish league, including the imposing Andoni Goikoetxea of Athletic Bilbao, who broke the Argentinian's ankle in September 1983, preventing him from playing for over three months. A year later, in the Copa del Rey final and in the presence of King Juan Carlos of Spain, Barcelona met Athletic Bilbao again. Maradona saw red in the face of his tormentor Goikoetxea and started a violent brawl on the pitch. This deepened European commentators' dim view of the undisciplined footballer, who was already notorious for his antics in Barcelona nightclubs and his growing addiction to cocaine.

In July 1984, the Argentinian prodigy arrived in Naples to join SSC Napoli, who had blown their budget on the *Pibe de Oro*. Maradona, welcomed like a messiah by 80,000 *tifosi* at the San Paolo stadium for his presentation to the fans, quickly became identified with a Naples stigmatised for its poverty and mafia crime. Popular, boisterous and volcanic, the player immediately felt at home in the decadent capital of southern Italy.

His stocky body, his black curls, his rites imbued with religion and superstition – kissing both his cross and the forehead of his masseur Carmano before taking to the pitch – as well as his spontaneity on the turf led Neapolitan fans to quickly identify him with the *scugnizzo*, the rascal from the working-class neighbourhoods of Naples who echoes the Argentinian character of the *pibe*.[8] In the words of Italian weekly *L'Espresso*:

> With his short legs, rounded body, ruffian's mouth and diamond in his ear, Diego became a true Neapolitan. His love for beautiful women and good food, his extravagant spending on racing cars [...] and, at the same time, his church and sacred family side – the whole family lives and prospers in Naples at the club's expense – his dirty, capricious, exuberant, undisciplined character, all this made him a true legitimate son of the city.[9]

With Maradona scoring 14 goals in his first season, SSC Napoli climbed up the first division, and in 1985–1986 his talents – coupled with those of freshly recruited forward Bruno Giordano – took the Neapolitan club to third place in the championship, to the delight of the *tifosi*.

Footballing divinity

After this second honourable season in Naples, Maradona was named captain of Argentina's national squad on the eve of the 1986 World Cup in Mexico. Carried by the fiery play of the inspired *Pibe de Oro*, the team had little trouble qualifying for the quarter-finals, where they faced England. On the eve of the match, the international media fanned the flames of rivalry by comparing it to the 1982 Falklands conflict between Great Britain and Argentina. The Spanish daily *El País* ran the headline: 'The Falklands War in football terms'.[10] 'Don't miss the re-run of the Falklands War', suggested the Mexican newspaper of reference *Excélsior*.[11] The British tabloid *The Sun* was as subtle as ever: 'It's war!'[12]

Four years earlier, Argentina's military junta, whose power was beginning to waver, had ordered the invasion of the Falkland Islands in the South Atlantic, occupied by the British since 1833. Despite attempts at conciliation on the part of the international community, Margaret Thatcher launched a vast military operation to recapture the Falklands, which ended on 14 June 1982 with the death of nearly

650 Argentinian soldiers and 250 British soldiers. Although the armed dictatorship never recovered from this humiliating defeat, the Falklands War remains synonymous with trauma for Argentinians.

On 22 June 1986, the day of the quarter-final match with England, Argentina fielded a generation of players most of whom had narrowly escaped recruitment to the 1982 armed conflict thanks to their status as international footballers. It was therefore with a great deal of media pressure and a fierce desire to erase the humiliation of the Falklands that the Argentinian eleven took to the pitch at the Azteca stadium in Mexico City in front of over 110,000 spectators. Under the hot Mexican sun, the first half ended 0–0. But six minutes into the second half, Maradona, wearing the number 10 shirt as always, suddenly broke through the English defence to make an impromptu pass to striker Jorge Valdano. As the ball clumsily bounced away from his team-mate's foot, England defender Steve Hodge, overwhelmed by the speed of the exchange, knocked the ball back to his keeper. Then the diminutive Maradona leapt to the height of the giant Peter Shilton's gloves and, with his left arm outstretched, knocked the ball into the back of the British net. The stands erupted and, despite the loud protests of the English players, the Tunisian referee Ali Bennaceur, not having seen the Argentinian's hand, validated the first goal.*

Exactly three minutes later, like a 'cosmic kite', in the words of Uruguayan sports commentator Victor Hugo Morales,[13] Maradona embarked on a wild run from the middle of the pitch and dribbled dazzlingly past half a dozen outflanked and panicked English players, to score a magnificent second goal, ensuring Argentina's advancement to the semi-finals. To this date, it is celebrated as one of the most beautiful goals ever scored. 'It all happened in four minutes', reported the Spanish daily *El Mundo*. 'The scoundrel and the genius, God and the devil, a high-flying crook and a footballing divinity, the best football player that a mortal mother has given birth to in the twentieth century'.[14]

* On 17 August 2015, while passing through Tunisia, Maradona paid a visit to Ali Bennaceur to gift him an Argentina jersey he dedicated with the words: 'For Ali, my eternal friend'.

At the post-match press conference, the Argentinian forward stirred the controversy by proudly accepting he had scored 'a little with the head of Maradona, and a little with the hand of God'. By assigning a divine dimension to this 'Hand of God' that passed into posterity, the captain of the Albiceleste avenged, in the eyes of Argentina, the wound of the Falkland Islands by breaking the rules of football. And if the irregularity of the Hand of God made the defeat even more bitter for the English, it was all the more appreciated by the Argentinian people because it was such a *criollo* gesture. In the face of England's physical domination, illustrated by the size of the English keeper (over 6 feet), little Diego had turned to the art of trickery to defeat the British Goliath. As he later claimed, 'It came from the deepest part of me. It was something I'd done before in the *potrero*, in Fiorito'.[15]

To counter the powerful and rational system of play of the English, Maradona deployed an astute creativity typical of the inhabitants of poor neighbourhoods.[16] 'In Fiorito, the pitch where Diego played was bumpy and strewn with rubbish and weeds. It was there that he developed his extraordinary physical abilities and his technique based on evasion', says Fernando Signorini, Maradona's physical trainer from 1984 to 1994. 'In this shanty town abandoned by the state, you had to be resourceful to get by. As a child, Diego was full of mischief when it came to taking the train or stealing an apple. This was reflected in his game'.[17] The second goal, meanwhile, recalls another characteristic of *criollo* football. 'He showed that dribbling is the essence of our style of play', says Juanjo, an Argentinian fan. 'He dribbled and dribbled some more, and those few seconds are engraved in my memory as if they were suspended forever in time'.[18]

In *Homo Ludens. A Study of the Play Element in Culture*, published in 1938, the Dutch historian Johan Huizinga already pointed out: 'To our way of thinking, cheating as a means of winning a game robs the action of its play-character and spoils it altogether [...] Archaic culture, however, gives the lie to our moral judgement in this respect, as also does the spirit of popular lore'. This 'popular lore', which sees in the Hand of God the very expression of Argentinian identity through the transgression of the law, has been, and still is, regularly probed by Argentinian intellectuals. 'We don't know if we are capable of maintaining a semblance of order and stability in our country', said the Argentinian journalist and writer Jorge Lanata in 1994. 'Can we really be a modern society that plays by the rules of modern countries, or are we just that boy from the slums who still thinks he can play by other rules as long as he is not caught red-handed?'[19]

With his Hand of God, Maradona laid out a founding social dichotomy of his nation. Since the mid-19th century, Argentina had asserted itself as a victory of 'civilisation', symbolised by the industrial metropolis of Buenos Aires, against the 'barbarism' represented by the pampa, the wild space where the gaucho roams, obeying only his own rules.[20] The *Pibe de Oro* and his fraudulent gesture thus reflect this indomitable part of Argentinian society that is furiously resistant to authority. An ambiguous relationship with Western modernity was noted as early as 1946 by the author Jorge Luis Borges in his essay *Our Poor Individualism*, in which he wrote that 'the Argentinian, unlike the North American and almost all Europeans, does not identify with the State [...] The Argentinian is an individual and not a citizen'.[21]

The 'individual' Maradona returned in early July 1986 to Naples having won the World Cup in Mexico, as well as the Golden Ball as best player. Raised to the ranks of football's mythical heroes, the *Pibe de Oro* spent his best years at SSC Napoli. In the 1986–1987 season, the club took home for the first time in its history the Scudetto, the Italian Premier League title, as well as the Coppa Italia. Assisted by strikers Bruno Giordano and Careca, Maradona carried the club to the top of European football by winning the UEFA Cup in 1989, and a second Scudetto the following year.

While SSC Napoli was accustomed to the threat of relegation and a lowly position in the table, Maradona's footballing exploits restored pride to the former capital of southern Italy. It was a symbolic revenge of the *terroni* ('peasants') of the deprived and stigmatised South against the industrial, haughty North. As if his goals were an extension of the miracles of San Gennaro, the patron saint of Naples, Maradona was elevated to the rank of a quasi-religious icon and became the object of a veritable popular cult. His very name is associated with 'Marònna', the name of the Virgin Mary in Neapolitan dialect, and prayers to win the Scudetto are said in his name such as: 'Our Maradona / You who come down to the pitch / We have sanctified your name / Naples is your kingdom / Don't bring us false hope / But lead us to victory in the championship'.[22]

Representations of the footballer referencing sacred iconography or on the knees of San Gennaro, and altars dedicated to the *pibe* adorn the streets of Naples, making Maradona 'a sort of saint, the new symbol of an archaic ritual to which popular culture turns to make its requests, to express its adversities, its needs, its sufferings and, less frequently, its joys'.[23] In a city then entirely draped in SSC Napoli blue, the demented carnival celebrations of the first Scudetto in 1987 were also an opportunity to communicate with the dead, a popular practice in Naples. On the wall of the Poggioreale cemetery, a giant inscription was painted reading 'You don't know what you missed!' before the following day the riposte 'Are you sure that we missed it?' appeared beneath it.[24] As for the thousands of *tifosi* who communicated with Diego each week from the stands, they draw on Naples slang like *malatia* (illness) or *patuto* (bewitched) to express their fervour. '*Diego, facce n'ata malatia!*' ('Diego, afflict us!') became a ritual invocation from Neapolitan supporters.[25] There are a score of unique chants dedicated to the *pibe*, including the famous refrain '*O mamma mamma mamma / Sai perche' mi batte il corazon? / Ho visto Maradona! / Eh, mamma', innamorato son*' ('Oh mamma, do you know why my heart beats? I've seen Maradona! And mamma, I'm in love').

Saint Maradona

Nevertheless, in early 1991, the star's nocturnal escapades and provocative remarks about his opponents and footballing institutions – he harboured a fierce hatred of FIFA's João Havelange and Sepp Blatter – increasingly attracted the attention of a press hungry for scandal. Accused of drug trafficking, of maintaining links with the Camorra clans and of having an illegitimate child with a young Neapolitan woman, Maradona tested positive for cocaine in March 1991 after a match against Bari. The case made headlines and the footballer, suspended for 15 months, decided to return to Buenos Aires on the sly. Barely a month later, a police raid on his flat led to a high-profile arrest of the *Pibe de Oro*, mercilessly handcuffed after drugs were found on him.

Maradona then embarked on a *via crucis*. He played for Sevilla, without much success, before returning to Argentina with Newell's Old Boys in 1993. He was resurrected by the Albiceleste for the 1994 World Cup, but, following a magical goal against Greece, he was ordered to leave after testing positive for ephedrine. He was suspended until September 1995, mocked by the international press, and fell into depression. 'They cut off my legs, but I was expropriated from my body', he said. 'I am empty […] I've been killed as a player and as a man'.[26] Despite a succession of drug rehabs and other affairs worthy of a bad telenovela, the *pibe* hung up his boots for good after a final positive test for cocaine in August 1997 following a match for Boca Juniors.

Paradoxically, the various convictions and suspensions for drug use did little to diminish the popularity of the footballing hero in Naples. In the eyes of Neapolitan youth, the chaotic career of the *Pibe de Oro* symbolised a certain emancipation from state oppression and the moral order of the dominant classes.[27] A few days after Maradona's suspension in 1991, a young Neapolitan woman interviewed on television retorted: 'He was right to do everything he did, to do drugs, to fuck, to have fun, to not give a damn about anything or anyone. How lucky he was!'[28]

Similarly, in Argentina, popular devotion to the rascal of Villa Fiorito did not wane, but the contrary. In the aftermath of his ephedrine test and ejection from the 1994 World Cup, the business daily *El Cronista comercial* reported:

> A real sadness and a certain madness were clearly perceptible in the streets of Buenos Aires. In the bars and restaurants, in the supermarkets, in the small neighbourhood shops, in the intense discussions on the bus and metro, a general reaction dominated among ordinary people: we will forgive Diego; we will always forgive Diego Maradona. The arguments presented were diverse.

> Some saw his doping test as a conspiracy against Maradona and Argentina; others accused Havelange, the Brazilian FIFA president, of being the main perpetrator because Maradona has always referred to him as his main enemy and criticised many of his decisions. But all of them, without distinction, said that Maradona was the essence of joy in football, and that if he had taken ephedrine, he was not responsible; others were responsible.[29]

Reacting to the impunity enjoyed by the *Pibe de Oro*, the Argentinian writer Mempo Giardinelli rebelled in 1994:

> Respect for the law has no prestige in this country [...] We could even say it is part of the Argentinian way of life. Believing that happiness is eternal, that it isn't important to follow rules or accept responsibilities. That it's easier to blame others, to imagine conspiracies, to tell oneself that, when we make a mistake, it's not our fault but someone else's.[30]

For those in favour of order and morality, Maradona had to repent and be punished for his actions. On the other hand, for many Argentinians, 'the more noise Maradona makes around him, the more he becomes the natural embodiment of a *pibe*'.[31] Drug addiction, obesity, drug trafficking, political support for Hugo Chávez and Fidel Castro: Maradona's disjointed career was the perfect reflection of what is expected of the *pibe*, the irresponsible and mischievous child who is forgiven everything.[32]

This childish nature, combined with a spirit of disobedience that is fundamentally rooted in Argentinian identity, is something that Maradona seems to have sought out tirelessly in his private life as well as on the pitch: 'I've been given a lot of nicknames, but Pelusa is the one I like best because it takes me back to my childhood in Fiorito', he said. 'I remember the Cebollitas, the bamboo poles and when we only played for a Coke and a sandwich. There was nothing as pure'.[33]

The Christ-like dimension of Maradona only grew in Argentina with the media coverage of his antics. The footballer, who was prone to bulimia (he gained and then lost more than 40 kg), and his addiction to alcohol, cigars and cocaine, as well as his major surgical operations in 2004 and 2007, were all televised weaknesses with which the Argentinian people could identify.[34] If Maradona was a mischievous and undisciplined *pibe*, his cracks made him a vulnerable being, who, like a cathodic martyr, sacrificed his tired body in a final sporting feat, that of going to the 1994 World Cup at the insistence of the Argentinian fans, before they 'cut off his legs' and 'killed him as a player'.

In order to prolong their devotion to Diego Maradona, barely a year after the end of his official career, three Argentinian fans created the Maradona Church in Rosario in October 1998. A Catholic syncretism entirely devoted to the cult of Maradona, renamed 'D10S', a typographical combination that refers to *Dios* ('God') and *Diez* ('ten', in homage to his jersey), the football-religious movement now has more than 120,000 followers across 60 countries.[35] 'The Maradona Church brings together Maradona fanatics from all over the world', explains Alejandro Verón, one of its founders. 'Our religion is football and, like any religion, it must have a god. Everything happens within the framework of football, with respect for all religious beliefs and without any desire to denigrate them'.[36]

The Maradonian calendar (which began in 1960, the year Maradona was born) is marked by two major rituals: Maradonian Easter, celebrated every 22 June to commemorate the two goals scored against England in 1986, and Christmas, which takes place on 29 October, the day before D10S's birthday. 'We show images of Diego's great goals on a giant screen and we invite some of his relatives to tell us stories about their experiences with our god', says Alejandro Verón. 'All this in a very festive atmosphere, while we wait for midnight'.[37]

At a Maradonian Christmas celebration in October 2008 in the back room of a Buenos Aires pizzeria, Hernan Amez, one of the three fans behind the movement, said: 'Argentinians are passionate, temperamental, sanguine. Maradona embodies this character on the football pitch. He is the one who never gives up [...] Maradona makes us so strong, that's why we love him like a god'.[38]

After 300 fans sang a Maradonian Our Father* – 'Our Diego, Who is on the pitches, May your left foot be blessed, May your magic open our eyes, Make us remember your goals, On earth as it is in heaven' – a good-natured ceremony begins amid a strange solemnity by ten apostle-teammates who bring various relics such as cleats, a bloody football decorated with a crown of thorns or a rosary with 34 beads recalling the number of goals scored by Diego for the national team. In the audience and after several beers, Anthony Bale, a young Scottish supporter and member of the Maradona Church, confessed: 'What did Jesus do that Maradona didn't? They both performed miracles, it's right that Maradona's are recognised'.[39]

* There are also ten Maradonian commandments, which include: 'Love football above all things', 'Spread the news of Diego's miracles throughout the universe', and even 'Name your first son Diego'.

17

'We are lovers, not fighters'

Istanbul's ultras and Turkish power

> Let's give the world to the children just for one day like a balloon in bright and striking colours to play with let them play singing among the stars.
>
> Nâzim Hikmet, *Exile is a Hard Job*

> The perfume of the lovers of Beşiktaş is the aroma of tear gas.
>
> A Çarşı ultra

It's an image that became a symbol of the protests that shook Istanbul in the spring of 2013. In the middle of a demonstration in Taksim Square, a bulldozer valiantly launches itself towards the stunned police. At the controls of the hijacked machine are Çarşı ultras, recognisable by their black and white striped scarves or jerseys, flocked with a bright red 'A' for anarchy.

These supporters of Beşiktaş JK, a football club from the eponymous Stambouliote district, were quick to join the wide-ranging protest movement against the Islamo-conservatives in power since 2002. The brutal police repression of a modest sit-in by environmental activists at the end of May 2013, against the planned destruction of Gezi Park, led to a wave of unprecedented uprisings throughout Turkey against the authoritarian excesses of Recep Tayyip Erdoğan, then the prime minister.

Angry at the police violence against marchers – the real bullets, tear gas and water cannons left eight dead and 8,000 injured[1] – the Beşiktaş ultras swiftly arrived to reinforce the young protestors. 'The Çarşı organised the defence of the occupied park', explains Tan Morgül, a journalist and host of a football programme on Açık

Radyo. 'They were on the front line against the forces of order, and a score of them were arrested in June 2013. In Turkey, football fans are one of the few social groups who know how to confront the police'.[2]

From the stadiums to Taksim Square

Beşiktaş fans maintain a boisterous rivalry with Istanbul's other two flagship clubs, Fenerbahçe SK and Galatasaray SK. Founded at the beginning of the 20th century, these three great Turkish clubs were, after the First World War, the vector of symbolic revenge against the teams of the British forces occupying Istanbul and brought together three very divided sporting and cultural communities. Fenerbahçe represents the posh, aristocratic club of the Asian side of the capital, while Galatasaray, which borrows its name from the prestigious French-speaking high school in Istanbul, is a symbol of the city's bourgeois elites. Since Beşiktaş is a working-class neighbourhood historically rooted in the left, this team forms a contrast as the 'people's club'.

After the military coup of September 1980, which banned all political gatherings and activities, the stadium became one of the privileged spaces of social expression for a whole section of Istanbul youth. 'Supporting one's team' became an essential feature of male identity in Turkey, and the stands a place of relatively free political association. 'We created the Çarşı in 1982, when we were just 15 years old', says Nizam, one of the group's founders.*

> We were a gang of seven or eight friends. Some guys from Fenerbahçe came to our neighbourhood to hang a flag of their team to provoke us and we quickly made them understand that they had to get out. At the same time, during matches against Fenerbahçe, we needed to physically defend ourselves against their fans who wanted to beat us up and prevent us from entering the stadium to support our team. We then simply called ourselves the Çarşı ['Central Market' or 'Bazaar' in Turkish], because we came from the bazaar of Beşiktaş.[3]

---

* Names have been changed at Çarşı's request.

After 1984, physical violence was the rule between the three rival brothers of Istanbul. Brawls between hundreds of supporters and fatal accidents in the stands were frequent because only the Inönü stadium in Beşiktaş hosted all the matches in the capital at the time – the other two stadiums being under renovation. 'We even slept at night in the stadium, the day before the match, to have the best seats so that our group was as visible as possible', adds Nizam. 'We then fought all night with the supporters of the other team to hold the end'. The gang's ranks in the Beşiktaş district grew as confrontations between supporters and with the police multiplied. Fists and stones were gradually replaced by knives, Molotov cocktails and revolvers. Pitched battles with the security forces outside the stadiums were legion, honing the first self-defence practices against the Turkish riot police. The brutal clashes between supporters would only subside after a truce between rival ultras was secretly negotiated at the turn of 1991, following the death of a Çarşı harassed by around 40 Galatasaray fans.[4] In the meantime, ten Çarşı ultras disappeared in the appalling inter-supporter ambushes dubbed the 'war of Inönü'.[5]

While these violent football antagonisms persist and still regularly spill out onto the streets of Istanbul, they were put on hold during the Taksim Square uprising. In early June 2013, at the height of the Gezi Park occupation, tens of thousands of Galatasaray and Fenerbahçe ultras, some of whom had roots in the left (such as Galatasaray's Tek Yumruk and Fenerbahçe's Vamos Bien), joined the Çarşı in chanting a slogan that would have previously seemed implausible: 'The Çarşı are our leaders!' Taksim Square burned with shouts of 'Who doesn't jump is for Tayyip', while an 'Istanbul United' flag was raised, sealing the alliance between the three enemy supporters' groups. In addition to the police violence, several events in the previous months convinced Galatasaray and Fenerbahçe fans to join forces with the Çarşı: government restrictions on alcohol consumption, rising ticket prices, the corruption scandals plaguing Turkish football, and the ban on ultras marching at the May Day parade in 2013.[6]

The supporters then set about passing on to the young Gezi demonstrators their long experience of urban struggle against the riot police by teaching them how to deal with tear gas, collectively repel police assaults, and erect barricades. More than just self-defence practices, though, it was a whole spirit of storytelling and humour that the Çarşı instilled in the movement.

While the supporters of the team in the black and white shirt regularly break official world records for noise in stadiums, the Çarşı are best known for the banners and other *tifos* they display in the stands. Using a play on words between Çarşı and karsı ('against' in Turkish), their messages are intended to be anti-fascist, anti-sexist or environmentalist. Banners were unveiled reading 'Çarşı against nuclear power' when the Turkish government decided to build power plants in the province of Sinop, or 'Çarşı against the construction of the Hasankeyf dam', a mega-dam project in Anatolia. 'The A of anarchy in our logo is because there are some anarchists among the Çarşı, but mostly because we are against everything, even ourselves!' quips Fahir, a member of the Çarşı since 1992.[7] The Beşiktaş ultras are also famous for their caustic humour, such as the occasion when, on the death of Michael Jackson, they held up a banner in their team's colours in tribute to the King of Pop: 'Half your life in black, the other half in white, rest in peace Michael, you were a great Beşiktaş fan'. When Pluto, because of its small size, was stripped of its rank as the ninth planet in the solar system, the Çarşı displayed a banner at the stadium proclaiming that they support the star, because 'it's not size that counts'.

Alongside these political messages and schoolboy humour, the Çarşı don't hesitate to actively show solidarity with social struggles, demonstrating their support for the Tekel workers' strike in 2010, and marching with mourning workers after the Soma mining disaster in 2014. Their militant commitment is also seen in their defence of numerous causes: mobilisation for the rights of people with disabilities, singing in the stands in sign language against racism, social actions for the poorest residents in their neighbourhoods, or campaigning for animal shelters.

'After the 2011 earthquake in Van, thousands of Beşiktaş supporters threw their scarves and jerseys onto the pitch both as a donation to the victims of the disaster and to denounce the government's inaction', says Cevat, 45, another co-founder of Çarşı. With a freshly damaged nose and a Beşiktaş pin in his buttonhole, he adds, 'Çarşı is a plural, heterogeneous movement, where you can have different political ideas – you can even find right-wing supporters – but which, in the end, speaks with one voice, with a spirit of solidarity among its members'.[8] The socio-political contours of this ultra group seem blurred at first, but a long poem written by the supporters and entitled 'What are the Çarşı?' reads:

> They are the people in the stands: a doctor, a worker, a businessman, an illiterate street child, a teacher. It is the leftist, the rightist, the atheist, the pilgrim, the Muslim, the Armenian, the Jew, the Christian who jump up and down side by side, tears in their eyes, crying out, 'My Beşiktaş, my one and only darling!'[9]

At each rally, which invariably begins at 7:03 pm (1903 being the date of the founding of the Beşiktaş club), the Çarşı are as likely to wave a flag showing Che Guevara as they are of Mustapha Kemal Atatürk, the father of the Turkish Republic and a popular icon whose penchant for alcohol the ultras celebrate in song: 'In the footsteps of our father / We will die of cirrhosis'.

This art of political composition, of the convergence of struggles and of permanent diversion was found within the Taksim Square movement, which brought together secular Kemalists as well as a collective of anti-capitalist Muslims, LGBT feminists and pro-Kurdish revolutionary militants. As for the anti-repression slogans of Gezi, they are as parodic and sarcastic as the slogans of the Çarşı, with lines like 'Gas me baby one more time', or 'Tayyip, join us, the water is lovely!', in allusion to the water cannon used by the forces of repression.

'There is a tradition of mutual aid in the Beşiktaş neighbourhood and Çarşı plays a prominent social role there', insists Fahir. Indeed, walking the streets of Beşiktaş reveals how deeply the club is embedded in the local identity, with ultras' banners and black eagle statues – the team's symbol – dotting the façades, squares and many bars of the neighbourhood. Fahir adds:

> Participating in Gezi was the natural thing to do. Çarşı initially got involved in a simple and direct way in the movement by defending themselves against the police and then, with our colours, we can both find each other and mass easily, spot each other, but also disappear in the crowd easily by taking off our jersey.[10]

'We are not hooligans', explains Deniz. 'We are lovers, not fighters. But when a fight comes, we fight better than anyone else'.[11]

Although, during the uprising, the Çarşı were on the front line of the street battles, they also militated in parallel in the stands, chanting one of the movement's key slogans every 34th minute of the match (34 being Istanbul's postal code): 'Taksim everywhere! Resistance everywhere!' Conversely, many of the supporters' chants were also taken up by the Gezi protestors. 'We defended the planet Pluto well, so we were obliged to defend Taksim Square, which is barely 15 minutes from our neighbourhood!' jokes Nizam.

> We found in this movement the spirit of the stadiums, where we are all united, whatever our social class or origin. But we were also touched by all these young people who, for the first time, were fighting against the authoritarianism of the government. For me, they are the real heroes of Taksim, and not the Çarşı, as the media tried to make people believe in order to criminalise us.[12]

Football under Erdoğan's thumb

No one knows how many members the Çarşı have. In the absence of an official card, a simple jersey and participation in matches as well as a certain motivation to chant songs and slogans are enough to be a Çarşı. There is no real leader either, just a few figureheads, such as Alen Markaryan, aka 'Amigo'. This Armenian Turk who owns a kebab shop in Beşiktaş was once the public face of the Çarşı, a real symbol in a country where the Armenian community is bitterly marginalised. 'Çarşı is not a group or an organisation', Markaryan stresses. 'We don't have a leader either. It is above all a shared state of mind'.[13] This culture of anonymity and horizontality that makes them elusive, their misbehaviour around stadiums as well as their involvement in popular struggles quickly brought the Çarşı into the crosshairs of the Turkish authorities. While the occupiers of Gezi Park were evicted by the military on 15 June 2013 and the revolt against the Islamo-conservative government was running out of steam, the Turkish authorities set about purging the country of its most virulent dissidents and targeted the Çarşı in particular, seen as the spearhead of the protest movement. Political songs and banners were prohibited in Turkish stands, and the government required fans to sign a text at the entrance to the stadiums in which they undertook not to take part in any activity likely to trigger 'ideological events'.

The cries of 'Taksim everywhere! Resistance everywhere!' continued to resound in sports grounds, inviting judicial repercussions. In September 2014, 35 Çarşı ultras were sentenced, in the words of the anti-terrorist prosecutor Adem Meral, for having formed an armed group to 'overthrow the democratically elected Turkish government [...] by seizing the offices of the prime minister in Ankara and Istanbul'.[14] On the eve of the trial, on 15 December 2014, Emma Sinclair-Webb, a researcher for Human Rights Watch in the country, stated: 'Charging these Beşiktaş football club fans as enemies of the state for joining a public protest is a ludicrous travesty. The indictment contains no evidence to support the coup attempt repressive charges and should never have come to court'.[15] The Çarşı ultras also responded with an official communiqué:

> The system wants our lives to be confined to 90 minutes during which we must either rejoice at the goals scored or lament the goals conceded [...] They want us to 'see nothing, hear nothing, and say nothing' that has anything to do with what happens off the pitch, as if the moments before kick-off are of no importance [...] The collective spirit and the shared memory, both of which are conveyed by football, offer us the opportunity to reach out to others, to be open to the world. This state of mind perpetuates human values and, in football grounds as in life, we must rebel against all these unfair red cards that stand in our way.[16]

While Fenerbahçe and Galatasaray ultras, families of victims of police violence as well as various collectives involved in the Gezi movement demonstrate in front of the court their support by chanting 'All united against fascism' and 'Çarşı will never walk alone', the judicial hearing starts with the Çarşı bursting into hilarity after the reading of the indictment charges. In front of his lawyers wearing the Beşiktaş jersey, the first defendant, called to the stand, honours the magistrates with an 'eagle salute', the distinctive sign of the Çarşı ultras. The judge then questions him: 'Are you the leader of the group? Did you participate in the coup attempt?' – 'No Çarşı can give orders to another Çarşı', the supporter replies mischievously. 'And if we had the ability to foment a coup, it would be to crown the Beşiktaş champion of Turkey!'[17] After a postponement of the trial in April, the Istanbul Prosecutor's Office refused to follow the Anti-Terrorism Bureau's demand for life imprisonment and acquitted the 35 defendants on 29 December 2015.

However, this judicial victory didn't put an end to Turkey's attempts to crack down on football. In 2011, Prime Minister Recep Tayyip Erdoğan – who had been a semi-professional player in his youth – tightened his grip on Turkish football in the hope of profiting from its potential to mobilise people. One month after the legislative elections in June of that year, which reinforced the position of his party, the AKP, a struggle between Erdoğan and his sworn enemy Fethullah Gülen for control of Fenerbahçe resulted in a huge corruption scandal, and subsequently saw men close to power being appointed to the club board in May 2012.[18] A year later, following the Taksim Square uprising, a new group of supporters, the 'Eagles of 1453' (the year the Ottomans conquered Constantinople), appeared in the Beşiktaş stands. Close to the AKP, the latter sought to sow discord in the stands and trigger violence at Beşiktaş matches in order to discredit the Çarşı. 'The party is trying to dominate all sectors of society, but football had escaped it so far, as we saw in June 2013. Yet stadiums are an important place of political protest', says Murat Sicakkanli, a member of the Çarşı. A colleague, Deniz Kiliç, agrees: 'We're talking about fifty guys who are given loaves of bread and free tickets to the game by the AKP. They are nothing'.[19] Other

AKP-led pseudo-supporter groups also tried to emerge in the ranks of Galatasaray and Fenerbaçe, chanting without vigour or rhythm 'Erdoğan' and other ominous pro-power slogans.

Certain football clubs have nevertheless become effective political showcases for the AKP, such as the one from Başakşehir, a residential area of Istanbul with a conservative electorate. Created from scratch in the 1990s, the modest municipal club initially known as Istanbul BB was renamed Medipol Başakşehir in 2015, after a sponsor whose CEO is none other than Erdoğan's personal doctor. Thanks to the flow of money from the AKP, the team, chaired by Göksel Gümüşdağ – husband of Erdoğan's niece, an AKP Istanbul politician and head of the Turkish Professional Clubs League – was able to compete with the capital's three big historical clubs and was crowned runner-up in the Turkish Cup in 2017.

The subsidies that the government generously distributes to football are, moreover, massively channelled towards teams that pledge allegiance to it, as demonstrated by the score of ultra-modern stadiums built in recent years for clubs in AKP strongholds such as Kayseri, Konya and Samsun.[20] Finally, in the ultimate sign of the government's stranglehold on football, the Turkish Football Federation publicly called on people to vote in favour of strengthening the powers granted to President Erdoğan in the constitutional referendum of April 2017.

Social cohesion vs. martial divide

'Since Gezi, the government has mistrusted ultras', says Gökhan, a Beşiktaş supporter. 'It can tame the population, the police, the judiciary, the media with threats of imprisonment, but it can't silence its opponents in a stadium. That's why it introduced the Passolig'.[21] Exasperated by the anti-Erdoğan militancy of the fans and their anti-authoritarian lifestyle that runs counter to the Islamo-conservative model advocated by the government, in 2014 the Turkish authorities decided to introduce the Passolig electronic ticket sales system. To purchase tickets, fans must now provide personal data, their seat number, and a bank account number.

'It's a way to track fans, to find troublemakers more easily, but also to secure and control the entrances and exits of the stadiums', explains Fahir from Çarşı.

> The '*Facholig*' also suits the club management, as they are fed up with us constantly criticising their mercantile and managerial delusions. We are witnessing a gentrification of football grounds in Istanbul, where they would like to evict the poorest and make room for the richest fans, those who consume and behave wisely during the matches.[22]

And Cevat adds: 'Not to mention that the company that implemented this electronic security system is run by Erdoğan's own son-in-law'.[23] From the very first days of its implementation, however, there was a massive nationwide boycott of the stands, leading to a significant drop in stadium attendance. A match in October 2014 between Beşiktaş and Eskişehirspor club, which would normally have been attended by 20,000 to 30,000 fans, for example, drew only 3,000 spectators to Istanbul's Atatürk Stadium. Ticket sales for Galatasaray and Fenerbahçe games, meanwhile, dropped by a staggering two-thirds in the space of a season.[24]

While the government claimed that the Passolig would increase tax revenues and ensure that sports venues are safe for families, a joint statement by some 40 ultras groups in April 2014 rejected it: 'The e-ticket system not only treats supporters like ordinary consumers, but also collects a whole range of private data. The system aims to prevent fans from organising and is intended to demolish stadium culture and the very identity of supporters'.[25] The only alternative to watching the matches live is to subscribe to the expensive TV sports package of Digiturk, a media group that is reputed to be close to AKP circles and is quick to turn off the stadium microphones when fans chant protest slogans.

This forced depoliticisation of football reached its climax with the opening of the Vodafone Arena, the new sports stadium in the Beşiktaş that replaced the old Inönü, demolished in 2013. On 10 April 2016, the stadium was officially inaugurated in the presence of Erdoğan (who became president in 2014), Prime Minister Ahmet Davutoğlu and Club President Fikret Orman. While the stadium capacity is 40,000, the ceremony was held in front of 6,000 hand-picked people including 1,000 activists from the AKP youth section.[26] This self-congratulatory celebration behind closed doors was upset by a video that provoked mockery on social networks, showing Ahmet Davutoğlu clumsily missing the ball twice during improvised passes with Erdoğan.

However, the very next day, during the stadium's inaugural match between Beşiktaş and Bursaspor, the Çarşı ultras reappeared both inside and outside the Vodafone Arena. With thousands of them not allowed to attend the match, violent clashes with the police broke out in the vicinity of the stadium. As soon as the smell of tear gas reached the fans in the stands, they defied the ban on political messages, chanting the most popular slogans of the Gezi movement, such as 'Gas us, gas us, take off your helmet, throw down your baton and we'll see who's the strongest'. With Digiturk's channel muting the sound as usual, Turkish social networks were suddenly flooded with the hashtag #korkmalabizizçarşı ('Don't be afraid, it's only us, Çarşı'), relaying the anti-government chants and slogans being shouted live in the stands. A 2.0 rebellion that was clearly not to Erdoğan's liking, as he was soon demanding prison sentences for the authors of these tweets for offending the head of state.

More than an actor in social struggles or a self-declared counter-power that dodges and weaves in response to the multiple faces of government repression, the Çarşı have played a social role of primary importance since Erdoğan's arrival to the presidency in maintaining the country's unity before a leader seeking to divide Turkish society in order to establish his autocratic regime. Thus, when the president of the Grand National Assembly, Ismail Kahraman, pleaded at the end of April 2016 for the abandonment of the principle of secularism within the framework of a constitutional reform, the Çarşı retorted in the stands with a slogan that was widely taken up by supporters: 'Turkey is secular and will remain secular!' Similarly, while the tensions between Kurdish demands for greater autonomy* and Erdoğan's nationalism were echoed on the pitches – some Turkish footballers make a military salute to the cameras after each goal against a Kurdish team – since spring 2016 Beşiktaş supporters have been chanting the famous verses of the Turkish poet Nâzım Hikmet, 'Beautiful days are ahead of us, my friends, sunny days!', as if to better urge an end to the militarisation of the country and friendly understanding between peoples.[27]

The Çarşı's refusal to endorse the Erdoğan regime's sinister nationalist and anti-Kurdish views was put to the test at the end of the year. On 10 December 2016, after a victorious match against Bursaspor, Beşiktaş fans were replaying the match just a stone's throw from the Vodafone Arena. Suddenly, a suicide bomber blew himself up among a group of police officers stationed nearby, while a car bomb was simultaneously launched at a riot police transport bus. Claimed by the Kurdistan Freedom Hawks, the Kurdish armed struggle's radical wing, the attack killed 44 people, including 36 policemen. While the club's management castigated 'terrorists [who] attacked our heroic security forces' and the Interior Minister Süleyman Soylu incited Turkish citizens to 'take revenge', the Çarşı called for a march at 7:03 pm on the following Monday to which, 'without separating anyone', 'young or old, man or woman, me or you' were invited. For the duration of a demonstration, the Çarşı, unfailing lovers of the Beşiktaş, thus thwarted the Turkish government's attempts at fomenting poisonous divisions by uniting people regardless of their age, gender or ethnicity behind a single banner bearing these words, 'This neighbourhood is ours, this country is ours, love is ours'.

* Following the example of the team from Diyarbakır, the largest Kurdish-majority city in the country, which renamed itself Amedspor, the breakdown of the ceasefire between the Turkish government and the Kurdistan Workers' Party (PKK) in the summer of 2015 led many Kurdish clubs to adopt a name that better asserts their Kurdishness.

PART V

Outflank

Facing the football industry: fight and reinvent

18

Football for footballers!

From May '68 to the fans' revolt

> Free football from the tutelage of the money of the pathetic pretend-patrons who are at the root of the decay of football.
>
> Footballers' Action Committee

Dull and boring. Such was French football during the 1960s – in the image of Gaullist society. Although General Charles de Gaulle's arrival in power coincided with France's third-place finish in the 1958 World Cup, French football was experiencing a period in the wilderness. Despite an exceptional boom in football after the war – the French Football Federation (FFF) had 440,000 members in 1950 compared to 188,000 in 1939 – the public was gradually deserting the stands. The rise of financial interests disrupted professional football. Professional clubs and the national team abandoned a quality game that prioritised offence and spectacle and favoured an efficient style of football that limited risk-taking on the pitch, with an eye on the final result. This evolution is directly linked to the rise of sponsorship: equipment manufacturers and other industrial companies want to be associated with the sporting successes of the teams they support financially, and want to make their investments profitable in the long term.

On the pitch, French coaches and trainers applied a defensive-based tactic popularised by the Franco-Argentinian Helenio Herrera. Called the *catenaccio* or 'lock' and inspired by the techniques of Nereo Rocco when he ran Padova and US Triestina, the defensive strategy developed by Herrera, coach at Inter Milan from 1960–1968, helped his club to victory in two European Champion Clubs' Cups, two Intercontinental Cups and three Italian championships.* This style of play, which relied wholly on counter-attacks to score goals, exasperated football lovers, who rapidly grew bored of this insipid game they nicknamed 'concrete' and that became synonymous with a series of sporting disasters for the French team from 1963 onwards.

The FFF and the Group of Professional Clubs are the home of the French football notables who, imbued with their social and material advantages, reign with authoritarianism and even nepotism over the French football world. Pierre Delaunay, the general secretary of the Federation, inherited the position from his father, and Louis Dugauguez, the coach of the French national team, was also the commercial director of Draperies Sedanaises and the coach of Sedan. Georges Boulogne, the national instructor nicknamed 'the Baron', was a supporter of rigorous, disciplined football. In his view:

> Any organisation aims for the best performance, that is, in this case, to increase the chances of victory. Since this victory can be achieved by the minimum gap (1–0), this gap is easier to obtain by a defensive reinforcement (number, quality and spirit of the players). This tendency is inescapable, because it is linked to the conditions and rules of the game.[1]

A fan of defensive rigour, Georges Boulogne thus made 'concrete' the tactical doctrine for the whole of French professional football.

'The players are slaves'

The authoritarianism of the FFF's tycoons was reflected in the working conditions of the professional players. René Hauss, coach of RC Strasbourg from 1967, later general manager of FC Sochaux, wrote in *L'Entraîneur français*, the Federation's newsletter: 'The only way to safeguard the spirit and mentality essential for sporting success is to develop a structure based on the model of military life

---

* Nereo Rocco, who coached the modest Padova team from 1953 to 1961, was aware of his team's sporting and physical inferiority and implemented an ultra-defensive system of play, with strict individual marking and players positioned very far back on the pitch. Known as *catenaccio*, this 'tactic of the weak', which consisted of solidifying defence and saving energy, was inspired by the strategies of the Italian resistance fighters.

[...] No consultation, no debate. A well-established hierarchy'.[2] The salaries of the best professional footballers were also relatively modest and many players had a second job. At the end of their careers, in the 1960s, the ultimate ambition of the international Roger Courtois was to buy a tobacco shop, and the French champion Bolek Tempowski declared that he wanted to take up farming, spending his match bonuses on buying cows.[3]

Similarly, the FFF texts codifying the status of professional players stipulated that 'every professional or semi-professional player is bound by contract until the age of 35 [...] to the club under whose colours he intends to play football'. As their sporting career rarely extends beyond the age of 35, players are thus bound 'for life' to their home club and almost never have a say in transfers, which depend on the exclusive will of the management. The rules state that 'the club wishing to acquire the services of a player on the transfer list [...] must contact not the player, but the club which has the player under contract'. By signing a professional contract, a footballer thus becomes capital that can be sold to the highest bidder.

Faced with the omnipotence of the governing bodies and sports employers, a few dissenting voices tried to shake up the patriarchal conservatism of French football. In November 1961, Just Fontaine, one of the best strikers of the time who played for the national team, and the Cameroonian Eugène N'Jo Léa, who was preparing for his doctorate in law while playing for AS Saint-Étienne, created the Union nationale des footballeurs professionnels (UNFP). This players' union intended to fight against the 'lifetime contract'.* In 1963, the English professional footballers' union succeeded in abolishing the retain and transfer system, which, as in France, tied players to club managers [see Chapter 3]. Inspired by this British victory, and after unsuccessfully attempting a strike during a qualifying match for the European Cup of Nations in February 1963, the UNFP decided to challenge the contracts of professional players before an industrial tribunal.

---

* A players' union had been founded in the 1930s but disappeared with the Second World War. The statutes of this union stated that its aim was 'to foster and develop among its football players feelings of comradeship and solidarity, to defend the interests of its members and to help players injured on the field of play'.

The 1958 Ballon d'Or winner, Raymond Kopa, four times French champion with Reims between 1953 and 1962, and three times winner of the European Champion Clubs' Cups with Real Madrid (in 1957, 1958 and 1959), then put a cat among the media pigeons. The son of a Polish immigrant and a survivor of the hell of the mines in the north of France, where he lost one of his fingers in a cave-in – 'That goddamn pit scared the hell out of me so much that I really thought I was doomed to this life of misery', he wrote[4] – Kopa was the archetypal modest and exemplary player who embodied the values of hard work and self-sacrifice fostered by football managers. However, on 4 July 1963, he expressed his anger in an article published by the weekly magazine *France Dimanche*, bluntly entitled 'Players are slaves'. 'Today, in the middle of the 20th century', he explained, 'the professional footballer is the only man who can be sold and bought without being asked his opinion'. The model player thus loudly denounced the leonine contract of professionals and raised an unprecedented controversy in the French footballing world. Kopa was given a six-month suspended sentence and withdrawn from the national team for a period because of his 'attitude'.

With no regrets, the insolent footballer publicly accepted his position and persisted: 'I find it shocking that managers can decide on a footballer's career on their own, negotiate his transfer without even warning him, and impose financial sanctions without him being able to defend himself'.[5] Four years after the scandal, Jean Sadoul, then president of the Groupement des Clubs Professionnels, publicly confessed that the 'lifetime contract' of footballers was illegal because it contravened French social legislation. However, this did little to encourage the Groupement to abolish it.

The monthly sports magazine *Le Miroir du football* was the other bastion of football protest. Part of the left-wing press movement, the journal was launched in January 1960. Although the monthly was published by Éditions J, owned by the French Communist Party, the journalistic team, led by editor-in-chief François Thébaud, was not affiliated to the Party and retained its freedom of expression. It was exclusively composed of journalists who militated for the beautiful game and who denounced the paternalism of the French football caciques and their deadening impact on the game. From the very first issue, François Thébaud used an incisive editorial to vilify the 'official aesthetes [who] cling to the outdated cult of the primordial manifestations of physical effort' and urged all footballers 'to become aware of their strength'. 'If you are looking for material in our pages to satisfy nationalistic pride, parochialism, or the commercial cult of the star', he concluded, 'read no further'.

Each month, *Le Miroir du football* offered readers theoretical articles advocating an offensive and creative style of football, as well as sections on the practice of the game – on short passing or line defence, for example – all illustrated with photographs that were both attractive and educational. 'They questioned the *catenaccio* of certain teams and called for zone defence and intelligent play instead', recalls André Mérelle, a professional player with Red Star in Saint-Ouen.[6] For the cheerful gang of activists at *Le Miroir*, football should embody the 'premonitory expression of a society worthy of the name' and, as early as August 1961, the sports monthly took a swipe at the 'lifetime contracts' of professional players in a long article entitled 'The status of the professional player, or slavery in 1961'.

A true exception among a conformist and unremarkable sports press, *Le Miroir* was at the forefront of social criticism of French football. It was 'critical of club and federation managers', 'polemical towards businessmen, politicians and technocrats who are always ready to exploit or manipulate sports' and 'unique in the cohesion of its team of journalists linked by their common passion for football'.[7] Finally, the editorial team devoted pages to the amateur game, where a certain sense of football as a 'collective art' persisted. 'Alongside objective and uncompromising commentaries on the "big" events in national and international news, we will continue to highlight the efforts of those who, at all levels of sporting practice (even the most modest), safeguard and enrich the true spirit of the greatest of all sports', the journalists of *Le Miroir* affirmed.[8]

Occupy Iéna

In April 1968, France experienced a historic sporting humiliation. Trained by the despotic Louis Dugauguez, the national team was swiftly eliminated from the European Championship when it was defeated 5–1 by Yugoslavia. In this debacle, fans glimpsed the exhaustion of the footballing authorities' retrograde policies. A month later, it was the turn of the Gaullist government to undergo a serious reverse: students rose up in the universities and the streets, shaking French society to its core. The Sorbonne and the Odéon were occupied, and on 13 May the workers' movement joined the wave of protest, declaring a general strike. Paris was in ferment when one evening, Pierre Lameignère, journalist at *Le Miroir du football*, put to the team his idea of occupying the headquarters of the FFF at number 60 bis, Avenue d'Iéna, in the chic 16th arrondissement.[9] For the small band of rebellious journalists, the month of May 1968 was the perfect opportunity to open a breach in the monolithic FFF.

At a second meeting, a date was set for the occupation: it would start on Wednesday 22 May. A few days in advance, they staked out the building to record the working hours of the staff and to draw up an evacuation plan in the event of an attack by the police. The building was a few streets from the Champs-Élysées, in an area dominated by embassies, well away from the barricades in the Latin Quarter. On the evening of Thursday 21 May, 10 million workers were on strike, and all industrial sectors blockaded. The next morning, about 60 individuals were stationed in cars along the Avenue d'Iéna or criss-crossing the district on bicycles. The squad was made up of journalists from *Le Miroir du Football* including François Thébaud, Francis Le Goulven, Jean Norval, Maurice Ragonneau and Daniel Watrin, players close to the monthly sports magazine as football partners on Sundays, and simple friends such as Jules Céron, a machinist at Chaillot and a footballer at Aubervilliers.

When a dozen employees emerged from the Federation to go for their morning coffee, a scout bent to touch his left shoe. This was the agreed signal to start the action.[10] The small band rushed into the mansion. In the marbled and carpeted hall of the Federation, the concierge burst out laughing: 'The Baron will be delighted!'[11] A quarter of an hour later, far from being happy, it was a surly Georges Boulogne who arrived at the headquarters of French football. Two occupiers grabbed the national coach and whispered to him: 'Come in, we invite you. The Federation is ours now'.[12] Over the plush façade of 60 bis Avenue d'Iéna, the demonstrators hoisted a red flag and unfurled two banners: 'Football for footballers' and 'The Federation, property of 600,000 footballers'. Pierre Delaunay, the FFF secretary general, and the 'Baron' remained confined to an office until mid-afternoon. 'Mr Boulogne, the footballers have things to say to you', announced the protesting players, before embarking on a vigorous discussion about the organisation and operation of the fortress of football.

Banners, slogans, occupations: the football agitators used the same techniques of struggle as the students and workers. 'Everyone was in revolt', recalls Jules Céron, who took part in the occupation of his factory in Chaillot as well as of the Federation. 'The guys from the *Miroir* were fighting against power and money in football. They decided to attack the citadel'.[13] On the same day the FFF was taken over, the occupiers wrote an explosive leaflet. Entitled 'Football for footballers' and subtitled 'The programme leaflet of the Footballers' Action Committee', it began with these sentences:

> As footballers belonging to various clubs in the Paris region, we have decided to occupy the headquarters of the French Football Federation today. Like workers occupy their factories. Like students occupy their faculties. Why? To give back to the 600,000 French footballers and their millions of friends what belongs to them: the football that the pundits of the Federation have expropriated from them to serve their selfish interests as profiteers from the sport.

The football rebels began with three measures taken by the FFF they saw as contradicting its primary mission: to develop and promote football throughout the country. They demanded the abolition of the 'B licence', which was initially introduced to limit amateurism, i.e. illegal payments by a club to a player who holds amateur status. However, in practice, this licence prevented amateur footballers who changed clubs during the year from playing for their new club before the following season.

A second measure that was derided was the limitation of the football season from October to May, when the summer months were more favourable for playing football. In 1961, Maurice Herzog, Secretary of State for Sport, had in fact decreed the suspension of the football season during the summer in order to encourage the development of other sports, such as athletics. In the eyes of the occupiers, this anti-popular measure demonstrated the Gaullist government's contempt for football, but also the class ties between the Federation's leaders and senior state officials.[14] Finally, the leaflet denounced the glaring lack of sports facilities for football players (in the Paris region, there was one football pitch for every four teams in 1968).[15] The notables of the FFF were accused in black and white of 'having worked against football and of having accelerated its decline by placing it under the tutelage of a government that was essentially hostile to popular sport'. The abolition of the 'slave contract for professional players', which 'flouts human dignity' and was still in force in 1968 despite its illegality being recognised a year earlier, was also among the demands of the angry football community.

For the Avenue d'Iéna activists, the social power relations within football reflected the class relations that structure French society. In the view of the French football historian Alfred Wahl, 'The protestors suggested that working-class players had been dispossessed of their rights for the benefit of the bourgeois. It was therefore necessary to claim them back and to manage the Federation directly'.[16] In their leaflet, the insurgents accused those they called the 'pontiffs' of French football of having 'shamelessly concentrated in the hands of a tiny minority the substantial profits we provide them with through our contributions'. Antoine Chiarisoli and Jean Sadoul, respectively presidents of the FFF and the Groupement des clubs professionnels, were accused of concealing 'illegal fees'. Georges Boulogne was described as the 'head of the coaching mafia', who 'reserves the best-paid jobs for his friends'. As for Pierre Delaunay, who had inherited the post of secretary general of the Federation from his father, in the eyes of the protestors he was nothing more than a 'vulgar Louis XVI'.

Finally, the Action Committee demanded the organisation of a referendum among the 600,000 affiliated footballers in order to rid the game of 'football profiteers and football insulters'. By inviting 'footballers, coaches, managers of small clubs, countless friends and football enthusiasts, students and workers' to the Federation's headquarters, the occupiers were de facto taking a revolutionary approach. 'Together', they concluded, 'we will make football what it should never have ceased to be: the sport of joy, the sport of the world of tomorrow that all workers have begun to build'.

The leaflet 'Football for Footballers' was swiftly distributed in the streets and in football grounds. Curious about this incongruous colleague-led action, journalists attended a press conference organised by the Footballers' Action Committee. The invitation of the press to the occupied headquarters resulted in the publication of a handful of articles that oscillated between condescension and disdain. The sports press denigrated the demonstrators' mode of action and would have appreciated 'a more rational revolution'.[17] Maurice Vidal himself, even though he was the director of the press group to which *Le Miroir du Football* belonged, showed little appreciation for this occupation carried out without the approval of the communist authorities. As for the Communist Party newspaper *L'Humanité*, it only saw in this action a demonstration with leftist overtones, one that above all was secondary to the workers' struggles.[18]

The football authorities were not slow to react either. Some of the Federation's 'pontiffs' didn't hesitate to describe the *Miroir* gang as 'bastards in spikes' and, on 23 May, the FFF published an official communiqué reaffirming the democratic validity of its statutes and condemning the occupation of its headquarters.[19] The next day, it was Georges Boulogne's turn, as leader of the Amicale des éducateurs de football, to 'energetically denounce the political and anti-democratic nature of this action'.[20] Nevertheless, the occupiers received messages of support from UNFP unionist footballers and clubs from all over the country. Amateur players from Malakoff, Pontoise, Mantes, and teams from the Saunier-Duval factory and the PTT Brune crossed the threshold of 'their' federation for the first time. 'I never thought that the world of football was capable of such a daring, irreverent gesture', recalls Serge Anger, an amateur footballer from Pavillons-sous-bois (Seine-Saint-Denis), who left his print shop for Avenue d'Iéna.[21]

The professional players, however, failed to mobilise. Only two footballers from the Red Star de Saint-Ouen, André Mérelle and

Michel Oriot, took part in the occupation, while declaring: 'We were not there as professionals, but to support the effort to democratise football being made by amateur players'.[22] The two professional players didn't hesitate to take a stand against the FFF's animosity and responded in the sports press:

> We should renounce the idea of the sponsoring club president and even the municipal subsidies. State subsidies should be allocated in proportion to the number of members and the activities of the club. Then, the leaders would be elected, and money would no longer be the criterion, but real ability. Under these conditions, it is not impossible to imagine that players could also participate in the management of the club.[23]

For five days, the occupation took place in a festive atmosphere. On the evening of the appropriation of the premises, cots were set up, people partied merrily in the Federation's smart lounges, and any suspicious movement outside was scrutinised from the roofs. May '68 was then at its height: on 24 May, the capital was the scene of fierce street battles between barricaded demonstrators and police forces. The Paris Stock Exchange was set on fire. The occupied headquarters of the FFF resounded to the tumultuous rhythm of the ongoing movement and was transformed into a veritable democratic agora. Intense debates about a different kind of football and film screenings of international matches were held, interspersed with improvised games on the spruce Avenue d'Iéna. On 27 May, the trade union leaders and student organisations began talks with the Gaullist government to reach the Grenelle agreements. The same day, the end to the occupation of the FFF headquarters was voted on at the general assembly. 'We had succeeded in publicising the movement', explained Faouzi Mahjoub, a journalist with *Le Miroir*. 'It had to take a new direction'.[24] When they left the premises, the occupiers were sure to take with them a list of the 12,000 French football clubs and their managers.

Taking over from the Action Committee, a French Footballers' Association (AFF) was created in the aftermath to carry forward the demands of 22 May. Chaired by Just Fontaine, co-founder of the UNFP, the association proposed that football should be rebuilt by the 600,000 amateur and professional players and received the support of players popular with the media such as Raymond Kopa, Rachid Mekhloufi and Yvon Douis. At the same time, the UNFP organised a match between AS Saint-Étienne and SCO Angers at the Bauer stadium in Saint-Ouen on 13 November 1968 as part of its union congress. The professional players' union wanted to use this match to demonstrate that football was free of its disciplinary shackles and synonymous with fun.[25] Feeling their authority threatened, the football governing bodies then asked for a fortnight's suspension for any footballer from Saint-Étienne or Angers who appeared on the turf of the Bauer stadium. Despite the FFF's intimidation, AS Saint-Étienne and SCO Angers took to the field on the day announced. The two teams reversed their colours to show the unity of the footballers and a blackboard in the dressing room read: 'To confound their detractors, the players' mission is to produce football worthy of its name'.[26] In the stands, a banner reading 'The players will win' was waved, and the match became a real footballing spectacle: the enthusiastic public witnessed an avalanche of goals, with the Stéphanois winning 5–4.

The popularity of the demands of 22 May, which were now supported by the French Footballers' Association, as well as the counter-power asserted by professional players within the UNFP, freed the voice of footballers, who no longer hesitated to collectively denounce their working conditions. With its back to the wall, the Federation was forced to give in. Immediately after the occupation of its headquarters, the FFF's federal bureau abandoned the 'B licence'. Players, coaches, amateur players and clubs were also better represented in the governing bodies. Some 'pontiffs' and other 'football profiteers' also bowed out, such as President Antoine Chiarisoli, who gave up his seat at the end of the year, and Pierre Delaunay, who resigned from his position as general secretary, which became an elected role. Finally, January 1969 saw the greatest victory won by the rebel footballers: the abolition of the 'slave' contract, which was replaced by a contract of freely determined length.

Nevertheless, French football was far from completing its revolution. Georges Boulogne was appointed coach of Les Bleus in 1969 (he remained until 1973, with the French team failing to qualify for the 1970 and 1974 World Cups, or the 1972 Euros). In 1970, the government appointed him to the newly created post of national director of football, a position that allowed him to manage the training of coaches with an iron fist. The Federation also tried to keep the 1968 footballers off the field. 'The Ligue de Paris [the regional level of the FFF] suspended our licences for a while', recalls Serge Anger, one of the amateur players who joined the occupation at Avenue d'Iéna. 'They wanted to prevent us from starting the 1968–1969 season'.[27] 'I had difficulty finding a professional club. I was the leftist', adds André Mérelle.[28] In the end, the 'pontiffs' of the Federation only wavered a little in the face of the footballers' revolt: 'Even though, in other social spheres, we are witnessing a questioning of the notion of authority, even though in schools and universities, new orientations are emerging [...] football remains the domain of unenlightened autocrats', sums up the historian Alfred Wahl. 'There was no question of them sharing power, they needed all of it, they needed to impose themselves if they could not be understood'.[29]

In 1972, professional footballers learned that the Groupement des Clubs Professionnels was working on a reform of the fixed-term contract that would once again restrict the relative freedom of players. After fruitless negotiations, the UNFP footballers officially declared themselves on strike on 3 December 1972: only two out of ten first-division matches would be played under normal conditions, the other eight being disrupted or cancelled.[30] In early 1973, under pressure, the club management adopted a Professional Football Charter to definitively regulate players' employment contracts.

Beneath the turf, the beach?

Despite these attempts by the sporting authorities to bring them to heel, the creative football of enjoyment and direct democracy promoted by *Le Miroir du Football* won disciples. The spirit of May '68 continued with the creation in 1972 of the Espoir Football Club in Neuilly-sur-Marne. Using the principles of play developed by the monthly magazine on the pitch and self-management practices in the changing rooms, the club brought together, among others, a few free-lancers from *Le Miroir* and young suburbanites. In Brittany, a land of attacking football synonymous with victory – Stade Rennais won the French Cup in 1971 and FC Nantes won the championship in 1973 – the club Stade Lamballais, in the Côtes-d'Armor, became the standard-bearer of a collective game constructed to encourage individual qualities and the pleasure of each player. For many militant footballers, this club was like a laboratory where the objective is the 'permanent search for emotions in the practice of "a different football", both aesthetic and moral, where beauty and goodness coexist', as the Breton player and coach Christian Gourcuff puts it.[31]

The club was coached by Jean-Claude Trotel, a local high school teacher, who favoured 'football made up of passes, made up of intelligence, a football that is intoxicating because it is a source of healthy joys, born of a collective game' and who liked to compare a team to 'a jazz orchestra' where 'all kinds of improvisation are possible'.[32] Initially close to the Communist Party, he was nonetheless attracted by the ideas of self-government that ran through May 1968. In 1973, Jean-Claude Trotel gave up his status as a coach to become a simple footballer and initiated the creation of a collective of 'player-coaches': four players elected at a meeting prepare the training sessions, select the teams and lead the discussions between matches. The collective is then renewed or altered by all the players every two months. The footballers published a newspaper, *La Passe lamballaise*, to assert their self-organisation while offering a space for debate with their supporters. 'We, the young people, were really into it', recalls Bernard Philippe, a player at Stade Lamballais.

> You have to remember the political context: we had seen May 1968 [and], in 1972, there was the big strike at the Joint français factory in Saint-Brieuc.* [On the ground] it was intellectually gratifying,

---

* From March to May 1972, the workers of the Joint français in Saint-Brieuc went on a tough strike for better working conditions. The movement was characterised by a surge of popular solidarity from Breton farmers, high school students, workers, artists, the local clergy and many media outlets.

> you had to play with your head. Moreover, I started as a defender and ended up as a striker: when you understood how to play, you could adapt to different positions, you could feel the game.[33]

To widespread astonishment, on 12 June 1973 a ministerial decree was issued obliging amateur clubs to hire a state-approved coach with a diploma from the national footballing body, still run by Georges Boulogne. The world of amateur football was concerned by this decision, seeing it as an authoritarian attempt to control even the sporting activities of the youth, treated as potentially subversive ever since May '68. The amateur players were equally worried at the idea of Boulogne training coaches who would spread his notions of disciplined, defensive play to clubs.

The Stade Lamballais players denounced, in a pamphlet and petition, 'an intolerable assault on players' freedom'. 'Imposing the services of a coach on a club is to seek to control people's leisure time, to take away their freedom'. On 2 February 1974, 200 footballers from 14 regional leagues, as well as sports teachers, sports educators from working-class neighbourhoods and journalists from *Le Miroir du Football* met in Yvelines. Initially motivated by the desire to mobilise en masse against this ministerial decree, the participants discussed their aspirations for a different kind of football, one that was more humane and emancipatory than that imposed by the Federation and the state.

After a day of discussions, the militant footballers and other lovers of the beautiful game put their collective thoughts into practice by forming a fully-fledged associative structure, the Mouvement Football Progrès (MFP). A three-point political platform was unanimously adopted. The first one takes up the social criticism of football developed by *Le Miroir*: 'Fight against the conformist conception of football characterised by the increasing commercialisation, by the growing hold of the government on its organisation, by the authoritarianism of the managers in place, by the search for results by all means in competitions'. The second point specifies the vision shared by the movement: 'To develop and spread a conception of football that respects the dignity of the player, his freedom of expression, his pleasure in playing and the development of his personality'. The last part of the platform reflects the MFP's desire to act as a counter-weight: 'To seek ways in which footballers themselves can contribute to the development of this football, by taking their own responsibilities, by fighting for better material conditions'.[34]

Initially, the MFP's action took the form of practical training courses whose spirit was the antithesis of those organised by the FFF. During these training sessions, inspired by the principles of popular education, the primary objective was to start from the experience of each participant to enable him to deconstruct, in an autonomous and non-directed way, his conditioned relationship with the ball. The training sessions aimed less at physical preparation than at developing the collective nature of the game and rediscovering the notion of individual enjoyment and improvisation. Sometimes, at the beginning of the course, a first match between trainees was filmed, viewed and criticised in order to collectively draw up the training programme for the following days. The participants were workers, postmen and teachers. Among players, coaches and club leaders alike, conviviality was the rule. Debates on the links between football and society – on education, group psychology, and so on – were the norm during these courses, as well as sessions viewing videos of matches where the absurdity of the ultra-defensive play of certain teams was humorously commented on.

If – like the student movement of May '68 – the militant footballers of the MFP rejected the verticality of power within the institutions of football as well as on the pitch, they also joined in the critique of industrial work by the striking workers. Thus, in an ideal and desirable organisation of work, just as in that of the game, the emancipation of each individual is intimately linked with the realisation of a collectively thought-out action where social relations are no longer governed by hierarchy and competition, but by horizontality and cooperation. 'We are well aware that the football we dream of cannot fully blossom in today's society', said three of the MFP's directors a year after its foundation. 'Our movement is necessarily part of a global action. But we believe that a struggle is possible within the institutions of cultural activities (of which football is a part) and that this struggle can contribute to "changing lives"'.[35]

The MFP aimed to foster in its followers a football viewed as a school of life, as well as of solidarity, in victory as in defeat. MFP tournaments were conceived as 'popular and artistic spectacles', like the one organised in June 1975 in Moëlan-sur-Mer, Finistère, with 48 teams taking part. The teams competed in matches lasting just 14 minutes, to put the focus on attacking football and the joy of playing, and the winner received a cup for the 'Best MFP Spirit' rather than a financial reward.[36] In cities and rural areas alike, MFP activists organised discussions about this 'other' football in youth and cultural centres, young workers' homes and municipal halls. Agit-prop also became part of the movement with the creation in 1976, in partnership with the Troupe rennaise d'action culturelle, of a puppet show called 'Les aventures de M. Ledur ('Mr Hard')', which attacked football pundits, and was a pun on the name of the president of Stade Rennais, one M. Lemoux ('Mr Soft'). Another play, 'Football Circus', was also staged with eleven actors and was intended to be a full-scale satire on the excesses of professional football.[37]

However, the MFP faced headwinds from the authorities. In December 1975, the deputy mayor of Locminé, in the Morbihan region, refused to make his municipal land available for a meeting of the movement, arguing that the structure was 'leftist and subversive' and using as a pretext an invective from the Ministry of Sport reminding him that the MFP was not a member of the Federation. Many players or coaches affiliated to the MFP were also gradually being ostracised from their clubs. This was the case, for example, of professional Raymond Kéruzoré of Stade Lavallois, who was banned from participating in the movement's championship.

The MFP was also riven by internal debate. For some, the movement was not political enough, and during the actions of the Committee for the boycott of Argentina's organisation of the 1978 World Cup (the COBA), some participated in the committee under the MFP label, others as individuals.[38] Some activists founded self-managed clubs, such as the Collectif Football Korrigans de Lesneven (Finistère) formed in 1975, in order to materialise the movement's political platform through affinity groups. Finally, *Le Miroir du football*, which provided media representation and political support for the MFP's actions, fell apart in 1976 after François Thébaud and most of the team left the paper in disagreement with the administration, which wanted to give the monthly a more commercial orientation. The administrators of the MFP confessed that their main enemy was the 'power of conditioning through sport' and noted that '[their] ideas are constantly at odds with the ideas that the mainstream press, radio and television "inoculate" people with on a daily basis'.[39] As the financial resources of the structure remained more than limited over the years, the Mouvement Football Progrès adventure came to an end in 1978. *Le Miroir du football* closed down a year later.

On a more modest scale, the torch of the MFP was taken up by a few players of the Stade Lamballais, such as Bernard Philippe, Alain Séradin and Tayeb Ikkène, who created in 1979 the association 'Le football, la vie' and a monthly magazine, *Le Contre-Pied*. The latter fought 'against authoritarianism at all levels' and the 'increasing commercialisation of football', while *Le Contre-Pied*, which lasted until 1985, dealt in its pages with women's football, trade unionism and popular education.

Playing without barriers

Today, the anti-authoritarian spirit instilled by *Le Miroir du Football* and the Mouvement Football Progrès still lives on in the form of self-refereed seven-a-side football, a practice whose roots date back to May 1968. At the height of the strike movement, Jo Dauchy, secretary of the Aubervilliers Municipal Club, decided to organise football matches between the various occupied factories in the town with the help of the Confédération Générale du Travail (CGT). At the municipal ground, the striking workers reclaimed the pleasure of playing football without constraints, whether you were an experienced player or a beginner, a young fan or an old-time supporter. One year after May '68, the desire to get together to play football in a friendly manner among the workers of Aubervilliers remained so strong that the CGT and the municipal club organised new meetings between factories, but also with the youth centres and other companies in the town. In order for everyone to play without discrimination during matches and training sessions, Jo Dauchy proposed dividing the pitch in two widthways and experimenting with football in teams of seven, without referees, tackles, or offsides.[40] Playing on a half-size pitch with seven on a team de facto eliminates specialisation, as each player can become a defender or a striker as the game proceeds. As for the self-management of refereeing – it is up to each team to claim a free kick when it deems one is required – it transforms the opponent into a partner in the game, without delegating to any authority the regulation of conflicts on the field. 'It was a luxury', recalls Jo Dauchy. 'The concept of sport for all, to simply have fun and not necessarily copy the elite, didn't exist'.[41] Every Monday evening, printers, butchers, high school students, postmen and workers from Aubervilliers met to play joyful, self-managed football together.

This seven-a-side game quickly spread throughout the Seine-Saint-Denis region, but also in the Ardèche, where it brought together miners and textile workers under the impetus of local trade unionists and communist militants. The first national seven-a-side football cup was organised in 1988 and the Fédération Gymnique et Sportive du Travail (FSGT) [see Chapter 5] decided to formalise a few rules: mixed teams were authorised, there was no limit to the number of substitutions, throw-ins were made with the foot and, of course, there was still no offside, no tackling and no referee. 'The rules are designed to encourage an attractive and lively game with lots of goals', says a departmental FSGT regulation for seven-a-side football. 'It is similar to football played in school. Seven-a-side football holds many promises: the spirit, the fun aspect, the growth in numbers without advertising, just word of mouth'. Moussa Dramé, a sports educator at the Association sportive forézienne in the Loire, adds: 'Self-refereeing carries the values of autonomy, responsibility, acceptance of mistakes, collective decision-making – including the opponent – and a sense of community life'.[42]

Popularised as far away as Japan, Mexico and Palestine, self-refereed seven-a-side football is now enjoyed by almost 30,000 players in France.[43] Numerous tournaments bring together several hundred teams – whose names reflect both the friendly spirit of the game and the players' self-mockery: 'Foiring Club de Paris', 'FC Fromage Blanc 0% United' or 'Monique's Bayern', who meet every week

> regardless of the cold that bites our legs for three quarters of the season (from October to May); regardless of the impression of being on the moon when we play on the cratered pitches of Choisy-le-Roi; and regardless of the suffocating humidity of the cramped dressing room shared with our opponents.[44]

From the occupation of the FFF headquarters, through the political adventure of the Mouvement Football Progrès, to the expansion of self-organised seven-a-side football, many players have worked hard to return 'football to the footballers'. As a symptom of a commercial world that always seeks – and often succeeds – to monopolise what remains, what resists, or what is born outside of it, football's governing bodies have gone so far as to appropriate some of the slogans of the May '68 rebels. In January 2007, Michel Platini became president of UEFA having adopted the slogan 'Football for footballers' for his campaign. Less than ten years later, the 'pontiff' was forced to resign for receiving illegal payments from FIFA. The 'football profiteers' so fiercely reviled by the occupiers of 60 bis Avenue d'Iéna are still legion – more than ever.

19
Tackling sexism
Women's football against the French sporting patriarchy

'For the first time, young women have played association football', the French sports daily *L'Auto* reported enthusiastically on 2 October 1917. The previous Sunday, two female teams affiliated to Fémina Sport, a Paris-based multi-sports club founded in 1912, played against each other under the intrigued gaze of a handful of onlookers and journalists. Following this unprecedented encounter on the capital's pitches, and in the absence of any female counterparts, the Fémina Sport players met throughout the autumn with the teams from Buffon and Charlemagne high schools, as well as with the seasoned players from the Union Sportive Commerciale and the Stade Français.

Although women's football was rapidly spreading on the other side of the Channel at the time [see Chapter 4], on the continent it remained at best secretive and was only played in very few institutions, such as the girls' school of Pont-à-Mousson in France or those of Uccle and Huy in Belgium.[1] However, the success of the mixed competitions initiated by Fémina Sport in 1917 led other women's teams to flourish in Paris during 1918 within sports societies such as En Avant!, the Académia or the Association sportive de la Seine. The following season, the first local women's tournament was set up.

A breath of emancipation

Benefitting from the growing sports movement in France – on the eve of the First World War there were over 2,000 football clubs[2] – women's football spread through France in the wake of the creation in January 1918 of a Fédération des sociétés féminines sportives de

France (FSFSF). Women's squads appeared in 1919 in Rouen and Reims, and the 1920–1921 season opened with a dozen female clubs.[3]

The socio-political context in the aftermath of the First World War also contributed to the integration of women into the football landscape. Although, after a long struggle, women had already won the right to freely dispose of their wages in 1907, the First World War, by mobilising more than 60 per cent of active men to the front, overturned the traditional division of the sexes in French society.[4] Having made up for the shortage of male labour by toiling in the war industry, women aspired to more egalitarian relationships and sought to free themselves from the patriarchal straitjacket. This desire for liberation was also expressed in and through sport. The physical emancipation of women through sports activities was celebrated by the former military officer and renowned educator Georges Hébert, who stated in 1919: 'Exercising, developing oneself, is a real liberation for women, both physically and morally [...] She becomes aware of both her strength and her valour'.[5] The magazine *La Vie féminine*, directed by the feminist activist Valentine Thomson, spoke for English women worker-footballers who 'never forget that they belong to a race where sport takes pride of place. We can see, as soon as they have any leisure time, how enthusiastically they indulge in the joys of football, which in England is almost a national pastime'.[6]

At the head of the FSFSF, Alice Milliat, a schoolteacher from Nantes, and her fellow association leaders made no secret of their feminism and intended to popularise football with the firm intention of 'preaching the virtues of sport among the working classes'.[7] The pioneers of French women's football were mostly modest office workers, students, seamstresses, workers or postmistresses who, in addition to their love of the ball game, were also involved in athletics. Ostracised first by the Fédération française de football-association (FFFA), founded in April 1919, and then by the hegemonic Union des sociétés françaises de sports athlétiques (USFSA), women footballers organised themselves on the fringes of the men's institutions. 'A sports federation is a miniature republic', declared *La Française*, the feminist weekly that was the voice of the National Council of

French Women.* 'By developing the FSFSF, by making it the equal of the big male federations, women will get used to directing their interests themselves. And they will prove that they are fit for the government of the nation by first governing themselves'.[8]

However, the dominant opinion, acutely aware of how the French population had been diminished by the First World War, was increasingly concerned with 'regenerating the race'. The idea that women had a patriotic duty to procreate was shared by even the most militant agitators for gender equality.[9] As the suffragette Marguerite de Witt-Schlumberger wrote in the columns of *La Française* in May 1917: 'All young, healthy households who, during the year following the war, refuse out of selfishness to give France a new child, should be treated like shirkers and deserters'.[10] Alice Milliat's commitment to sport and feminism also took this hygienic and natalist view. 'To give France the physical supremacy necessary for its tranquillity and prosperity', she wrote in 1920, 'we need robust women capable of giving it healthy, vigorous and numerous children'.[11] Beyond the physical and ultimately political emancipation of women, the women's sports movement advocated physical activities for its members with a view to constituting 'solid human engines, through better pregnancies, healthier and more fertile maternities'.[12]

The FSFSF also issued recommendations on football practice. Women's matches should not exceed 60 minutes and should be played on small pitches, while any rough contact between players was prohibited. The federation's rules also prohibited the mixing of the sexes during competitions and training sessions, and the dress code for women's football was strictly regulated. The sleeves of their tunics must cover a quarter of the arm and the knickerbockers must be dark in colour and reach down to 10 centimetres from the knee. These physical and clothing restrictions undoubtedly reflect the federation's absorption of gender norms and even certain stereotypes about the so-called 'weaker sex', but above all they indicate the desire of female sports leaders to avoid any hostility from male spectators.

---

* A federation of women's associations campaigning for women's rights, created in 1901. In 1929, the National Council of French Women organised the General Assembly of Feminism.

In the spring of 1920, a team of Parisian players played a series of four matches in England's most prestigious grounds against the brilliant Dick, Kerr Ladies of Preston, with the British players crossing the channel in November to play four matches in Paris, Roubaix, Le Havre and Rouen, attracting a total of 56,000 spectators [see Chapter 4].[13] 'While too many backward minds pity the natural weakness of women and find a remedy only in the social subordination of women to men, a great movement is developing to restore to women all the beauty, all the primitive strength that civilisation deprives them of', reported *La Française* on 5 November 1921 after a match between Parisian and English players. 'It is edifying to follow the sports columns on this subject, where women's exploits are given almost as much importance as those of the stronger sex'.

Gradually, the FSFSF expanded its membership. According to Laurence Prudhomme-Poncet, author of a reference work on the history of women's football, the federation had 130 affiliated clubs at the beginning of 1922 and 17 sports societies offering women's football, in some 40 teams, in 1923.[14] The game took root in the north of France, in Marseille and in the working-class suburbs of the capital (Pantin, Aubervilliers and Saint-Ouen). A Paris championship was created in 1921 and was a great success, with 18 teams entering in the first season, such as the Fauvettes from Argenteuil, the Muguettes from Charenton, and Parisiana. Finally, after launching an Encouragement Cup, then an Esperance ('Hope') Cup aimed at beginners, the FSFSF organised the *La Française* Cup, on the initiative of the eponymous feminist magazine. After the final of this first tournament in April 1922, Jane Misme, founder of *La Française*, urged readers to attend women's events and expressed her certainty 'that sport would provide feminism with strong women who are determined to win their rights'. She concluded: 'Sport, whether we like it or not, will have social consequences for women. And as such, it is of interest to feminism'.[15] The growing success of women's football also filled Alice Milliat with optimism:

> It is not our intention to point out what progress still needs to be made in order for society to be organised on an equitable basis,

but we would like to point out that our work on women's physical education and sport is, in short, a feminist manifestation of the highest order.[16]

Women's football turns male

While women's football was asserting itself as a new area of emancipation for French women at the beginning of the 1920s, the sports press was becoming increasingly cautious. It is true that *L'Auto* was satisfied that women's football allowed them to 'maintain and improve their health, to be better able to fulfil the duties that nature imposes on women'.[17] At the end of 1921, however, the sports daily gloatingly reported on a player confessing her trouble reconciling football with her marital duties: 'Witness how sport, which is said to take over everything, has only occupied the place it should in their gentle brains [...] Oh, the adorable little fiancées! Oh, the adorable little wives and mothers-to-be'.[18]

The violent nature of football was also regularly invoked by the detractors of women's sport. The journalist Maurice Pefferkorn deplored the fact that 'the being of grace, elegance and charm that is woman risks losing so many refined qualities and subtle virtues in violent sports like football [...] The roughness of this sport and the vigour it requires are virile qualities which it is not desirable for women to acquire'.[19] Moreover, football was said to 'masculinise' women to the extent that it endangered their ability to procreate. 'Kicking a ball exerts a very intense abdominal pressure that could have the most serious effects on a woman's organs', claimed Professor Georges Racine. 'The practice may have a harmful influence on the child in gestation'.[20] Medical conjecture was mobilised to demonstrate that football causes women to develop a 'narrow pelvis', 'immature vaginas', or simply the loss of their reproductive functions.[21]

This virulently sexist backlash can be explained by the natalist ideology which, under pressure from conservative and Catholic leagues, was enshrined in July 1920 and March 1923 in a body of laws that prohibited the advertising of anti-conceptives and made abortion a crime. The publication in 1922 of the novel *La Garçonne* ('The Tomboy') by Victor Margueritte caused a national scandal by narrating the unbridled sexual mores of a young woman seeking independence. With a growing number of 'garçonnes', characterised by their androgynous silhouettes and short hair, asserting their right to do what they liked with their bodies, in the eyes of its slanderers women's football exacerbated this gender confusion.[22] 'Women have become virilised, their breasts and hips have ceased to develop, and they have become "neutral"', *L'Éducation physique et sportive féminine* reported in exasperation on 1 July 1924. The tempestuous footballer Violette Morris,* a member of Fémina Sport and then Olympique de Paris, attracted the wrath of men for '[her] men's trousers, [her] cap on the side and [her] cigarette in the corner of her lip'[23] and for her right hook to the chin of a supporter who had called her a 'fat cow' and a 'fat arse' during a match in December 1924.[24]

By distracting women from their domestic and maternal duties, women's football represented a threat to the gendered division of French society, reaffirming the fundamentally masculine identity of football. In order to vilify women footballers, some invoked the most reactionary moral order, such as Henri Desgrange, editor-in-chief of *L'Auto*:

> Let young girls play sport among themselves, in a strictly enclosed area, inaccessible to the public: yes, that's fine. But for them to make a spectacle of themselves on certain festival days, where the public is invited, and even to dare to chase a ball around a field that is not surrounded by thick walls, that is intolerable![25]

From 1925 onwards, women's football began to disappear from the sporting landscape. The efforts of the FSFSF, which exhibited photographs of the newborn babies of Fémina Sport members at the Élisabeth stadium or refused to renew the licence of the tumultuous Violette Morris in 1928, changed little.[26] Moreover, the quality of the sporting spectacle offered by women's football was gradually declining, as *Le Miroir des sports* pointed out in early 1925: 'The

---

* A great sportswoman of the interwar period, Violette Morris also practised boxing, cycling, car racing and aviation, with the slogan: 'What a man does, Violette can do!' She was shot in 1944 by maquisards following her involvement with the Gestapo.

game is worthless [...] the most crude technique, the most basic knowledge of football do not exist in women's teams'.[27] Tired of witnessing poor matches, the public gradually lost interest, like the one between Fémina Sport and the Cadettes de Gascogne in 1926: 'Only a few locals take the trouble to come and reinforce the small, thin troop of children from the neighbourhood who have slipped into the ground through the well-known gaps in the fence or the hedge', noted the same newspaper. 'Is the public wrong to abstain? You can't blame them. Among sportswomen, football is not a very eventful game, lacking in passes and exciting action'.[28]

The disenchantment with women's football was the result of the ageing teams and the lack of training. The pioneers learned to kick the ball 'on the job' and without a real coach, as Lucienne Laudré-Viel, a female footballer in her own right, testified: 'I learned by playing. There wasn't much advice. I don't know if they had a coach at Fémina, but we didn't have one. There was advice from dad but [...] seeing the men play is how you learn'. Her sister, Jacqueline, added: 'There was no training. Nothing was planned for that. We were summoned, we met in the changing room and that was that. We would get ready, we would go and play'.[29] Similarly, the lack of sports facilities, especially those equipped with changing rooms, further hindered the development of women's football as the number of men's teams – unwilling to share the few available pitches – exploded during this period. Finally, novice sportswomen were being channelled towards basketball, which was considered more graceful and less brutal, and didn't suffer the patriarchal ire of medical and sports institutions. 'I believed for a while in the future of women's football; I don't believe in it any more', lamented Alice Milliat in the summer of 1926.

> In England, it has more or less fallen; in other countries, such as Czechoslovakia and Yugoslavia, it has been very badly received; the national game *hazena* [Czech handball] has easily dethroned it; in Germany, it is handball; in America and Canada, the number of basketball teams far outnumbers the few that play football.[30]

Over the course of the seasons, fewer teams enrolled for the French championship (founded in 1919), and several disappeared altogether due to lack of players. From 1928, the matches organised by the FSFSF sometimes involved incomplete teams. The same year, sports bodies took their distance from women's football. 'We are wholly opposed to football for women and we are happy to ignore it', pronounced the secretary of the FFF.[31] A few months after the 1928 Summer Olympics, Baron Pierre de Coubertin stated: 'If there are women who want to play football or box, they are free to do so, provided that it is without spectators, because the spectators who gather around such competitions do not come to see sport'.[32] Although the socialist fringe of the working-class sports movement had previously looked favourably on women's football as a sign of the democratisation of physical activities, it now turned its back on it. Following the Prague Congress of 1929, the educational programme of the Socialist Workers' International recommended that women play 'ball games with the exception of football' because 'the various branches of women's sport must be practised with due regard for the special conditions of women'.[33]

At the end of the 1932–1933 season, after a French championship that crowned Fémina Sport for the last time, women's football was officially banned by the FSFSF, which cited growing financial difficulties as well as the disastrous image of a sport that, according to its detractors, tainted women's sport as a whole. In the wake of this, a short-lived and autonomous Women's Football League was created on the initiative of a few Parisian sports societies, before disappearing at the end of 1937.

In the meantime, the second edition of the Football World Cup, organised in Italy in 1934 under the aegis of the Mussolini regime, exalted the warrior masculinity of the players and established football as a mass spectacle that could stir up European nationalism [see Chapter 6]. A few years later, the discrediting of women's football was confirmed by the Vichy regime, which 'vigorously prohibited' its practice on 27 March 1941 under the pretext that it was 'harmful to women'.

Our desires cause disorder

Played in Europe only in an improvised, quasi-clandestine manner since the end of the 1930s, women's football did not make its official return until 1955. In locations as distinct as The Hague, Manchester, and the Vienna region, high school girls' teams appeared, coached by a father or a brother. After the German national team's victory over Hungary in the 1954 World Cup final, renewed popular enthusiasm for football gave rise to a dozen women's teams in West Germany.[34] An initial international match with Holland was arranged in Essen in 1956, followed by two more in Stuttgart and Munich (the latter drawing a crowd of 14,000).[35] Established in 1957, the Associazione Italiana Calcio Femminile (AICF) comprised six women's teams from Rome, Naples and Sicily. In Murgenthal, Switzerland, a dozen young female players founded FC Goitschel in 1964.

In France, Pierre Delaunay, secretary general of the French Football Federation (FFF), issued a warning about women footballers in 1965: 'It is beyond our comprehension to admit that they can really play [...] Any organised attempt can, it seems, only be doomed to failure, even if it were to be encouraged; once again, football is, in our opinion, only for men'.[36] In spite of this official disregard, women's football in France developed within a most unexpected festive framework: that of charity fairs in support of sports associations. In September 1965, on the occasion of the annual festival of the Club sportif d'Humbécourt, in Haute-Marne, a women's team was formed at short notice to play against a group of firemen from the neighbouring villages. Intended as a burlesque attraction, the aim of the game was to raise funds for the club's coffers. But it was so successful that more and more women's football matches were offered as comic entertainment at club celebrations in eastern France. To celebrate its 45th anniversary, the Association Sportive Gerstheim in the Bas-Rhin region attracted a thousand onlookers on 20 August 1967 with a women's football exhibition.[37]

In Reims, a journalist from the daily *L'Union*, Pierre Geoffroy, launched an appeal in his columns in July 1968 to organise a women's football match as part of the annual fair of the Union Sports club. The previous year, the sports association opened the festivities with a 'midget-wrestling' match. About 30 young women responded, and two teams were organised and trained twice a week under the guidance of Geoffroy and his colleague Richard Gaud to prepare the public entertainment. 'What started out merely as a promotional stunt soon took a more serious turn, because the players didn't just want to "put on a display" for the audience, but absolutely wanted to play a real match', recalled the sports journalist. 'Most of them had already been playing for several years with their brothers and did so very well [...] There was an unimaginable number of girls playing improvised football on the outskirts of Reims'.[38] Gaud added 'We had to admit it was a pleasant surprise because they weren't just messing around. It wasn't a parody of football. On the contrary, they held themselves so well that a representative of the professional Stade de Reims who was there asked us [...] to do a curtain raiser'.[39]

On the eve of the fair, on 24 August 1968, the women's Football Club of Reims faced FC Schwindratzheim of Alsace in an opening match prior to the men's game between Stade de Reims and Valenciennes in the Auguste-Delaune ground. 'When we took the field, we were worried about the reaction of the spectators', says Nicole Mangas, a player from Reims. 'Initially, there were a few snickers [but] with the way the game was constructed (one-two, counter-attacks, dribbling, etc.), the crosses and the well-struck shots, the crowd couldn't believe it and were soon cheering'.[40] The next day, 2,000 people flocked to the Union Sports festivities to watch the spectacle of these footballers who, to great applause, won the game against the girls from Schwindratzheim.

While these 'exhibition matches' proliferated, leading to the creation of women's teams, the Alsace League, with its score of women's sections, became an early home for women's football and launched a championship for the 1969–1970 season. The encouragement of Pierre Geoffroy – who in the pages of *L'Union* urged the young women of the region to set up their own team – as well as the footballing quality of the Reims players, led to the creation of a regional challenge in March 1969 with more than a dozen squads.

Backed into a corner by the explosion in the number of female players seeking recognition in the sport (they numbered nearly 2,000 by 1970), the FFF officially recognised women's football on 29 March 1970. This decision reflected the growth of women's football across the continent. Dutch women's footballers established the Algemene

Nederlandse Damesvoetbalbond in 1955, while a Women's Football Association was formed in Great Britain in 1969. The Federazione italiana di Calcio femminile, founded in 1968 on the initiative of businessmen from Turin, began with about 50 teams competing in a national championship with two divisions.

First conceived by this Italian association and with a view to increasing profits, an initial European Competition for Women's Football took place in November 1969, without the oversight of any official – male – authority. The same businessmen founded, with the support of the Martini & Rossi brand, the International Federation of European Women's Football (FIEFF). In July 1970 the first women's World Cup was held near Naples, bringing together seven teams: six from Europe and one from Mexico. Regardless of the lack of recognition from international football bodies, the final between Denmark and Italy in Salerno on 15 July drew 10,000 spectators.[41] The following year, the Italian businessmen thumbed their noses even harder at FIFA, with the second Cup bringing a crowd 90,000 strong to the Azteca stadium in Mexico to watch the Mexico-Denmark final.[42]

Troubled by this uncontrolled, mercantile evolution of women's football, the European football federations decided to officially recognise the practice. Yet it was more out of fear at seeing the women's game escape from them, than out of a real ambition to promote and support women's football, that the male hierarchs of the federal authorities changed their views. This recognition by default and desire to control women players are made clear by the grudging words of the FFF's director general at a July 1970 meeting of the federal council:

> This is the way our time wants it. In football as in other areas, women have had their rights recognised. Let us not complain. The members of your council are not misogynists [and recognise] women's football, which article 1 of the statutes therefore instructs the FFF to organise, develop, and control.[43]

The rise of women's football in France was down to three factors: the introduction of obligatory schooling for girls after the war, co-ed schools becoming the norm following the Berthoin ordinance of 1959, and sports becoming a school subject in 1967. These social advances made the school institution a place where young French women could discover and learn team sports. While most of the first female footballers initially played basketball, handball or volleyball, many of them were quickly tempted by football when they saw their male entourage indulging in the joys of the game: 'My father supported the Véloce Vannetais and dragged us to the La Rabine stadium every Sunday. We had to eat at 11 o'clock to be on time for the opening match!' recalls Michèle Carado, a pioneer of women's football in Brittany. 'I naturally became friends with the players' wives and daughters, and at some point we felt like going onto the pitch and kicking the ball around'.[44] Annie Fortems, the famous captain of Étoile sportive de Juvisy, who played from the age of 6 with her five brothers, says that after May '68:

> A life of possibilities for women opened up for the young teenagers we were. Speech was liberated and some of us expressed our ambitions to our elder brother or our father: 'We want to play football in a real team, like the boys!' [...] In Juvisy, in September 1971, the older brother of a 14-year-old girl spoke up for us and asked the president of the local club to create a girls' team.[45]

The first French women footballers were often schoolgirls or ordinary workers and office employees who had to take unpaid leave to be able to combine their work with their passion. 'After long journeys by minibus, to Marseille, for example, and a night sharing a hotel room with four or five others, we would return after the match', recalls the illustrious Rémoise Ghislaine Royer-Soef, known as 'Gigi'. 'On the Monday morning, it was a struggle to get to work on time'.[46] The working-class origins of these young women who were passionate about football particularly appealed to the anti-establishment sports press, such as *Miroir-Sprint*, a weekly magazine close to the French Communist Party, which saw these players as 'worthy descendants of those beret-wearing women who, in 1918, took advantage of the emancipation due to the First World War to start kicking a ball' and actively supported the practice as 'an expression of the feminist movement and a factor of emancipation'.[47] As for the monthly *Le Miroir du football*, it praised the collective and attacking dimension of women's football as opposed to the physical and ultra-defensive men's football then promoted by the pundits of the FFF [see Chapter 18]. 'It is quite obvious that if men consider, when financial interests are at stake, that football consists of preventing the opponent from scoring by blocking the goal with eight players and by using unsportsmanlike methods, women are under no obligation to treat this as the truth', the monthly magazine joked on 21 February 1973.

Following the political effervescence of May '68, the fight for female emancipation and gender equality continued with the creation of the Women's Liberation Movement (MLF) in 1970. However, while the female body was at the heart of the feminist movement's most mobilising demands through the struggle for the right to abortion and contraception, the denunciation of male violence and sexism in advertising – one of the MLF's earliest flagship slogans was 'Our bodies belong to us' – the issue of sport was not a focus of women activists. Conversely, most women footballers, while sensitive to the social movement of the time and its questioning of the patriarchal order, didn't make explicit the feminist dimension of their involvement in a sport seen as key to the construction of virile masculinity. 'I wasn't campaigning for feminism, I was campaigning for women's football', says Marilou Duringer, a pioneer of FC Schwindratzheim.

> There was no reason why girls shouldn't play football like they play basketball or handball. It wasn't really about feminism but more about claiming our place on the football field. I don't really like it when people compare us to men's football because it's a female form of physical engagement and a female game, gentler, more graceful and not manly, that's all.[48]

The pioneers of women's football challenged male domination and their disqualification from the heavily gendered sport in a straightforward manner: with a ball on the ground every Sunday, on what was seen as male turf. However, despite the official legitimisation of women's football, this feminism in action was harshly attacked from the outset in both the hushed confines of the governing institutions, and in the sports pages of the French press.

Institutional abuse

On the ground, in the absence of any real federal financial support and available sports facilities, women's teams were forced to join men's football clubs. Of the 315 teams listed in 1973, only 20 or so were organised as autonomous women's associations.[49] The cohabitation between women players and men's teams was all the more difficult as it was regularly the latter that benefited from the best pitch, the best equipment and the most convenient training times. Dominique Rinaudo recalls her first steps at FC Lyon:

> We had a hard time, we had no pitch, we had no changing room. There was a small, potholed car park. We were given old balls, which were oval because they couldn't put up with the boys [sic] any more, torn jerseys, old jerseys from the under-16s, some of them barely fit us. It was horrible. We weren't allowed to use the changing rooms, we couldn't shower after training. You really had to be passionate, want to do it and keep going to accept that.[50]

Meanwhile, the FFF kept up its stereotypes about the supposed 'weaker sex' by limiting, until the summer of 1970, women's matches to a duration of two 35-minute halves.* In addition, any kind of mixing was strictly forbidden during training sessions as well as in tournaments, while young players couldn't become members until the age of 11 (unlike their male counterparts who could access the club from age 5).

With the network of clubs with a women's section still weak, the late introduction of girls to football and the impossibility of joining a men's team – even when there was a shortage of players – considerably slowed the development of women's football. Though the federation set up an official French women's team in 1971 and launched the first national championship in the 1974–1975 season, top-level

* The standard two 45-minute halves would only be imposed by UEFA in 1992.

female footballers were not fooled. 'I was astonished to realise that the FFF didn't give a damn about women's football and treated the national squad like second-class players', says Annie Fortems, recalling a training camp for the French women in 1977. 'This contempt was demonstrated by the lack of resources and skills dedicated to its development. As a woman and a feminist, I was appalled at the prevalent macho backwardness'.[51] She soon withdrew from the national team to devote herself to her club, Étoile sportive de Juvisy.

The lack of interest in women's football by the press also reflected sexist attitudes. The weekly *France Football* devoted only seven articles to the subject between 1971 and 1976, while *L'Équipe* Magazine published an average of only one article per year on the subject between 1980 and 2011.[52] In the rare reports and interviews with female footballers, the female body was systematically at the centre of attention. The press never failed to emphasise the femininity and physical beauty of female players, as if to reassure their male readers that they are not 'tomboys'.[53] The daily *Paris-Jour* thus described a young French national team player on 21 September 1970 as 'harmoniously proportioned. And cute, yes! Curly black hair. Laughing eyes. A caressing voice. Adorable. Since she also plays football very well, we can only be seduced'. As for *Libération*, it referred, with wanton chauvinism, to 'big lanky girls, little plump ones, sweeties with multicoloured bands in their hair and cheekbones reddened by effort. They come in all models and temperaments. With slightly muscular thighs among the elite who train twice a week. Not enough to make a lover go limp, though'.[54]

This constant focus on the appearance of women footballers and the reassuring refrain of women easily moving 'from cleats to heels' locked the players into a gendered normativity. The magazine *Lectures pour tous*, in January 1970, revelled in the fact that 'fashion is still a hot topic among these young women. These fierce female footballers aren't abandoning their powder puffs. Far from it'. In 1988, *L'Équipe* Magazine described Martine Puentes, a player in the French national team, as 'elegant, cute – she's no virago', before subtly pointing out that the newspaper 'didn't take the most beautiful one' and that among the female players 'there aren't [only] fatties'.[55]

This media denigration, with the passive complicity of the sports authorities, did little to boost attendance at grounds. In the early 1980s, the stars of the women's team in Reims, already five-time French champions, were barely able to attract 200 to 300 spectators per match.[56] As for the number of registered female members, it grew so imperceptibly that by 2000 they still only represented 1.4 per cent of FFF membership, equivalent to some 28,000 women footballers.[57] This is very different to Sweden and Germany, where, by the late 1970s, women footballers made up 15 per cent and 9 per cent of the total membership respectively.[58] For the historian Xavier Breuil, who has studied the history of women's football in Europe, this disparity is linked to different feminist mobilisation strategies: the French, Italian and British movements were more inclined to fight for women's rights to have free use of their bodies, while activists for gender equality in Northern Europe focused their demands primarily on conquering the places of power monopolised by men.[59] In this sense, Scandinavian and German women footballers have fought to impose within their respective federations the conditions required for the development of the practice, namely co-education in clubs, the promotion of school football, and the possibility for girls to play the sport from a very young age.

A crumbling bastion

In November 1991, after seven unofficial World Cups, women's football entered the realm of commercial football with the first FIFA Women's World Cup, held in China. The US team won the final against Norway, playing before a crowd of 63,000, and went on to become the leading international squad, winning world titles in 1999 and 2015, as well as four Olympic titles. Played above all in the Italian and Latino communities, 'soccer'* has also emerged in the United States as a school sport for women and girls. While American football, ice hockey and baseball are considered to be authentically national, masculine sports, soccer became particularly popular among women in the late 1990s: half of the 8 million American

* The term comes from 'assoccer', which in the 19th century referred to association football, in the same way that 'rugger' referred to rugby.

soccer players are women.[60] This staggering success among women led to the fact that in 2014, North America had an average of 450 female football players per 10,000 inhabitants, compared to just 71 in Europe.[61]

In France, it was not until a fourth-place finish in the 2011 Women's World Cup that women's football timidly began to win the hearts of fans and sportswomen alike. Following the dismaying sporting and media spectacle offered by the men's team in 2010 at the World Cup in South Africa, the public became enamoured of the women's team, which was as warm as it was talented.* Some 2.3 million French viewers watched the French women's semi-final against the United States, an unprecedented audience record for women's football. 'We had a real sympathy rating, people identified with this team', said Bruno Bini, the coach of Les Bleues during this World Cup.

> It's a kind of sociological phenomenon. In a society where the rich are getting richer and the poor are getting poorer, where there is not much work, the French saw 21 simple girls go down to the wire. They saw 21 ordinary girls with an ordinary coach, and they liked it.[62]

However, from 2005 onwards, the FFF, stubborn in its desire to govern the bodies of female players, embarked on a veritable campaign to 'feminise' female footballers. Les Bleues were forced to pose nude as part of a campaign to promote women's football in 2009, model and footballer's wife Adriana Karembeu was recruited as an ambassador for women's football, 'skirt days' were organised at the big clubs to teach players how to wear a suit or make-up, and the FFF's school programme for girls was given the name 'Football for Princesses' in 2011, with lots of pink.[63] The FFF's obsession with 'femininity' was not limited to women.

---

* Although Les Bleus were quickly eliminated from the World Cup in 2010, they also suffered public and media opprobrium for their antics, notably following a training strike in support of player Nicolas Anelka, who was sent off after insulting coach Raymond Domenech.

Obsessed with the 'femininity' of female footballers, the federation even turned to lesbophobia. 'All the girls who were not feminine enough were suspected of being gay, and some were selected less often for the French team', says Annie Fortems.[64] This discrimination against lesbian players expressed the federation's anxiety that the figure of the female footballer – like that of the gay player – might disrupt traditional social sex and gender relations. Sports sociologist Béatrice Barbusse says:

> The constant injunction to femininity, expressed as if there were only one, single way to be a woman is present in all areas of [women footballers'] lives: wearing their hair tied back and long if possible, using make-up off the pitch, showing up on stage or at events in dresses and heels, etc.
>
> Sportswomen are appreciated first and foremost for their perceived body, rather than for the body 'in itself'. In short, do they play football for themselves or for the male gaze? We are faced with an institutional and political instrumentalisation of women's bodies and therefore of women footballers.[65]

This systemic sexism and homophobia led feminist movements to turn to football in order to denounce male domination in the sports industry. A first step was taken on a European scale on the occasion of the 2006 Men's World Cup in Germany. The opening in Berlin of Artemis, a giant 3,000 m^2 complex for sex workers, a few months before the opening of the competition, provoked the ire of certain feminist groups. In January 2006, the Coalition Against Trafficking in Women denounced this sex supermarket adjacent to the sporting event in a media campaign entitled 'Buying sex is not a sport'. The German association for the defence of the rights of sex workers, for its part, alerted public opinion to the human exploitation of 40,000 young women from Eastern Europe.[66] 'When we see that the next men's football World Cup is associated with prostitution, we feel doubly affected, as women and as former footballers and pioneers', says Annie Fortems, president of the association Les Pionnières du football féminin.

> Thirty-five years ago, it was the same people, with their deep sexism, that we had to suffer and fight against before we could impose ourselves. Today, women's dignity is still shamelessly sacrificed on the altar of the God of football and of money. This is the sad proof, if any were needed, that sexism and contempt for women are still alive and well in the world of football.[67]

In France, some feminist activists are gradually taking over the pitch, fed up with sexist or homophobic remarks made by players, sports commentators and managers. Former 1998 world champion Didier Deschamps, then coach of Juventus, said in 2007 about the pink colour of the team's shirt: 'I don't like this colour because in France it's the colour of gays'. As for Bernard Lacombe, manager of Olympique Lyonnais (whose women's squad is one of the best in Europe), he belched out in March 2013: 'I don't talk about football with women [...] Let them deal with their pots and pans and things will be fine'.*

Formed in Paris in 2012, the Dégommeuses are a football team politically committed to the fight against sexism, homophobia and all forms of discrimination. 'Our struggle is through and in sport, which specifically means providing a calm space for lesbians and trans boys to be on a football field', explains Marine Romezin, a Dégommeuse.[68] She adds: 'If you don't take your place, nobody will give it to you. Football is a metaphor for this, we take over the space on the pitch'.[69] The team even pays particular attention to access to sport for women refugees and the most vulnerable, while regularly challenging the governing bodies on homophobia and sexism in football.[70] In parallel to their sporting and political activities, in June 2012, as part of a week of action against sexist and lesbophobic violence, the football activists invited a delegation from the Thokozani Football Club, a South African women's team made up of lesbian and trans players from the townships of Durban.** Four years later, on the sidelines of the Euro 2016 men's tournament, the Dégommeuses

* Three years after these sexist remarks, Nathalie Boy de la Tour became the first female president of the French football league.

** The name pays homage to Thokozani Qwabe, a young South African player murdered in 2007 for her homosexuality.

also organised 'Foot for Freedom', a mixed football tournament with refugees persecuted in their country because of their sexual orientation or gender identity.

Many women no longer hesitate to 'take their place' by getting together in amateur competitions such as the Bernard Tapine Cup, a Parisian futsal* tournament that, since 2015, has seen teams with punning names like the Cacahuètes Sluts, Olympique de Marcelle, and the Joga Bonitas. The Dégommeuse player Veronica Noseda adds: '[Playing football] is a political issue because women's bodies, and lesbians' bodies in particular, have always been subject to such social control and disapproval that seeing these girls reclaim their bodies is thrilling [...] It's an enormous power that we have over ourselves'.[71]

From the first emancipatory paths traced by the valiant female pioneers of the 1970s to the activism of the Dégommeuses, women's football has succeeded in breaking open the fortress of male chauvinism and heteronormativity embodied by the FFF, and in sketching out an image of football that is far removed from the model of femininity conveyed by sporting institutions. It is a long road that is still full of pitfalls. 'Thirty years later, the city of Reims has finally put up a plaque at the Auguste-Delaune stadium celebrating our five French championship titles', sighs former Reims midfielder Ghislaine Royer-Souef. 'They only displayed the men's titles before [...]'[72]

* Futsal is a form of football played in teams of five on a handball court in two 20-minute halves. Created in the 1930s in South America, futsal (a contraction of the Spanish term *fútbol de salón*) was initially a team sport for students at Young Men's Christian Associations (YMCA). The game is governed by two bodies, the World Futsal Association (since 1971) and FIFA (since 1989), which each organise their own competitions.

20

'Here it's about punk football'

Fan-owned clubs in England

I carry my awareness of defeat like a banner of victory.

Fernando Pessoa, *The Book of Disquiet*, 1913–1935

At the start of the 1990s, the quiet town of Northampton, mid-way between London and Birmingham, was better known for its rugby team, The Saints, than for its football team. Usually hovering between the third and fourth divisions, Northampton Town FC's greatest sporting feat was securing runner-up status in the second division in 1965. Worse, the club was on the verge of bankruptcy, unable to pay its players at the start of the 1991–1992 season. Due to the disastrous management of Northampton Town FC by then-chairman Michael McRitchie, the team nicknamed the Cobblers had accumulated £1.6 million in debts, the equivalent of two years' worth of business.[1] To save the club from ruin, ten players were sacked and much cheaper young footballers were hastily recruited. But the modest club sank to the bottom of the fourth division.

Trying to cheer themselves up in the pub after yet another disappointing game, a handful of supporters including Rob Marshall, editor of the fanzine *What A Load of Cobblers*, discussed the club's dire situation. One of them, Brian Lomax, mentioned between pints that he had been impressed by a Lancaster University student rent strike his daughter had been involved in, convincing him that in these difficult times Cobblers fans needed to take on a more active role. 'It was clear as the financial crisis deepened and time passed that there was no one coming along to save us, no white knight charging to our rescue', recalls Lomax. 'In response to this, a few of us arranged a meeting of the supporters to see what could be done'.[2]

In fans we trust

Crammed into a 250-capacity hall, 600 Cobblers fans gathered in a feverish atmosphere one evening in January 1992. The meeting began with a man displaying a club badge that had been given to his father in the 1950s. At the request of Northampton Town's governing body, the fans had paid for expensive floodlights for their stadium out of their own pockets. As a thank you for their generosity, donors were given these badges and the right, for some, to have a drink once a year with the management.

The current management's disregard for the Cobblers' crisis encouraged the angry supporters to take back their club. Brian Lomax, who was director of the Mayday Trust, a cooperative that helps former prisoners, drug addicts and victims of domestic violence to find housing, came up with the idea of using a similar cooperative structure to collectively buy out part of Northampton Town FC. This type of organisation allows its members, as an association recognised as being of public benefit, to pool capital for non-profit purposes. Any cooperative, by virtue of its statutes, must also be managed democratically and in an egalitarian manner, with each of its members having one vote, regardless of the capital contributed. 'It was clear to me that the kind of structure I was involved in was the perfect tool for supporters to get together to buy a piece of the club and thereby democratically influence club policy', recalls Brian Lomax. 'There was no reason why what works elsewhere in society couldn't be transferred to football'.[3] A few weeks later, the Northampton Town Supporters Trust was officially founded, a first in football.

Scouring pubs, city streets and workplaces, the Trust's members collected donations of anything between £1 and £1,000. The initiative won popularity when, during a match, the Cobblers' chairman, under the eye of the television cameras, attempted to violently expel the rebel supporters who had managed to collect £3,500 inside the stadium itself.[4] In a few months, the supporters' trust raised nearly £30,000, enough to buy a share in the club, which was then under administration. Combined with the skills and local knowledge networks of the various members of the Northampton Town Supporters' Trust, this initial financial contribution made it possible to renegotiate the gradual payment of debts to creditors and to offer a guarantee of solvency. Two representatives of the trust were then elected to the club's board of directors, ensuring that the supporters had a countervailing power within the Cobblers' management. Within a year, Northampton Town FC was saved from financial collapse. A decade later, with the supporters' cooperative now owning more than 8 per cent of the Cobblers' capital, Brian Lomax was jubilant: 'Managers and players come and go. We will always be here. We keep football alive. Why shouldn't we have a say?'[5]

This is how, from the sleepy banks of the River Nene, an unprecedented shockwave spread, leading to an upsurge of assembly democracy within the monolithic football industry. The Northampton Town FC supporters' venture was quickly emulated by the Kettering Town 'Poppies' Supporters' Trust, created in 1992, and the Lincoln City and Crystal Palace supporters' cooperatives, set up in 2000. That same year, under the impetus of the indefatigable Brian Lomax, Supporters Direct was founded, a platform to support the creation of supporters' trusts and to promote this model of democratic management of clubs. 'Fans were becoming more militant, a reaction to a profound change in football', explains Dave Boyle of Supporters Direct.

> The advent of Sky TV and the Premier League was reshaping the game, disrupting the traditional relationship between fans and their clubs. Ticket prices were rising, clubs were spiralling into debt, the whole notion of 'going to the game' was altering. But football fans were really not prepared to accept this.[6]

Since the turn of the 1990s, English football has undergone profound economic upheaval. The rights to broadcast matches on television, which began in 1964 with the BBC's *Match of the Day*, were shared equally among the four divisions of professional football that make up the Football League. But in 1988, the major English clubs decided to put an end to this egalitarian distribution: of the £44 million in broadcasting rights negotiated for the next four years, half was to go to the first division, 25 per cent to the second and the remaining 25 per cent to the last two. However, the earthquake came in 1992 with the creation of the Premier League, which brought together the top 20 or so clubs in the upper division and broke away from the Football League, which was now reduced to three divisions [see Chapter 14]. BSkyB, the package of satellite channels owned by tycoon Rupert Murdoch, then paid £305 million over five years to broadcast the matches of this prestigious Premier League, conceived as a television show in its own right. When the contract was renewed in 1997, the cost of rights rose to a staggering £670 million, and in 2013 reached the astronomical sum of £3 billion for a three-year period.[7]

This massive influx of money radically reconfigured the financial model of English professional football. Anticipating the lucrative windfall from broadcasting rights and merchandising revenues, clubs took on huge debts in order to attract the best players and remain among the country's footballing elite. Between 1992 and 2010, the salaries of Premier League players increased by 1,508 per cent compared to an average increase of 186 per cent for an English worker over the same period.[8] Locked in an inflationary spiral caused by the hunt for talented footballers, driven by a race to save money based on extensive borrowing, 18 of the 20 clubs operating in the Premier League were loss-making in 2014.

In the lower divisions, the avalanche of cash and the logic of club debt was turning into a nightmare. In 2002, the pay-TV channel ITV Digital, which two years earlier had committed £315 million in broadcasting rights to the Football League, went bankrupt.[9] While viewers were not reluctant to spend £20 a month to watch Chelsea and Manchester United, few were willing to subscribe to ITV to watch matches between obscure teams in the fourth tier. There was one problem: in anticipation of the miraculous revenues from broadcasting, many clubs had already bought players at a premium, or embarked on expensive stadium renovations. Between 2002 and 2011, no fewer than 36 Football League clubs went into insolvency, and it is estimated that the 72 clubs in the three divisions had a total debt of £1 billion in 2013.[10]

Faced with this financial haemorrhage and fed up with the irresponsibility of the clubs' governing bodies, the supporters of Football

League teams saw their chance to save their clubs in the cooperative experience modelled by the supporters' trusts. Yet the financial excesses of the football business were so great that supporters' trusts began to set their sights higher than merely taking shares in clubs facing bankruptcy: they were now trying to take control of them.

Taking stock of a different football

One of the most emblematic cases of the fans' revolt against the autocracy of incompetent and unscrupulous managers is that of Exeter City, the first fully professional Football League club to be majority owned through popular ownership. By the end of 1994, the legendary Devon club, then in the fourth tier, was up to its eyeballs in debt. After selling its historic stadium, St James Park, for a pittance, in 2002 two businessmen were called in to rescue the Grecians, as they are known, under the watchful eye of the supporters. The first, John Russell, had just left the management of Scarborough FC with a huge debt, while the second, Mike Lewis, had sold Swansea City for a symbolic £1 to a consortium. Uri Geller, a former TV conjurer with a notorious reputation for greed, was appointed chairman of the club. In order to replenish the coffers, this fine management team even had the crazy idea of inviting Michael Jackson to the stadium on 14 June 2002, where nearly 10,000 people flocked to see the singer, who donned an Exeter shirt for the occasion and was made an honorary member of the club.

With the King of Pop bailing out the coffers and a spoon-bending club chairman, the bewildered fans feared they had become the laughing stock of English football. They were further dismayed when in May 2003 John Russell and Mike Lewis were arrested by the police for fraudulent trading. The two businessmen had been making dubious transactions with the club's money and their proposed financial package to save Exeter City from bankruptcy was shown to be a complete sham. The club was in a dire economic state and its list of creditors growing longer. No buyer was in sight as the Grecians plummeted to the fifth tier in the 2003–2004 season, relegated from the Football League.

Founded a few years earlier to support the club financially, the 700-strong Exeter City Supporters' Trust voted at a meeting in

February 2003 for a new strategy: to become the sole owner of the club to put an end to the shenanigans of the two crooked businessmen. By dint of donation campaigns and after having bought the shares of a former director at a low cost, Exeter City became the collective property of the supporters' trust within a few months. The club's new board of directors, drawn directly from the cooperative, decided to put democratic transparency and economic sobriety at the heart of the Grecians' management policy. As early as October 2003, a debt consolidation plan was approved. As for the price of tickets and season tickets, it is defined by the Exeter City fans themselves. 'We are a democracy', says Laurence Overend of the Exeter City Supporters' Trust. 'Supporters have the right to vote and any member can become chair of the club. Trust members pay just £2 a month'.[11]

In 2008, the Grecians succeeded in regaining the fourth tier and the following season entered League One (third tier). The club dropped back down to the lower division in 2012 but, as Paul Tisdale, the team's illustrious manager, argued:

> You know, it would have been the easiest thing in the world last season to borrow money to splash out on players in an effort to stay in League One. But what would have been the point if in doing so we would have betrayed everything that Exeter and the supporters' trust have worked so hard to build over the past decade.[12]

Laurence Overend added:

> It's more about investing your time and love into a local club for the simple joy of watching football and feeling part of something that matters to your community. Exeter are very, very unlikely to ever win the Champions League but then that doesn't matter. That's not why we support them.[13]

If, on the ruins of these bankrupt Football League teams, supporters manage to resurrect their clubs by buying them and managing them democratically – they are known as 'phoenix clubs' – the cooperative model also allows a new strategy to be honed to counter the financial appetites of certain predatory Premier League managers: that of founding a type of dissident sporting entity that is distinct from the original football club.

In the early 1990s, Wimbledon FC, the Premier League club from south-west London and 1988 FA Cup winners, wanted to abandon its dilapidated Plough Lane ground and move to a new sports venue. Faced with increasing economic difficulties, the club's management responded positively in 2001 to repeated requests from the Milton Keynes Stadia Consortium to host Wimbledon FC. The aim of this business cartel, made up of multinationals such as Ikea, was to launch a vast economic development programme in Milton Keynes, a famously bland new town in Buckinghamshire, including the construction of a sports arena. But the small local amateur team was in no position to fill the 30,000 seats in the brand new arena, prompting the consortium to hunt down indebted professional clubs and approach the struggling Wimbledon FC.

However, with Milton Keynes about 60 miles away from their historic home, supporters of the Dons did their best to remind Charles Koppel, the club's chairman and now their bête noire, of the absurdity of such a move – the club had been rooted in Wimbledon since 1889. The supporters, united in the Wimbledon Independent Supporters' Association, mobilised. They organised strikes on cheering, mass towing, and die-ins to block the access roads to the ground on match days. All to no avail. At the beginning of 2002, the board of directors agreed to the club's move, scheduled for September 2003.

The Wimbledon Independent Supporters' Association refused to accept this decision and decided to form an alternative club that was rooted in its historical territory and that it would fully own. In the days that followed, the Dons Trust, a cooperative of nearly a thousand supporters, was hastily set up despite the shared feeling of conceding victory to Charles Koppel and abandoning the beloved club, Wimbledon FC. After raising enough money to rent a ground in Kingsmeadow, a short distance from Wimbledon, AFC Wimbledon was formed in June 2002, while supporters organised a summer recruitment drive open to all players motivated by this crazy project. Within six weeks, the foundations of a new club had been laid.

'People tend to think: "Football fans? What the hell do they know?"' says Kris Stewart of the Dons Trust. 'But we are a society in miniature with accountants, lawyers, journalists, delivery people, teachers. They all have their own skills and they are all very useful to us'.[14] The young cooperative club even managed to join the Combined Counties League (D9) just in time to start the new 2002–2003 season. 'That first season was wonderful', says Ivor Heller, an elected member of the club's board. 'After the hell of the previous few years, I think that there was a sense of release among those following the club. We were all just having a laugh again, travelling around London, often visiting places some of us had never heard of'.[15]

The secessionist team made an incredible comeback. From the depths of the ninth division, it reached League One, the third English division, in 2016, where it faced, ironically, Wimbledon FC, which, in 2004, had renamed itself Milton Keynes Dons FC. Despite the club's meteoric rise in the Football League, which allows it to breathe financially, Erik Samuelson, one of AFC Wimbledon's fan managers, insists:

> We won't borrow money to fund transfers or pay exorbitant wages. If the club can't afford a player, then that's too bad. And if a player is demanding a salary in excess of what we can manage then we can't afford to keep him; it's as simple as that. Other clubs might be happy to borrow or turn to a benefactor but not us.[16]

As for the power granted to supporters, the cooperative club remains viscerally attached to it. 'AFC Wimbledon is a club collectively created, owned and run by its fans', reads its charter. 'In everything we do, we strive to provide the very best football club we can possibly be – for our supporters, our visitors and our community. And, as a fans-owned club, everything we do is for fans, and much of it is done by fans'.

'Our club, our rules'

'LUHG'. At the turn of 2005, these four enigmatic letters invaded the red brick walls of some of Manchester's working-class neighbourhoods. Only a few stickers shed light on the mystery: 'Love United, Hate Glazer'. Malcolm Glazer, an American billionaire known for having bought the Tampa Bay Buccaneers football club, had incurred the wrath of a large part of the former cotton city. Glazer took a stake in Manchester United in March 2003 and bought all the club's shares on 12 May 2005 for nearly £800 million.[17] To finance the deal, the cynical billionaire borrowed £660 million from New York hedge funds and mortgaged the club's future.[18] As a result, for the first time since 1931, Manchester United was in debt and found itself in a grotesque situation: the club was expected to repay the loan necessary for its purchase by Malcolm Glazer with monstrous interest payments amounting at the time to £60 million a year.

The Red Devils' fans were furious. All the more so as they had already experienced an attempt to buy the club by the unspeakable Rupert Murdoch in 1998, via his television group BSkyB. The Independent Manchester United Supporters' Association was founded in 1995 to protest against the renovation of the popular Old Trafford stands. At the time, it organised the anti-Murdoch protest and brought together five lawyers who, free of charge, tried to legally dismantle the Australian-American businessman's bid. At the same time, a group of small, rebellious shareholders, Shareholders United Against Murdoch, was formed to counter the businessman on the financial front. The pressure from both organisations combined with the public campaign of the supporters persuaded the British government to subject Murdoch's proposal to analysis by the Monopolies and Mergers Commission. In April 1999, the Commission rejected the bid as being both anti-competitive and damaging to the football economy. 'To say we were overjoyed was an understatement', recalls Andy Walsh, a founder of the Independent Manchester United Supporters' Association.

> It wasn't just an example of the power of supporters in action; it was an example of the power of supporters winning against a powerful person in English society. It was Murdoch after all, the man who will do anything to get what he wants. But we organised, we persevered and eventually we triumphed.[19]

Following this victory, the Supporters' Association, Shareholders United Against Murdoch – now the Manchester United Supporters' Trust – and a number of Mancunian fanzines joined forces in a collective, the 'Not For Sale Coalition', in order to prevent any attempt at a predatory takeover of the club. But six years later, in the face of Malcolm Glazer's financial capacity, the popular shareholding initiatives launched by the Manchester United Supporters' Trust and the 'Love United, Hate Glazer' protest campaign were like spitting into the wind.

On 12 May 2005, the day Glazer took control of the club, Luc Zentar, a Red Devils fan, recalls: 'On the evening of the 12th, I got drunk. Same thing on the 13th, same thing on the 14th. And on the 15th we decided to act'.[20] Malcolm Glazer's takeover of Manchester United increased the feeling of dispossession among fans, a growing malaise since the creation of the Premier League in 1992. Between 1990 and 2011, the cost of the cheapest seats at Old Trafford Stadium rose by 454 per cent, driving out the least affluent fans.[21] Price inflation has also been accompanied by increasing security in the stands, which are strictly monitored by stewards. The only way to support your team without paying a fortune for tickets is to go to the pub to watch the Sky pay-TV channel. The club's policy and the behaviour of the overpaid players are disconcerting to many. 'I supported Manchester United until the early 2000s', says Mike, a long-time fan. 'At that time, [defender] Rio Ferdinand was suspended for failing a drug test. When he returned, he asked for a raise. And twenty big ones for his agent. Now I thought, this is not right'.[22] 'The problem, from our perspective, was that clubs, especially in the top flight, were treating their fans in a way that I would describe as dismissive', adds Andy Walsh. 'At Old Trafford you could see this in the growing heavy-handedness of stewards during the game, [or in the] moving of match times to accommodate the Sky TV channel'.[23]

Malcolm Glazer's victory and widespread dissatisfaction quickly prompted some Manchester fans to envisage a 'protest club', directly inspired by the AFC Wimbledon experiment begun three years earlier. Barely a month after the billionaire's financial transaction, the independent associations of Manchester United supporters and the three fanzines *Red Issues, Red News* and *United We Stand* officially founded FC United of Manchester on 14 June 2005. On 5 July, 700 Red Rebels voted for their club to be structured as a cooperative and wrote the FC United manifesto on the fly. 'Our aim', they declared, 'is to create a sustainable club for the long term which is owned and democratically run by its members, which is accessible to all the communities of Manchester and one in which they can participate fully'.[24]

The very next day, nearly 4,000 Mancunians pledged donations and membership fees to the cooperative – including celebrities such as Peter Hook of Joy Division and New Order, and Mani, the bassist of the Stone Roses – with the result that the mutinous club raised £150,000 within days.[25] Nearly 900 players were quickly auditioned by the fans and 17 footballers were recruited in the summer of 2005. They included one Jonathan Mitten, a plumber, who is the great-nephew of Charles Mitten, winner of the FA Cup in 1948 with none other than Manchester United. Quite a symbol.

Starting out in the lowly North West Counties Football League (tiers 9–10), the Red Rebels played their first official game in Leigh on 16 July 2005. More than 2,500 enthusiastic fans turned out for the game, which ended with a joyous pitch invasion – a practice banned and harshly punished at Old Trafford – and players hoisted on shoulders like heroes. A week later, FC United played AFC Wimbledon in a friendly match that sealed the solidarity between the two clubs, forged in revolt against the excesses of business football. While their regional league usually only brings in a handful of onlookers, FC United managed to mobilise an average of over 3,000 supporters at the end of the season,[26] who had fun singing protest songs in the stands: 'His name is Malcolm Glazer, he thinks he's rather flash / He tried to buy a football club, but didn't have the cash / He borrowed lots of money, he made the fans distraught / But we're FC United, and we won't be fucking bought!'[27]

Many hands keep FC United running on a daily basis. More than a hundred volunteers work every week to manage the ticket office, maintain the pitch, and run the refreshment stall.[28] The coach still gets up at 3 am to make his rounds before heading to the ground. But they are all happy to be back in the warm and friendly atmosphere of a certain kind of popular football. 'Going to see FC United feels like it used to do when I'd go and watch Manchester United when I was younger', says Simon Howles, editor of *Under the Boardwalk*, the club's fanzine.

> Going down with your mates on a Saturday, paying to get in at the gate, and then being with them in the ground. It's so different to what was on offer at Old Trafford, where you'd be lucky to get a ticket at all and if you did get in then you'd probably be sitting on your own, policed at every moment by ever-present stewards.[29]

Ticket prices are also set directly each year by the fans. A ticket to a Red Rebels game costs between £5 and £9 (£2 for children) compared to around £60 for a black market ticket at Old Trafford. The season ticket is £100 but everyone pays according to their means (in 2009, free tickets were even made available). 'We just want to have a good time', says Vinny, an FC United supporter. 'Football shouldn't be about "How can I afford such-and-such a ticket", it should be about "I want to have a weekend like the last one"'.[30] As for the club, it is now owned by 4,000 supporters who pay £12 a year for a share in FC United and a vote in the cooperative. The annual general meeting is an opportunity for the supporters to renew the eleven volunteer members of the board of directors and to set the club's policy. For example, the supporters decided to refuse all advertising on shirts. FC United also worked hard to develop a social action programme for prisoners, schoolchildren and disadvantaged young people in the suburbs of Manchester. 'Our club, our rules', as the Red Rebels like to display in their stands.

However, fan members don't hesitate to lash out. For example, there was an outcry when club officials appeared alongside politicians in 2015. Three of the eleven board members had to resign in 2016 after protests and pitch invasions to demand more transparency and democracy at the club. 'This is punk football', says one FC United supporter. 'We have kept this rebellious side'.[31] This doesn't stop some supporters from meeting up in the pub to watch their former passion, Manchester United, after supporting FC United at the stadium a few hours earlier.* The internal debates were also extremely heated when members had to pay £800,000 out of their own pockets to reach the £6.3 million sum needed to build their own stadium.[32] Opened in May 2015, the 4,400-capacity Broadhurst Park is both a further step towards the small insurgent club's autonomy and a means of ensuring some economic sustainability. 'Of course you need money, it's not a fairy tale', says Veronica, a fan in her 60s. 'But it's honest money, ours, not that of billionaire capitalists who don't know what to do with their money and who decide to put it into a club'.[33]

Despite the ups and downs of running an entirely DIY club, the red, black and white team has risen through the ranks to the National League North, in the sixth tier, and the fans have become known throughout England for their wild cheering and hijacking of songs, such as their cover of the Sex Pistols' 'Anarchy In The UK': 'I am an FC fan / I am a Mancunian / I know what I want and I know how to get it / I wanna destroy Glazer and Sky / Cos I wanna be at FC!'

The success of protest clubs such as AFC Wimbledon and FC United shows all football lovers that it is possible to break out of the passive consumer role that the football industry seeks to reduce them to. Swansea City, a prestigious Premier League club, has been over 20 per cent owned by its supporters since 2013 through the Swan Trust – allowing them to sit on the board – while being one of the few Premier League clubs to be debt-free.[34] Portsmouth FC, which also played in the Premier League for a time, was saved from bankruptcy in 2013 by more than 2,000 supporters in the Pompey Supporters' Trust. The greed of Saudi and later Russian businessmen had led Portsmouth FC into administration and a plunge into the fourth tier. The cooperative has since become the majority owner of the club.

In the smaller teams of the Football League and the lower divisions, popular ownership provides both a strong club identity and a space for local community involvement. 'We have given power back

* In Ken Loach's *Looking for Eric* (2009), a classic humorous scene highlights this tug of war among FC United fans between their protest club and their original club, Manchester United.

to the people by trying to have an egalitarian system. You have a badge, a shareholder card and you decide the policy of the club', explains Trevor, a Lewes FC supporter.[35] Bought out by its supporters in 2010, the small Sussex club, which plays in the eighth division, is now known throughout England for its match posters, which are inspired by rock festivals, films and punk concerts.

However, not everything is perfect in the land of cooperative football, which sometimes has to make concessions, accept compromises or suffer major setbacks. As AFC Wimbledon climbed into the third tier, it became increasingly clear to fans that they needed to own their ground. However, the costly acquisition of a sports venue required the help of outside investors, despite a slight loss of fan power within AFC Wimbledon – although the Dons Trust still owns over two-thirds of the club. Another 'protest club' founded in 2008 by a thousand fans exasperated by Liverpool FC's prohibitively high ticket prices, AFC Liverpool can only attract an average of 100 fans per game and is clinging on in the ninth division. In the hope of reaching elite levels of English football, some cooperatives, such as those owning Notts County (tier 4) or York City (tier 5), have opted to give up majority control of their club in order to bring in investors. This was a decision they sometimes bitterly regretted when their clubs failed to move up to higher divisions.

Despite these setbacks, Supporters Direct estimates that it has backed the creation of around 100 supporters' trusts across the country since 2000. More than 30 football teams in England are now majority owned by their fans, four of which – Portsmouth FC, Wycombe Wanderers, AFC Wimbledon and Exeter City – are fully professional. This momentum is being emulated in Scotland (with clubs such as Stirling Albion and Brechin City), Ireland (Shamrock Rovers in Dublin), Spain (UC Ceares in Gijón or Atlético Club de Socios in Madrid*) and Italy (CS Lebowski in Florence). While France is still in the early stages of popular ownership with initiatives

* It should be noted that in Spain, Athletic Bilbao, FC Barcelona, Real Madrid and CA Osasuna have a legal structure that allows each of their supporters to hold a share in the club. In these large clubs, each *socio* has one vote and the right to vote in elections for the club president and other important elections.

such as the À La Nantaise association, founded in 2010 to buy shares in FC Nantes, Germany enacted a law in 1998 obliging professional clubs not to be more than 49 per cent owned by a single investor.*

This European development constitutes an increasingly serious alternative to the neoliberal management model advocated by the champions of commercial football. It shows that clubs can place at their hearts the voices of those who, as the pioneer of the supporters' trusts movement Brian Lomax, who died in 2015, liked to remind us, come to the stadium to find 'emotion, sharing and comradeship'. These are all 'deeply rooted human needs and I believe that that is at the root of people's love for football and loyalty for their clubs'.[36]

* With the exception of VFL Wolfsburg and Bayer Leverkusen, which historically belong to Volkswagen and Bayer respectively.

21

Playing on the left wing

Hamburg's FC Sankt Pauli or the pirates of the football business

Who are the rats who betray us? The social democrats!
Who will never betray us? Sankt Pauli, for sure!

Slogan of FC Sankt Pauli fans, 1986–1987 season

'No place for homophobia, fascism, sexism, racism'. From the entrance to its Millerntor ground, Hamburg's FC Sankt Pauli makes its political engagement clear, in English and in red and black letters. The side stands are draped in two giant slogans: 'No football for fascists' and 'No human being is illegal'. Following an unchanging ritual, the players in their brown and white strips take to the pitch as a thunderous burst of *Hells Bells* by AC/DC resounds around the stadium. The terraces, surprisingly full for a second-division Bundesliga match, pulsate with enthusiasm as soon as the Blur hit *Song 2* is heard, the traditional marker of a Sankt Pauli goal. It's an ordinary match day in the cauldron of the Millerntor, but the musical references and political slogans accompanying this professional team encapsulate the militant and non-conformist spirit of a club that counters the trend of institutional football.

Used to treading the depths of the second-division 2. Bundesliga, FC Sankt Pauli is more popular than its home city rival, the giant Hamburger Sport-Verein (HSV), even though the latter has hoisted more national and European trophies. Despite its modest and uneven sporting successes – five titles as second-division champions between 1964 and 1977 and four third-division wins between 1981 and 2007 – the rebel squad claims 11 million fans worldwide,[1] including the largest number of female supporters in Europe,[2] and more than 480 supporters' clubs* who are committed to 'opposing all forms of discrimination, all forms of racism, sexism and hooliganism, as well as all forms of discrimination based on sexual preferences'.[3]

This outsize passion for a second-tier German team is explained by the fact that since the end of the 1980s the club has embodied an anti-establishment image in the very civilised landscape of professional football, on top of a real resistance to the commodification of the football business. As early as 1963, FC Sankt Pauli was the first German team to sign a player from sub-Saharan Africa, the Togolese player Guy Acolatse. In the 1990s, the club was the only one in Germany to officially threaten any attendee using a racist slogan or symbol with expulsion from their ground. Known as the *Braun und Weiß* (Brown and Whites), they also distinguished themselves by removing sexist advertising for a men's magazine from the stadium in 2002, and by electing an openly gay president between 2003 and 2010 (Corny Littmann, a figure in Hamburg's LGBT community and proprietor of the Schmidt-Theater cabaret). Finally, in November 2009, the club became the first in the country to adopt its own 'guiding principles' (*Leitlinien*). This charter, a kind of political manifesto, establishes that

> FC Sankt Pauli is a club made up of all of its members, employees, supporters and volunteers. The club forms a part of the society and the social fabric that surrounds it and as a result is directly or indirectly influenced by political, social and cultural changes [...] FC Sankt Pauli is a club rooted in a specific district. It owes its identity to this district and is committed to investing in it socially and politically.[4]

Red-light district and *Autonomen* activists

The roots of this political activism are found in the close relationship woven between FC Sankt Pauli and the district that gives it its name. Situated on the right bank of the Elbe and cut off from the centre of

* Although most are based in Germany, clubs are also found as far away as the United States, Brazil and Cambodia.

Hamburg, Sankt Pauli has always been marginalised. Home in the 17th century to a quarantine hospital and ravaged by a terrible fire in 1842, the district was only officially incorporated into the Hanseatic city in 1894.[5] Sankt Pauli quickly acquired a seedy reputation thanks to the many brothels, cabarets and bars for sailors on shore leave, and the rowdy dockworkers of the merchant port who lived there. In the late 19th century, the district developed into a hotspot of German trade union activity, with the year 1896 marked by one of the greatest social conflicts in the German empire: an eleven-week wildcat strike organised by 16,000 Hamburg dockers and stevedores.[6] Finally, Sankt Pauli was one of the city districts where Ernst Thälmann, leader of the German Communist Party, launched a workers' uprising on 23 October 1923, storming police stations across Hamburg to try and take the city by force and overthrow the Weimar Republic.

Ten years later, with Sankt Pauli under the Nazi yoke, the local football team that had been founded in 1910* was forced to submit to the Aryan Laws of 1933, like all sports bodies at the time. The managers of FC Sankt Pauli, unlike the venerable HSV, were slow to exclude Jews, as ordered by the Hitler regime, and to join the Nazi party. (Like all sports executives in the country, they did so later on, in the hope of protecting the club's interests.) Barely two months after Hitler's arrival to power, FC Sankt Pauli even hosted two Jewish brothers, Otto and Paul Lang, who established a rugby section within the club, following their exclusion from SV St. Georg, another Hamburg football club.[7]

Due to the importance of the port, from 1943 onwards the district was bombed by British planes. The team's football ground south of Heiligengeistfeld was completely destroyed, but resurrected by members of the club in November 1946, before a modern enclosure, the Millerntor-Stadion, was built in 1961. With its sex shops, brothels and dealers around the Reeperbahn, Sankt Pauli was the city's red-light district. Also home to many clubs and concert halls, the area hosted some of the Beatles' earliest concerts between 1960

---

* In 1910, a few members of the Hamburg-Sankt Pauli Turnverein 1862 gymnastics club decided to set up a football section, and in 1924 it became independent under the name Fußball-Club Sankt Pauli.

and 1962. Swiftly falling in love with this infamous neighbourhood, the Liverpudlians helped to shape the international and cosmopolitan aura of Sankt Pauli.

In the subsequent decades the quarter was transformed, first by the oil crises of 1973 and 1979, which triggered mass layoffs in the port industry, and then by the AIDS epidemic, which hit the Reeperbahn hard. The number of residents plummeted from 31,000 in 1970 to 22,000 in 1985.[8] Yet from October 1981 industrial warehouses and other empty properties began to be occupied by anarchist and punk collectives and *Autonomen* ('autonomous groups'). The Hafenstraße and its dozen buildings converted into living spaces and alternative cultural centres became the focal point of Hamburg's radical left. As the leaders of a real bastion of liberty at the heart of the second-largest city in Germany, the squatters of Hafenstraße dedicated as much energy to anti-nuclear and anti-military struggles as they did to forging close links with the dock workers of their district who had lost their jobs in the recession.

Since the Millerntor (renamed the Wilhelm-Koch-Stadion in 1970 in homage to a former club president) was right next door to the squats, the radical militants gradually began to make their presence felt on the stands. At the time FC Sankt Pauli was still a fairly little-known club, with just 2,000 official supporters, having briefly entered the first-division Bundesliga before being relegated again. 'There was never any plan to get involved in the stadium', recalls Sven Brux, a well-known punk figure from the district who today is employed by the club. 'The folk from Hafenstraße and the surrounding area started to go the stadium for the same reasons as any other fan: to spend a nice afternoon with their friends with a few beers, and to watch a good football match'.[9]

From the mid-1980s, a hundred *Autonomen* would regularly gather in a section of the stands behind the dugout, from which they acquired their nickname: the *Gegengerade*. Raising a 'Black Block' banner, these new supporters with their Mohicans stood out in the small family stadium as they chanted slogans like 'Fascism no more! War no more! The third division no more!' or 'Hamburg without the Hafenstraße is like the Bundesliga without FC Sankt Pauli!'[10]

Goalkeeper for the Brown and Whites from 1981 to 1991, Volker Ippig played a big role in the identification with the club by the district's radical political militants. Himself a veteran of the Hafenstraße squats, the charismatic keeper with his long blond mane had campaigned for a time with a Sandinista brigade in Nicaragua. Taking leave from his goalkeeping duties to go on demonstrations or work in a nursery for disabled children, Volker Ippig stood out on the pitch for his clenched fist salute addressed to the Black Block supporters.

The small group of activist fans adopted the Jolly Roger skull-and-crossbones emblem, the same as the pirate flag flown above the squats of Sankt Pauli. 'The first time I went to see FC Sankt Pauli play was in 1976', recalls Doc Mabuse, a well-known punk from the district's bustling streets.

> I lived on Hafenstraße and I was always bringing new people with me. After one match, I was totally plastered, and I walked by a church where there was a stall selling flags. I saw one with a skull-and-crossbones that cost 10 marks. I don't remember if I nailed or stapled it to a broom handle, but next time I took it to the stadium. And that's how it came to be.[11]

A symbol of protest, the flag also references the tradition of piracy in Hamburg embodied in the figure of Klaus Störtebeker, known as the 'Red Corsair' and beheaded in 1401 by the city authorities.* This popular local figure, who by stealing from the rich merchants of the port city represents the rebellion of the poor, was glorified by FC Sankt Pauli's fan punk group Slime, who dedicated a song to the freebooter in 1983. And two years later, the occupants of Hafenstraße opened an anti-fascist militant space called the Störtebeker Centre.[12]

While the young *Autonomen* activists were turning their attentions to the FC Sankt Pauli stadium, German football was riddled with far-right hooliganism and groups of neo-Nazis that flourished in the stands. In Hamburg itself, the HSV stadium – the Volksparkstadion – had become a notorious meeting point for nationalist skinheads.

---

* The legend tells that new recruits had to be able to swallow a 4-litre tankard of beer in one go.

'Football and far-right violence are closely connected in the West stands of the Volksparkstadion', warned the weekly *Der Spiegel* in 1983.[13] Michael Kühnen, the leader of the neo-Nazi party Aktionsfront Nationaler Sozialisten, ordered his followers to recruit new members in football stadiums. Openly racist slogans and physical assaults on supporters with immigrant backgrounds or labelled as far-left proliferated both on the terraces and in the streets. Exiting a match in December 1984, far-right fans of HSV and Borussia Dortmund attacked the Hafenstraße squats with Molotov cocktails. Less than four years later, on 21 June 1988, the residents of the district were again assaulted by a mob of neo-Nazi HSV supporters leaving a Volksparkstadion match between West Germany and the Netherlands.

'With the growing number of Nazis among the fans of Hamburg's other team, a lot of people didn't want to go to their stadium any more', Sven Brux recalls. 'As a result, they turned to FC Sankt Pauli to watch football peacefully, since there were no hooligans'.[14] These HSV supporters, fed up with the violence on the terraces steadily swelled the ranks of their city rival, especially after FC Sankt Pauli experienced a resurgence in popularity when it re-entered the Bundesliga in 1988.

However, by 1990, the stands of the Wilhelm-Koch-Stadion too had become the scene of regular attacks on supporters from the Turkish community. Under pressure from *Gegengerade* activists, who unfurled banners at each match (example slogan: 'Against racist hate, self-defence here and now!') and who put the club management on the spot in their fanzine *Millerntor Roar!*, in late 1991 FC Sankt Pauli invited the Istanbul team Galatasaray to a friendly match, and declared that any supporter making racist comments would be expelled from the grounds.[15] Taking such a firm stand was unprecedented at the time and set the small club apart, forging an association in people's minds between Sankt Pauli and strong values. 'It wasn't planned this way, but spontaneously it became an anti-fascist club', Sven Brux emphasises. 'For us, fighting racism wasn't even a political act, just a normal human attitude'.[16]

Founded in July 1989, the first of its kind in Germany and following the style of the British fanzine movement [see Chapter 14], *Millerntor Roar!* not only asserted the anti-racist views of the supporters, but also expressed its solidarity with the social struggles of the Sankt Pauli district by allocating a number of pages to the squatters of Hafenstraße. Since 1983, the occupants had been engaged in a fierce battle with the municipality and real estate developers in Hamburg who wanted to redevelop this urban area. Intense police repression was felt by the *Autonomen*, who periodically barricaded Hafenstraße in order to defend themselves. On 20 December 1986, forcible expulsions of squats led to a 12,000-strong demonstration of support in the streets of Sankt Pauli.[17] In 1990, special forces raided the district, following rumours that occupants were hosting members of the Red Army Faction, a far-left terrorist organisation. Meanwhile, accounts of the struggle against property speculation appeared in *Millerntor Roar!*, and banners reading 'Hafenstraße – You'll Never Walk Alone!' appeared on the stands from 1991, while club players publicly expressed their support for the squatters.

In January 1989, local residents and supporters of FC Sankt again united in protest against an urban development project – but this time it was one put forward by the club's own governing body. They were dreaming of building a giant 50,000-seat 'Sport-Dome' to replace the Wilhelm-Koch-Stadion. Benefitting from the financial support of a Canadian consortium, the Sport-Dome was to include a pool, tennis courts, the ability to host international concerts as well as a shopping centre and vast car parks. A titanic undertaking that in the protestors' eyes would have utterly transformed their district and triggered huge rent increases. In response, they deployed the militant savvy developed in recent years in Hafenstraße. Before a match against Karlsruher SC, they distributed thousands of flyers at the stadium entrance. Just before the end of the first half, all 19,000 spectators fell completely silent in the stands for five whole minutes, leaving the managers of FC Sankt Pauli flabbergasted.[18] Two months later, the Sport-Dome project was abandoned once and for all.

With a smart mix of supporter action and political activism, using the stands as a sounding box for issues that concerned the club and the district, the alliances among residents, militants and fans meant the rebel identity of the quarter became linked with that of FC Sankt Pauli.[19] The *Kiezkicker* – the neighbourhood footballers – became the new local nickname for the team, and the number of club members climbed to nearly 20,000 at the start of the 1990s.[20] 'If the stadium had been located outside the neighbourhood, I don't think all this would have happened, confesses Mike Glindmeier', a sports journalist who is a Hamburg native and an active supporter of FC Sankt Pauli. 'This area brought together dock workers, junkies, sex workers, petty crooks and radical political activists. This offered unique social conditions'.[21]

The pirates of the league

Inspired by the autonomous strategy of the district's political activists, FC Sankt Pauli fans set up the *Fanladen* (fan store) in 1990. Independent from the club, it was run by and for supporters. Headquartered in a shipping container located behind the North Stand of Wilhelm-Koch-Stadion, the *Fanladen* initially offered tickets and memberships to followers of the team and organised trips to away matches. Volunteers distributed the *Millerntor Roar!* fanzine and self-financed the operation by selling T-shirts screen-printed with the pirate flag unearthed by Doc Mabuse.

Swiftly, the *Fanladen* became more than a simple shop. With their strong anti-fascist identity, fans used it to distribute stickers reading *St. Pauli Fans Gegen Rechts* ('St. Pauli Fans Against the Right') and profited from the convivial nature of group travel to discuss politics with young fans from the district who showed signs of being drawn to nationalist and racist viewpoints.[22] Subsequently, having learned in 1997 that Wilhelm Koch, the former president of the club after whom the stadium had been named,* had been a member of the Nazi party, the *Fanladen* launched a long and ultimately successful campaign to officially rename it the Millerntor. Likewise, since 2004, it has organised an anti-racist football tournament each year for fans from some ten different countries, where matches alternate with debates on the current state of the anti-fascist struggle.

* From 1931–1945 and again from 1947–1969.

The sporting and political activism of the *Fanladen* also serves as a springboard for numerous independent social projects. Each week since 2002, the *Kiezkick* programme has offered free football training for underprivileged girls and boys from the neighbourhood. The U18 Ragazzi, a group of supporters under the age of 18, coordinates with social workers to organise both football matches and travel to away games. Finally, the *Fanladen* promotes a series of initiatives against sexism, homophobia and racism in sport, through the partnerships it has forged with the *F_in – Frauen im Fußball* (Women in Football), the *Queer Football Fanclubs* and the *Bündnis Aktiver Fußball Fans* (Alliance of Active Football Supporters). Now integrated into the stadium, the *Fanladen* has succeeded in becoming the voice of the club supporter community, and in making football a vector of social and political actions.

On top of their political activism, the supporters engage in strategies that give FC Sankt Pauli its punk and subversive image. From the 1990s this earned the team the nickname among sports journalists of the *Freibeuter der Liga* (Pirates of the League). One of the first media coups by fans was in 1991 when, to sell more tickets and fill the club's coffers, the club management decided to play the Kiezkicker games in the HSV, much larger than their own. They failed to account for the creativity of the most rebellious fans. On 5 March they decided to boycott a match with Hertha Berlin at the Volksparkstadion and instead climbed over the fences to get into the Millerntor. There, some 1,500 fans followed the match on the radio, broadcast over the stadium's loudspeakers. During the 90 minutes, they cheered on their team before an empty pitch illuminated by the stadium lighting, celebrating each goal with a resounding blast of *No Sleep Till Brooklyn* by the Beastie Boys.

FC Sankt Pauli's fans also cultivated self-mockery as a way of embroidering the rare sporting successes of the club, and asserting its status as the eternal 'magnificent loser'. Striker for the team from 1989 to 1996, the Brazilian footballer Leonardo Manzi, due to his distressing inability to control the ball or to score goals, became the darling of the public, fêted with the title 'the only Brazilian who doesn't know how to play football'.[23] As the former vice-president of the club, Christian Hienzpeter, jokes: 'Here, everyone has problems in their daily lives, with their boss, with their job, or their wages. Leo had problems with the ball: perhaps that's why he became so popular'.[24] The midfielder and team captain, Fabian Boll, was adulated for his strong attachment to FC Sankt Pauli since he joined in 2002. However, he also worked part-time as a police inspector, which should have drawn the wrath of the supporters who had struggled against police repression for 30 years. Yet his athletic and personal qualities prompted fans to transform their banners and placards bearing the traditional anti-police acronym to 'ACABAB', meaning 'All Cops Are Bastards Außer Boll' – except Boll. 'Once you become part of the club, you realise the meaning of what you can do for these people, both on the stands and in the district. We always said loud and clear that when the club does well, the district does well', Fabian Boll is moved to recall. 'This flame, this unconditional feeling that flows from the stands onto the pitch, these steadfast fans: at the time we felt that nothing bad could happen'.[25]

When the club briefly rejoined the Bundesliga for the 2001–2002 season, FC Sankt Pauli beat the league giants Bayern Munich 2–1 on 6 February 2002. The Bavarians having recently won the Intercontinental Cup, Sankt Pauli mischievously claimed the title of *Weltpokalsiegerbesieger* ('defeater of the winner of the Intercontinental Cup'). This wit, however, could not conceal the fact that the economically fragile pirate ship was beginning to take on water where it came to sport. The following season was a nightmare for the club, and in 2003 it was relegated to the third-division Regionalliga Nord. Crippled by debts and close to bankruptcy, FC Sankt Pauli quickly sold off its training centre and launched a major fundraising campaign. Fans sold nearly 130,000 T-shirts in the club colours with the inscription *Retter* ('Saviour') and engaged in operation *Saufen für St. Pauli* ('Drink for Sankt Pauli'), with a few cents from each Astra-brand beer consumed being donated by the brewer to the club. Almost 11,500 stadium memberships were taken out and various events, such as a gala match against Bayern Munich and a concert with a reading by Nobel Prize-winning writer Günter Grass, were organised.

Despite raising over 2 million euros, the Pirates of the League were still on borrowed time as they gradually surrendered to a growing merchandising of the club's identity. With the aim of securing the economic stability of FC Sankt Pauli, the management embarked on a commercial shift in the 2000–2001 season by making the famous Jolly Roger a registered trademark and one of the official logos of the club. As the bridgehead of this foray into merchandising, the corsair flag appeared on a vast range of items from clothing to mugs, toasters to toothbrushes. In 2013 alone, the club estimated that it made nearly 8 million euros from the sale of products bearing the image of the pirate skull.[26] This selling-out of the neighbourhood's political and social symbol marked a turning point: 'If I'd known what it was going to become, I would have trademarked it myself', lamented Doc Mabuse in 2015. 'I felt aggrieved seeing the Jolly Roger being exploited commercially. The whole FC Sankt Pauli scene changed around that time. Going to the stadium became a more "trendy" thing. It was the end of people's real identification with the club'.[27]

Countering the commercial world

In the early 2000s, the district of Sankt Pauli found itself in the grip of gentrification on a massive scale. The arrival of artists and young people working in the digital industry triggered a rapid rise in rents and a mushrooming of art galleries, commercial buildings and hostels focused on clubbers, to the detriment of the area's bars, squats and local shops. The change in social make-up of the district also brought about the arrival of new audiences at Millerntor, more attracted by the alternative identity of a club from a fashionable city quarter than by the football team itself.

The community that had built up around FC Sankt Pauli was torn. Some wanted to see their favourite team rise up the Bundesliga and stay there, which would force the club to attract more and more spectators and generate substantial profits in order to be able to invest in top-level footballers. For others, it was the identity of the club that mattered, and not its performance. 'It's more important to have a club with a unique identity and no commercial atmosphere during games', as one fan put it. 'We're really happy when the team succeeds, but we don't want this to be at the cost of our identity and our values'.[28] A political tightrope-act hard to maintain when the pirate spirit of FC Sankt Pauli had itself become a source of profit. 'The club's identity – at bottom the brand – is its principal asset', the club's commercial manager for 2004–2015 Michaël Meeske candidly remarks. 'This allows it to access new economic opportunities'.[29] The legendary goalkeeper Volker Ippig – who has since become a dock worker and amateur coach – laments this: 'The Millerntor was once an open-air laboratory for German football, and the close relationship between supporters, players and management really worked. Today all that is artificially orchestrated, and only the myth remains. So much nonsense is talked'.[30]

Soon, in order to prevent the pirate club from becoming a vulgar consumer product and losing its soul with the arrival of new, less politicised fans, several groups of radical supporters merged to give birth, in 2002, to the Ultrà Sankt Pauli. Assembling in the Südkurve (south stand) of the Millerntor, they are responsible for bringing the stands to life with passionate chants and spectacular *tifos*. These supporters assert their role as guardians of the club's anti-fascist identity and don't hesitate to fuel historical and political rivalries by punching neo-Nazi supporters of clubs in Rostock, Dresden or Cottbus. In November 2007, they set up the Alerta! Network, an international network of ultras committed to the fight against fascism and racism in the stands. Along with other Millerntor activists, the Ultrà Sankt Pauli constitute a force of over 1,000 supporters who are particularly vigilant in the face of any drift towards commercialisation.[31]

Of the 30,000 faithful supporters of the Brown and Whites, 14,800 are members of the Abteilung Fördernde Mitgleider, or AFM: the Department of Active Members. Each member has the right to vote at the annual general meeting of FC Sankt Pauli, meaning the AFM can exercise a degree of countervailing power. When in 2007 the management announced renovation works at Millerntor, intense pressure from fans ensured that the AGM voted to prohibit the sale of the stadium name to a sponsor. The marketing practice of 'naming' had become widespread when sports venues were renovated in Germany (since 2001, HSV's Volksparstadion has successively been known as the AOL Arena, the HSH NordBank Arena, and the Imtech Arena). Likewise, the supporters successfully ensured that after the refurbishment of the stadium, the Millerntor had more standing (and therefore low-cost) places than seats.

In the stands and in the AGM alike, this balance of power between supporters and management allows FC Sankt Pauli to perpetuate the political traditions of the club. During a match against Paderborn in March 2013, fans deployed a striking *tifo* reading 'Love whoever you like – Fight homophobia'. A few days earlier, the retired US international footballer Robbie Rogers had declared to the press that it had been impossible to reveal his sexuality during his professional career. Four months later, the club decided to fly the rainbow flag over the Millerntor on a permanent basis. The next year, after the arrival of more than 300 refugees in Hamburg who had landed on the Italian island of Lampedusa, FC Sankt Pauli fans launched the 'Refugees Welcome' campaign. They deployed banners reading 'Destroy fortress Europe – Abolish Dublin II' and raised 120,000 euros to pay for travel passes and SIM cards for the migrants.[32] Invited to the stadium and to the players' training sessions, the young refugees set up a team known as FC Lampedusa. Coached by five Sankt Pauli players, the squad, who adopted the slogan 'Here to stay, here to play' was officially incorporated into the club in July 2016. Subsequently, FC Lampedusa entered the local amateur championship and regularly played in tournaments across Europe. A recent illustration of the political intransigence of the fans came in January 2017 when the club management had to apologise for allowing an automobile advertisement to be displayed in the Millerntor with the slogan: 'Not for sissies'. As soon as the ad appeared in the stadium, the supporters inundated the club's marketing department via social media: 'Does anyone find that funny? Creative? It's just sexist shit. You haven't understood anything about our operation and our club'.[33]

The fight against the commodification of the club saw a huge turning point in 2011 with the wave of anti-commercial protests led by the *Sozialromantiker*. Thumbing their noses at Corny Littman, then president who had described his club's most radical supporters as 'social romantics', the movement emerged at the end of 2010 with a simple petition stating, 'Enough is enough'. Their demands? A reduction in the amount of advertising inside the stadium, the removal of 'business class' seating in the stands, a ban on the erotic entertainment company Susis Show Bar having a private box, and to allow the kids at the Piraten-Nest (the Millerntor crèche) to paint its external walls themselves.

Treated by the management as a movement restricted to a handful of supporters (at the turn of 2011, the petition had barely gathered 3,000 signatures), the *Sozialromantiker* nevertheless called on fans to come to the stadium with a Jolly Roger on a red background, recalling the social roots of FC Sankt Pauli. On 4 January 2011, as AC/DC's *Hells Bells* played the teams into the stadium, the Millerntor's stands suddenly turned red as 10,000 spectators held up red cards, scarlet pirate flags were unfurled, and a giant banner appeared declaring 'Give us back Sankt Pauli'. A scale of mutiny against the club leadership that surprised even the *Sozialromantiker*, and obliged the management to take their claims seriously.

'It's true that for 25 years now some managers have tried to distinguish the club from its politically militant fan base. Some even tried to prevent people wearing club colours to political demonstrations', points out supporter and journalist Mike Glindmeier. 'But it doesn't work like that with Sankt Pauli. There is a constant struggle between commercial and political forces. And both sides have had to make compromises. I think that a certain balance has been maintained, which is what makes Sankt Pauli still a unique club today'.[34]

The real hidden treasure of Germany's football pirates, this distinctive political identity of FC Sankt Pauli was again to the fore in July 2017 with the protests against the G20 meeting held in Hamburg. After being illegally evicted from numerous militant camps, 200 demonstrators were welcomed into the Millerntor where a mobile kitchen and sleeping arrangements were made available. As for the radical supporters, they took full part in the demonstrations and the street battles against the police forces in the districts of Schanzenviertel and Sankt Pauli. A few days earlier, they had invited all Kiezkicker fans to meet in the street to protest, stressing that 'FC Sankt Pauli, as a club based on the idea of solidarity, represents a counter-model to the world of G20 leaders and the misery produced by global capitalism'.[35]

22

Wild balls, balls on the margins

Street football wrong-foots the institutional game

> I learned to play in the street and if you do me the honour of finding me elegant on the pitch, it's because I had elegance on the street.
>
> Johan Cruyff, *L'Équipe*, 13 December 2014

'It lasts five months, people go mad and they find it much more interesting than the national championship', enthuses Amadou, coach of the football team in the Gueule Tapée, a poor neighbourhood in Dakar.[1] In this month of September 2011, Senegal is in full swing. From June to October, while the country is slowing down due to the rainy season, the Senegalese are in thrall to the feverish rhythm of the *navétanes*, the country's most popular sporting event. Derived from the Wolof word *nawetaan* – literally 'to spend the rainy season' – this nationwide inter-district championship attracts far larger crowds than the professional league run under the auspices of the Senegalese Football Federation (FSF). And with more than 3,500 neighbourhood clubs, the *navétane* movement can boast the densest fabric of associations in the country: this street football is played by no fewer than 500,000 members, ten times more than the FSF.[2]

Senegal: football at the heart of the neighbourhood

Navétane football emerged in the 1950s in Dakar, when a few enthusiasts began to organise informal street football tournaments at the beginning of the rainy season to keep the young people in their neighbourhood busy. This winter period coincides with the school holidays and the break in the national football championship. Originally involving a dozen teams from different neighbourhoods of Dakar, the *navétanes* grew in importance after Senegal's independence in 1960. A modest trophy as well as a crate of coffee, condensed milk and oranges were then offered to the winner of the improvised tournament, while a multitude of new street teams and inter-neighbourhood championships gradually sprang up in other cities.[3]

The unbridled urbanisation of Dakar is closely correlated with the meteoric rise of these street football teams. After the Second World War, the capital received a massive influx of Senegalese from the rural areas of the country. They settled in overcrowded shantytowns near the city centre before being forcibly relocated, from 1952 onwards, to newly built suburbs, such as Pikine and Guédiawaye.[4] Uprooted from their villages, coming to Dakar to try to sell their labour, expelled from the shantytowns by force, and then settled in suburbs lacking in both soul and infrastructure, they threw themselves into the creation and running of local *navétanes* teams, which became one of the few sources of recreation and social activity in their bleak dormitory towns.[5]

After independence, institutional football suffered from the disaffection of the Senegalese. The national team, formed in 1961, put in a series of disappointing performances at every African Cup of Nations and World Cup until the early 2000s. No Senegalese club has won an African Cup of Champions since the trophy was created in 1964. The official tournaments, managed by the FSF, are of poor quality. Contested refereeing decisions, match cancellations, boycotts by some clubs, violent riots by spectators: for all these reasons and more the Senegalese championship has failed to attract crowds.

Navétane football is no better structured. Teams rarely have access to municipal grounds, and tournaments are improvised on empty fields where the playing area is poorly defined and where it is, according to sports writers in the 1960s, 'courageous to play and fall down'.[6] The refereeing was inconsistent and the game was frequently interrupted. In August 1964, *Dakar-Matin*, for example, didn't hesitate to denounce the 'overheated atmosphere', or even the 'total insecurity', of the *navétanes*.[7] However, these matches fuelled the footballing passions of a whole group of precarious young people who, by playing in the streets and on makeshift pitches, appropriated the urban territory and forged a strong collective identity for themselves. The names of the first *navétane* teams reflect the desire to put down local roots while at the same time connecting with world footballing culture: Monaco of Pikine, Juventus of Thiaroye, Brazil of Wakhinane and Blackpool of Rebeuss. Other teams prefer to draw on the political imagination by expressing their attachment to the Afro-American (Harlem of Médina), pan-African (Renaissance Africaine, Africa Sports of Pikine) or communist (Progrès, Beijing Football Club) movements.

Following the student revolts in Dakar, the general strike of Senegalese workers and the spontaneous demonstrations of the 'unschooled urban sub-proletariat' in the spring of 1968,[8] a whole tranche of high school and university students became involved in the working-class neighbourhoods, and more specifically in informal *navétane* football teams. In a logic of opposition 'from below' to the authoritarian grip of the state, these groups went beyond the strict framework of football to become Sports and Cultural Associations (ASC) and serve as a support for local socio-cultural projects such as the creation of theatre groups and micro-libraries or the organisation of educational outings with schoolchildren. Women's football tournaments as well as basketball and handball matches were also developed. On the fringes of the government's youth and sports policy, the activities of the CSAs become a pretext for all members of the community to get involved in their neighbourhood and ultimately improve their own living conditions. 'We were very critical', admits a former *navétane* activist and co-founder of the ASC Disso in Guédiawaye. 'In a certain sense, we were communists'.[9]

ASCs took on a more inclusive and family-based dimension. Residents become involved because 'a parent, brother or uncle is responsible for these inter-neighbourhood sports or cultural meetings' and 'houses and dwellings become places for meetings or gatherings'.[10] Women, who are actively involved in the *navétane* supporters' groups, play an important role in the development of cultural activities and become the instigators of large-scale fundraising operations at the neighbourhood level in order to finance their ASC. The names of the newly founded *navétane* teams emphasise their ambitions for solidarity and social cohesion, such as the ASC Diouboo ('Be United'), Walli Daan ('Come Together and Win') or Bokk Diom ('Mutual Respect'). Others prefer to display their fierce independence, such as the ASC Lat Dior (referring to the Wolof ruler who fought hard against French troops in the 19th century) or Cayor (an allusion to the pre-colonial kingdom of Senegal).[11] At the turn of the 1970s, the suburbs of Dakar were overflowing with sports and cultural activities, reflecting both the appropriation by the inhabitants of their living space and the failure of the state to provide public services. In November 1972, the daily newspaper *Le Soleil* ran the headline: 'Pikine, the dormitory town, has long been awake'.[12]

The Senegalese state, however, took a dim view of this autonomy of the neighbourhoods and the popular craze for street football. Faced with this *navétane* movement which escaped its control, the Ministry of Youth and Sports denounced the 'anarchy' of inter-neighbourhood matches as well as the 'incompetence' and 'improvisation' of the organisers and participants.[13] As a result, in the early 1970s, the ministerial authorities created the Organisme national de coordination des activités de vacances (ONCAV) and encouraged all *navétane* teams, via their ASC, to join this official structure. Behind the declared ambition to promote an annual 'popular national championship', the ministerial bureaucracy wanted to include amateur *navétane* football in its official youth policy. Although this attempt at institutional absorption ended in failure, as the ONCAV was unable to take control of the teams, this state intervention reinforced the competitive nature of inter-district matches. On the one hand, the pyramidal structure of the championship under the aegis of an official body exacerbated the rivalries between the teams while intensifying the identification of the supporters with their district. On the other hand, the ONCAV, by implicitly recognising the formal existence of the *navétane* clubs and their respective neighbourhoods as administrative entities, was obliged to facilitate the access of the teams to municipal and even national stadiums.

The gradual formalisation of a popular national championship – quickly nicknamed the 'National Pop' – aroused the curiosity of the country's daily newspapers. The latter regularly devoted two to four pages to *navétane*, while confessing that the best football in Dakar was not to be found in the big stadiums but in the street.[14] The excitement of the matches and the heated atmosphere in the stands impressed the sports commentators. 'You had to be present at the explosions of joy that occurred after each goal', reported Le Soleil, for example, on the occasion of the 1970 *navétane* final. 'You had to experience the tension of the match, the enthusiasm of the crowd. You had to see the shimmering colours of the women's outfits. In short, you had to be there to be able to say that the final […] restored football to its origins as a popular festivity'.[15]

Each neighbourhood cheers on its team to the rhythm of the sabar and tama drums and, as with big festivities, some supporters appear in the stands with their own musicians. As Chimère Gueye, administrator of ASC Walidane, points out, 'beyond the sporting stakes, it is the honour of a neighbourhood, that of a family, that must be raised so that your relatives are proud of you'.[16] The popular excitement before each match is also reflected in the street. Banners, balloons and garlands in the team's colours are hung among the trees, while the walls are embellished with frescoes of trophies or portraits of local footballers. Before each major match, residents march through the neighbourhood excitedly singing about their ASC, while a myriad of tailors rush to finish the women fans' colourful dresses and banners.

Relying on the voluntary commitment of countless helpers during the rainy season, the 'National Pop' lasts three to four months and the physical training of the footballers takes place in the street with unqualified coaches. *Navétane* football therefore emphasises collective play to the detriment of individual physical performance, while focusing on the players' mental state. Throughout the championship, the players are called upon to play *dem ba diekh*, a Wolof expression which means 'to go all the way'. This injunction to surpass oneself is all the more crucial as it is supported by the *khon*, a set of mystical practices that are very widespread in Senegalese sports circles, particularly during the *navétanes*. So in addition to the traditional pre-match meeting devoted to discussing tactics, the footballers take part in various rituals organised by the team's official marabout with the aim of protecting the players from injury, or warding off the spell cast by the opposing team. Before taking the field, each player is also given a talisman and amulets are buried near the goals. As Chimère Gueye of ASC Walidane attests, 'the mystical pre-match preparations are part of the psychological preparation of the teams'.[17]

On the strength of the popular success of the national *navétane* championship, by the mid-1980s Senegal had more than 600 ASCs – including 200 in Dakar – registered with the ONCAV.[18] The rapid growth of neighbourhood associations with amateur football teams gradually transformed the ASCs into key players in local development. A new Wolof community practice is even emerging through this network of Sports and Cultural Associations: the *set setal*. Literally translated as 'to be clean and to make clean', *set setal* consists of a broad popular movement that encourages residents to collectively clean up, sanitise and beautify their neighbourhood. In 1990 *Sud Hebdo* wrote about the *set setal* and the power of mobilisation of the ASCs: 'The neighbourhood replaces the commune. Everything is decided there [...] The young people take the initiative and make their rules [...] The street is controlled by those who live there'.

However, the rapidly growing mass of young members of the ASCs – in 1999, Dakar alone had more than 50,000 registered members and 400 clubs[19] – gradually attracted the interest of Senegalese politicians who saw an undeniable electoral potential in them. From the presidential and legislative campaigns of 1993 onwards, politicians in search of popularity systematically attended presentation ceremonies for *navétane* trophies to offer a financial reward and sports equipment to the victorious team. Some ASC leaders have been unable to resist the siren calls of clientelism, and are even beginning to flirt with the Dakar political establishment or to use the club as an electoral springboard. Moreover, the gradual takeover of the various local ONCAV committees by the presidents of the ASCs is completing the rapprochement between certain *navétane* clubs and the councillors in search of new voters. 'It's an effective tool, and the local councillors have also understood this', complains Foutihou Ba, president of the ASC Liberté 3, a Dakar neighbourhood. 'They shower the clubs with subsidies, because where there is amateur football, there are votes to be won'.[20]

At the same time, the sporting and economic stakes of the *navétanes* have become increasingly important. The popular folklore of the opening and closing ceremonies, animated by the theatre and dance troupes of the ASCs, has been firmly regulated and, thanks to financial support from the Senegalese diaspora living in Europe and North America, the players are now equipped with shoes with studs and real shirts in the colours of the club (and no longer makeshift T-shirts with a number painted on the back). Teams no longer hesitate to recruit 'mercenaries', i.e. players from outside the neighbourhood who are paid for their footballing skills. Some *navétane* clubs even have ambitions to reach the elite of Senegalese professional football, following the example of ASC Niarry Tally, one of the most popular teams in the capital, which managed to enter Ligue 1 in 2009 before becoming official Senegalese runners-up in 2010 and 2015.

Despite these political excesses and a relative standardisation of the 'National Pop', the popular enthusiasm for *navétane* matches and, above all, the sporting vitality of this street football remain intact. As proof of this, the neighbourhood teams are now considered to be training grounds in their own right, and this is only thanks to the voluntary dedication of passionate coaches. Renowned Senegalese international players such as El-Hadji Diouf, Diafra Sakho and Papiss Demba Cissé all emerged from *navétane* teams. This unique character was all the more noticeable when, in 2002, Senegal finally managed to shake off its footballing lethargy by reaching the quarter-finals of the World Cup, and shortly after this making the final of an African Cup of Nations for the first time. The role of *navétane* football in this success cannot be understated since, of the 22 internationals selected, almost all had participated in the 'National Pop' – and only three of them had ever worn a shirt of the official professional league. This completed an amateur outflanking of institutional football which, despite the FSF's displeasure, comes directly from the street.

Futebol without pitches or boundaries

On the other side of the Atlantic, another country also explores its passion for football on the margin of the game's institutions. Just 1 per cent of Brazilians are members of a football club.* Even though in Brazil 77 per cent of the population – both men and women – state that *futebol* is their greatest passion, most of them play it outside of the institutional bounds of the Confederação Brasileira de Futebol (CBF).[21] Ever since it was first introduced to São Paulo in the 19th century, football has been played in the street in Brazil, a version of the game affectionately known as *pelada*.** This word, literally 'naked', refers as much to the players, who are often barefoot, as to the bare ground that provides the improvised pitches. The expression could also come from *péla*, the name given to children's balls, but regardless, the name itself highlights a practice that is both poor and playful, far removed from the exaltation of competition instilled by the official football authorities.

The *pelada* is first and foremost an informal, convivial game of football that can be played in any space made available for the duration of a game. 'This might be in the street, on a hillside, between train tracks, inside a bus or in a swamp, on wet sand or anywhere else', says artist-musician Chico Buarque. 'It is a sport without a pitch, all boundaries are imaginary [...]'[22] The keystone of the *pelada* remains the pleasure of sharing a moment of football without constraints. Although there are no specific times or days for the *pelada*, it is generally in the late afternoon, at dusk, that the frenzied matches begin. Saturdays and Sundays, as well as public holidays, are traditionally devoted to kicking the ball around in the street. The game usually ends either after a team has scored two goals, or after ten minutes of play.[23]

The materials needed to play are minimal and mobile. The goals are formed by bricks, shoes or pieces of wood. The ball can be a discarded leather ball or a *bola de leite* (a child's plastic ball) or even be made on the spot out of socks or plastic bags. The players of the two teams are easily distinguished: those who keep their shirts on and those who play shirtless. The number of players on the field can vary, from 2 to 22, depending on the space and the *peladeiros* avail-

* That is, only 2.14 million registered players in a country of over 200 million, according to FIFA's last *Big Count 2006*. For comparison, Germany and France reported 6.5 and 2 million, respectively.

** It is also known as *baba*, *racha* and *rachão*.

able at the time. Whether it is a young dribbler from the favelas, a teenage girl who loves *futebol*, an old shopkeeper or a child who has just finished his schoolwork, the *pelada* brings together people of all ages and sexes. There are many ways to play the game: *golzinho*, with mini-goals about 1.5 metres wide and no goalkeeper; *golzão*, with real goals and two goalkeepers; *bobinho*, a passing game with a central player who has to try to recover the ball; or a *roda de embaixadinhas*, the players, arranged in a circle, kick the ball to each other without letting it touching the ground. There is no referee; instead, the footballers collectively regulate disputes and trust whoever calls a foul or shouts when the ball goes outside the pre-determined boundaries.[24] The two structuring elements of the *pelada* are thus improvisation and flexibility, with any constraint being overcome by the imperative need to kick the ball. 'I can play in trainers or barefoot, on the pitch or on asphalt, it doesn't matter, what matters is to have fun, to always play and to give your best football', says Fabiano, a young footballer from the Sinhá neighbourhood, a favela in São Paolo.[25]

In Rio de Janeiro, football is played on makeshift pitches often located at the top of a hill. Over the years, some of these spaces have become part of a collective memory forged over the course of games, defining residents' sense of belonging to their ground. Since the late 1970s, a small, dusty field on the heights of Babilônia has seen *peladeiros* from the eponymous favela flock to it every Sunday. 'At the time, further down the road, there was a pitch where only adults were allowed to play', recalls *peladeiro* Paulo Cesar de Souza.

> I was only 12 years old and there was an old man who had been living up there for many years. With eight or nine friends, we climbed up to his house to kick the ball around. One day he caught our ball, came up to us and said, 'You want to play football? Here's what we're going to do: I'm going to help you clear up this area and then you'll have your own pitch to play on'. Every weekend we came here to dig, clear, level, and he helped us as promised. Then we set up mini-goals and even today I still feel the same pleasure of playing there with my children and friends.[26]

In São Paulo, where rapid urbanisation has eaten up any vacant space, *pelada* fields can give rise to neighbourhood struggles. This was the case when, in the early 2000s, the residents of Morro da Lua had to mobilise against the construction of housing on the site of their football pitch, known as 'América'.[27] 'In Brazil, football has always been very dependent on public spaces, and most of them are simply vacant lots', says Thiago Hérick de Sá, a researcher at the University of São Paulo. 'But these spaces have come under pressure from the real estate market for the construction of flats or offices, the city centres and in the suburbs alike'.[28]

Locals' affection for the places they play is explained by the social dimension of street football. In Vila Andrade, a poor district of São Paolo, a PE teacher demonstrated how a simple cul-de-sac lined with garages in the Jardim Elisa district has been a favoured *pelada* playground for four generations.[29] Taken over in the afternoon first by 10-year-olds and then by teenagers at nightfall, this stretch of asphalt, which is used by car mechanics during the day, becomes a pitch for local youth. For many inhabitants, the occupation of the cul-de-sac by football is also a way to bring life to the street at night and to increase the security of this otherwise deserted area. In their eyes, it is a shared space where young people can practice their passion for free and where the youngest are supervised by the older youths, giving the parents a break.[30]

In São Paulo, which is suffocated by concrete, street football is popular in the *quadras*, small fenced areas enclosed in the dense urban network. The *quadras* see a less informal *pelada*, known as *futebol de várzea*, named after the alluvial plains surrounding the river that runs through São Paulo where the very first football games were played. In the poor suburbs of São Paulo, which are plagued by drug-related violence, the small local *futebol de várzea* clubs occupy a key social role. 'Our main objective is to bring people together, to create a family spirit, a group cohesion', says Wellington, leader of one of these clubs, Nove de Julho Futebol Lazer. 'We try to integrate everyone, to show that we can make new friends here. We are taking an alternative approach to those who spread violence in the neighbourhood'.[31] An escape from the daily reality of crime, many volunteers are involved in organising *pelada* meetings to keep young people busy and try to give meaning to their lives in neighbourhoods that have been totally abandoned by the state.

Formerly known as Desafia ao Galo and recognised by the regional football authorities in the 1990s, an annual amateur tournament, the Copa Kaiser, brings together around 200 *futebol de várzea* teams from São Paulo's favelas. This Copa and, more generally, each weekend match, have become an opportunity to mobilise local drumming groups, to set up a sound system and to organise *churrascos* (barbecues) for local families in a convivial atmosphere, united in fervour for their respective teams.

On a national scale, an astonishing amateur championship not affiliated to the Confederação Brasileira de Futebol takes place every year in Manaus, in the middle of the Amazon. Conceived in 1973 as a social project by journalists from the daily newspaper *A Crítica* and named the Peladão, this vast popular event combines amateur football with a very Brazilian peculiarity: a beauty queen contest, with each queen representing a team. Assembling nearly 1,100 teams and 23,000 *peladeiros*, the event requires some 60 improvised pitches across the city – on some, car headlights enable play to continue after dark – and draws some 40,000 spectators to the Vivaldo Lima stadium.[32]

The Peladão includes some rules of play that would drive a FIFA executive mad. If a 'beauty queen' qualifies for a stage of the competition but her team does not, the *peladeiros* can replay in a parallel tournament to try to re-enter the competition. Meanwhile, yellow cards can be wiped out if players commit to buying balls for disadvantaged children. Multiple divisions structure this tumultuous championship* to allow teams of men, women, teenagers, veterans and even Native American communities to compete. 'There is no separation of social classes', insists Arnaldo Santos, in charge of the championship. 'Some people don't even know what they are going to

---

* In 2013, the goalkeeper of the Amigos do Tonho team, Paulo Christian Bezerra Silva, was murdered by a fan of the opposing team after saving a penalty that was decisive for his team's qualification.

eat on Monday, but on Sunday they play and the spectators applaud them'.[33]

In addition to these large-scale amateur competitions, which are not subject to any institutional authority, the freedom of practice inherent in the *pelada*, the many obstacles that define the playing area – kerbs, walls, cars, uneven ground, etc. – and the narrowness of the pitches force the players to acquire superb control over the ball. Brazilians call this virtuosity the *ginga*, a term that designates both the basic footwork of capoeira and the swaying gait of the street thug (the *malandro*) [see Chapter 12]. 'It is in the *pelada* that you learn to play football, to develop your style, to take shots, to get the ball out of difficult situations, to fake things, things that even professional footballers don't know', says Neto, a former SC Corinthians and Brazilian national team player. 'Footballers from the *peladas* have this *ginga* in them, unlike other players who are totally robotic nowadays'.[34] The *futebol de várzea* tournaments, the *quadras* and other open fields are effectively a hotbed for promising talent for the big professional clubs. Garrincha in the 1950s and 1960s, Romário, Ronaldo and Rivaldo in the 1990s and 2000s, and more recently Neymar, are all hardcore former *peladeiros*. 'Brazilian football, this joyful football of lightness, improvisation and skill, comes from the *pelada*', says Luís Fabiano, an international player and striker for the Brazilian team in the 2000s. And the professional footballer recalls his street games with a touch of nostalgia: 'With or without a shirt, barefoot, with a makeshift ball, we had fun. It allowed us to put aside all our problems, our daily lives, our responsibilities. It was really great, pure *pelada*, the kind that comes from the neighbourhoods [...]'[35]

Inner-city football: playing to survive

Institutional football is also in crisis in France. While the French Football Federation (FFF) has had around 2 million members for the past 20 years, many French men – and a growing number of French women – play the sport outside the institutional framework. 'There is a parallel football developing outside the clubs', observed former French footballer and coach Laurent Blanc in 2012. 'It's a wild football – this is not pejorative – unregulated, with no referees. More than a million people play like this. Because they enjoy it'.[36]

This is particularly the case in the *banlieues*, which have seen the emergence of an authentic, alternative street football. By appropriating open spaces – car parks, the courtyards of low-income housing estates, central reservations of roads – or the small local sports facilities built from the 1980s onwards,[37] a totally improvised and self-organised form of inner-city football has broken free from dominant footballing practices. Like the Brazilian *peladas*, and in order to return to the purely playful aspect of football, this street football takes certain liberties with the official rules. 'We play without rules, well, without any specific rules', explained Stéphane, a player from the Grenoble suburbs, responding to a sociological survey carried out at the end of the 1990s.

> If there is a problem, we discuss it and decide [...] We don't put limits on the pitch, or if a player runs like crazy to catch a ball and it goes a bit behind the goal line, we give him the chance to make a beautiful cross. It's the beautiful actions that we care about [...] For the pleasure of dribbling a bit more, a striker might wait for his defender to catch up before shooting at the goal.[38]

Spontaneous street games are played without referees and certain constraints on the game, such as offside, are frequently abandoned. Teams usually play five against five, but players can change during the game to balance the forces – if one team is too dominant, the game loses all its meaning[39] – or to include other footballers who want to have a go. 'We have fun, it's not competitive football, we're free, we dribble, we don't dribble, there's no coach, no club supervisor who would nag us, who would tell us what to do', insists Salah from the Cité des Œillets in Toulon. 'We aren't imprisoned in a framework. It's not rigid'.[40] Self-arbitration is practised horizontally and can sometimes give rise to verbal or even physical violence. But altercations are rare, insists Salah: 'It's managed well; it goes on like that despite the fact that there is a lot of grumbling and shouting'.[41] The main thing is the flexibility of the game and not the rigid application of federal rules. The choice of the playing area itself embodies this radical break with the institutional sports framework and its standardised football pitch. 'The pitch ends at the car park on one side and the slope on the other. That's where the touchlines are! The length depends on the number of players', says one player.[42]

The sense of detachment from conventional practice is also achieved by the reversal in the logic inherent in football, whereby the individual is at the service of the collective with the productive aim of scoring goals. In inner-city football, the collective is a pretext for showcasing the technical skills of each player through a series of purely aesthetic actions.[43] Nutmegs, roulette turns, step-overs, back-heels, flip-flaps and *ailes de pigeon* (pigeon's wings) are all skill moves that are worked tirelessly to perfection and that allow each player to be recognised and valued on the pitch. 'We want to please ourselves, without pleasing the team', confesses Choukri, from the Cité des Œillets in Toulouse.[44] As for those who can't control the ball, they are mercilessly teased on the estate, says Dounia Homms, a footballer from Choisy-le-Roi. She explains: 'The nutmeg is looked down on, if you're nutmegged, it means you don't know how to play, you don't know how to close your legs'.[45] For Maxime Travert, lecturer at the Faculty of Sports Sciences in Marseille, this primacy of individual technical skill should not be interpreted 'as an attack on the collective spirit of the game, or even as the expression of an infidelity to the discipline of the game, but rather as an ephemeral attempt to exist in a community context'.[46]

Virtuosity with the ball is transformed into a body language that allows players who are too often described as an indistinct mass of 'estate kids', ignored and unseen, to freely assert themselves as individuals in their own right.

Ferhat Cicek, a football coach-educator on the 'Plateau', a pitch in a working-class neighbourhood south of Paris, says:

> Street football allows you to let off steam because at some point you feel hatred, you don't understand anything at school, there's no one to help you, you have money problems and when you find yourself [on the pitch] you are free, you're free of all your problems, of all the barriers you have outside, in society, and there, it's a breath of fresh air.[47]

Street footballers cultivate a certain distrust of traditional eleven-a-side football, which they see as erasing their individuality. 'It's impersonal [...] you no longer have your own identity [...] you're drowned in a group', says Choukri. And Sami, from the same housing estate in Toulon, agrees: 'We're non-existent, we aren't seen!'[48] The many constraints imposed by club football, such as regular weekly training sessions, the match schedule, the formation of teams or the spirit of rigour and discipline, also form a stark contrast to the spontaneity of street football. 'In an eleven-a-side football club, you don't choose your partners, the coach does. Street football is made up of younger and older kids from the neighbourhood, it's your second family. The best definition [of street football] is freedom', explains Ferhat Cicek.[49] 'The "among us" that characterises street football doesn't apply to clubs, which value the confrontation between "them" and "us" instead'.[50] Franck, from the Cité des Œillets, says: 'I prefer street football because club football is more physical, more violent. On the housing estate, since we all know each other, we don't do nasty stuff; whereas in the club we don't know the opposing players, we want to destroy them, so we go for a nasty tackle'.[51]

More prosaically, it is often a lack of financial resources that prevents young footballers from these areas from joining their local club. 'There were five boys in our house alone', says Yannick Mendy, an educator in Argenteuil. 'So paying for membership, boots, studs, tracksuits, etc., was very expensive. Our parents couldn't afford it, it added up to a lot of money'.[52] Meanwhile, kicking a ball around in the street, 'requires nothing, even if you have no kit and shoes with holes in them, you play with your friends, you don't need anything', says Bernard Messi, also from Argenteuil and initiator of a five-a-side football tournament in the Ile-de-France for 14–16 year-olds.[53]

The sports club are also sometimes seen by footballers from the housing estates as a social institution that represents state authority – like the police force.[54] The emergence in the 1980s of that media villain, the unruly 'estate youth', notably following the revolts in the Lyon suburbs – the Minguettes housing estate in Vénissieux, and later in Villeurbanne and Vaulx-en-Velin – led the public authorities to turn sport into a tool of social pacification.[55] Regarded with suspicion by local elected officials, street football became part of city policies introduced in the 1990s, as the public authorities sought to bring young players from the inner city 'to a "higher stage" of socialisation, that is to say, to insert them into sports associations or clubs that are repositories of a higher form of sociability and citizenship'.[56]

Financed by the municipality and affiliated to the FFF, the local amateur club is perceived by the footballers from the housing estates as a place where a certain social order is perpetuated. As street players from Fontaine, in the Grenoble suburbs, complained at the end of the 1990s:

> It's easy to see, there's no room for everyone. So they give you the patter. They say that what's-his-name is in good shape, or that he's holding his place well. OK, he wasn't up to it last week, but he'll be better next time. And in the meantime you're waiting on the bench. Then you understand and you don't even bother coming anymore. Hamed, he stays at home! So the coach takes the opportunity to tell you that you have a bad temper and you don't know how to play as a team. The truth is that he can't stand Arabs. But he'll never say that. So all that's left is to form a team of Arabs, and why not, a team of Algerians, of Tunisians [...] The veteran players form teams like that, but they do it to remember the good times back in their villages. For us, it doesn't make sense. Or it only means that we aren't wanted.[57]

If street footballers prefer to distance themselves from the official clubs, it is also because they are attached to their pitch, where players and local residents alike build up a collective memory over the course of feverish matches. In the Cité des Musiciens in Argenteuil, a pitch named 'San Siro', after the mythical Milan stadium, has been a venue for Sunday football matches for over 25 years. 'At the time, the Italian championship was one of the best in the world', recalls Toufik, a local figure. 'The benchmark clubs were Inter and AC Milan'.[58] The San Siro does not look like much. The pitch is not rectangular, the playing area is not marked out, and the rough asphalt has scratched many a footballer's hands and knees.

However, when in 2013 the municipality announced plans to demolish the San Siro in order to build a car park, the residents of the estate mobilised to stubbornly defend their ground. 'Beyond football, San Siro is very important to us', insists Tarek Mouadane, a local association leader.

> It's where we meet to celebrate our dead [young people from the neighbourhood who died prematurely]. It's where many conflicts have been resolved. It's where we talk about the problems of the neighbourhood, and it has become a symbol of our ability to make things happen, to fight together. We had written the names of our disappeared on the walls, we knew every square inch of the land. Destroying it meant destroying our history.[59]

The pitch has been used for charity tournaments in solidarity with the relatives of the deceased to raise money for funerals, or to help families affected by a fire in a nearby block of flats. 'It's also where everyone meets, footballers or no, it's where we have barbecues, it's where the little ones can hang out with the older ones for a while, it's where we can talk', adds Fabrice Ngoma, a sports educator. 'In fact, it's not just a football pitch, it's a whole, it's really the heart of the neighbourhood'.[60] After three years of difficult negotiations and night-time sabotage of the construction site, the city council gave in on condition that the San Siro be renovated and brought up to current standards.

In housing estates on the north side of Paris, street football pitches are also used to keep alive the memory of victims of police violence. In Seine-Saint-Denis, on 27 October 2005, a dozen teenagers from Clichy-sous-Bois were returning from a day spent playing football when they ran into police officers responding to a call about an attempted robbery. Scared, two of them – Zyed Benna, from the Chêne-Pointu estate, and Bouna Traoré, from the Pama estate – died when they sought refuge in an electricity transformer to escape an identity check that would have meant they got home too late, in the middle of Ramadan. Three weeks of revolt followed, setting the country's inner-city estates ablaze. Ever since, one of Traoré's brothers

– he was known to be a good, very technical player – has organised a football tournament on 27 October in memory of the two young victims. 'Bouna was a legend', says Fariz, a classmate. 'When they lost, the guys from the Pama said it was because Bouna wasn't there. He was the star'.[61] Mustapha Otmani, who, like Zyed Benna, comes from the Chêne-Pointu estate and is now a professional futsal player, recalls the makeshift matches that used to take place in Clichy-sous-Bois: 'We often organised tournaments between neighbourhoods: Chêne-Pointu, Stamu [...] Each player came with a bottle of Coke or fruit juice. The winning team would go home with all the bottles. It was a bit like our Champions League'.[62] In the summer of 2017, in the Paris suburbs, a tournament was also set up in Champagne-sur-Oise, then at the Boyenval pitch in Beaumont-sur-Oise, in tribute to Adama Traoré. The 24-year-old football fan died a year earlier when he was arrested by the local police.

The dummies of the football business

Like the *navétane* championship in Senegal, or pitches in Brazilian favelas, French inner-city estates are a reservoir of elite players in the eyes of the football industry. While Zinedine Zidane remains the emblematic 'footballer from the estates', Paul Pogba from La Renardière in Roissy-en-Brie, Hatem Ben Arfa from Butte-Rouge in Châtenay-Malabry, and Ousmane Dembélé from Évreux are also footballers playing in top-flight European teams.

Famed for their technical skills learned on asphalt, these stars of the ball are a model for many young players from the city. Yet the recruitment of these street footballers also allows professional football to transform the playful, appealing logic of its wilder cousin into a competitive value. Technical virtuosity or dribbling ability, synonymous with individual recognition and popular spectacle in neighbourhood football matches, become simple variables that allow each player to be coldly evaluated on the world football market. 'We're going to reach to a point where it's all about who puts in the most sidesteps, the most fakes', commented Karim Benzema, Real Madrid's star striker and a native of Bron, an estate in Lyon, in 2017. 'Maybe we'll add points based on that. Today we talk a lot more about creative players, dribblers [...] When you watch a match on TV, they only talk about statistics. They don't talk about football anymore'.[63]

This institutional and commercial appropriation of street football is also reflected in the new competitions organised under the aegis of major sponsors in the football industry. Since the mid-1990s, the equipment manufacturer Puma has organised street football matches in European cities with a great deal of merchandising aimed at inner-city youth.[64] Recently, Adidas and Nike have launched the Tango League and Winner Stays respectively, international four-a-side and five-a-side street football tournaments, which serve primarily as a promotional tool for their latest sports shoes. Some events, such as the Red Bull Street Style (created in 2012) and the European Street Cup (2013), go so far as to take up playing practices invented in the street, such as *panna* (a one-on-one game in which bonus points are awarded for each nutmeg of an opponent) or Freestyle (a player has to perform as many tricks as possible within a set time limit).

FIFA, for its part, has standardised and codified *pelada* games on Brazilian beaches in an attempt to open up a new sports market and get its hands on a popular informal practice. In May 2005, it created a professional beach football World Cup with Beach Soccer Worldwide (a beach football federation founded in 1992). In the same year, the FIFA Street video game series was launched by the international footballing body's franchise, considered by its producer to be the 'first true quality street football experience'.[65]

As if to regenerate itself and acquire new legitimacy, the football business is eagerly drawing on the image of street football. For the 2006 World Cup, Adidas, an official partner, filmed its advertising campaign on a makeshift pitch in a working-class Spanish neighbourhood. It featured two children playing an improvised game of football in the street with stars such as David Beckham, Djibril Cissé and even Franz Beckenbauer, before their mother calls them in from a balcony to end the game. Entitled *José+10*, this memorable advert mobilises the universal imagery of street football (a courtyard pitch, a hand game to choose team members, a ball hitting a car, a disputed goal) as much as the playful, childlike dimension of the game. In 2014, it was Nike's turn to launch a global advertising campaign invoking street football. In a perfect metaphor for the commercial institutionalisation of grassroots football, a modest neighbourhood football game between teenagers gradually evolves into a televised international match, with the young footballers turning into Cristiano Ronaldo or Neymar whilst the sparse grass pitch metamorphoses into an international stadium packed with fans.

In referencing improvised football, commercial tournaments fuelled by sponsorship money and huge marketing campaigns try to convince us that there is a natural continuity between street football and the global football industry. However, the proponents of the football business forget that they will never be able to capture one of the core values of football: the sheer joy of playing together. 'The number one pleasure for someone who plays street football is the relationship between them, the ball and their friends in the neighbourhood', says street coach Ferhat Cicek. 'Whether it's the favelas of Rio or the inner-city estates of France, the pleasure is exactly the same because street football is all about a ball, a pitch and your mates. There – the world is yours!'[66]

Postscript to the English edition

Prolongations

Steal from the rich and organise with the poor.

Call to a general strike by Colo-Colo supporters
in Santiago de Chile, 21 October 2019

'Less democracy is sometimes better for organising a World Cup', Jérôme Valcke, General Secretary of FIFA confided to the press on 24 April 2013. Five years later, when *A People's History of Football* first appeared in French bookshops, the football world was abuzz with excitement for the World Cup 2018, held in Russia. Putin spared no expense, investing more than 9.5 billion euros to attract fans. 'Everything was extremely beautiful and efficient [...] This World Cup has changed the world's perception of Russia', concluded Gianni Infantino, FIFA's new boss.

Apart from the pitch invasion in the 52nd minute of the France–Croatia final by three members of the anti-Putin punk collective Pussy Riot, nothing had disrupted the smooth running of this heavily-policed World Cup. The change in the 'perception of Russia' was a resounding success. The authoritarianism of the Russian state and its cynical attacks on human rights were carefully swept beneath the green carpets of the stadiums. The image of Putin bombing civilians in Syria just months earlier to prop up the dictatorial Assad regime vanished into thin air. The World Cup was a diplomatic triumph for the Kremlin.

In 2022 it was the turn of another authoritarian state, Qatar, to host the tournament. Just like in Russia, police surveillance and LGBT-phobia were to the fore. Yet the flagship product of world football had never raised so many questions and doubts. The exact number of workers who died on building sites linked to the Qatari World Cup is unknown. But it is said to be at least 6,500. On top of these deaths are the living and working conditions of hundreds of thousands of migrant workers who have been the terrible face of a proletariat so many had believed consigned to history. It's all the same to FIFA: it counts the dollars, not the deaths.

Boycott for equality

A year after winning the 2018 World Cup, France hosted the women's version of the tournament. With unprecedented audience figures, it was a real popular success: some 1.12 billion viewers watched official television broadcasts. This media spotlight only emphasised how much football remains a male bastion, and yet can become a space of feminist assertion.

The US world champion Megan Rapinoe spearheads this struggle for equality. Since coming out in 2012, she has fiercely defended both LGBT+ and women's rights. On 8 March 2019, International Women's Day, she and other players sued the US Soccer Federation for 'institutionalised gender discrimination'. A few days before the World Cup began, Rapinoe put the boot in, criticising FIFA's lack of interest in women's football: 'For the resources and for the ability that I feel like FIFA has to implement that change, I think they're not doing nearly enough'.[1] In 2016, she was the first white person to take the knee during the national anthem to protest police violence in the US, in solidarity with American football player Colin Kaepernick. The forward also refused to sing the US anthem in protest at Donald Trump's policies towards minorities. On the eve of the tournament, Rapinoe announced that she would not accept a visit to the White House: 'I am not going to fake it, hobnob with the president, who is clearly against so many of the things that I am [for] and so many of the things that I actually am'.[2]

Another figure fighting for equality between men and women in football, the Norwegian Ada Hegerberg boycotted the women's World Cup. Crowned footballer of the year in 2018, the 23-year-old forward has refused to wear the jersey for her country since 2017 to denounce the lack of resources allocated to women's teams compared to men's. On 7 June 2019, she told the press: 'The NFF has never taken the women's national team seriously. It's a feeling I've had since I was called-up as a dead serious young girl to the U15 squad'.[3]

Echoing the demands of football's female players, the stands didn't remain silent either. On 11 June, at a Chile–Sweden match in Rennes, a choir of 600 women sang 'Debout les Femmes', the emblematic protest song of the French women's liberation movement. After the US won against Holland in the final on 7 July, the sports sociologist Béatrice Barbusse assured 'Even if the organisers didn't intend it, this World Cup will be remembered as feminist'.[4]

Supporters united

Football supporters have again emerged as political actors in their own right at the heart of social movements. Just like in Tunis, Cairo and Istanbul, Algerian fans have been at the forefront of protest against the authoritarian regime of Abdelaziz Bouteflika. From Friday 22 February 2019, date of the first peaceful anti-government march, 'La Casa del Mouradia' became the anthem of the demonstrations.[5] This song emerged from the stands of the Union sportive de la médina d'Alger (USMA), one of the most important football clubs in the country. Composed by the Ouled El-Bahdja supporters collective, the song depicts the despair of Algerian youth before jeering the 20 years of Bouteflika's reign.

For the last 15 years, Algerian football ground chants have developed into a musical culture in their own right. The words for these popular songs draw on themes as diverse as the drugs young people take, government authoritarianism, corruption, clandestine migration and mass unemployment. 'Since independence in 1962, stadiums have been the sounding board for social demands among male youth', explains the Franco-Algerian political scientist Youcef Fatès, a specialist in the history of Algerian sport. 'Historically, football clubs have always been a space for protest. They take on a socio-political dimension of resistance and anti-colonial struggle'.[6]

As the most popular and first Muslim club in Algeria, since it was founded in 1921 Mouloudia Club d'Alger (MCA) has represented Algerian and anti-colonial identity. What's more, Yacef Saâdi – military leader of the National Liberation Front during the Battle of Algiers in 1957 – and revolutionary Zoubir Bouadjadj both played for USMA, recruiting fighters during their time there. Some 40 'martyrs of independence' have come from the ranks of the Algiers football club.

From the beginning of the protest movement, Algerians were struck by the presence of football supporters in the demonstrations, singing songs hostile to the government. In Constantine, they were there at the first marches, escorting and providing bottles of water to the demonstrators. The different supporter groups in Algiers even declared themselves *khawa* ('brothers'). Fans of MCA, USMA, Union Sportive de Madinet El Harrach and Chabab Riadhi Belouizdad put aside their rivalries to unite against the regime.

On Thursday 14 March 2019, USMA and MCA faced each other in the Algiers derby, renowned for its fervour in the stands and its spectacular *tifos*. But on the morning of the match, an MCA-stamped pamphlet declared: 'You don't go to a wedding party when your mother is ill [...] Let's boycott the stands in the interests of the country and the club'. For the first time in the history of Algerian football, the Stade du 5-Juillet-1962 was virtually empty at kick-off. The founding members of Ouled El-Bahdja said: 'We cancelled the *tifo* that was to be displayed because the beauty of the stands during previous Algiers derbies has been used by the state to show a distorted image of the social reality of the country. Football should not be a way to hypnotise and distract the people'.[7]

Four months later, the Algerian team beat Senegal in the final of the Africa Cup of Nations. The sporting success of the Algerian team, which had not won the trophy since 1990, was seen as a continuation of the popular victories that led to the departure of former president Abdelaziz Bouteflika. 'The Algerian people have been an example to the world with these peaceful demonstrations over the last few months', said Algerian international Adlene Guedioura. 'That's why we were so determined to give them this Africa Cup'.[8]

'No football without justice!'

In Chile, the day after protests broke out against President Sebastián Piñera, football players and supporters also relayed the demands of the people. On 19 October, 2019, Claudio Bravo, then Manchester City goalkeeper and former captain of the Chilean team, denounced 30 years of neoliberal policy in Chile by tweeting: 'They sold our water, electricity, gas, education, health, pensions, roads, forests, the Atacama salt flats, the glaciers, transport. What's left? Not much. We don't want a Chile of the few, but of the many'.

The Chilean midfielder playing at FC Barcelona, Arturo Vidal, exhorted politicians to 'listen to the people', while international Fernanda Pinilla openly called for the president to step down: 'You still haven't understood that we want you to go? [...] You succeeded in bringing us together, and now we're never going to back down'.

Through their social structures known as *corporaciones*, the clubs got involved in the social movement. The *corporación* of the Santiago Wanderers made a commitment to provide financial support to the victims of police repression. The most popular club in Chile, the Colo-Colo[9] *corporación* organised assemblies at its stadium to enable Chileans to voice their grievances and ultimately prepare a constituent assembly.

As in Algiers just months earlier, the supporter groups of Santiago's three biggest clubs (Universidad de Chile, Colo-Colo and Universidad Católica) put aside their rivalries to join street demonstrations. Even though the Garra Blanca (Colo-Colo) and Los de Abajo (Universidad de Chile) ultras were confronting each other a few days earlier at matches, the groups fraternised at the demos and called for a general strike.

The Chilean professional championship was suspended from 19 October. A month later, the football authorities, advancing the interests of the government as well as club owners, sought to restart matches. Supporters, however, saw it as an attempt to restore social peace and revive the industry. The resumption of the league on 22 November 2019 was an outright failure. For the first match of the day between Unión La Calera and Deportes Iquique, the stands were almost empty, a minute's silence was held for demonstrators killed, and for the pre-match photo the players placed one hand over their left eye, alluding to the frequent blinding of protestors by police-fired rubber bullets. Finally, Colo-Colo supporters invaded the ground in the 67th minute and interrupted the game. At this, the teams that had matches scheduled later that day refused to play.

Faced with this setback, the Chilean Football Federation announced on 29 November the premature end of the 2019–2020 season. This was a heavy defeat for the Chilean football business and for Sebastián Piñera, but a victory for the fans, who had been clamouring since the beginning of the protest: 'No football without justice!'

One of the most recent outbursts from the stands dates from November 2022. In Brazil, football fans rose up against the far-right partisans of former president Jair Bolsonaro, who had erected barriers blocking highways across the country in their refusal to accept Luiz Inácio Lula da Silva's victory in the hard-fought presidential elections of 30 October 2022.

The Supreme Court had sent the federal police to clear the roads. Yet some police officers were colluding with these pro-Bolsonaro demonstrations, meaning some 100 blockades remained. Where the security forces failed to break the blockades, supporters took matters into their own hands. On their way to their respective teams' matches, ultras from SC Corinthians, Atlético Mineiro, Coritiba FC and Cruzeiro Esporte Clube tore down Bolsonarist barricades in the states of Minas Gerais, São Paulo and Paraná.

Showing continuity with the politically engaged history of SC Corinthians, which rebelled against the Brazilian military dictatorship in the early 1980s, its supporters also hung a banner on a motorway bridge bearing the words: 'We believe in democracy'.

More than ever, on the pitch, in the stands and in the street, an alternative history of football continues to be written.

Endnotes

Introduction

1. Cited in Florent Torchut, 'Le Barça, une marque mondiale qui agace les socios', *L'Équipe*, 18 August 2017.
2. Matt Woosnam, 'Premier League season tickets: 11 clubs raise prices for 2022–23', *The Athletic*, 19 June 2022.
3. 'Price of football: Full results 2015', *BBC News*, 14 October 2015; David Conn, 'The Premier League has priced out fans, young and old', *The Guardian*, 16 August 2011.
4. Cited in Florent Torchut, op. cit.
5. Christian Bromberger, Alain Hayot and Jean-Marc Mariottini, 'Allez l'O.M., Forza Juve. La passion pour le football à Marseille et à Turin', *Terrain*, no. 8, 1987, pp. 8–41.
6. Cited in *So Foot*, no. 150, October 2017, p. 22.
7. Eric Hobsbawm, 'La culture ouvrière en Angleterre', *L'Histoire*, no. 17, November 1979, pp. 22–35.
8. Paul Dietschy, *Histoire du football*, Perrin, Paris, 2010, p. 10.

Chapter 1

1. Cited in Norbert Elias and Eric Dunning, *Sport et civilisation. La Violence maîtrisée*, Fayard, Paris, 1994, p. 240.
2. Émile Souvestre, *Les Derniers Bretons*, Second edition, vol. 2, Charpentier, Paris, 1836, p. 56.
3. Cited in Ronald Knox and Shane Leslie, *The Miracles of King Henry VI*, Cambridge University Press, Cambridge, 1923.
4. Norbert Elias and Eric Dunning, op. cit.
5. Nicolas Bancel and Jean-Marc Gayman, *Du Guerrier à l'athlète: éléments d'histoire des pratiques corporelles*, PUF, Paris, 2002.
6. Charles Gondouin and Jordan, *Le Football: rugby, américain, association*, Pierre Lafitte & Cie, Paris, 1914, p. 273.
7. Nicolas Bancel and Jean-Marc Gayman, op. cit.
8. Louis Gougaud, 'La soule en Bretagne et les jeux similaires du Cornwall et du pays de Galles', *Annales de Bretagne*, vol. 27, no. 4, 1911.
9. Nicolas Bancel and Jean-Marc Gayman, op. cit.
10. Michel Pitre-Chevalier, *La Bretagne ancienne*, Didier, Paris, 1859, p. 552.

11. Patrick Vassort, *Football et politique. Sociologie historique d'une domination*, Les Éditions de la Passion, Paris, 1999.
12. Siméon Luce, *La France pendant la guerre de Cent Ans*, Hachette, Paris, 1890.
13. Hippolyte Violeau, *Pèlerinages de Bretagne (Morbihan)*, Ambroise Bray, Libraire-éditeur, Paris, 1859, p. 163.
14. Nicolas Bancel and Jean-Marc Gayman, op. cit.; Patrick Vassort, op. cit.
15. Jean-Michel Mehl, *Les Jeux au Royaume de France, du XIII*e *au début du XVI*e *siècle*, Fayard, Paris, 1990.
16. Émile Souvestre, 'La soule en Basse-Bretagne', *Musée des familles*, vol. 3, 1836.
17. James Walvin, *The People's Game. The History of Football Revisited*, Mainstream Publishing, Edinburgh, 2000, p. 26.
18. Ibid., p. 27.
19. Siméon Luce, op. cit.
20. Patrick Vassort, op. cit.
21. Ibid.
22. James Walvin, op. cit.
23. Ibid.
24. Norbert Elias and Eric Dunning, op. cit.
25. Ibid.
26. Jean-Jules Jusserand, *Les Sports et les jeux d'exercice dans l'ancienne France*, 1901, reprinted Slatkine, Paris, 1986.
27. Patrick Vassort, op. cit.
28. Louis Gougaud, loc. cit.
29. Nicolas Bancel and Jean-Marc Gayman, op. cit.
30. Patrick Vassort, op. cit.
31. Norbert Elias, *La Civilisation des mœurs*, Pocket, Paris, 2011 [1939].
32. Patrick Vassort, op. cit.
33. *Sports en Morbihan, des origines à 1940, textes et documents réunis et présentés par Louis Tascon*, Association pour la diffusion et l'animation du patrimoine historique en Marbihan, Vannes, 1980.
34. Anatole de Barthélemy, 'Recherches historiques sur quelques droits et redevances bizarres au Moyen Âge', *Revue de Bretagne et de Vendée*, vol. 3, 1859.
35. Guillotin de Corson, 'Usages et droits féodaux en Bretagne', *Revue de Bretagne, de Vendée et d'Anjou*, vol. 25, January 1901.
36. Emmanuel Laot, *Le Sport dans les Côtes d'Armor. Des origines à 1940*, Service éducatif des Archives des Côtes-d'Armor, Saint-Brieuc, 1997.
37. Nicolas Bancel and Jean-Marc Gayman, op. cit.
38. Ibid.

39. Edward P. Thompson, 'Modes de domination et révolutions en Angleterre', *Actes de la recherche en sciences sociales*, no. 2–3, June 1976, pp. 140–141.
40. Eric Hobsbawm, *Histoire économique et sociale de la Grande-Bretagne, tome 2: De la révolution industrielle aux années 70*, Seuil, Paris, 1977, p. 92.
41. Ibid.
42. Edward P. Thompson, *La Guerre des forêts. Luttes sociales dans l'Angleterre du XVIIIe siècle*, La Découverte, Paris, 2014.
43. Eric Hobsbawm, op. cit.
44. Edward P. Thompson, op. cit.
45. James Walvin, op. cit., p. 27.
46. Norbert Elias and Eric Dunning, op. cit.
47. James Walvin, op. cit., p. 29.
48. Eric Hobsbawm, op. cit., p. 93.

Chapter 2

1. Thomas Hughes, *Tom Brown's Schooldays*, Oxford University Press, Oxford, 2008 (1857).
2. John Lawson and Harold Silver, *A Social History of Education in England*, Methuen, London, 1973.
3. Ibid.
4. James Walvin, op. cit., p. 32.
5. Paul Dietschy, op. cit.
6. James Walvin, op. cit.
7. Cited in Richard Holt, *Sport and the British, a Modern History*, Oxford University Press, Oxford, 1989.
8. Nicolas Bancel and Jean-Marc Gayman, op. cit.
9. James Walvin, op. cit., p. 36.
10. Nicolas Bancel and Jean-Marc Gayman, op. cit.
11. Bernard Andrieu, 'La fin du fair-play? Du "self-government" à la justice sportive', *Revue du MAUSS permanente*, 3 August 2011 (available at www.journaldumauss.net).
12. James Walvin, op. cit., p. 38.
13. Colin Shrosbree, *Public Schools and Private Education: The Clarendon Commission, 1861–64, and the Public Schools Acts*, Manchester University Press, Manchester, 1988.
14. Nicolas Bancel and Jean-Marc Gayman, op. cit.
15. Cited in 'Football: A Survival Guide', *Colors*, no. 90, 2014, p. 5.
16. Daniel Denis, '"Aux chiottes l'arbitre". À l'heure du Mundial, ces footballeurs qui nous gouvernent', *Politique Aujourd'hui*, no. 5, 1978, p. 12.

17. James Anthony Mangan, *Athleticism in the Victorian and Edwardian Public School. The emergence and consolidation of an educational ideology*, Cambridge University Press, Cambridge, 1981, p. 57.
18. James Walvin, op. cit., p. 41.
19. Patrick Mignon, *La Passion du football*, Odile Jacob, Paris, 1998.
20. Richard Holt, op. cit.
21. Sébastien Nadot, *Le Spectacle des joutes. Sport et courtoisie à la fin du Moyen Âge*, Presses universitaires de Rennes, Rennes, 2012.
22. Johan Huizinga, *Homo ludens. Essai sur la fonction sociale du jeu*, Gallimard, Paris, 1972, p. 162.
23. Peter McInstosh, *Fair Play: Ethics in Sport and Education*, Heineman, London, 1979, p. 27.
24. Paul Dietschy, op. cit.

Chapter 3

1. Nicolas Bancel and Jean-Marc Gayman, op. cit.
2. Paul Dietschy, op. cit.
3. James Walvin, op. cit., p. 45.
4. Ibid.
5. Cited in Charles Korr, 'West Ham United, une rhétorique de la famille', *Actes de la recherche en sciences sociales*, vol. 103, no. 1, 1994, p. 57.
6. James Walvin, op. cit.
7. Tony Mason, *Association Football and English Society, 1863–1915*, Harvester Press, Brighton, 1980.
8. Cited in James Walvin, op. cit., p. 69.
9. Ibid., p. 79.
10. Eric Hobsbawm, 'La culture ouvrière en Angleterre', loc. cit.
11. Charles Burgess Fry, 'Football', in *Badminton Library of Sports and Pastimes*, Longmans Green & Co, London, vol. 1, 1895.
12. *La Vie au grand air*, 24 December 1899.
13. *Bell's Life in London and Sporting Chronicle*, 18 December 1869.
14. Richard Sanders, *Beastly Fury, The Strange Birth of British Football*, Bantam, London, 2009, p. 66.
15. Charles Alcock, *Football: Our Winter Game*, Nabu Press, London, 1874, p. 83.
16. James Walvin, op. cit., p. 83.
17. Jean-Claude Michéa, *Le Plus beau but était une passe*, Climats, Paris, 2014, p. 62.
18. Paul Dietschy, op. cit.
19. Cited in Keith Warsop, *The Early FA Cup Finals and the Southern Amateurs*, SoccerData, Nottingham, 2004.
20. *The Morning Post*, 2 April 1883.

21. Hunter Davies, *Boots, Balls and Haircuts. An Illustrated History of Football from Then to Now*, Cassell llustrated, London, 2004, p. 36.
22. James Walvin, op. cit., p. 85.
23. Charles Korr, 'Angleterre: le "foot", l'ouvrier et le bourgeois', *L'Histoire*, no. 38, October 1981.
24. James Walvin, op. cit., p. 84.
25. Ibid., p. 87.
26. Ibid., p. 85.
27. Ibid., p. 90.
28. John Harding, *Football Wizard. The Billy Meredith Story*, Robson Books, London, 1998, p. 130.
29. Claude Boli, 'Le premier syndicat de joueurs. La création du syndicat des footballeurs professionnels anglais', *WeAreFootball*, www.wearefootball.org, 2007.
30. John Harding, op. cit., p. 126.
31. Ibid., p. 135.
32. Ibid., p. 143.
33. Cited in Stefano Pivato, *Les Enjeux du sport*, Casterman, Paris, 1994.
34. Pierre Lanfranchi, 'La réinvention du foot en Italie', *Football et sociétés*, no. 7, December 1998.
35. Fabien Archambault, 'L'autre continent du football', *Cahiers des Amériques latines*, no. 74, 2014.
36. Peter Alegi, *African Soccerscapes. How a Continent Changed the World's Game*, Ohio University Press, Athens, 2010.
37. Allen Guttmann, *Sports. The First Five Millennia*, University of Massachusetts Press, Amherst, 2007, p. 241.
38. James Walvin, op. cit., p. 105.
39. Ibid., p. 98.
40. Ibid.
41. Alfred Wahl, *Les Archives du football. Sport et société en France (1880–1980)*, Gallimard Julliard, Paris, 1989.
42. Cited in Joseph Mercier, *Le Football*, PUF, Paris, 1966, p. 13.

Chapter 4

1. Cited in Hesketh Pearson, *Oscar Wilde. His life and wit*, Harper & Bros., London, 1946, p. 147.
2. Claude Boli, Football. *Le triomphe du ballon rond*, Les Quatre Chemins, Paris, 2008, p. 123.
3. Jennifer Hargreaves, *Sporting Females. Critical issues in the history and sociology of women's sports*, Routledge, London, 1994, pp. 88–111.
4. Tim Tates, *Girls With Balls. The Secret History of Women's Football*, John Blake Publishing, London, 2013, p. 9.

5. *The Manchester Guardian*, 22 June 1881.
6. James Walvin, op. cit., p. 69.
7. Kathleen E. McCrone, *Sport and the Physical Emancipation of English Women 1870–1914*, Routledge, London, 1988, p. 201.
8. Cited in *Quel Corps?*, no. 12–13, 1979.
9. James F. Lee, 'The Lady Footballers and the British Press, 1895', *Critical Survey*, vol. 24, no. 1, 2012.
10. *Paisley and Renfrewshire Gazette*, 4 May 1895.
11. Jean Williams, *A Game for Rough? A History of Women's Football in Britain*, Routledge, London, 2003.
12. Tim Tates, op. cit., p. 103.
13. Archives of the Imperial War Museum, Women's Work Collection, cited in Xavier Breuil, *Femmes, culture et politique. Histoire du football féminin en Europe de la Grande Guerre jusqu'à nos jours*, Doctoral Thesis, Université Paul Verlaine, Metz, 2007, p. 37.
14. Fabienne Broucaret, *Le Sport féminin. Le sport, dernier bastion du sexisme?*, Michalon, Paris, 2012, p. 20.
15. Claude Boli, op. cit., p. 124.
16. Patrick Brennan, 'Munition Girls' Football in Cumbria 1917–1919', *Donmouth*, www.donmouth.co.uk, 2016.
17. Cited in Xavier Breuil, op. cit., p. 34.
18. Tim Tates, op. cit., p. 127.
19. Ibid., p. 129.
20. Marie-Noëlle Bonnes, 'Les Anglaises et l'effort de guerre de 1914–1918', *Guerres mondiales et conflits contemporains*, no. 198, June 2000, pp. 79–98.
21. Tim Tates, op. cit., p. 159.
22. Ibid., p. 185.
23. *L'Auto*, 14 May 1920.
24. *Le Miroir des sports*, 21 October 1920.
25. Alfred Wahl, op. cit., p. 195.
26. Tim Tates, op. cit., p. 197.
27. Cited in John Simkin, 'Lily Parr', *Spartacus Educational*, https://spartacus-educational.com/FparrL.htm, September 1997.
28. Gail J. Newsham, *In the League of Their Own! The Dick, Kerr Ladies Football Team*, Scarlett Press, London, 1997, pp. 47–49.
29. Tim Tates, op. cit., p. 212.
30. Claude Boli, op. cit., p. 125; Xavier Breuil, op. cit., p. 92.
31. Tim Tates, op. cit., pp. 241–241.
32. Ibid., p. 228.
33. Ibid., p. 229.

34. John Williams and Jackie Woodhouse, 'Can play, will play? Women and football in Britain', in John Williams and Stephen Wagg, *British Football and Social Change: Getting into Europe*, Leicester University Press, Leicester, 1991, pp. 85–109.
35. Xavier Breuil, op. cit., p. 94.

Chapter 5

1. *L'Auto*, 3 April 1904, cited in Julien Sorez, *Le Football dans Paris et ses banlieues. Un sport devenu spectacle*, Presses universitaires de Rennes, Rennes, 2013, p. 131.
2. *Le Sport Universel Illustré*, 24 December 1898.
3. Alfred Wahl, op. cit.
4. Ibid., p. 79.
5. Julien Sorez, op. cit., p. 139.
6. Ibid., p. 141.
7. *Le Football Association*, 21 May 1921, cited in Julien Sorez, op. cit., p. 142.
8. Alfred Wahl, op. cit.
9. *La Revue Athlétique*, 25 March 1890.
10. Alfred Wahl, op. cit.
11. Neville Tunmer and Eugène Fraysse, *Football Association*, Armand Colin, Paris, 1897, p. 76.
12. *Les Jeunes*, 5 February 1903.
13. *Les Sports athlétiques*, 24 February 1894.
14. Cited in Jean Legoy, *Cultures havraises. 1895–1961*, EDIP, Saint-Étienne-du-Rouvray, 1986.
15. Alfred Wahl, op. cit.
16. Patrick Fridenson, 'Les ouvriers de l'automobile et le sport', *Actes de la recherche en sciences sociales*, vol. 79, no. 1, 1989.
17. Jean Ferette, *La Société métallurgique de Normandie. Grandeur et déclin d'une communauté ouvrière*, L'Harmattan, Paris, 2012.
18. Jean Legoy, op. cit.
19. Cited in Patrick Fridenson, loc. cit.
20. Jean-Marie Brohm, *Sociologie politique du sport*, Presses universitaires de Nancy, Nancy, 1992 [1976].
21. Cited in Patrick Fridenson, loc. cit.
22. André Mouroux, 'Du ballon rond à la tôle. Club Olympique de Billancourt', *De Renault frères constructeurs automobiles à Renault Régie Nationale*, vol. 4, no. 23, December 1981.
23. Ibid.
24. Ibid.
25. *Le Pays de Montbéliard*, 21 August 1929.

26. Patrick Fridenson, loc. cit.
27. Nicolas Kssis-Martov et al., *La FSGT. Du sport rouge au sport populaire*, La Ville Brûle – *Sport et plein air*, Montreuil, 2014, p. 11.
28. Léon Jouhaux, 'Huit heures de loisirs, qu'en ferons-nous?', *Floréal*, numéro programme, August 1919.
29. *La Petite République*, 6 December 1903.
30. *L'Humanité*, 29 March 1910, cited in 'Exista-t-il un foot "rouge" en France?', *Never Trust a Marxist in Football!* (So Foot Blog), 11 September 2010.
31. *L'Humanité*, 2 June 1914.
32. *L'Humanité*, 26 January 1914.
33. *Le Socialiste*, 9–16 May 1909, cited in Nicolas Kssis-Martov et al., op. cit., p. 12.
34. *L'Humanité*, 17 April 1911, cited in ibid., p. 22.
35. Nicolas Kssis-Martov, 'Le movement ouvrier balle au pied, culture populaire et propagande politique: l'exemple du football travailliste en région parisienne (1908–1940)', *Cahiers d'histoire. Revue d'histoire critique*, no. 88, 2002, pp. 93–104.
36. Patrick Dubechot and Henri Ségal, *CPS X, Un club populaire et sportif au cœur de l'histoire du Xe arrondissement de Paris*, Éditions du CPS X, Paris, 2002.
37. Ibid.
38. Ibid.
39. *Le Sport Alsacien*, 3 March 1922, cited in Alfred Wahl, op. cit., p. 194.
40. André Gounot, 'Le sport travailliste européen et la *fizkul'tura* soviétique: critiques et appropriations du modèle "bourgeois" de la compétition (1893–1939)', *Cahiers d'histoire. Revue d'histoire critique*, no. 120, 2013, pp. 33–48.
41. *Le Sport ouvrier*, 5 October 1923, cited in Patrick Fridenson, 'Les ouvriers de l'automobile et le sport', loc. cit.
42. Fabien Sabatier, 'Essai sur les mémoires militantes du sport communiste français. Première approche du cas colonial (1923–2011)', *Migrations Société*, vol. 137, no. 5, 2011, pp. 129–144.
43. *Le Sport ouvrier*, 20 November 1924, citéd in 'Quand patrons et ouvriers se disputaient le foot entre les deux guerres', *Never Trust a Marxist in Football!* (So Foot Blog), 12 December 2012.
44. Marc Giovaninetti, '1928–1929, "classe contre classe": les sportifs ouvriers peuvent-ils se mesurer aux sportifs bourgeois?', *Cahiers d'histoire. Revue d'histoire critique*, no. 120, 2013, pp. 49–60.
45. Madeleine Leveau-Fernandez, *Histoire du Val de Bièvre des origines aux années 1970*, Éditions de l'écomusée du Val-de-Bièvre, Fresnes, 2015.

46. Franz Vandersmissen, *Le Sport ouvrier*, Publications de la Centrale d'éducation ouvrière, no. 3, L'Églantine, Bruxelles, 1929.
47. Cited in Alfred Wahl, op. cit.
48. Nicolas Kssis-Martov, 'Le movement ouvrier balle au pied', loc. cit.
49. See 'Les sociétés coopératives de consommation', *Revue des Deux Mondes*, vol. 47, 1908; and Lucien Mercier, *Les Universités populaires: 1899–1914. Éducation populaire et mouvement ouvrier au début du siècle*, Les Éditions ouvrières, Paris, 1986.
50. Nicolas Kssis-Martov, 'La Bellevilloise et le sport ouvrier', in Jean-Jacques Meusy (ed.), *La Belleviloise. Une page de l'histoire de la coopération et du mouvement ouvrier français (1877–1939)*, Creaphis, Grane, 2001.
51. Cited in Patrick Dubechot and Henri Ségal, op. cit.
52. Nicolas Kssis-Martov, 'La Bellevilloise et le sport ouvrier', loc. cit.
53. Ibid.
54. Nicolas Kssis-Martov et al., *La FSGT*, op. cit.
55. 'Union sportive d'Ivry: histoire d'un club travailliste en banlieue rouge', *Never Trust a Marxist in Football!* (So Foot Blog), 11 October 2013.
56. Julien Sorez, op. cit., p. 110.
57. Nicolas Kssis-Martov et al., *La FSGT*, op. cit.
58. *Journal des débats politiques et littéraires*, 31 December 1929; and *Journal de Roubaix*, 30 December 1929.
59. Julien Sorez, op. cit., p. 197.
60. *L'Humanité*, 9 April 1928.
61. Julien Sorez, op. cit., p. 195.
62. Nicolas Kssis-Martov et al., *La FSGT*, op. cit.
63. Ibid.
64. André Gounot, 'Les Spartakiades internationales, manifestations sportives et politiques du communisme', *Cahiers d'histoire. Revue d'histoire critique*, no. 88, 2002, pp. 59–75
65. Ibid.
66. Franz Vandersmissen, *Le Sport ouvrier*, op. cit.
67. André Gounot, loc. cit.
68. Ibid.
69. André Gounot, 'Le sport travailliste européen et la *fizkul'tura* soviétique [...]', loc. cit.
70. Nicolas Kssis-Martov et al., *La FSGT*, op. cit.
71. Ibid.
72. Julien Sorez, op. cit., p. 114.
73. Alain Ehrenberg, 'Note sur le sport rouge (1910–1936)', *Recherches*, no. 42, April 1980.
74. Cited in Nicolas Kssis-Martov, 'Le réseau Sport libre et la persécution des sportifs juifs sous l'Occupation. La Résistance face à l'antisémitisme

d'État dans le sport', in Georges Bensoussan et al. (ed.), *Sport, corps et sociétés de masse. Le projet d'un homme nou-veau*, Armand Colin, Paris, 2012.

75. Ibid.
76. André Gounot, Denis Jallat and Benoît Caritey, *Les Politiques au stade. Étude comparée des manifestations sportives du XIX*[e] *au XXI*[e] *siècle*, Presses universitaires de Rennes, Rennes, 2007.
77. Cited in Pascal Boniface, *JO politiques. Sport et relations internationales*, Eyrolles, Paris, 2016. p. 59.

Chapter 6

1. Angela Teja, 'Italian sport and international relations under fascism', in Pierre Arnaud and James Riordan, *Sport and International Politics. The Impact of Fascism and Communism on Sport*, E & FN Spoon, London, 1998, p. 162.
2. Fabien Archambault, 'Les passions sportives des dirigeants italiens', *Histoire@Politique*, no. 23, 2014.
3. Paul Dietschy, op. cit., p. 202.
4. Pierre milza, 'Le football italien. Une histoire à l'échelle du siècle', *Vingtième Siècle*, no. 26, April–June 1990.
5. Ibid.
6. UNESCO/ST/R/1, Service de statistique, *Statistique du nombre de postes récepteurs de radio pour 128 pays et territoires*, Paris, December 1950.
7. Lando Ferretti, *Il libro dello sport*, Libreria del Littorio, Milan-Rome, 1928, p. 227.
8. Daphné Bolz, 'La mise en scène sportive de l'Italie fasciste et de l'Allemagne nazie: la Coupe du monde de football (1934) et les Jeux olympiques de Berlin (1936)', in André Gounot, Denis Jallat and Benoît Caritey, op. cit., 2007.
9. Christian Hubert, *50 ans de Coupe du Monde*, Arts et voyages, Brussels, 1978, p. 33.
10. Daphné Bolz, loc. cit.
11. Paul Dietschy, op. cit., p. 172.
12. Cited in Daphné Bolz, loc. cit.
13. Cited in Pascal Boniface, *La Terre est ronde comme un ballon. Géopolitique du football*, Seuil, Paris, 2002, p. 33.
14. Christian Hubert, op. cit., p. 34.
15. *Il Piccolo di Trieste*, 3 June 1934.
16. *Berliner Tageblatt*, 11 June 1934, cited in Fabio Chisari, '"Une organisation parfaite": la Coupe du monde de football de 1934 selon la presse européenne', in Yvan Gastaut and Stéphane Mourlane (eds.), *Le*

Football dans nos sociétés. Une culture populaire 1914–1998. Autrement, Paris, 2006, pp. 174–189.
17. Cited in *Miroir du football*, no. 130, May 1970.
18. Jules Rimet, *L'Histoire merveilleuse de la Coupe du monde*, René Kister, Geneva, 1954, p. 98.
19. Paul Dietschy, 'Le sport italien entre modernité et fascisme', in Georges Bensoussan et al. (ed.), op. cit., pp. 73–89.
20. David Goldblatt, *The Ball is Round. A Global History of Football*, Penguin Books, London, 2007, p. 323.
21. Ibid.
22. Cited in Stéphane Mourlane, 'Le jeu des rivalités franco-italiennes des années 1920 aux années 1960', in Yvan Gastaut and Stéphane Mourlane (eds.), op. cit.
23. James Riordan, *Sport in Soviet Society. Development of Sport and Physical Education in Russia and the USSR*, Cambridge University Press, New York, 1977, p. 106.
24. André Gounot, 'Le sport travailliste européen et la *fizkul'tura* soviétique [...]', loc. cit.
25. Ibid.
26. Cited in Robert Edelman, *Serious Fun. A History of Spectator Sports in the USSR*, New York Oxford University Press, New York, 1993, p. 55.
27. Paul Dietschy, op. cit., p. 213.
28. Cited in Robert Edelman, op. cit., p. 46.
29. Ibid., p. 48.
30. Ibid., p. 47.
31. *Krasnyi Sport*, 23 November 1938.
32. Robert Edelman, op. cit., p. 54.
33. Ibid., p. 48.
34. Robert Edelman, 'Le Football sous Staline. Le Spartak au Goulag, 1937–1945', in Georges Bensoussan et al. (ed.), op. cit., pp. 134–145.
35. Ibid.
36. Robert Edelman, 'A small way of saying "no". Moscow working men, Spartak soccer, and the Communist Party, 1900–1945', *The American Historical Review*, vol. 107, no. 5, December 2002, pp. 1441–1474.
37. Robert Edelman, 'Le Football sous Staline [...]', loc. cit.
38. Cited in Paul Dietschy, op. cit., p. 210.
39. Robert Edelman, 'A small way of saying "no"', loc. cit.
40. Robert Edelman, *Serious Fun. A History of Spectator Sports in the USSR*, op. cit., p. 70.
41. Cited in Robert Edelman, 'A small way of saying "no"', loc. cit.
42. Ibid.
43. Simon Kuper, *Football against the Enemy*, Orion, London, 1994, p. 46.

44. Nikolai Starostine, *Futbol skvoz gody*, Sovetskaya Rossiya, Moscow, 1989, p. 83.
45. Victor Peppard and James Riordan, *Playing Politics: Soviet sport diplomacy to 1992*, Jai Press, Greenwich (Connecticut), 1993, pp. 120–121.
46. Robert Edelman, 'A small way of saying "no"', loc. cit.
47. Ibid.
48. Robert Edelman, *Serious Fun* [...], op. cit., p. 72.
49. Robert Edelman, 'Le Football sous Staline [...]', loc. cit.
50. Ibid.
51. Nikolai Starostine, op. cit., pp. 80–81.
52. Cited in James Riordan, 'The Strange Story of Nikolai Starostin, Football and Lavrentii Beria', *Europe-Asia Studies*, vol. 46, no. 4, 1994.
53. Teresa González-Aja, 'Le sport dans l'Espagne franquiste', *International Review on Sport & Violence*, no. 6, *Sport et totalitarisme*, pp. 5–21.
54. Cited in David Goldblatt, op. cit., p. 304.
55. Duncan Shaw, *Fútbol y franquismo*, Alianza Editorial, Madrid, 1987, p. 58.
56. Jean-Stéphane Duran Froix, 'Le football: le loisir par excellence des Espagnols sous le franquisme (1939 – début des années soixante)', *Les Travaux du CREC en ligne*, no. 2, 2006, pp. 40–65.
57. Raymond Carr and Juan Pablo Fusi, *Spain: Dictatorship to Democracy*, Oxford University Press, Oxford, 1980, p. 118.
58. Jean-Stéphane Duran Froix, loc. cit.
59. Michael Eaude, *Catalonia. A Cultural History. Landscapes of the imagination*, Oxford University Press, Oxford, 2008, p. 258.
60. Teresa González-Aja, loc. cit.
61. David Goldblatt, op. cit., p. 305.
62. Henry de Laguerie, *Les Catalans. Lignes de vie d'un peuple*, Ateliers Henry Dougier, Paris, 2014.
63. '1930–39. Luchando contra la historia', www.fcbarcelona.es.
64. David Goldblatt, op. cit., p. 305.
65. Jean-Stéphane Duran Froix, loc. cit.
66. Michael Eaude, op. cit.
67. Emma Kate Ranachan, *Cheering for Barça. FC Barcelona and the shaping of Catalan identity*, Thesis of Art History and Communication Studies, McGill University, Montréal, Canada, 2008.
68. Simon Kuper, op. cit. p. 87.
69. Emma Kate Ranachan, op. cit.
70. Jimmy Burns, *Barça. A People's Passion*, Bloomsbury, London, 1999, pp. 40–41.
71. Emma Kate Ranachan, op. cit.
72. Duncan Shaw, op. cit. p. 63.

73. Henry de Laguerie, op. cit.
74. Jimmy Burns, op. cit. p. 140.
75. Jean-Stéphane Duran Froix, loc. cit.
76. Alfred Wahl, *La Balle au pied, histoire du football*, Gallimard, Paris, 1995.

Chapter 7

1. Paul Dietschy, op. cit., p. 202.
2. Guillaume Robin, *Les Sportifs ouvriers allemands dans la lutte antifasciste (1919–1945)*, Doctoral Thesis in German Studies, Université Paris 3 Sorbonne Nouvelle, 2006.
3. Ibid.
4. Paul Dietschy, op. cit., p. 198.
5. Ulrich Pfeil, 'Le football allemand sous le national-socialisme', in Georges Bensoussan et al. (ed.), op. cit., pp. 117–133.
6. Merkel Udo, 'The hidden social and political history of the German football association (DFB), 1900-50', *Soccer and Society*, vol. 1, no. 2, 2007.
7. Kevin E. Simpson, *Soccer under the Swastika. Stories of Survival and Resistance during the Holocaust*, Rowman & Littlefield Publishers, Lanham, Maryland, 2016.
8. 'Much more than a game', *The Guardian*, 20 July 1999.
9. Paul Dietschy, op. cit., p. 203.
10. Ibid., p. 205.
11. Kevin E. Simpson, op. cit.
12. Daphné Bolz, loc. cit.
13. Ibid.
14. Michel Caillat, *Le Sport*, Le Cavalier bleu, Paris, 2008.
15. Cited in Johann Chapoutot, 'La Grèce et la guerre: corps et sport sous le IIIe Reich', in Georges Bensoussan et al. (ed.), op. cit., p. 114.
16. Guillaume Robin, op. cit.
17. *Die Fußball-Woche*, 17 October 1934, cited in Guillaume Robin, op. cit.
18. Cited in ibid.
19. Guillaume Robin, op. cit.
20. William L. Shirer, *Le IIIe Reich. Des origines à la chute*, Stock, Paris, 1990, p. 380.
21. David Goldblatt, op. cit., p. 258.
22. Olivier Villepreux, Samy Mouhoubi and Frédéric Bernard, *Débordements. Sombres histoires de football 1938–2016*, Anamosa, Paris, 2016, p. 43.

23. Matthias Marschik, 'Between manipulation and resistance. Viennese football in the Nazi era', *Journal of Comptemporary History*, 1999, vol. 34, no. 2, pp. 215–229.
24. David Goldblatt, op. cit., p. 312.
25. Matthias Marschik, loc. cit.
26. Olivier Villepreux, Samy Mouhoubi and Frédéric Bernard, op. cit.
27. David Goldblatt, op. cit., p. 311.
28. Karl-Heinz Schwind, *Geschichten aus einem Fußball-Jahrhundert*, Carl Ueberreuter, Vienna, 1994, p. 121.
29. Matthieu Sartre and Stéphane Siohan, 'Gol! #Ukraine2012', *Le Monde*, 15 June 2012.
30. Ibid.
31. 'Football', *Citrus* no. 1, May 2014, p. 159.
32. Matthieu Sartre and Stéphane Siohan, loc. cit.
33. David Goldblatt, op. cit., p. 328.
34. Kevin E. Simpson, op. cit.
35. David Goldblatt, op. cit., p. 328.
36. 'Much more than a game', loc. cit.
37. *Season '40–'45, Football during World War II*, Exhibition catalogue, Het Verzetsmuseum Amsterdam, 2009 (available at www. verzetsmuseum. org).
38. Kevin E. Simpson, op. cit.
39. David Goldblatt, op. cit., p. 326.
40. Simon Kuper, *Ajax, the Dutch, the War: Football in Europe during the Second World War*, Orion, London, 2003, p. 107.
41. Ibid.
42. Ibid.
43. Kevin E. Simpson, op. cit.
44. *Season '40–'45, Football during World War II*, op. cit.
45. Ibid.
46. Paul Dietschy, op. cit., p. 230.
47. Christophe Pécout and Luc Robène, 'Sport et régime autoritaire : le cas du gouvernement de Vichy (1940-1944)', *International Review on Sport & Violence*, no. 6, 2012.
48. *Éducation Générale et Sportive*, official review of the CGEGS, no. 1, January–April 1942.
49. Patrick Dubechot and Henri Ségal, op. cit.
50. Ibid.
51. Edmond Ronzevalle, *Paris 10e: Histoire, monuments et culture*, Martelle Éditions, Lyon, 1993.
52. Nicolas Kssis-Martov et al., *La FSGT*, op. cit.

53. Bernard Prêtet, *Le Monde sportif parisien: 1940–1944*, in Pierre Arnaud, Thierry Terret, Jean-Philippe Saint-Martin and Pierre Gros, *Le Sport et les Français pendant l'Occupation: 1940–1944*, vol. 1, L'Harmattan, Paris, 2002, pp. 105–118.
54. Nicolas Kssis-Martov *et al.*, *La FSGT*, op. cit.
55. Bernard Busson, *Héros du sport, héros de France*, Éditions d'Art Athos, Paris, 1947, p. 187.
56. Adrien Pécout, 'Football: le Red Star se souvient de ses résistants', *Le Monde*, 24 February 2014.

Chapter 8

1. James N. Green, 'Paradoxes de la dictature brésilienne', *Brésil(s)*, no. 5, 2014.
2. Ibid.
3. Maud Chirio and Mariana Joffily, 'La repression en chair et en os: les listes d'agents de l'État accusés d'actes de torture sous la dictature militaire brésilienne', *Brésil(s)*, no. 5, 2014.
4. Ibid.
5. Carlos Fico, 'La classe média brésilienne face au régime militaire. Du soutien à la désaffection (1964–1985)', *Vingtième Siècle*, vol. 10, no. 105, 2010.
6. Roberto da Matta 'Futebol: opio do povo vs. drama social', *Novos Estudos Cebrap*, vol. 1, no. 4, 1982.
7. Matthew Shirts, 'Sócrates, Corinthians and questions of democracy and citizenship', in Joseph L. Arbena (ed.), *Sport and Society in Latin America. Diffusion, Dependency and the Rise of Mass* Culture, Greenwood Press, Westport, 1988.
8. Francis Huertas, 'La démocratie corinthiane', *Revue La Courte échelle*, no. 10, 1999.
9. Ibid.
10. Ibid.
11. Cited in Eric Delhaye, 'Au Brésil, la crise politique réveille la Démocratie corinthiane', *So Foot*, 17 April 2016.
12. *Democracia em preto e branco. Futebol, política e rock 'n' roll*, documentary by Pedro Asbeg, 80 min, TV Zero, Miração filmes & ESPN Brasil, 2014.
13. Francis Huertas, loc. cit.
14. Ibid.
15. Cited in *Ser Campeão é Detalhe – Democracia Corinthiana*, documentary by Gustavo Forti Leitão and Caetano Biasi, 25 min, DNA Filmes, Instituto de Artes da Unicamp, 2011.

16. Alex Bellos, *Futebol. The Brazilian Way of Life*, Bloomsbury Publishing, London, 2002.
17. Gilles Dhers, 'Socrates, un Brésilien trépasse', *Libération*, 5 December 2011.
18. Francis Huertas, loc. cit.
19. Laurent Vergne, 'La démocratie corinthiane, cette parenthèse enchantée', *Eurosport*, 11 July 2014.
20. Jérôme Latta, 'Socrates et la "Démocratie corinthiane"', *Cahiers du football*, 4 December 2011.
21. David Ranc and Albrecht Sonntag, 'La "démocratie corinthiane", un exemple d'organisation créative dans le football au temps de la dictature brésilienne', *Humanisme & Entreprise*, no. 313, May–June 2013.
22. Gilles Dhers, loc. cit.
23. Cited in *Democracia em preto e branco*, loc. cit.
24. Claudette Savonnet-Guyot, 'Brésil 1984: la re-démocratisation tranquille. Chronique d'une campagne présidentielle', *Revue française de science politique*, vol. 35, no. 2, 1985, pp. 262–278.
25. *Gazeta Esportiva*, 25 May 1984.
26. Cited in *Democracia em preto e branco*, loc. cit.

Chapter 9

1. Lina Khatib and Ellen Lust, *Taking to the Streets. The Transformation of Arab Activism*, Johns Hopkins University Press, Baltimore, 2014.
2. *Soccer News and Scores*, www.espnfc.com, 23 April 2007.
3. Michel Raspaud and Monia Lachheb, 'A Centennial Rivalry, Ahly vs Zamalek: Identity and Society in Modern Egypt', in Chuka Onwumechili and Gerard Akindes (eds.), *Identity and Nation in African Football. Fans, Communities and Clubs*, Palgrave Macmillan, Basingstoke, 2014, pp. 99–115.
4. Michel Raspaud, 'Cairo Football Derby. Al Ahly-Zamalek', in John Nauright and Charles Parrish, (eds.), *Sport Around the World. History, Culture and Practice*, ABC-Clio, California, 2012, pp. 283–284.
5. Razan Baker, 'Egypt, sport and Nasserism', in John Nauright and Charles Parrish, (eds.), op. cit., p. 287.
6. Anna Zacharias, 'Only a game? Not in Egypt', *The National*, 24 June 2014.
7. Ibid.
8. Steve Bloomfield, *Africa United. Soccer, Passion, Politics, and the First World Cup in Africa*, Harper Collins, New York, 2010.
9. Alaa al-Aswany, 'Egypt's enduring passion for soccer', *The New York Times*, 16 April 2014.
10. Michel Raspaud, 'Cairo Football Derby […]', op. cit.

11. Alaa al-Aswany, loc. cit.
12. Michael Slackman, 'This Time, Egyptians Riot Over Soccer, Not Bread', *The New York Times*, 20 November 2009.
13. James M. Dorsey, 'Pitched Battles. The Role of Ultra Soccer Fans in the Arab Spring', *Mobilization. An International Journal*, vol. 17, no. 4, 2012, pp. 411–418.
14. James Montague, 'The world's most violent derby. Al Ahly v Zamalek', *The Guardian*, 18 July 2008.
15. James M. Dorsey, loc. cit.
16. Ghada Abdel Aal, *La Ronde des prétendants*, L'Aube, La Tour d'Aigues, 2012. See also Michel Raspaud and Monia Lachheb, op. cit.
17. Michel Raspaud, op. cit.
18. Amin Allal, 'Supporters ou révolutionnaires? Les ultras du Caire' (interview with Céline Lebrun), *Mouvements*, no. 78, 2014.
19. 'Interview with Ultras Ahlawy', www.ultras-tifo.net, 7 January 2008.
20. Ibid.
21. Amin Allal, loc. cit.
22. 'Interview with Ultras Ahlawy', loc. cit.
23. Amin Allal, loc. cit.
24. 'Interview with Ultras Ahlawy', loc. cit.
25. Claire Talon, 'Égypte: génération ultras', *Le Monde*, 17 October 2011.
26. Ibid.
27. Anna Zacharias, loc. cit.
28. Claire Talon, loc. cit.
29. James Montague, 'Egypt's politicised football hooligans', *Aljazeera English*, 2 February 2012.
30. James M. Dorsey, 'Soccer fans play key role in Egyptian Protests', *Bleacher Report*, 26 January 2011.
31. Saïd Aït-Hatrit, 'En privé, les ultras égyptiens se préparaient aux manifestations'. Interview with James Dorsey, *So Foot*, 3 December 2012.
32. Cited in Kelly Gene Poupore, 'New Actors in Egyptian Post-Revolutionary Politics. Soccer Hooligans', *Law School Student Scholarship*, no. 548, 2014.
33. Cited in James M. Dorsey, loc. cit.
34. Claire Talon, loc. cit.
35. Cited in 'Honneur du prolétariat', broadcast on 16 January 2016, Radio Canut, Lyon.
36. Claire Talon, loc. cit.
37. Cited in Marie-Lys Lubrano, 'Égypte: les Ultras d'Al-Ahly, gardiens de l'après-révolution à Tahrir', *Les Inrocks*, 10 December 2012.
38. Ibid.
39. Amin Allal, loc. cit.

40. Anna Zacharias, loc. cit.
41. James M. Dorsey, loc. cit.
42. Kelly Gene Poupore, loc. cit.
43. Patrick Kingsley, 'The long revolution of the Ultras Ahlawy', *Roads & Kingdoms*, November 2013.
44. Marwan Chahine, 'Nuit d'effroi à Port-Saïd', *So Foot*, 2 February 2012.
45. Marion Guénard, 'Tuerie de Port-Saïd: l'armée en accusation', *Le Figaro*, 2 February 2012.
46. Cited in 'Honneur du prolétariat', loc. cit.
47. James M. Dorsey, loc. cit.
48. '#OpEgypt: Ultras Ahlawy chanting "Oh Council of Bastards"' (available at www.youtube.com/watch?v=3XvnIOzX64I).
49. Christophe Larcher, 'Ultras contestataires', *L'Équipe Magazine*, 27 April 2013.
50. Saïd Aït-Hatrit, loc. cit.
51. AFP, 'Égypte: la justice interdit les mouvements ultras de foot', *HuffPost Maghreb*, 17 May 2015.
52. Ibid.
53. Eslam Omar, 'Egypt's Ahly apologises to police and army for "fans offence"', *Ahram online*, 27 December 2015.
54. Claire Talon, loc. cit.
55. Amin Allal, loc. cit.
56. Patrick Kingsley, loc. cit.
57. James M. Dorsey, loc. cit.
58. Patrick Kingsley, loc. cit.
59. Claire Talon, loc. cit.

Chapter 10

1. Cited in Anver Versi, 'Striking Power. Arab Football Kicks Off', *The Middle East*, March 1988, p. 10.
2. Albert Camus, 'Pourquoi je fais du théâtre?', in Œuvres complètes (1957–1959), Gallimard, Paris, 2008, p. 607.
3. Abderrahmane Zani, *Les Associations sportives d'Algérie 1867–1952*, Éditions ANEP, Alger, 2003, p. 5. Cited in Philip Dine and Didier Rey, 'Le football en Guerre d'Algérie', *Matériaux pour l'histoire de notre temps*, no. 106, 2012, pp. 27–32.
4. Cited in Philip Dine and Didier Rey, loc. cit.
5. *L'Écho d'Oran*, 30 March, 1936.
6. Philip Dine and Didier Rey, loc. cit.
7. Youssef Fatès, 'Le club sportif, structure d'encadrement et de formation nationaliste de la jeunesse musulmane pendant la période coloniale', in Nicolas Bancel, Daniel Denis and Youssef Fatès, *De l'Indochine à*

l'Algérie. La jeunesse en mouvements des deux côtés du miroir colonial 1940–1962, La Découverte, Paris, 2003, p. 157.

8. Didier Rey, 'Le temps des circulaires ou les contradictions du football colonial en Algérie (1928–1945)', *Insaniyat. Revue algérienne d'anthropologie et de sciences sociales*, Centre de recherches en anthropologie sociale et culture de l'Université d'Oran, 2007, pp. 29–45.
9. Philip Dine and Didier Rey, loc. cit.
10. Cited in Didier Rey, 'Le temps des circulaires [...]', loc. cit.
11. Philip Dine and Didier Rey, loc. cit.
12. Paul Dietschy, op. cit., p. 316.
13. Michel Nait-Challal, *Dribbleurs de l'indépendance*, Prolongations, Paris, 2008, p. 36.
14. Michaël Attali, '*Paris Match* et la fabrique sportive de la figure de l'immigré au cours des années 1950: entre naturalisation et assignation', *Migrations Société*, vol. 137, no. 5, 2011, pp. 161–176.
15. Michel Nait-Challal, op. cit., p. 118.
16. Paul Dietschy and David-Claude Kemo-Keimbou, *Le Football et l'Afrique*, EPA, Paris, 2008, p. 94.
17. 'Interview de Rachid Mekhloufi', poteaux-carres.com, 28 March 2007.
18. Cited in Olivier Villepreux, Samy Mouhoubi and Frédéric Bernard, op. cit., p. 87.
19. Ibid., p. 88.
20. 'Interview de Rachid Mekhloufi', loc. cit.
21. Michel Nait-Challal, op. cit., p. 183.
22. 'Interview de Rachid Mekhloufi', loc. cit.
23. Faouzi Mahjoub, *Le Football africain*, ABC, Paris, 1978.
24. Cited in the documentary by Awaly and Olivier Monot, *L'Aventure du football africain: naissance d'une passion*, 52 min, Caméra Lucida Productions, TV Rennes 35, Histoire, Institut national de l'audiovisuel, 2010.
25. Faouzi Mahjoub, op. cit.
26. Michel Nait-Challal, op. cit., p. 204.
27. 'Interview de Rachid Mekhloufi', loc. cit.

Chapter 11

1. Cited in Mahmoud Darwich, *La Trace du papillon – Pages d'un journal (été 2006–été 2007)*, Actes Sud, Arles, 2009.
2. James Montague, 'No place like home as Palestine redefine the meaning of winning', *The Guardian*, 28 October 2008.
3. James M. Dorsey, 'Constructing national identity. The Muscular Jew vs. the Palestinian Underdog', *RSIS Working Paper Series*, no. 290, 2015.
4. David Goldblatt, op. cit., p. 872.

5. Christophe Boltanski, 'À Gaza, le foot par la bande', *Libération*, 21–22 October 1995.
6. Daniella Peled, 'Asian Cup 2015: Palestinians hope footballers can put them on the map', *The Guardian*, 3 January 2015.
7. Benjamin Barthe, '"Match historique" en Palestine', *Le Monde*, 25 October 2008.
8. Daniella Peled, loc. cit.
9. Jean-Chistophe Collin, 'Le sport au pied du mur', *L'Équipe Magazine*, 1 September 2012.
10. Patrick Strickland, 'Palestinian soccer players tell FIFA Israel violates their "basic rights"', Aljazeera America, 20 May 2015.
11. Olivier Pironet, 'Mahmoud Sarsak, une jeunesse brisée', *La Valise diplomatique* (Les blogs du '*Diplo*'), 15 May 2013.
12. Video interview with Mahmoud Sarsak in the context of the international campaign 'Carton rouge à l'apartheid israélien', 10 April 2013 (available at www.youtube.com/watch?v=cNjHF9dixoo).
13. Dave Zirin, 'After latest incident, Israel's future in FIFA is uncertain', *The Nation*, 3 March 2014.
14. Benjamin Barthe, loc. cit.
15. Tamir Sorek, 'Palestinian nationalism has left the field. A shortened history of Arab soccer in Israel', *International Journal of Middle East Studies*, vol. 35, no. 3, 2003.
16. Issam Khalidi, 'Sports and Aspirations. Football in Palestine 1900-1948', Jerusalem Quarterly, no. 58, 2014, pp. 74–89.
17. James M. Dorsey, 'Constructing national identity', loc. cit.
18. Ibid.
19. *Filastin*, 16 April 1929, cited in Issam Khalidi, 'The coverage of sports news in *"Filastin"* 1911–1948', *Jerusalem Quarterly*, no. 44, 2010, pp. 45–69.
20. Tamir Sorek, loc. cit.
21. Issam Khalidi, loc. cit.
22. James M. Dorsey, loc. cit.
23. Benny Morris, *Victimes. Histoire revisitée du conflit arabo-sioniste*, Complexe, Bruxelles, 2003, pp. 147–153.
24. James M. Dorsey, loc. cit.
25. Ibid.
26. Ibid.
27. Elia Xureik, *The Palestinians in Israel. A Study in Internal Colonialism*, Routledge and Kegan Paul, London, 1979, pp. 130–133.
28. Tamir Sorek, loc. cit.
29. Sabri Jiryis, *The Arabs in Israel*, Institute for Palestine Studies, Beirut, 1969, p. 138.

30. Tamir Sorek, 'Le foot est, pour les Arabes d'Israël, un terrain contesté entre deux tendances', *So Foot*, 3 March 2017.
31. Tamir Sorek, loc. cit.
32. Nicolas Kssis-Martov, 'L'histoire du premier et seul France-Palestine', *So Foot*, 20 January 2015.
33. J.-E. D., 'Les Palestiniens ont joué contre le Variété', *L'Humanité*, 9 October 1993.
34. Eric Hobsbawm, *Nations et nationalisme depuis 1780*, Gallimard, Paris, 1992, p. 183.
35. James M. Dorsey, loc. cit.
36. Oz Rosenberg, 'Hundreds of Beitar Jerusalem fans beat up Arab workers in mall. No Arrests', *Haaretz*, 23 March 2012.
37. Patrick Strickland, loc. cit.
38. Cf. Omar Barghouti, *Boycott, Désinvestissement, Sanctions. BDS contre l'apartheid et l'occupation de la Palestine*, La Fabrique, Paris, 2010.
39. Patrick Strickland, loc. cit.
40. 'We call on FIFA to suspend the Israel Football Association', *The Guardian*, 15 May 2015.
41. Iyad Anou Gharqoud, 'FIFA Should Give Israel the Red Card', *The New York Times*, 28 May 2015.
42. Gershon Baskin, 'Encountering Peace. FIFA, soccer and the Palestinians', *The Jerusalem Post*, 13 May 2015.
43. Barak Ravid, 'Israel steps up diplomatic action as fears grow over FIFA Suspension', *Haaretz*, 13 May 2015.
44. Peter Beaumont, 'Palestinians withdraw call to suspend Israel from FIFA', *The Guardian*, 29 May 2015.
45. 'Israel/Palestine. FIFA Sponsoring Games on Seized Land. Israeli Settlement Football Clubs Contribute to Human Rights Violations', *Human Rights Watch*, 24 September 2016.
46. Ibid.
47. 'La FIFA sous pression après le vote de l'ONU sur les colonies israéliennes', *L'Équipe*, 29 December 2016.
48. Steven Morris, 'Protesters greet Israel in Cardiff before Euro 2016 match with Wales', *The Guardian*, 6 September 2015.
49. Rodolphe Ryo, 'Des ultras du Celtic rendent hommage à la Palestine face à un club israélien', *L'Express*, 18 August 2016.
50. 'Coupée du monde, Gaza organise son proper Mondial de football', *rfi.fr*, 15 May 2010.
51. Abaher El-Sakka, 'Supporters à distance. Les fans du Barça et du Real en Palestine', in *Jeunesses arabes. Du Maroc au Yémen: loisirs, cultures et politiques*, La Découverte, Paris, 2013, pp. 105–113.

52. Jon Donnison, 'Why Spain's greatest football match, El Clasico, matters to Palestinians', *BBC News*, 7 October 2012.
53. Ibid.
54. Cited in 'Protestations attendues suite à l'invitation VIP du soldat israélien Shalit par le FC Barcelona', www.bdsfrance.org, 28 September 2012.
55. Cited in Abaher El-Sakka, loc. cit.
56. 'Gazans stage soccer protest at Israeli Shalit's Barcelona visit', *Reuters*, 7 October 2012.

Chapter 12

1. Eduardo Galeano, *Football in Sun and Shadow*, tr. Mark Fried, Penguin, London, 2018.
2. José Sergio Leite Lopes and Jean-Pierre Faguer, 'L'invention du style brésilien. Sport, journalisme et politique au Brésil', *Actes de la recherche en sciences sociales*, vol. 103, no. 1, June 1994.
3. Ibid.
4. Clément Astruc, 'Le métier de footballeur: origines, ascension sociale et condition des joueurs brésiliens des années 1950 à 1980', *Cahiers des Amériques latines*, no. 74, 2013.
5. Olivier Guez, Éloge de l'esquive, Grasset, Paris, 2014.
6. Cited in Marcelin Chamoin, 'Football et racisme, le Brésil fête aujourd'hui le jour de la conscience noire', *Lucarne opposée*, lucarne-opposee.fr, 20 November 2016.
7. Ibid.
8. José Sergio Leite Lopes and Jean-Pierre Faguer, loc. cit.
9. Eduardo Galeano, op. cit.
10. José Sergio Leite Lopes and Jean-Pierre Faguer, loc. cit.
11. Cited in Paul Dietschy, op. cit., p. 257.
12. Ibid., p. 258.
13. Eduardo Galeano, op. cit.
14. Mauricio Murad, 'Um ícone chamado Pelé', *Caravelle*, no. 98, 2012, pp. 171–182.
15. Paul Dietschy, op. cit., p. 259.
16. Cited in Astolfo Cagnacci, *Pays du foot. Une passion et des styles*, Autrement, Paris, 1998, p. 73.
17. Mário Filho, *O negro no futebol brasileiro*, Mauad X, Rio de Janeiro, 2003.
18. *Correio da Manhã*, 15 June 1938.
19. Cited in Paul Dietschy, op. cit., p. 263.
20. Eduardo Galeano, op. cit.

21. Alex Bellos, 'Au Brésil, le sombre destin des gardiens noirs', *Libération*, 1 July 2006.
22. Hubert Artus, *Donqui Foot, Dictionnaire rock, historique et politique du football*, Don Quichotte, Paris, 2011, p. 46.
23. David Goldblatt, op. cit., pp. 368–369.
24. Mauricio Murad, loc. cit.
25. David Goldblatt, op. cit., p. 370.
26. Ibid., p. 371.
27. Ruy Castro, *Garrincha. The Triumph and Tragedy of Brazil's Forgotten Footballing Hero*, Yellow Jersey, London, 2004, p. 101.
28. *The Times*, 30 June 1958.
29. Marcelin Chamoin, 'Pelé, une histoire auriverde', *Lucarne opposée*, lucarne-opposee.fr, 3 August 2016.
30. *The Times*, loc. cit.
31. Andreas Campomar, *Golazo! A History of Latin American Football*, Quercus, London, 2014, p. 252.
32. Florent Dupeu, 'Des Indiens sous le Maracanã', *Les Cahiers du football*, 7 May 2012.
33. Olivier Guez, op. cit.
34. Cited in *L'Orient littéraire*, July 2014.
35. 'Matériaux pour une histoire politique du dribble', Les Cahiers d'Oncle Fredo, onclefredo.wordpress.com.
36. *Caros Amigos*, July 2012.
37. João Sette Whitaker, 'Salve a Seleção! Les villes brésiliennes et la Coupe du monde de football 2014', *Cahiers des Amériques latines*, no. 74, 2013.
38. Ibid.
39. Ravi Tala, 'La Coupe du monde n'aura pas lieu', *CQFD*, June 2014.
40. Ibid.
41. Cited in the documentary by Alexandre Bouchet, *Les Aigles de la forêt*, 52 min, Kwanza and Yemaya Productions, France Télévisions, 2014.
42. Ibid.
43. Ibid.
44. Cited in Nicolas Cougot, 'Mushuc Runa, quand les indigènes utilisent le football pour gagner en reconnaissance', *Lucarne oposée*, lucarne-opposee.fr, 26 October 2014.
45. Cited in Francesco Martino, 'Il Mundialito nell'Amazzonia peruviana. Dove il calcio è una gran fiesta', *Zona Cesarini*, zonacesa-rini.net, 18 March 2016.
46. Subcomandante Marcos, 'Tribulations poétiques d'un footballeur sur la défensive', *Le Monde*, 20 June 1998.
47. Guillermo Aramburo, 'Où sont les Indiens?', *Le Monde Diplomatique*, May 1994, p. 24.

48. 'Otro futbol es posible. Zapatistas FC (Parte I)', *Futbol rebelde*, www.futbolrebelde.org, 12 April 2016.
49. Sophie Arie and Jo Tuckman, 'Soccer stars support guerrillas', *The Guardian*, 19 October 2004.
50. *BBC News*, 20 December 2004.
51. Paco Ignacio Taibo II and Subcomandante Marcos, tr. Carlos López, *The Uncomfortable Dead*, Serpent's Tail, London, 2007.
52. Ibid., p. 37.
53. Kristine Vanden Berghe, 'Goooaal. La politique du football dans Des morts qui dérangent (2006) par le sous-commandant Marcos et Paco Ignacio Taibo II', *Amerika. Territories*, no. 1, 2010.
54. Extract from the 'First declaration of La Realidad for humanity and against neoliberalism', *https://schoolsforchiapas.org/library/1st-declaration-la-realidad-humanity-neoliberalism/*, 1996.

Chapter 13

1. Nicolas Bancel and Jean-Marc Gayman, op. cit., p. 332.
2. *L'Éducation physique aux colonies*, École supérieure d'éducation physique, Imprimerie de l'école, Joinville-le-Pont, 1931, cited in Jacques Dumont, 'Joinville et l'éducation physique aux colonies dans les années 1930', *Staps*, vol. 71, no. 1, 2006, pp. 85–97.
3. Sergent (Cdt), *L'Éducation physique au service de la colonisation*, École supérieure d'éducation physique, Joinville-le-Pont, 1937, cited in Jacques Dumont, loc. cit.
4. Peter Alegi, *African Soccerscapes. How a Continent Changed the World's Game*, Ohio University Press, Athens, 2010, p. 3.
5. Nicolas Bancel and Jean-Marc Gayman, op. cit.
6. Pierre de Coubertin, *Essais de psychologie sportive*, Payot & Cie, Lausanne, 1913, p. 237.
7. Pierre de Coubertin, 'Les sports et la colonisation', *Revue olympique*, January 1912.
8. David Goldblatt, op. cit., p. 491.
9. Paul Darby, *Africa, Football, and FIFA. Politics, Colonialism, and Resistance*, Routledge, Oxford, 2002, p. 12.
10. Peter Alegi, op. cit.
11. Cited in Paul Dietschy, 'Du sportsman à l'histrion: les cultures sportives de trois leaders africains (Nnamdi Azikiwe, Nelson Mandela et Joseph-Désiré Mobutu)', *Histoire@Politique*, vol. 23, no. 2, 2014.
12. Ibid.
13. François Dupaire, 'Sport et colonisation. Le cas du Congo belge (1950-1960)', *Bulletin de l'Institut Pierre Renouvin*, no. 16, Autumn 2003.

14. Catherine Coquery-Vidrovitch, 'De la nation en Afrique noire', *Le Débat*, no. 84, March–April 1995, p. 128.
15. Bernadette Deville-Danthu, 'Le développement des activités sportives en Afrique occidentale française: un bras de fer entre sportifs et administration coloniale (1920–1956)', *Revue française d'histoire d'outre-mer*, vol. 85, no. 318, 1st quarter 1998.
16. Nicolas Bancel and Jean-Marc Gayman, op. cit., p. 337.
17. Bernadette Deville-Danthu, *Le Sport en noir et blanc. Du sport colonial au sport africain dans les anciens territoires français d'Afrique occidentale (1920–1965)*, op. cit., pp. 250–252.
18. Bernadette Deville-Danthu, 'Le développement des activités sportives en Afrique occidentale française', loc. cit.
19. Paul Dietschy, *Histoire du football*, op. cit., p. 312.
20. Frederick Cooper, *Décolonisation et travail en Afrique. L'Afrique britannique et française 1935–1960*, Karthala, Paris, 2004, p. 213.
21. Nicolas Bancel and Jean-Marc Gayman, op. cit., p. 329.
22. *La Dernière Heure*, 20 June 1953, cited in François Durpaire, loc. cit.
23. *Le Moustique*, 21 June 1953, cited in ibid.
24. François Durpaire, loc. cit.
25. *Le Courrier d'Afrique*, 17 June 1957, cited in ibid.
26. François Durpaire, loc. cit.
27. David Goldblatt, op. cit., p. 488.
28. Ibid., p. 489.
29. Paul Darby, op. cit., p. 26.
30. Ossie Stuart, 'The lions stir. Football in African society', in Stephen Wagg (ed.), *Giving the Game Away. Football, Politics and Culture on Five Continents*, Leicester University Press, Leicester, 1995, pp. 24–51.
31. Paul Dietschy, 'Du sportsman à l'histrion', loc. cit., pp. 123–141.
32. Ibid.
33. Peter Alegi, op. cit., p. 39.
34. Ibid., p. 40.
35. Wiebe Boer, 'Football, mobilization and protestation. Nnamdi Azikiwe the goodwill tours of World War II', *Lagos Historical Review*, vol. 6, 2006.
36. Paul Dietschy, 'Du sportsman à l'histrion', loc. cit.
37. Cited in the documentary by Awa Ly and Olivier Monot, *L'Aventure du football africain*, op. cit.
38. Paul Darby, 'Football, colonial doctrine and indigenous resistance. Mapping the political persona of FIFA's African constituency', *Culture, Sport, Society*, vol. 3, no. 1, 2000.
39. David Goldblatt, op. cit., p. 488.

40. Peter Alegi, '"Amathe Nolimi" (it is saliva and the tongue): contracts of joy in South African football c. 1940–76', *International Journal of the History of Sport*, vol. 17, no. 4, December 2000.
41. Bernard Magubane, *Sport and Politics in an Urban African Community. A Case Study of African Voluntary Organisations*, M.Sc. Thesis, University of Natal, 1963, p. 53.
42. Paul Dietschy and David-Claude Kemo-Keimbou, *Le Football et l'Afrique*, EPA, Paris, 2008, p. 218.
43. Cited in ibid., p. 220.
44. Peter Alegi and Chris Bolsmann, 'From Apartheid to Unity. White capital and Black power in the racial integration of South African football, 1976–1992', *African Historical Review*, vol. 42, no. 1, 2010.
45. Jean-Baptiste Onana, 'Le sport sud-africain entre déclin et renaissance, raisons d'un relatif recul', *Outre-Terre*, vol. 3, no. 8, 2004.
46. David Goldblatt, op. cit., p. 497.
47. Peter Alegi and Chris Bolsmann, loc. cit.
48. David Goldblatt, op. cit., p. 498.
49. Chuck Korr and Marvin Close, *More Than Just a Game. Football v Apartheid*, Collins, New York, 2008.
50. Denis Müller, 'Pulsion de victoire et passion de justice. Un petit coup de projecteur trois ans avant les Championnats du monde de football en Afrique du Sud (2010)', *Revue d'éthique et de théologie morale*, vol. 4, no. 247, 2007.
51. 'L'Afrique du Sud reconnaît avoir versé 10 millions de dollars à la FIFA', *lemonde.fr*, 31 May 2015.

Chapter 14

1. James Walvin, op. cit., p. 80.
2. Ibid., p. 79.
3. Rogan Taylor, *Football and its Fans. Supporters and their relations with the game 1885–1985*, Leicester University Press, Leicester, 1992, p. 8.
4. Patrick Mignon, 'Supporters et hooligans en Grande-Bretagne depuis 1871', *Vingtième Siècle*, vol. 26, no. 1, April–June 1990.
5. Sean Ingle and Mark Hodgkinson, 'When did football hooliganism start?', *The Guardian*, 13 December 2001.
6. Eric Dunning and Patrick Murphy, 'Working class social bonding and the socio-genesis of football hooliganism', *SSRC Report*, 1982, p. 43.
7. Steve Frosdick and Peter Marsh, *Football Hooliganism*, Willan Publishing, London, 2005.
8. Patrick Mignon, *La Passion du football*, Odile Jacob, Paris, 1998, p. 102.
9. Sean Ingle and Mark Hodgkinson, loc. cit.

10. John Hutchinson, 'Some aspects of football crowds before 1914', *The Working Class*, University of Sussex Conference Report, 1975.
11. Patrick Mignon, op. cit., p. 106.
12. James Walvin, op. cit., p. 123 and 139.
13. Eric Dunning, Joseph Maguire, Patrick Murphy and John Williams, 'The social roots of football hooliganism', *Leisure Studies*, vol. 1, no. 2, 1982.
14. Richard Holt, *Sport and the British. A Modern History*, Oxford University Press, Oxford, 1989, p. 334.
15. Patrick Mignon, op. cit., p. 108.
16. Ibid., p. 98.
17. Ian Taylor, '"Football Mad". A speculative sociology of soccer hooliganism', in Eric Dunning (ed.), *The Sociology of Sport*, Franck Cass, London, 1971, pp. 353–377.
18. James Walvin, op. cit., p. 165.
19. Alain Ehrenberg, *Le Culte de la performance*, Hachette, « Pluriel », Paris, 1991, p. 57.
20. Patrick Mignon, op. cit., p. 146.
21. Paul Dietschy, *Histoire du football*, op. cit., p. 477.
22. Sean Ingle and Mark Hodgkinson, loc. cit.
23. Steve Frosdick and Peter Marsh, op. cit.
24. Richard Holt, op. cit.
25. Patrick Mignon, op. cit., p. 116.
26. Richard Holt, op. cit.
27. Eric Dunning, Patrick Murphy and John Williams, *The Roots of Football Hooliganism*, Routledge, Oxford, 1988, p. 172.
28. Bill Buford, *Among the Thugs*, Martin Secker & Warburg, London, 1991, p. 29.
29. Philippe Broussard, *Génération Supporter. Enquête sur les ultras du football*, So Press, Paris, 2011, p. 42.
30. Bill Buford, op. cit., p. 63.
31. Patrick Mignon, op. cit., p. 118.
32. Stuart Hall, 'The treatment of football hooliganism in the press', in Roger Ingham (ed.) *Football Hooliganism. The Wider Context*, Interaction in Print, London, 1978.
33. Alain Ehrenberg, op. cit., p. 59.
34. Ibid., p. 60.
35. Peter Marsh, *Aggro. The Illusion of Violence*. Dent, London, 1978.
36. Cited in Patrick Mignon, op. cit., p. 117.
37. Ibid., p. 125.
38. Steve Frosdick and Peter Marsh, op. cit.
39. Patrick Murphy, Eric Dunning and John Williams, 'Soccer crowd disorder and the press. Processes of amplification and de-amplification

in historical perspective', *Theory, Culture and Society*, vol. 5, no. 4, 1988, pp. 645–673.

40. Eric Dunning, Patrick Murphy and John Williams, op. cit.
41. Merrill J. Melnick, 'The mythology of football hooliganism. A closer look at the British experience', *International Review for the Sociology of Sport*, vol. 21, no. 1, 1986.
42. *Daily Mirror*, 4 April 1977.
43. *Public Disorder and Sporting Events: a report*, Sports Council and the Social Science Research Council, London, 1978.
44. Eugene Trivizas, 'Offences and offenders in football crowd disorders', *British Journal of Criminology*, vol. 20, no. 3, 1980.
45. Steve Frosdick and Peter Marsh, op. cit.
46. *Le Monde*, 23 November 2016.
47. Philippe Broussard, op. cit., p. 45.
48. Cited in 'Le Kop d'Anfield Road: vie et mort d'une tribune populaire', *Les Cahiers d'Oncle Fredo* (<onclefredo.wordpress.com>), 30 July 2016.
49. *Os Cangaceiros*, no. 2, November 1985, pp. 78-79.
50. Patrick Mignon, 'La violence dans les stades supporters, ultras et hooligans', *Actes des entretiens de l'INSEP, Les Cahiers de l'INSEP*, no. 10, 1995.
51. Jon Garland and Mike Rowe, 'Racism at work. A study of professional football', *The International Journal of Risk, Security and Crime Prevention*, vol. 1, no. 3, 1996.
52. Alain Ehrenberg, op. cit., p. 59.
53. Cécile Collinet, Denis Bernardeau Moreau and Julien Bonomi, 'Le *Casual*, un nouveau genre de hooligan. Loin du stade et de la police', *Les Annales de la recherche urbaine*, no. 105, 2008.
54. Ibid.
55. Jamie Cleland and Ellis Cashmore, 'Football fans' views of violence in British football: evidence of a sanitized and gentrified culture', *Journal of Sport and Social Issues*, vol. 40, no. 2, 2016, pp. 124–142.
56. Max Clos, 'Éditorial', *Le Figaro*, 30 May 1985.
57. Cited in David Goldblatt, op. cit., p. 598.
58. Jamie Cleland and Ellis Cashmore, loc. cit.
59. Steve Frosdick and Peter Marsh, op. cit.
60. Richard Hayes, *The Football Imagination. The Rise of Football Fanzine Culture*, Arena, London, 1995.
61. Nicolas Hourcade, Ludovic Lestrelin and Patrick Mignon, *Livre vert du supportérisme. État des lieux et propositions d'actions pour le développement du volet préventif de la politique de gestion du supportérisme*, Secrétariat d'État aux Sports, Paris, 2010, p. 65.
62. Steve Frosdick and Peter Marsh, op. cit.

63. Manuel Comeron, 'Hooliganisme: la délinquance des stades de football', *Déviance et société*, vol. 21, no. 1, 1997.
64. 'Hard luck stories', *When Saturday Comes*, no. 114, August 1996.
65. David Conn, 'The Premier League has priced out fans, young and old', *The Guardian*, 16 August 2011.
66. Kevin Quigagne, '20.2.1992: naissance de la Premier League', *Teenage Kicks* (Blog), *Les Cahiers du football*, 20 February 2012.
67. 'Price of Football: Full results 2015', BBC News, 14 October 2015.
68. Nicolas Hourcade, Ludovic Lestrelin and Patrick Mignon, op. cit.
69. Adrian Tempany, 'How football lost touch with its young fans', *The Guardian*, 8 March 2014.
70. Kevin Quigagne, loc. cit.
71. Nicolas Hourcade, Ludovic Lestrelin and Patrick Mignon, op. cit.
72. *Football and Football Hooliganism*, Sir Norman Chester Centre for Football Research, University of Leicester, Fact Sheet no. 1, January 2001.
73. Jacques Besnard, 'Cass Pennant, ex-hooligan: "On ne naît pas violent"', *Rue89*, 7 July 2013.
74. *Football and Football Hooliganism*, op. cit.
75. 'Londres: la réaction anglaise aux violences entre supporters à Marseille', *France info*, 12 June 2016.
76. Ruth Mosalski, 'Facial recognition software will be used on anyone in Cardiff for the Champions League final', (walesonline.co.uk), 27 April 2017.
77. John King, Football Factory, Points, Paris, 2006, p. 87.

Chapter 15

1. Paul Dietschy, 'The Superga disaster and the death of the "Great Torino"', *Soccer and Society*, vol. 2, no. 2, 2004, pp. 298–310.
2. Ibid.
3. Hubert Artus, op. cit., p. 409.
4. *Tuttosport*, 10 November 1951, cited in Paul Dietschy, *Histoire du football*, op. cit., p. 472.
5. Paul Dietschy, 'The Superga disaster [...]', loc. cit.
6. Paul Dietschy, *Histoire du football*, op. cit., p. 473.
7. Ibid.
8. Fabien Archambault, 'La violence des *ultrà* au tournant des années 1970: une violence politique?', *Storicamente*, no. 10, 2014.
9. Alessandro Dal Lago and Rocco De Biasi, 'Italian Football Fans: culture and organization', in Richard Giulianotti, Norman Bonney and Mike Hepworth (eds.), *Football, Violence and Social Identity*, Routledge, London, 1994.

10. Ibid.
11. Nanni Balestrini and Primo Moroni, *La Horde d'or. Italie 1968–1977. La grande vague révolutionnaire et créative, politique et existentielle*. L'Éclat, Paris, 2017.
12. Ibid.
13. Fabien Archambault, loc. cit.
14. Alessandro Dal Lago and Rocco De Biasi, op. cit.
15. Paul Dietschy, *Histoire du football*, op. cit., p. 474.
16. Cited in Christian Bromberger, Alain Hayot and Jean-Marc Mariottini, *Le Match de football. Ethnologie d'une passion partisane à Marseille, Naples et Turin*, Éditions de la Maison des sciences de l'homme, Paris, 1995, p. 51.
17. Cited in Alessandro Dal Lago and Rocco De Biasi, op. cit.
18. Citation taken from the documentary by Andrea Zambelli, *Farrebero tutti silenzio*, Malamela Productions, 28 min., 2011.
19. Marc Lazar and Marie-Anne Matard-Bonucci (eds.), *L'Italie des années de plomb. Le terrorisme entre histoire et mémoire*, Autrement, Paris, 2010, p. 6.
20. Fabien Archambault, loc. cit.
21. Philippe Broussard, op. cit., p. 132.
22. Cited in Daniele Segre, *Ragazzi di stadio*, Gabriele Mazzotta, Milan, 1979, p. 21.
23. Ibid., p. 30.
24. Paolo Sollier, *Calci e sputi e colpi di testa. Riflessioni autobiografiche di un calciatore per caso*, Gammalibri, Milan, 1976.
25. Valerio Marchi, 'Italia 1900–1990: dal supporter all'ultrà', in *Ultrà: Le sottoculture giovanili negli stadi d'Europa*, Koinè, Rome, 1994, p. 202.
26. Alessandro Dal Lago and Roberto Moscati, *Regalateci un sogno. Miti e realtà del tifo calcistico in Italia*, Bompiani, Milan, 1992, p. 118.
27. Fabien Archambault, loc. cit.
28. Alessandro Dal Lago and Rocco De Biasi, op. cit.
29. Sébastien Louis, *Ultras, les autres protagonistes du football*, Mare et Martin, Paris, 2017, p. 61.
30. *So Foot* hors-série no. 5, Winter 2012, Spécial Supporters, p. 112.
31. Daniele Segre, op. cit., p. 30.
32. Ibid., p. 36.
33. Fabien Archambault, loc. cit.
34. Ibid.
35. Ibid.
36. Nanni Balestrini and Toni Negri, 'En Italie, une amnistie politique qui ne passe pas', *Libération*, 18 May 2004.
37. Daniele Segre, op. cit., p. 125.

38. Sébastien Louis, *Le Phénomène ultras en Italie*, Mare & Martin, Paris, 2008.
39. Philippe Broussard, op. cit., p. 131.
40. Christian Bromberger, Alain Hayot and Jean-Marc Mariottini, op. cit., pp. 46–47.
41. Philippe Broussard, op. cit., p. 167.
42. Sébastien Louis, op. cit.
43. Christian Bromberger, Alain Hayot and Jean-Marc Mariottini, op. cit., p. 300.
44. Ibid.
45. Ibid., p. 66.
46. Ibid., pp. 24–26.
47. Nicolas Hourcade, 'La place des supporters dans le monde du football', *Pouvoirs*, no. 101, 2002.
48. Christian Bromberger, Alain Hayot and Jean-Marc Mariottini, op. cit., p. 43.
49. Jean-Michel Faure, 'Le sport et la culture populaire: pratiques et spectacles sportifs dans la culture populaire', *Les Cahiers du LERSCO*, no. 12, 1990.
50. Paul Bartolucci, *Sociologie des supporters de football. La persistance du militantisme sportif en France, Allemagne et Italie*, Doctoral Thesis in sociology, University of Strasbourg, 2012.
51. Christian Bromberger, Alain Hayot and Jean-Marc Mariottini, op. cit., p. 32.
52. Antonio Roversi, 'The birth of the "ultras". The rise of football hooliganism in Italy', in Richard Giulanotti and John Williams (eds.), *Game without Frontiers. Football, Identity and Modernity*, Arena, Aldershot, 1994; Alessandro Dal Lago and Roberto Moscati, op. cit., p. 118.
53. Alessandro Dal Lago and Rocco De Biasi, op. cit.
54. Ibid.
55. Citation taken from the documentary by Andrea Zambelli, op. cit.
56. Antonio Roversi, loc. cit.
57. Nicolas Hourcade, loc. cit.; Alessandro Dal Lago and Rocco De Biasi, op. cit.
58. Ibid.
59. Nicolas Hourcade, Ludovic Lestrelin and Patrick Mignon, op. cit., p. 88.
60. Citation taken from the documentary by Andrea Zambelli, op. cit.
61. Piero Calabrò, 'La violenza negli stadi: approccio storico e risposte normative', *Altalex*, 26 November 2013.
62. Tobias Jones, 'Inside Italy's ultras: the dangerous fans who control the game', *The Guardian*, 1 December 2016.

63. Nicolas Hourcade, Ludovic Lestrelin and Patrick Mignon, op. cit., p. 89.
64. Matthew C. Guschwan, 'La Tessera della Rivolta: Italy's failed fan identification card', *Soccer & Society*, vol. 14, no. 2, 2013.
65. Nicolas Hourcade, Ludovic Lestrelin and Patrick Mignon, op. cit., p. 89.
66. Paul Bartolucci, op. cit.
67. Matthew C. Guschwan, loc. cit.
68. 'Gli ultras dicono "no" alla tessera del tifoso', *Giornale di Sicilia*, 24 July 2010.
69. 'Boys. Cancellieri, elimini la tessera del tifoso', *La Repubblica*, 16 November 2011.
70. Cited in Roberto Stracca, 'Tessera del tifoso: i tifosi doriani scrivono al presidente della Samp', Blog *Dentro lo stadio*, *Corriere della Sera*, 2 August 2010.

Chapter 16

1. Eduardo P. Archetti, 'The spectacle of a heroic life. The case of Diego Maradona', in David L. Andrews and Steven J. Jackson (eds.), *Sport Stars. The Cultural Politics of Sporting Celebrity*, New York, Routledge, 2001, pp. 151–163.
2. Ibid.
3. Bartlomiej Brach, 'Who is Lionel Messi? A comparative study of Diego Maradona and Lionel Messi', International Journal of Cultural Studies, vol. 15, no. 4, 2012.
4. Ibid.
5. Julio D. Frydenberg, 'Football à grand spectacle et identification de quartier à Buenos Aires', *Cahiers des Amériques latines*, no. 74, 2014.
6. Bartlomiej Brach, loc. cit.
7. Ibid.
8. Vittorio Dini, 'Maradona, héros napolitain', *Actes de la recherche en sciences sociales*, vol. 3, no. 103, June 1994.
9. *Le Monde*, 24 August 1989, cited in Christian Bromberger, Alain Hayot and Jean-Marc Mariottini, op. cit., p. 137.
10. Matías Baldo, 'México 86: el día que los futbolistas usaron la guerra de Malvinas como una motivación', *La Nación*, 23 June 2016.
11. Hubert Artus, op. cit., p. 266.
12. Thomas Goubin, 'Main de Dieu et but du siècle: ce que vous ignoriez sur le jour où Maradona est entré au Panthéon', *Eurosport*, 22 June 2016.
13. Ibid.

14. Olivier Bras, 'Maradona. Le mythe du divin démon a vingt ans', *Courrier international*, 14 April 2009.
15. Bartlomiej Brach, loc. cit.
16. Eduardo P. Archetti, loc. cit.
17. Alexandre Juillard, 'Le but diabolique du dieu argentin', *L'Équipe Magazine*, 20 May 2006.
18. Eduardo P. Archetti, loc. cit.
19. Cited in Nathaniel Nash, 'Argentina is booming but there is no rest for its tortured soul', *The New York Times*, 17 July 1994.
20. Ksenija Bilbija, 'Maradona's left. Postmodernity and national identity in Argentina', *Studies in Latin American Popular Culture*, vol. 14, 1995.
21. Jorge Luis Borges, 'Notre pauvre individualisme', in *Œuvres complètes*, book 1, Gallimard, La Pléiade, Paris, 1993, p. 698.
22. Christian Bromberger, Alain Hayot and Jean-Marc Mariottini, op. cit., p. 142.
23. Marino Niola, 'San Gennarmando le disavventure del símbolo', in Vittorio Dini and Oscar Nicolaus, *Te Diegum*, Milan, Leonardo, 1991.
24. Vittorio Dini, loc. cit.
25. Ibid.
26. *Clarín*, 3 September 1994, cited in Eduardo P. Archetti, loc. cit.
27. Vittorio Dini, loc. cit.
28. Ibid.
29. Eduardo P. Archetti, loc. cit.
30. Mempo Giardinelli, 'El video del adios', *Noticias de la semana*, 3 July 1994, cited in Ksenija Bilbija, loc. cit.
31. Bartlomiej Brach, loc. cit.
32. Eduardo P. Archetti, *Masculinities. Football, Polo and Tango in Argentina*, Berg, Oxford, 1999, p. 184.
33. 'Diego Armando Maradona: El "Pibe de Oro" cumple 55 años', *El Universo*, 30 October 2015.
34. Ksenija Bilbija, loc. cit.
35. Jonathan Franklin, 'He was sent from above', *The Guardian*, 12 November 2008.
36. Diego Borinsky, '7,000 Adeptos en México, Llegó la Iglesia Maradoniana', *Milenio* supplement, no 20, August 2007.
37. Ibid.
38. Jonathan Franklin, loc. cit.
39. Rupert Howland-Jackson, 'La Iglesia Maradoniana. Argentina's real religion?', *The Argentina Independent*, 1 December 2008.

Chapter 17

1. 'En Turquie, des manifestants de la place Taksim condamnés à des peines de prison', *Le Monde*, 23 October 2015.

2. Personal interview with the monthly *CQFD*: 'Football populaire *vs* foot business', June 2014.
3. Personal interview, ibid.
4. James M. Dorsey, 'Government and fans battle in court and on the pitch in Egypt and Turkey', *Centre for Policy and Research on Turkey*, vol. 4, no. 1, London, January 2015.
5. Elif Batuman, 'The view from the stands', *The New Yorker*, 7 March 2011.
6. Dağhan Irak, 'Istanbul United? Le supportérisme comme lutte culturelle et résistance au pouvoir politique en Turquie', in Thomas Busset and William Gasparini (eds.), *Aux frontières du football et du politique*, Peter Lang Academic Publishers, Berne, 2016.
7. Personal interview, ibid.
8. Ibid.
9. Elif Batuman, loc. cit.
10. Personal interview, ibid.
11. Elif Batuman, loc. cit.
12. Personal interview, ibid.
13. Elif Batuman, loc. cit.
14. James M. Dorsey, loc. cit.
15. 'Turkey: football fans on trial for "coup"', Human Rights Watch, 15 December 2014.
16. 'Çarşı' dan açıklama: la biz size n'ettik?', *Cumhuriyet*, 16 December 2014.
17. 'Çarşı' darbeye karşı', *Cumhuriyet*, 17 December 2014.
18. Hay Eytan Cohen Yanarocak, 'The last stronghold. The Fenerbahçe Sports Club and Turkish politics', *Tel Aviv Notes, An Update to Middle Eastern Developments*, vol. 6, no. 10, 28 May 2012.
19. Gokan Gunes, 'Qui veut la peau du Besiktas?', *So Foot*, 4 October 2013.
20. Rico Rizzitelli, 'Le football turc en coupe réglée', *Libération*, 13 February 2017.
21. Ibid.
22. Personal interview, ibid.
23. Ibid.
24. James M. Dorsey, loc. cit.
25. Ibid.
26. 'Turquie': Erdogan contre les supporters du Besiktas Istanbul, un match inamical', *L'Obs*, 18 April 2016.
27. James M. Dorsey, 'Turkish soccer pitches tell the story of hardening fault lines', *The Huffington Post*, 21 March 2016.

Chapter 18

1. Revue EP&S, no. 117, September–October 1972, cited in Loïc Bervas, 'Le MFP ou la révolte des amateurs, Épisode 4', *Miroir du football* (www.miroirdufootball.com), 30 November 2015.
2. François-René Simon, Alain Leiblang and Faouzi Mahjoub, *Les Enragés du football. L'autre Mai 68*, Calmann-Lévy, Paris, 2008.
3. Alfred Wahl, op. cit.
4. Raymond Kopa and Paul Katz, *Mon football*, Calmann-Lévy, Paris, 1972.
5. Cited in Nicolas Jucha, 'Raymond Kopa, un destin qui dépasse le football', *So Foot*, 23 May 2016.
6. Floréal Hernandez, 'Quand la FFF était occupée […]', *Le Journal du Dimanche*, 1 May 2008.
7. François Thébaud, *Le Temps du 'Miroir'. Une autre idée du football et du journalisme*, Albatros, Paris, 1982.
8. *Le Miroir du football*, August 1973, cited in 'Le Foot-business par François Thébaud réactualisé', *Miroir du football* (www.miroirdufootball.com), 25 February 2015.
9. François-René Simon, Alain Leiblang and Faouzi Mahjoub, op. cit.
10. Jean Norval, *Des années de braise aux années* […] *de pèze*, Auto-édition, 2001.
11. Ibid.
12. François-René Simon, Alain Leiblang and Faouzi Mahjoub, op. cit.
13. Floréal Hernandez, loc. cit.
14. Alfred Wahl, 'Le mai 68 des footballeurs français', *Vingtième Siècle*, no. 26, April–June 1990.
15. François-René Simon, Alain Leiblang and Faouzi Mahjoub, op. cit.
16. Ibid.
17. *France-Football*, 11 June 1968.
18. Jean Norval, op. cit.
19. François-René Simon, Alain Leiblang and Faouzi Mahjoub, op. cit.
20. Ibid.
21. Floréal Hernandez, loc. cit.
22. *France-Football*, 18 June 1968.
23. *France-Football*, 11 June 1968.
24. Floréal Hernandez, loc. cit.
25. François-René Simon, Alain Leiblang and Faouzi Mahjoub, op. cit.
26. Ibid.
27. Floréal Hernandez, loc. cit.
28. Ibid.
29. Alfred Wahl, loc. cit.
30. François-René Simon, Alain Leiblang and Faouzi Mahjoub, op. cit.

31. Loïc Bervas, *Christian Gourcuff, un autre regard sur le football*, Liv' éditions, coll. 'Documents et témoignages', Le Faouët, 2013.
32. Loïc Bervas and Bernard Gourmelen, *Le Mouvement Football Progrès et la revue Le Contre-Pied. Un combat des footballeurs amateurs, 1970–1980*, L'Harmattan, Paris, 2016.
33. Ibid.
34. Ibid.
35. *Le Miroir du Football*, January 1975, cited in Loïc Bervas, 'Le MFP ou la révolte des amateurs, troisième partie, Épisode 10', *Miroir du football* (www.miroirdufootball.com), 26 December 2015.
36. François-René Simon, Alain Leiblang and Faouzi Mahjoub, op. cit.
37. Loïc Bervas and Bernard Gourmelen, op. cit.
38. Ibid.
39. *Le Miroir du Football*, January 1975, loc. cit.
40. Nicolas Kssis-Martov, 'Mai 68: gazon maudit!', *So Foot*, May 2008.
41. Nicolas Kssis-Martov et al., *La FSGT: Du sport rouge au sport populaire*, op. cit.
42. *Sport et plein air*, no. 561, June 2012.
43. Ibid.
44. Henri Seckel, 'Le football est un sport qui se joue à sept', *Le Monde*, 28 April 2012.

Chapter 19

1. Laurence Prudhomme-Poncet, *Histoire du football féminin au xxe siècle*, L'Harmattan, Paris, 2003, p. 25.
2. Alfred Wahl, op. cit., p. 126.
3. André Drevon, Alice Milliat. *La Pasionaria du sport féminin*, Vuibert, Paris, 2005, p. 31.
4. Françoise Thébaud, 'La Grande Guerre. Le triomphe de la division sexuelle', in Georges Duby and Michèle Perrot (eds.), *Histoire des femmes, le xxe siècle*, book 5, Plon, Paris, 1992.
5. Georges Hébert, *L'Éducation physique féminine. Muscle et Beauté plastique*, Vuibert, Paris, 1919.
6. *La Vie féminine*, 3 March 1918, cited in Xavier Breuil, op. cit., p. 49.
7. *L'Auto*, 1 December 1921, cited in Laurence Prudhomme-Poncet, op. cit., p. 57.
8. *La Française*, 11 June 1921, cited in ibid., p. 105.
9. Wendy Michallat, 'Terrain de lutte. Women's Football and Feminism in "Les années folles"', *French Cultural Studies*, vol. 18, no. 3, 2007.
10. Cited in Xavière Gauthier, *Naissance d'une liberté. Contraception, avortement : le grand combat des femmes au xxe siècle*, Robert Laffont, Paris, 2002, p. 44.

11. Alice Milliat, 'Considérations générales', *Bulletin des sociétés féminines françaises de sports et gymnastique*, October–November 1920.
12. Philippe Tissié, *L'Éducation physique et la race: santé, travail, longévité*, Flammarion, Paris, 1919, p. 3.
13. Tim Tates, op. cit., p. 193.
14. Laurence Prudhomme-Poncet, op. cit., p. 70 and 140.
15. Cited in ibid., pp. 104, 106.
16. Ibid., p. 102.
17. Cited in Wendy Michallat, loc. cit.
18. Ibid.
19. Maurice Pefferkon, *Le Football association. Théorie et pratique du jeu de football*, Flammarion, Paris, 1921, pp. 288–289.
20. *L'Éducation physique et sportive féminine*, 1 December 1923, cited in Laurence Prudhomme-Poncet, op. cit., p. 127.
21. Xavier Breuil, op. cit., p. 99.
22. Wendy Michallat, loc. cit.
23. Cited in Laurence Prudhomme-Poncet, op. cit., p. 136.
24. Ibid., p. 119.
25. Ibid., p. 134.
26. Wendy Michallat, loc. cit.
27. Cited in Xavier Breuil, op. cit., p. 141.
28. Ibid., p. 142.
29. Cited in Laurence Prudhomme-Poncet, op. cit., p. 144.
30. Cited in Xavier Breuil, op. cit., p. 121.
31. *L'Auto*, 12 September 1928, cited in Laurence Prudhomme-Poncet, op. cit., p. 65.
32. *Le Sport suisse*, 21 November 1928, cited in ibid.
33. Franz Vandersmissen, *Le Sport ouvrier*, op. cit.
34. Ulrich Pfeil, *Football et identité: en France et en Allemagne*, Presses universitaires du Septentrion, Villeneuve-d'Ascq, p. 188.
35. *Kicker*, 25 March 1957, cited in Xavier Breuil, op. cit., p. 174.
36. *France Football*, 23 February 1965, cited in ibid., p. 169.
37. Laurence Prudhomme-Poncet, op. cit., p. 190.
38. *France Foot 2*, 5 January 1979.
39. Remarks taken from 'Les filles de Reims, premières footballerines en équipe de France', *L'Heure du documentaire*, *France Culture*, 30 July 2012.
40. Laurence Prudhomme-Poncet, op. cit., p. 192.
41. Vera Botelho, Bente Ovedie Skogvang, 'The pioneers. Early years of the Scandinavian emigration of women footballers', *Soccer & Society*, vol. 14, no. 6, 2013.
42. Paul Dietschy, op. cit., p. 504.

43. Christine Mennesson, 'La gestion de la pratique des femmes dans deux sports "masculins": des formes contrastées de la domination masculine', *Staps*, vol. 63, no. 1, 2004.
44. Mathieu Pélicaet, 'Football féminin. Michèle Carado, la pionnière', *Le Télégramme*, 3 June 2016.
45. 'Annie Fortems, pionnière de l'Étoile sportive de Juvisy', *50/50 Magazine*, 3 August 2012.
46. Anthony Hernandez, 'Foot féminin: sur les traces des pionnières rémoises', *Le Monde*, 8 February 2015.
47. *Miroir-Sprint*, 22 September 1970.
48. Remarks taken from 'Les filles de Reims [...]', loc. cit.
49. Xavier Breuil, op. cit., p. 258.
50. Laurence Prudhomme-Poncet, op. cit., p. 274.
51. 'Annie Fortems, pionnière de l'Étoile sportive de Juvisy', loc. cit.
52. Xavier Breuil, op. cit., p. 187; Laurence Prudhomme-Poncet, op. cit., p. 257.
53. Maxime Travert and Hélène Soto, 'Une passion féminine pour une pratique masculine: le football', *Sociétés*, vol. 103, no. 1, 2009.
54. Cited in Laurence Prudhomme-Poncet, op. cit., p. 261.
55. Ibid.
56. Laurence Prudhomme-Poncet, op. cit., p. 252.
57. Christine Mennesson, loc. cit.
58. Xavier Breuil, op. cit., p. 274.
59. Quentin Girard, 'Football féminin: "en France, on ne veut pas s'identifier aux femmes"', *Libération*, 12 July 2011.
60. Emmanuelle RIchard, 'Aux États-Unis, certaines l'aiment rond', *Libération*, 12 July 1999.
61. FIFA, *Enquête sur le football féminin. Rapport de synthèse*, 2014, p. 17.
62. 'Bini: "La popularité des Bleues est une sorte de phénomène sociologique"', *Le Monde*, 17 July 2011.
63. Christine Mennesson, 'Le gouvernement des corps des footballeuses et boxeuses de haut niveau', *Clio. Femmes, genre, histoire*, no. 23, 2006; and Annie Fortems, 'Le football féminin face aux institutions: maltraitance et conquêtes sociales', *Mouvements*, vol. 78, no. 2, 2014, pp. 90–94.
64. Marie Kirschen, 'Foot féminin: sport ou concours de miss?', i-d.vice.com, 28 October 2015.
65. Nicolas Kssis-Martov, '"Il vaut mieux être un gars qui perd qu'une fille qui gagne". Entretien avec Béatrice Barbusse', *So Foot*, 23 November 2016.
66. Mark Landler, 'World Cup Brings Little Pleasure to German Brothels', *The New York Times*, 3 July 2006.

67. Audrey Keysers and Maguy Nestoret Ontanon, *Football féminin. La femme est l'avenir du foot*, Le Bord de l'eau, Lormont, 2012, p. 25.
68. 'Foot For Freedom', *Radio Campus Paris*, 1 June 2016.
69. 'Foot For Freedom, du foot pour lutter contre les préjugés', (*Paris.fr*), 7 June 2016.
70. Cf. their columns: Les Dégommeuses, 'Est-ce de ce football que nous voulons?', *Mediapart*, 16 March 2017 and Les Dégommeuses, 'Le sexisme toujours pas hors jeu', *L'Équipe*, 7 June 2015.
71. Citation taken from *Les Dégommeuses, footballeuses militantes*, documentary film by Emily Vallat and Assia Khalid, *France Culture*, 'Sur les docks', 2 December 2014.
72. Anthony Hernandez, loc. cit.

Chapter 20

1. Richard Foster, 'What does the Northampton Town case teach us about fans' role in football clubs?', *The Guardian*, 16 October 2015.
2. Jim Keoghan, *Punk Football. The Rise of Fan Ownership in English Football*, Pitch Publishing, Durrington, 2014, p. 71.
3. Ibid., p. 72.
4. Richard Foster, loc. cit.
5. Christophe Boltanski, 'Liverpool: le blues du supporter prolétaire', *Libération*, 28 June 2002.
6. Jim Keoghan, op. cit., p. 78.
7. Ibid., p. 36.
8. Ibid., pp. 37–38.
9. Christophe Boltanski, 'Des clubs anglais privés de leur télé vache à lait', *Libération*, 29 March 2002.
10. Jim Keoghan, op. cit., p. 37.
11. Nick Moore, 'We shout about it being shit, but we are the owners', *FourFourTwo*, December 2014, pp. 66–69.
12. Jim Keoghan, op. cit., p. 116.
13. Ibid., p. 103.
14. *AFC Wimbledon – Case Studies*. Supporters Direct, www.supporters-direct.org.
15. Jim Keoghan, op. cit., p. 97.
16. Ibid., p. 99.
17. Adam Brown, '"Not For Sale"? The destruction and reformation of football communities in the Glazer takeover of Manchester United', *Soccer & Society*, vol. 8, no. 4, October 2007.
18. Steve Wilson, 'Glazer family ownership of Manchester United: timeline', *The Telegraph*, 14 August 2010.
19. Jim Keoghan, op. cit., p. 66.

20. Alban Traquet, 'Les dissidents du FC United', *Le Journal du dimanche*, 16 October 2005.
21. David Conn, 'The Premier League has priced out fans, young and old', *The Guardian*, 16 August 2011.
22. Yann Bouchez, 'This is United', *So Foot*, Hors-série no. 5, Winter 2012.
23. Jim Keoghan, op. cit., pp. 144–145.
24. 'The Manifesto. Who we are and what we mean', www.fc-utd.co.uk.
25. Adam Brown, loc. cit.
26. Adam Brown, '"Our club, our rules": fan communities at FC United of Manchester', *Soccer & Society*, vol. 9, no. 3, July 2008.
27. Yann Bouchez, loc. cit.
28. Adam Brown, '"Our club, our rules": fan communities at FC United of Manchester', loc. cit.
29. Jim Keoghan, op. cit., p. 149.
30. Yann Bouchez, loc. cit.
31. Ibid.
32. Jim White, 'How FC United rose to the brink of the big time', *The Telegraph*, 15 April 2015.
33. Yann Bouchez, loc. cit.
34. David Conn, 'FC United of Manchester: the success story that proves what fans can achieve', *The Guardian*, 26 May 2015.
35. Romain Molina, 'Les supporters propriétaires de leur club: un modèle britannique', *Barré*, http://barremag.info, no. 1, Spring 2015.
36. David Conn, 'Football mourns Brian Lomax, the founding father of supporter activism', *The Guardian*, 2 November 2015.

Chapter 21

1. Mick Totten, 'Sport activism and political praxis within the FC Sankt Pauli fan sub-culture', *Soccer & Society*, vol. 16, no. 4, 2015.
2. Carles Viñas and Natxo Parra, *St. Pauli. Otro fútbol es posible*, Capitán Swing, Madrid, 2017.
3. 'Supporters clubs', www.fcstpauli.com.
4. 'Guiding principles', www.fcstpauli.com.
5. Petra Daniel and Christos Kassimeris, 'The politics and culture of FC St. Pauli: from leftism, through anti-establishment, to commercialization', *Soccer & Society*, vol. 14, no. 2, 2013.
6. Nick Davidson, *Pirates, Punks & Politics*, SportsBooks, York, 2014, p. 27.
7. Ulrich Pfeil, 'Le football allemand sous le national-socialisme', in Georges Bensoussan et al. (ed.), op. cit., p. 125.

8. René Martins, 'Here to stay with St Pauli', in Mark Perryman, *Hooligan Wars: Causes and Effects of Football Violence*, Mainstream Sports, Edinburgh, 2001, pp. 179–190.
9. Nick Davidson, op. cit., p. 80.
10. René Martins, loc. cit.
11. Cited in 'FC St. Pauli. Zwischen Mythos und Realität', *Vice Sports*, 20 mins., 2015.
12. Nick Davidson, op. cit., p. 73.
13. René Martins, loc. cit.
14. Cited in 'FC St. Pauli. Zwischen Mythos und Realität', op. cit.
15. Petra Daniel and Christos Kassimeris, loc. cit.
16. Renaud Dely, 'Sankt Pauli, très à gauche du terrain', *Libération*, 7 September 1998.
17. Nick Davidson, op. cit., p. 76.
18. Ibid., p. 98.
19. Udo Merkel, 'Football fans and clubs in Germany. Conflicts, crises and compromises', *Soccer & Society*, vol. 13, no. 3, 2012.
20. Nick Davidson, op. cit., p. 96.
21. Gabriel Kuhn, *Soccer vs The State. Tackling Football and Radical Politics.* PM Press, Oakland, California, 2011, pp. 136–140.
22. Nick Davidson, op. cit., pp. 124–125.
23. Renaud Dely, loc. cit.
24. Ibid.
25. Cited in 'FC St. Pauli. Zwischen Mythos und Realität', op. cit.
26. Petra Daniel and Christos Kassimeris, loc. cit.
27. Cited in 'FC St. Pauli. Zwischen Mythos und Realität', op. cit.
28. Mick Totten, loc. cit.
29. Cited in 'FC St. Pauli. Zwischen Mythos und Realität', op. cit.
30. Cited in Gabriel Kuhn, op. cit., p. 115.
31. Mick Totten, loc. cit.
32. Hubert Artus, 'Sankt Pauli l'autre modèle allemand', *Marianne*, 8 August 2015.
33. 'Banderole sexiste à Sankt Pauli', *So Foot*, 30 January 2017.
34. Gabriel Kuhn, op. cit.
35. 'G20 Summer Schedule (Hamburg)', alerta-network.org, 25 June 2017.

Chapter 22

1. Renée Greusard and Julien Duriez, 'Au Sénégal, le foot qui passionne, c'est celui des quartiers', *Le Nouvel Observateur*, 16 October 2011.

2. Papa Alioune Sow, 'Coups et contrecoups du "navétane" dans le développement du football au Sénégal', *Langues et Littératures*, no. 18, Université Gaston Berger, Saint-Louis, Senegal, January 2014.
3. Susann Baller, 'Urban football performances. Playing for the neighbourhood in Senegal, 1950s–2000s', *Africa: The Journal of the International African Institute*, vol. 84, no. 1, February 2014.
4. Gérard Salem, *La Santé dans la ville. Géographie d'un petit espace dense: Pikine (Sénégal)*, Karthala, Paris, 1998.
5. Susann Baller, 'Transforming urban landscapes. Soccer fields as sites of urban sociability in the agglomeration of Dakar', *African Identities*, vol. 5, no. 2, 2007.
6. Cited in Susann Baller, loc. cit.
7. Ibid.
8. Françoise Blum, 'Sénégal 1968: révolte étudiante et grève générale', *Revue d'histoire moderne et contemporaine*, no. 59-2, 2012.
9. Susann Baller, 'Urban football performances', loc. cit.
10. Tado Oumarou and Pierre Chazaud, *Football, religion et politique en Afrique. Sociologie du football africain*, L'Harmattan, Paris, 2010.
11. Papa Alioune Sow, loc. cit.
12. Cited in Marc Vernière, *Dakar et son double Dagoudane Pikine*, Comité des travaux historiques et scientifiques, Bibliothèque nationale, Paris, 1977, p. 211.
13. Susann Baller, 'Urban football performances', loc. cit.
14. Ibid.
15. *Le Soleil*, 18 September 1970, cited in Susann Baller, 'Urban football performances', loc. cit.
16. Cited in Olivier Monlouis, *Navétanes. La Mousson des Champions*, documentary film, 26 mins., Idé Prod Production, 2002.
17. Ibid.
18. Susann Baller, 'Urban football performances', loc. cit.
19. Ibid.
20. Christophe Gleizes and Barthélemy Gaillard, 'Le meilleur tournoi de foot au monde se tient au Sénégal', *Vice Sports*, 7 February 2017.
21. 'Futebol é "maior paixão" para 77% dos brasileiros, aponta pesquisa Ibope', *O Globo*, 17 December 2012.
22. Cited in Laurent Rigoulet, 'L'art du dribble ou comment les Brésiliens ont transcendé le foot', *Télérama*, 16 June 2014.
23. Alexsander Batista e Silva and Eguimar Chaveiro, 'O jogo de bola: uma análise socioespacial dos territórios dos peladeiros', *Silva*, no. 10, vol. 1, 2007.

24. Jorge Hideo Tokuyochi, *Futebol de rua: uma rede de sociabilidade.* Masters Dissertation, Escola de Educação Física e Esporte, Universidade de São Paulo, 2006, p. 48.
25. Cited in Alex Miranda, *Pelada. Futebol na Favela*, documentary film, Trator Filmes, 98 mins, São Paulo, 2013.
26. Cited in Sam Borden, 'Pickup Soccer in Brazil Has an Allure All Its Own', *The New York Times*, 18 October 2013.
27. Jorge Hideo Tokuyochi, op. cit., p. 23.
28. Hérika Dias, 'Cai o número de brasileiros que joga futebol no lazer', *Agência USP de Notícias*, 21 August 2014.
29. Jorge Hideo Tokuyochi, op. cit., p. 37.
30. Ibid.
31. Alex Miranda, op. cit.
32. Jeré Longman, 'Brazil's Other Beautiful Games', *The New York Times*, 6 July 2014.
33. Ibid.
34. Cited in Alex Miranda, op. cit.
35. Ibid.
36. Henri Seckel, loc. cit.
37. Gilles Vieille Marchiset, 'La construction sociale des espaces sportifs ouverts dans la ville. Enjeux politiques et liens sociaux en question', *L'Homme et la société*, vol. 165–166, no. 3, 2007.
38. Jean-Charles Basson and Andy Smith, 'La socialisation par le sport, revers et contre-pied: les représentations sociales du sport de rue', *Les Annales de la recherche urbaine*, no. 79, 1998.
39. Pascal Chantelat, Michel Fodimbi and Jean Camy, 'Les groupes de jeunes sportifs dans la ville', *Les Annales de la recherche urbaine*, no. 79, 1998.
40. Maxime Travert, 'Le "football de pied d'immeuble": Une pratique singulière au cœur d'une cité populaire', *Ethnologie française*, no. 27, April–June 1997.
41. Ibid.
42. Christophe Mauny and Christophe Gibout, 'Le football "sauvage": d'une autre pratique à une pratique autrement […]', *Mouvement & Sport Sciences*, no. 63, 2008.
43. Ibid.
44. Maxime Travert, loc. cit.
45. Cited in Jesse Adang and Syrine Boulanouar, *Ballon sur bitume*, documentary film, 52 mins, Yard, 2016.
46. Maxime Travert, loc. cit.
47. Cited in Jesse Adang and Syrine Boulanouar, op. cit.
48. Maxime Travert, loc. cit.

49. Cited in Jesse Adang and Syrine Boulanouar, op. cit.
50. Jean Griffet and Maxime Travert, 'La distinction footballistique', *Libération*, 18 June 1998.
51. Maxime Travert, loc. cit.
52. Cited in Jesse Adang and Syrine Boulanouar, op. cit.
53. Ibid.
54. Jean-Charles Basson, 'Sports de rue et politiques sportives territoriales', in Catherine Louveau and Anne-Marie Wazer (eds.), *Sport et cité. Pratiques urbaines, spectacles sportifs*, Presses universitaires de Rouen, Rouen, 1999.
55. Gilles Vieille Marchiset, loc. cit.
56. Pascal Chantelat, Michel Fodimbi and Jean Camy, *Sports de la cité, anthropologie de la jeunesse sportive*, L'Harmattan, Paris, 1996.
57. Jean-Charles Basson and Andy Smith, loc. cit.
58. Cited in Jesse Adang and Syrine Boulanouar, op. cit.
59. Barthélemy Gaillard, 'Dans le San Siro du 9-5', *Vice Sports*, 21 March 2017.
60. Cited in Jesse Adang and Syrine Boulanouar, op. cit.
61. 'Clichy-sous-Bois: le destin tragique de Zyed et Bouna', *Le Parisien*, 16 March 2015.
62. Mathieu Habasque, 'Non, Clichy-sous-Bois n'est pas une "no-goal zone"', *Vice Sports*, 26 October 2015.
63. Maxime Brigand, 'Benzema: "Je ne suis pas dans une compétition"', *So Foot*, 7 September 2017.
64. Jean-Louis Ivani, 'Splendeurs et misère du "fast-foot"', *Le Monde diplomatique*, September 1996.
65. Tom Pakinkis, 'Interview. FIFA Street: "The first true quality street football experience"', computerandvideogames.com, 24 October 2011.
66. Cited in Jesse Adang and Syrine Boulanouar, op. cit.

Postscript

1. 'US soccer star slams sport's leadership for how it invests in women', *CNN*, 26 May 2019.
2. Emily Caron, 'Megan Rapinoe won't visit White House if USWNT wins 2019 World Cup', *Sports Illustrated*, 29 May 2019.
3. Marius Lien and Lars Johnsen, 'Miss selfishness?', *Josimar*, 7 June 2019.
4. Adrien Franque, 'Ce mondial 2019 restera comme féministe', *Libération*, 7 July 2019.
5. The song title refers to the presidential palace in the Algiers district of El-Mouradia, as well as to *La casa de papel* (Money Heist), a Spanish television series about a band of professional thieves.

6. Mickaël Correia, 'En Algérie, les stades contre le pouvoir', *Le Monde Diplomatique*, May 2019.
7. Ibid.
8. 'Guedioura: "Cette Coupe est un peu notre Hirak"', *Dzfoot.com*, 20 July 2019.
9. The name and badge of the club refer to a chief of the Mapuche resistance to Spanish colonisation in the 16th century.

Acknowledgements

I would particularly like to thank Lico for his valuable help with research and for his wise advice during the writing of this book. My gratitude also goes to my fellow travellers from CQFD and Jef Klak for their kind support, as well as to Julia Zortea and Mathieu Léonard. A huge thank you also to my friends, my family and especially to Lo for providing encouragement.

For their time or providing access to their work, my thanks to Paul Dietschy, Xavier Breuil, Nicolas Kssis-Martov, Guillaume Robin, Nicola Hudson of Supporters Direct, Claude Boli, Jean-Bruno Tagne, Bernard Gourmelen, Loïc Bervas, Giulia Delfini, Pascal Bordes, Nicolas Barré of the FIFA Museum, Olivier Monlouis, the ultras Çarşı, the members of FC United of Manchester and FC Sankt Pauli, the Dégommeuses.

This book is dedicated to my late father, in memory of our afternoons on the pitch at the Étoile sportive mouvalloise.

People's History

History tends to be viewed from the perspective of the rich and powerful, where the actions of small numbers are seen to dictate the course of world affairs. But this perspective conceals the role of ordinary women and men, as individuals or as parts of collective organisations, in shaping the course of history. The People's History series puts ordinary people and mass movements centre stage and looks at the great moments of the past from the bottom up.

The People's History series was founded and edited by William A. Pelz (1951–2017).

Also available:

A People's History of Tennis
David Berry

A People's History of Catalonia
Michael Eaude

A People's History of the Russian Revolution
Neil Faulkner

Long Road to Harpers Ferry
The Rise of the First American Left
Mark A. Lause

A People's History of the German Revolution, 1918–19
William A. Pelz
Foreword by Mario Kessler

A People's History of Modern Europe
William A. Pelz

A People's History of the Portuguese Revolution
Raquel Varela

A People's History of Europe
From World War I to Today
Raquel Varela

Index

For topics related to foothall, *see* the topic, e.g. co-operative clubs; racism; women's football. *n* refers to a note

Aal, Ghada Abdel *I Want to Get Married!* 138
Abbas, Ferhat 153, 160, 160*n*, 163
Adidas Company 385
Africa 42–3, 204–19
see also specific countries
African Cup of Nations 212, 213, 215, 368, 390
African National Congress (ANC) 217–8
Agnelli family 248, 256, 258
Aguirre, Javier 199
AIDS epidemic 356
Ajax Amsterdam FC 117–8
Al Ahly SC 134–8, 140–2
Al Masry FC 146, 147
Al-Sissi, Marshal Abdel Fattah 148, 149
Alberto, Carlos 182
Alcock, Charles W. 35
Algeria 137, 139, 153–63, 388–90
Ali, Mohamed 192
Allam, Mohamed 162, 163
Almond, Hely Hutchinson 26
Alves, Adilson Monteiro 125–7, 129, 133
Amado, Jorge 130
Amerindians 194–203
anti-colonial movements 208–19
Anti-Comintern Pact (1937) 86
anti-fascist movements 72–7, 87, 254–8, 266–7, 353
anti-Semitism 87, 105–6, 117, 120, 266
anti-World Cup campaign 272*n*
Arab Palestine Sports Federation (APSF) 169, 170
Arab Revolt (1936-39) 169–70
Arab-Israeli War (1948) 165, 171
Arafat, Yasser 165
Argentina 185, 271–83
Arnold, Thomas 24–5
Arpinati, Leandro 82
Arribi, Mokhtar 158, 160
Arsenal FC 32, 242
Aru, Paulo 196
AS Roma 72, 82, 260, 261
Aston Villa FC 31, 224, 243
Astor, Nancy 55
Atatürk, Mustapha Kemal 288
Athletic Bilbao FC 43, 97, 98*n*, 274
Atlético Celaya FC 201
Austria 110–3
Auto, L' 53, 85, 87, 318, 322
Autonomen (anarchist group) 356–7, 359
Autonomia Operaia 254
Azikiwe, Nnamdi 210–1, 212
Azzurri FC 83, 84–6, 87

Bafana-Bafana FC 219
Bala'c, Peta 218
Balestrini, Nanni 251
Bamako, Mali 208

Bancel, Nicolas 208
Bandung Conference (1955) 208
Bangerter, Hans 239
Bangu AC 182
Barbosa, Moacir 187–8, 188*n*
Barbusse, Béatrice 335, 389
Barcelona FC 1, 43, 98, 99, 100–3, 178–80
Baskin, Gershon 175
Basto, Guilherme Pinto 44
Beatles, The 355–6
Beckenbauer, Franz 385
Beckham, David 385
Beitar Jerusalem FC 174
Belgian Congo 206, 209
Bell's Life in London 33, 35
Ben Ali, Zine El Abidine 143
Ben Arfa, Hatem 384
Ben Bouali, Abdelkader 154
Ben Tifour, Abdelaziz 158, 159
Bennaceur, Ali 276, 276*n*
Benouna, Ali 154
Benzema, Karim 384–5
Berger, John 175
Beria, Lavrentiy 94–5
Berlusconi, Silvio 264, 266
Beşiktaş FC 284–8, 296
Best, George 229
'bicycle kick' 185
Biko, Steve 218
Bini, Bruno 334
Black Stars FC 212
Blackburn Olympic 36–7
Blatter, Sepp 167, 279
Blaugranas see Barcelona FC
Bleus, Les FC 310, 334, 334*n*
Boca Juniors FC 272, 272*n*
Boll, Fabian 362
Bolsonaro, Jair 392
Boomsma, Rein 118
Booth, William 31
Borges, Jorge Luis *Our Poor Individualism* 278
Bosio, Edoardo 43
Bosman, Jean-Marc 264*n*
Botafogo FC 183, 192
Bouadjadj, Zoubir 390
Bouazizi, Mohamed 142
Boubekeure, Abderrahmane 157, 163
Bouchouk, Abdelhamid 157, 158
Boulogne, Georges 300, 304, 306, 307, 310, 312
Boumezrag, Mohamed 157, 158, 160
Bourdieu, Pierre 30
Bouteflika, Abdelaziz 389, 390
Bouvier, Father 205
Boy de la Tour, Nathalie 336*n*
Brahimi, Saïd 158, 159
Bravo, Claudio 391
Brazil 4, 123–33, 181–97, 374–8, 392
Breuil, Xavier 333
Britain 4, 17–29, 30–44, 225
  see also England; Scotland
British colonialism 41–2, 209
British Ladies' Football Club 47–9
British Union of Fascists 236
Brittan, Leon 239
'broken time' payments 37
Brux, Sven 356, 358
BSkyB 243, 341, 346
Buarque, Chico 124, 130, 192, 374
Buford, Bill *Among the Thugs* 230
Burumbo, Benjamin 210

Caballero, Ernesto Giménez 97
Camp Nou stadium 101–2
Camus, Albert 153
Cantona, Eric 30, 167
caracoles 200*n*
Carado, Michèle 329

Carreras, Narcís de 102
Çarşi Ultras 284–91, 294–5
Carvalhaes, João 189–90
Casagrande, Walter 126, 128, 130, 131–3
'casuals' 237–8, 246
Catalonia 97–8, 100–3, 178–9
Catanzaro FC 257–8
catenaccio tactic 299–300, 300*n*, 303
Catholic Church 15–16, 60–2, 68, 205, 322
Chabri, Hassan 158
Chiapas, Mexico 197–9, 201, 203
Chiarisoli, Antoine 306, 309
Chile 390–1
Chomsky, Noam 175
church football clubs 31–2
Cicek, Ferhat 380, 381, 386
Clarendon Commission (1864) 26
Clarke, Emma 49
Club athlétique socialiste (CAS) 71
Club Atlético Peñarol 42
co-operative clubs 339–40, 342–52
Coalition Against Trafficking in Women 335
Colo-Colo FC 391–2
Combi, Giampiero 83
'combination game' 35
Combined Counties League 345
Comintern 74, 76
Commandos Rossoblu 254, 256
company clubs 63–6
Confédération Générale du Travail (CGT) 66, 315
Confederation of African Football (CAF) 212, 215
Contre-Pied, Le 315
Copa Kaiser Tournament 377
Coquery-Vidrovitch, Catherine 207
Corinthians FC 41–2, 125, 127–33
Coubertin, Pierre de 61, 63, 108, 205, 206, 325
'criollo' style 272–3, 277
Cruyff, Johan 102–3, 367
CSKA Moscow FC 90, 91–2, 94
Cucchiaroni, Tito 270

Daily Express 234
Daily Mail 57
Daily Mirror 234, 238
Daily Sketch 47, 48
Daily Telegraph 33
Dakar 208, 367–9, 372
Dauchy, Jo 315–6
Davutoğlu, Ahmet 294
De Volewijckers FC 118, 119
Dégommeuses FC 336–7
Delaunay, Pierre 300, 305, 306, 309, 326
Delegación National de Deportes (DND) 96, 97
della Negra, Rino 122
Dembélé, Ousmane 384
Deschamps, Didier 336
Desgrange, Henri 323
Deutscher Fußball-Bund (DFB) 104, 105
Dick, Kerr Ladies team 51–4, 57–8, 321
Didi (Vinicius José Ignacío) 190, 191
Digiturk Media Group 293, 294
Diretas Já movement 131, 132
Dixie, Florence 47, 48
Domínguez, Maribel 201
Dons Trust 344–5, 351
Dorsey, James M. 138, 150
Douis, Yvon 309
Drew, Bryan 245
'dribbling game' 25, 27, 34, 182–3, 277
Dugauguez, Louis 300, 303
Duringer, Marilou 330
Dynamo Kyiv FC 113

Dzerzhinsky, Felix 73

Easton Cowgirls and Cowboys FC 177, 200
Eberhard, Generalmajor Kurt 113, 114
Ecuador 196–7
Egypt 134–50
Eini, Ofer 176
Elias, Norbert 15, 16
Emkachkhines 138–9
En Avant! FC 53, 318
England 14, 223–46
English Civil War (1642-46) 17–19
Erdoğan, Recep Tayyip 284, 291–2, 294
Espérance Sportive de Tunis FC 138, 142
Ethiopia, invasion by Italy of 86
Eton College 22, 23–4, 25, 26, 36
European Championship (Euro 96) 243, 245, 303–4
Evian Accords (1962) 163
Exeter City FC 'Grecians' 341–2

Factory Act (1850) 30
Falk, Richard 167
Falklands Conflict (1982) 275–6, 277
fanladen (fan stores) 360–1
Fanon, Frantz 204
fanzines 241–2, 348
Farndone, Nicholas, Lord Mayor of London 9
Farouk I, King of Egypt 138
fascist movements 236, 358
Fatès, Youcef 389
Fausto (Fausto dos Santos) 183–4
Fedelissimi Granata 249–50
Fédération des sociétés féminines sportives de France (FSFSF) 318–9, 321, 323, 325
Fédération française de football-association (FFA) 63, 319
Fédération gymnastique et sportive des patronages de France (FGSPF) 61–2, 205
Fédération Internationale de Football Association (FIFA) 2, 3, 61, 83, 86, 160, 161–3, 165, 168, 174–7, 201, 213, 215, 218–9, 385, 388
Fédération sportive athlétique socialiste (FSAS) 68, 70, 71
Fédération sportive du travail (FST) 69, 70, 73
Fédération Sportive et Gymnique du Travail (FSGT) 77, 120, 173, 316
Fémina Sport FC 53, 318, 323, 325
Fenerbahçe SK 285–6, 291–2
Ferdinand, Rio 347
Ferrari, Giovanni 83
Fiat Company 65, 248, 251, 256
FIFA see Fédération Internationale de Football Association
Figueiredo, General João 124
Firm, The (film) 246
Flamengo FC 183, 184
folha seca (dry leaf) 190
Fontaine, Just 161, 301, 309
football
  class attitudes to 61–3, 223–4
  films and novels about 245–6, 273, 350*n*
  history of 4, 9–21
  rules of 3, 25–9
  seven-a-side matches 315–7
  street football 378–86
  as a working-class sport 4–5, 33, 36, 68–9
Football Association (FA) 27–40, 54–5

Football Association Cup (FA Cup) 29, 37–8, 55, 226
Football Factory, The (film) 246
football fans
behaviour of 224, 228–33
demonising of 233–5
Football League 33–4, 38–40, 54–5, 234, 341–2
Football Offences Act (1991) 240
Football Spectators Act (1989) 240, 240*n*
footballers
amateur players 37–8, 61, 106, 312–5
professional players 39, 301–2
salaries and transfer fees for 39–40, 264, 341
see also Jewish footballers; mixed-race players; women's football
Fortems, Annie 329, 332, 335
Fossa Dei Leoni Ultras 252, 262, 266
Française, La 319–20, 321
France 10, 12–17, 44, 53–4, 59–77, 299–317, 378–84
1968 protests 304–5
Vichy France 119–22
France Football 158, 185, 332
Franco, General Francisco 77
Frankland, Alfred 51, 52
Fraysse, Eugène 62
French colonialism 153–4, 204–8, 204*n*, 206*n*
French Football Federation (FFF) 2*n*, 156–7, 159, 299, 300–1, 306, 309, 325, 327, 328, 331, 334, 378
occupation of 304–9
Freyre, Gilberto 186
Friededreich, Arthur 182–3
Fry, Charles Burgess 34
Fuchs, Gottfried 106
futsal 337*n*

G20 Summit (2017) 366
Galatasaray SK 285, 291–2
Galeano, Eduardo 184, 198, 201, 271
Gallice, René 122
Gamblin, Lucien 185
Garrincha (Manuel Francisco dos Santos) 188–9, 192–3, 193*n*, 203, 378
Garvey, Marcus 212
Gaud, Richard 326–7
Gavião Kyikatejã FC 196
Gayman, Jean-Marc 208
Geller, Uri 342
Geoffroy, Pierre 326–7
George, Walter Goodall 55–6
Germany 354–6
Nazi era 74–5, 104–22
Ghana 212, 213
Gharqoud, Iyad Abou 175
Ghrayeb, Najwan 172
Giáp, General 162–3
Giardinelli, Mempo 281
Gil, Gilberto 123, 124, 130
Gilbert, Nellie 48
Giraud, General Henri 154
Glazer, Malcolm 346, 347–8
Glindmeier, Mike 360, 366
Goebbels, Joseph 104–5
Goikoetxea, Andoni 274
Gold Coast (later Ghana) 211
Gontcharenko, Makar 114, 115
Gramsci, Antonio 5, 132
Granata Supporters' Group 248–9
Green Brigade Ultras 177–8
Green Street Hooligans (film) 246
Grimbaum, Bernard 121
Groupement des Clubs Professionnels 302, 306, 310

Gueye, Chimère 371–2
Guez, Olivier 182–3, 192
Guia, Domingos da 184, 185
Guinea 212
Gülen, Fethullah 291
Gümüsdağ, Göksel 292
Guyot, Raymond 76
Gyamfi, Charles Kumi 211–2

Hall, Stuart 231
Halvorsen, Asbjørn 116–17
Hamburg 355–8
Hamburger Sport-Verein (HSV) 353, 357–8, 364
Hamdy, Hassan 148
Hamzeh, Izzar 166
'handling game' 25, 27
Hapoels sports associations 168–9, 171
Harder, Otto 'Tull' 117
Hauss, René 300–1
Havelange, João 188, 279, 281
Hébert, Georges 319
Hegerberg, Ada 388–9
Heller, Ivor 345
Hells Bells (song) 353, 366
Herrera, Helenio 299
Hewitson, Dave *The Liverpool Boys are Back in Town* 245
Heysel stadium disaster (1985) 238–9
Hikmet, Nâzim 284, 295
Hills, Arnold F. 32
Hillsborough stadium disaster (1989) 242, 242*n*
Himmler, Heinrich 116
Hirsch, Julius 106, 106*n*
Histadrut 168, 171
Hitler, Adolf 74, 76, 106–8, 119, 355
  Mein Kampf 104
Hobsbawm, Eric 5, 34, 173
Hogg, Thomas and James 42
Hollander, Hartog 'Han' 117
homophobia 335, 353, 365
Honeybell, Nettie 47
Hook, Peter 348
'hooligan' culture 223–42, 231*n*, 232*n*, 238–6
Horn, Leo 117, 119
Hough, Ian *Perry Boys* 245
Hughes, Thomas *Tom Brown's Schooldays* 22, 25
Huizinga, Johan 28
  Homo Ludens 277
Human Rights Watch 176–7, 290

Ikkène, Tayeb 315
Independence Eleven 160, 162–3
India 43
Inter Milan FC 82, 200, 252, 260
International Olympic Committee (IOC) 83, 107–8
Ippig, Volker 357, 364
Israel Football Association 167, 171, 174*n*, 175
Israel-Palestine 165–80
  Boycott, Divestment and Sanctions movement (BDS) 174–5
Israeli football clubs 168–9, 171, 174, 177
Italian Communist Party (CPI) 248, 250
Italy 43, 248–70
  fascist era 74, 81–7, 185
ITV Digital (tv channel) 341

Jackson, Michael 287, 342
Jalco Cup 211
Jaurès, Jean 67, 73
Jewish footballers 87, 106, 117–18, 154*n*, 170*n*, 355

Joint Français Company 311–12, 311*n*
Joubert, Jimmy 218
Jouhaux, Léon 67
Juventus FC 248–9, 256, 257, 260, 261

Kahraman, Ismail 294
Kaizer Chiefs FC 218–9
Kamil, Mustafa 135
Kanafani, Marwan 136*n*
Karembeu, Adriana 334
Kennedy, Benjamin Hall 24
Kermali, Abdelhamid 158
Kfouri, Juca 129
Kgongoane, Ariel 218
'kick and rush' strategy 34, 35
King, John *The Football Factory* 245
Kinnaird, Lord Arthur Fitzgerald 29, 36
Kleynhoff, Abraham Henri 68
Klymenko, Olensky 115
Knighton, Albert Leslie 57
Koch, Wilhelm 360, 360*n*
Kop *see* Spion Kop
Kopa, Raymond 161, 302, 309
Koppel, Charles 344
Kordik, Josef 113–4
Korotkikh, Nikolaï 115
Kossarev, Alexander 90
Kouzmenko, Ivan 115
Kssis-Martov, Nicolas 73
Kühnen, Michael 358
Kurds 295, 295*n*

Lacombe, Bernard 336
Lampedusa FC 365
Lanata, Jorge 278
Landauer, Kurt 106
Lang, Otto and Paul 355
Laudré-Viel, Lucienne 324
Léa, Eugène N'Jo 158, 301
Lee, Geoff 175
Leoni della Maratona Ultras 253, 266
Lewis, Mike 342
Ligue de Paris 310
Lins do Rego, José 184
Lions of Canaan FC 165, 171
Littmann, Corny 365
Littoriali dello Sporto 82
Liverpool 235, 237
Liverpool FC 231, 243, 351
Lloyd George, David 50
Loach, Ken 175, 350*n*
Lomax, Brian 338, 339–40, 352
Looking for Eric (film) 350*n*
Lula da Silva, Ignacio 124, 392
Lunatics FC 200
Luthuli, Albert 217

Mabuse, Doc 357, 360, 363
Maccabi Tel-Aviv FC 168, 171
Maccabiah Games 168
Mahieu, Johan 239
Makana Football Association 217–8
malandro (mythical figure) 191–2
Manchester United FC 32, 40–1, 233, 346–50
  Stretford End 233–4, 242, 244
Mandela, Nelson 217
Mangin, General Charles 204
Mansour, Mortada 148
Manyoba, Sipambaniso 210
Manzi, Leonardo 361–2
Maouche, Mohamed 158
Maradona, Diego 201, 260, 271–83, 283*n*
  The 'Hand of God' 276–8
Marcos, Subcomandante 181, 198–9, 200–1
  The Uncomfortable Dead 202–3

Margeuritte, Victor *La Garçonne* 322–3
Markaryan, Alen 289
Marrane, Georges 71–2, 76
Marzbach, George 137
Match of the Day (tv programme) 340
Matheus, Vicente 125, 129
Matta, Roberto da 124
Matthews, Helen 46–7, 48
Mattler, Étienne 122
Mayday Trust 339
McRitchie, Michael 338
McWilliam, Peter 57
Meazza, Giuseppe 83
Médici, General Emílio 193
Medipôl Başakşehir FC 292
Meeske, Michaël 364
Mehl, Jean-Michel 13
Mekhloufi, Rachid 157–8, 159, 160–1, 162–3, 309
Men's World Cup (2006 Germany) 335
Meral, Adem 290
Mercet, René 85
Meredith, Billy 40, 41
Mérelle, André 303, 307–8, 310
Mexico 197–204
Mignon, Patrick 227, 233
Milan AC 43, 250–2, 253, 256, 260, 264
Miles, Eustace 56
Miles, Robert 47
Miller, Charles William 42
Millerntor Roar! 358, 359, 360
Millerntor stadium 355–6, 360, 364–6
Milliat, Alice 53, 319, 320, 321–2, 324–5
Millwall FC 224, 230, 232*n*, 234
Milton Keynes 344
Miroir des sports, Le 70, 323–4, 330
Miroir du football, Le 302–4, 307, 310–1, 312, 315, 330
Misme, Jane 321
Mitten, Jonathan and Charles 348
mixed-gender games 201
mixed-race teams 182–4, 185, 215–6, 218–9
Mobutu, Sese Seko 213
Moll, Herbert 106–7
Molotov, Vyacheslav 95
Môquet, Guy 121
Moraes, Vinícius de 181, 192
Morales, Victor Hugo 276
Moratti, Massimo 200–1
Moro, Aldo 256, 258
Morocco 139, 156
Moroni, Primo 251
Morris, Violette 323, 323*n*
Morsi, Mohamed 148
Moscow Dynamo FC 43, 90–4
Motaung, Kaizer 218
Mother City Girls FC 216
Mouvement Football Progrès (MFP) 312–4, 315
Mubarak, Alaa 137
Mubarak, Hosni 134, 137, 141, 144, 145
Murdoch, Rupert 243, 341, 346
Muscular Christians Association 24–5, 210
Mushuc Runa FC 196–7
Muslim Brotherhood 141–2, 148
Muslim football clubs 154–6, 170–1, 389
Mussolini, Benito 74, 81–2, 85–6
Mwepu, Ilunga 213

Nasser, Gamal Abdel 135
National Football Intelligence Unit 241, 243
National Indigenous Congress 203, 203*n*

National Professional Soccer League 218-9
Navétane event 367-73
Netherlands 117-9, 327-8
Niarry Tally FC 373
Niemeyer, Oscar 130
Nigeria 211, 212
Nike Company 385-6
Nkrumah, Kwame 212-3
Northampton Town FC 'Cobblers' 338-40
Norway 115-7
Noseda, Veronica 337
Nxele, Makana 217

Old Etonians FC 29, 36-7
Olechchuk, Yuri 90, 91, 92
Olivetto, Washington 129
Olympic Games (1936 Berlin) 77, 86, 107-8, 116
Oriot, Michel 308
Orlando Pirates FC 214
Orlando Pirates Women's FC 216
Oslo Accords (1993) 165, 173
Otmani, Mustapha 384
Ouled El-Bahdja supporters 389, 390
Overend, Laurence 343

Palestine 136, 164-80
see also Israel-Palestine
Palestine Liberation Organisation (PLO) 171, 172-3
Palestinian Football Association 154, 168, 169, 173, 175-6
Pan-African Congress (PAC) 217-8
Pankhurst, Emmeline 49
Parr, Lily 54
Pasolini, Pier Paolo 247
'passing game' 36, 37
Passolig ticket sales system 292-3
Pefferkorn, Maurice 185, 322
Peladáo event 377
pelade football 374-8, 385
Pelé (Edson Arantes do Nascimento) 188-93, 195
Pelota de Trapo (film) 273
Pelser Harry 118, 119
Pennant, Cass 244
Terrace Legends 245
People's Olympiad, Barcelona 77
Pereira, Jingles 218
Pessoa, Epitácio 183
Pessoa, Fernando *The Book of Disquiet* 338
Peugeot Company 64, 66
Philippe, Bernard 311-2, 315
Philips Company 65
'phoenix clubs' 343-4
Piantoni, Roger 161
Piñera, Sebastián 390, 392
Pinilla, Fernanda 391
Pires, Waldemar 125, 129
Platini, Michel 195, 239*n*, 260, 317
Pogba, Paul 384
Popular Front 76, 77, 87
Portugal 43-4
Praag, Jaap Van 118
Prague Congress (1925) 325
Premier League 243, 244, 340, 341, 347
Preston North End FC 38, 51, 224
Primo de Rivera, José 98
Proudhomme-Poncet, Laurence 321
public schools 22-6, 42
Public Order Act (1986) 240
pubs 33
Puma Company 385
Putin, Vladimir 387

Queen's Park FC 34-5, 224
Queen's Park Rangers FC 41-2

Qwabe, Thokozani 336*n*

Racine, Georges 322
racism 174, 181–4, 188, 206–9, 236, 241, 266, 358
Radwan, Ahmed 143–4, 146–7, 150
Rajoub, Jibril 164–5, 174, 179
Rapinoe, Megan 388
Real Madrid FC 96–7, 99
Red Devils *see* Al Ahly SC; Manchester United
Red Sport International (RSI) 69, 73–4, 88
refugees 365
Reiss, Hugo 106
Renault Company 63, 64
Representation of the People Act (1918) 55
Rimet, Jules 85, 187
Rinaudo, Dominique 331
Rivaldo (Vitor Borba Ferreira) 378
Robben Island prison football team 217–8, 219
Roberts, Charles 40, 41
Rocco, Nereo 299, 300*n*
Rodrigues, Nelson 191
Rogers, Robbie 365
Romani, José Escrivá de 99
Romário (Romário de Souza Faria) 378
Romezin, Marine 336
Ronaldo, Cristiano 193, 378
Ronsard, Pierre de 9, 12
Rook, Clarence *The Hooligan Nights* 224
Roossens, Albert 239
Royal Engineers AFC 35
Royer-Soef, Remoise Ghislaine 'Gigi' 329, 337
Rubatto, Mario 249
Rugby Football Union 28
Rugby School 22, 23, 24, 25
Rukh Kyiv FC 114
Russell, John 342
Russia 43, 387
see also Soviet Union
Russian Revolution 69
Ryhove, Raphaël de la Kethulle 206–7

Saâdi, Yacef 389–90
Sadat, Anwar 136
Sadoul, Jean 302, 306
Salvation Army 31
Sampdoria Ultras 252, 260, 266, 269
Samuelson, Erik 345
San Andrés Accords (1996) 198
Sankt Pauli FC 353–66
Santana, Telé 193
Santos, Arnaldo 377–8
Santos, Nilson 188
Sarsak, Mahmoud 167, 179
Schalke 04 FC 107, 112–3
Scotland 35–6, 35*n*, 225
Segal, Ze'ev 173–4
Sékou Touré, Ahmed 212
Seleçáo FC 124, 183–4, 185–7, 189, 190–1
Senegal 367–73
Séradin, Alain 315
Sesta, Karl 111
Sevilla FC 177
sex workers, trafficking in 336
sexism 331–7
Sexta, La (tv channel) 203
Shabat al-Arab FC 169
Shalit, Gilad 179–80
Shankly, Bill 223
Sheffield FC 27
Signorini, Fernando 277
Silva, Leônidas da 184, 185
Silva, Nélson 'Dida' de Jesus 188*n*

Silva, Paulo Christian Bezerra 377*n*
Sinclair-Webb, Emma 290
Sindelar, Matthias 110–2, 112*n*
Sixth Declaration of the Lacandon Jungle 200, 202
skinheads 230, 236, 236*n*
Slime (punk group) 357
Soares, Elza 192
soccer 333–4, 333*n*
Sochaux FC 66
Socialist Workers' Sports International (SWSI) 70, 73–4
Sócrates 3, 126, 127–9, 131, 132, 193, 260
Solé I Sabaté, Josep 97, 100
Sollier, Paolo 255
Sono, Eric 'Scara' 214
soule (game) 10, 11–17, 232
South Africa 43
  apartheid era 214–9, 218*n*
South African Football Association (SAFA) 215, 218, 219
South African Soccer Federation (SASF) 215, 216
South America 42
South America Championship 182, 183
Southern Rhodesia (later Zimbabwe) 210
Souvestre, Emile 10, 11–12, 14
Soviet Union 69, 74, 88–95, 113
Sozialromantiker 365–6
Spain 43
  Franco era 74, 77, 95–103
Spanish flu epidemic (1918) 52*n*
Spartak FC 90–5
Spartakiads sports event 74
Spion Kop stadiums 229, 229*n*
Sporting Events Act (1985) 240
SSC Napoli 274–5, 278–9
Stade Lamballais 311–2, 315
stadiums 238, 242–3, 264
Stalin, Joseph 88, 91
Starostin brothers 90, 93, 94–5, 95*n*
Start FC 114–5
Störtebeker, Klaus 357
Stubbes, Philip *The Anatomie of Abuses* 13
Stylianou, Lucky 218
Suddel, Willliam 38
suffragette movement 49
Sun, The 234, 242, 275
Sunyol, Josep 99
Supporters Direct 340, 351
Szepan, Fritz 107

Tahir, Muhammad Pasha 170
Takriz (cyber network) 142
Tantawi, Marshal Mohamed 145–7, 149
Taylor, Lord Peter 242
television, impact on football of 227, 233, 265, 340–1
Thälmann, Ernest 75–6, 355
Thames Ironworks FC 32, 38
Thatcher, Margaret 235
Thébaud, François 302–3
Thokozani FC 336
Thompson, E.P. 18
Thomson, Valentine 319
Thornton, Phil *Casuals* 245
ticket prices 2, 243–4, 292–3, 347, 349
Tisdale, Paul 343
Tompousky, Georges 121
Torino FC 247, 260
  plane disaster (1949) 247–8, 261
Tours Congress (1920) 69
Tovey, Neil 'Makoko' 219
Trade Disputes and Trade Union Act (1927) 225
trade unions 30, 66, 225–6
Trades Union Congress 30, 39, 225

Transvaal United FC 216
Travert, Maxime 380
Troussevitch, Nikolaï 113–4, 115
Trotel, Jean-Claude 311
Tschammer und Osten, Hans von 104
Tunisia 142, 156
Tunmer, Neville 62
Turk, Rifaat 172, 173
Turkey 43, 284–95

Uganda 43
Ukraine 113–5
Ultrà Sankt Pauli 364
Ultras movement 138–42, 150, 252–70
Ultras Ahlawy 134–5, 139–48
Ultras Tito Cucchiaroni 252, 270
Ultras White Knights 139, 143, 146–7, 148
Union des sociétés françaises de sports athlétiques (USFSA) 60–2, 68, 319–20
Union des sociétés sportives et gymnique du travail (USSGT) 69, 70
Union national des footballeurs professionnels (UFPF) 301, 309–10
Union of Independent Egyptian Women 150
Union sportif de Gorée 205
United States 42, 333–4
United States Soccer Federation 388
Uruguay 4, 42, 185

Vaccaro, General Giorgio 83, 85
Valdano, Jorge 4, 276
Valke, Jérôme 387
Valley Parade stadium fire (1985) 238
Vargas, Getúlio 186
Variété Club de France FC 173
Vasco da Gama FC 183–4
Vassort, Patrick 13
Veloso, Caetano 124
Vidal, Arturo 391
Vidal, Maurice 307
Villaplane, Alexandre 122*n*
Violeau, Hippolyte 13
Vodafone Arena 293–4
Volata (game) 82*n*

Wagenaar, Gerben 118–9
Wahl, Alfred 59–60, 306, 310
Walsh, Andy 346, 347
Warburton, Albert 36, 37
West Ham United FC 32, 38, 224, 230, 246
What a Load of Cobblers (magazine) 338
White Defence League 236
Wijnbergen, Jan 118
Wilde, Oscar 45, 48
Wilhelm-Koch Stadion (later Millerntor) 356, 358, 389
Wimbledon FC 344–5, 351
Witt-Schlumberger, Marguerite de 320
Wladimir (Rodrigues dos Santos) 126, 127, 131–3
women
  role in society of 45–6, 150
  sexist attitudes to 331–7
women' football 45–58, 165, 216, 262–3, 318–37, 369, 388–9
  opposition to 46–8, 55–8, 322–6, 331–3
women Ultras 262–3
women's liberation movement 330
Women's Social and Political Union 49

Women's World Cup 328, 333–4, 388
Workers Football World Cup 75–6
working class 67–73, 224–33, 235
World Cup
(1930 Uruguay) 83, 183
(1934 Italy) 81, 83–6, 325
(1938 France) 87, 112, 185
(1950 Brazil) 4, 186–7
(1954 Switzerland) 326
(1958 Sweden) 188, 189, 299
(1962 Chile) 192
(1966 England) 193, 213
(1970 Mexico) 124, 193
(1978 Argentina) 3, 272, 314
(1982 Spain) 274
(1986 Mexico) 275–6
(1990 Italy) 264
(2002 South Korea-Japan) 193
(2006 Germany) 166, 188*n*, 335
(2010 South Africa) 178, 219, 334
(2014 Brazil) 194–6
(2018 Russia) 387
(2022 Qatar) 1, 387–8
World War I: 49–52, 225, 319

Yates, Sydney 36
Yekutielo, Yosef 168
young people 67, 228

Zaghoul, Pacha Saad 135
Zaire 213
Zamalek SC 136, 137–8, 142
Zamalkawy Ultras 148
Zandkorn, Albert 121
Zanetti, Javier 200
Zapatista Army of National Liberation (EZLN) 197–203
Zaqout, Ahed 167
Zé Maria (José Marcelo Ferreira) 127
Zeca (José Carlos Rodrigues) 196
Zedillo, Ernesto 199
Zico, Arthur 193, 260
Zidane, Zinedine 384
Zik Athletic Club (ZAK) 211
Zitouni, Mustapha 157, 158, 159, 161, 163

Thanks to our Patreon subscriber:

Ciaran Kane

Who has shown generosity and comradeship in support of our publishing.

Check out the other perks you get by subscribing to our Patreon – visit patreon.com/plutopress.

Subscriptions start from £3 a month.